BOMBSHELL

BOMBSHELL

*The Secret Story of America's
Unknown Atomic Spy Conspiracy*

JOSEPH ALBRIGHT
MARCIA KUNSTEL

TIMES BOOKS
RANDOM HOUSE

NEW YORK

Library of Congress Cataloging-in-Publication data is available.

Book Design by Robert C. Olsson
ISBN 0-8129-2861-X
http://www.randomhouse.com/
Manufactured in the United States of America
9 8 7 6 5 4 3 2
First Edition

For Josephine Patterson Albright
and Marguerite C. Kunstel

Prologue

The scientist the Russians called Mlad almost always walked home for lunch. So he was in his Chicago apartment when he heard the radio bulletin that "within recent weeks an atomic explosion occurred in the USSR." President Harry Truman made the announcement on the morning of September 23, 1949—close to fifty years ago. Like most Americans, the president had been shocked when an Air Force sniffer plane picked up radioactive dust from the sky east of the Kamchatka Peninsula. Truman was only beginning to realize that the breaking of the U.S. monopoly on atomic weapons would touch the lives and pocketbooks of each new generation, right on into the twenty-first century.

Mlad knew something Truman didn't: how espionage had helped the Russians perfect the atomic bomb much faster than the CIA had projected. Five years earlier, Mlad had been so passionately convinced that a U.S. atomic monopoly was dangerous to the world that he decided to contact America's wartime ally, the Soviet Union. It was the middle of World War II; Mlad was working in the Manhattan Project. He felt that by passing information, he was giving some insurance against future war to millions of Americans, as well as to the rest of the world.

After that, the Soviets had no trouble cobbling together the reports in Mlad's cramped handwriting with the later data furnished by their other spy Klaus Fuchs and perhaps from other sources as well. The Soviet bomb turned out to be a replica of the one Truman ordered dropped on Nagasaki. And that was not to be the end of Mlad's involvement.

Mlad is a real person—a living American with an authentic biography, real rationales, and genuine co-conspirators. Along with everyone else who enters these pages, Mlad appears with his own full name, his own historical roots, and his own career. A few identifying details about living relatives have been omitted, but nothing about the acts of Mlad and his partners in espionage has been disguised.

Back in 1947, Mlad met a young woman who was as idealistically passionate and intellectually remarkable as he. Just before they took out a marriage license at Chicago's City Hall, Mlad let her in on the secret of his wartime espionage. Like Mlad, she concluded that he had taken a grave risk for a good purpose, that he had performed a deeply moral act that might make the world a safer place.

"We were sitting in the kitchen," Mlad's wife said many years later, as she tried to re-create the day of Truman's 1949 announcement. "I was really proud of him. It was as though he had done it all by himself."

Mlad was already finishing his doctorate in atomic physics at the University of Chicago, an academic halfway house for former Manhattan Project scientists. Mlad and his wife had painted the kitchen yellow, and in a corner was a big gas stove, the old-fashioned kind that stood on legs. "We had a table in the window above a very crummy-looking backyard," Mlad's wife remembered. "But the sun used to come in. And we had curtains there. It was extremely pleasant, that kitchen. . . . I remember pinning up some photographs on the curtains sometimes."

When they heard Truman's announcement, Mlad and his wife were disciplined enough to leave the apartment without saying a word. Lucky for them: If Mlad's house was not bugged already, it was about to be. The Army's legendary cryptanalyst Meredith Gardner was soon to break the Soviet espionage cable that tipped off the FBI to Mlad's wartime contact with Soviet intelligence.

Once outside their apartment, Mlad and his wife walked east past the ugly old Stagg Field, the one the chancellor left standing for football games among the Aristotelians, the Platonists, and other intramural teams. By then, the ivy that used to cover most of the gray stone exterior of the stadium was dead. Even the controversy over the end of intercollegiate football was fading; there was talk on campus of demolishing the whole sports complex. Some of Mlad's physicist colleagues were against that; after all, it had been in one of the old Stagg Field squash courts that Enrico Fermi had built the world's first atomic reactor only seven years earlier. Mlad didn't much care about Fermi's former squash court, though he admired the way Professor Fermi lectured on quantum mechanics, which was Mlad's favorite course. The only squash court at Stagg Field that Mlad had ever visited was the one where he sometimes played.

Once Mlad and his wife were out on Fifty-sixth Street and beyond range of microphones, they talked and talked. A new day had dawned for the world, they hoped. Now another world war was less likely, and perhaps there would be breathing room for socialism to grow. As they strolled toward Lake Michigan, they shared a furtive exhilaration. Mlad had done his bit to stave off a catastrophe, they thought—but they could not even tell their parents.

That was a traumatic day all over the country for Manhattan Project veterans. J. Robert Oppenheimer looked "worried, drawn," remembered David Lilienthal, chairman of the Atomic Energy Commission. The AEC chief also wrote in his diary that Robert Bacher, who had helped Oppenheimer create the American bomb at Los Alamos, was "deeply worried." Stalin's nuclear explosion came three to five years before the Truman White House expected, and from the first intelligence reports Lilienthal foresaw "a whole box of trouble." The president pondered for three days, finally deciding to make a preemptive disclosure to avoid "great fear, troubles" if the news came from Moscow first. Truman told Lilienthal he needed to show he was "not scared, hence others needn't be." Despite the weight of the radiological intelligence, it didn't fully persuade Truman and his inner staff that the Soviets really had the bomb. The filters of the WB-29 weather plane might just have found the debris from a runaway Soviet reactor, said Admiral Sidney Souers, director of the National Security Council. That's why Truman downplayed his wording, not even referring to the Soviet explosion as a bomb. Later, Truman told a senator he doubted that "those Asiatics" could ever master the complexities of building an atomic bomb.

The radio was full of worried commentary, but the next day's *Chicago Daily Tribune* quoted a surprising number of scientists who discerned some good in the sudden breaking of the American monopoly. Carnegie Tech physicist Edward Creutz, who had also worked in the Manhattan Project, said, "It is really a good thing this happened. Now people have been awakened and will realize there is no such thing as an atomic secret." The *Trib* quoted another nuclear pioneer, Arthur Snell, the chief physicist at Oak Ridge, as saying, "The moral of Russia having the bomb is pretty clear—the world must get together and make atomic energy everybody's business." And from West Germany, there on page 3 was an Associated Press dispatch quoting Otto Hahn, a pioneer of uranium fission: "If both the United States and Russia have it, there will be no war."

Nearly five decades were to elapse before the world got the first

inklings of who Mlad was and what he had done. A piece of his story finally broke into the open in 1995. After that, Mlad and his wife decided
it was finally time to tell what had happened—or, at least part of what
had happened. Though seriously ill, Mlad granted us more than 100
hours of interviews over a year and a half. They wouldn't tell everything—not with the risk of prosecution still in the back of their minds
even fifty years later. So the rest of Mlad's history—intertwined as it is
with the deeds of an elusive Soviet espionage ring called "the Volunteers"—had to be accumulated from sources around the world. Much of
this book is based on recently opened intelligence archives in Washington and Moscow; the rest is from personal letters, private document collections, and interviews. As the Notes will indicate, most of our
interviews were "on the record," although a number were conducted
"on a background basis" with a promise to our sources that the information would be attributed only to a "confidential source."

Is Mlad a "viper in our bosom" of the sort Rebecca West condemned in her book *The New Meaning of Treason*? Or is he the unsung
hero of the nuclear age—a man of conscience who risked the electric
chair because he could see that nuclear parity would lessen the risk of
war? No court has ever tried Mlad for anything, although he was the
target of a decade-long espionage investigation. The only court he is
likely to face is one such as this—a court of historical hindsight where
readers are the judge and jury. It is a court with no rules of evidence, except truth—a venue where specific acts count, but so do motivations
and ultimate results. It is a tribunal of uncomfortable dilemmas: one that
asks whether an illegal act can be justified if it turns out to benefit humanity in the long run.

Though Mlad admits he acted illegally, the crude calculus of history
has yet to refute Mlad's view that he helped decrease the risk of war.
Even Terry Hawkins, who fifty years later was the head of the nonproliferation division at Los Alamos National Laboratory, said: "If you look
at the history of the world, nuclear parity has probably had a stabilizing
effect. In the first half of this century, the number of people killed in war
was escalating beyond all bounds. You had eighty-odd million people
killed in the years leading up to 1945. After that, there was a precipitous
drop in the number of military deaths on the battlefield. The demarca-
tion is very clear. There will be historians who will say that this wasn't
significant, that many other factors were involved, but I think the Trinity explosion was the breakpoint. And after Trinity, I think the nuclear
parity which existed between ourselves and the Russians probably

bought us this fifty-year respite of peace that allowed the world to come to perhaps a rational conclusion of a Russia-U.S. conflict that would have certainly happened if there had not been nuclear weapons. Had we had nuclear weapons only on our side, we may have been tempted to use them on occasion."

Can Mlad legitimately claim some share of the responsibility for the avoidance of World War III? Perhaps. Does that exculpate him? That is a far different question. For as Terry Hawkins went on to say about the half-dozen known spies in the Manhattan Project, "The fact is they violated U.S. law. And at the time they acted, they did not know what the consequences would be. You can postulate a scenario where the United States might have hit some kind of stone wall in our weapons program, where we were not technically able to proceed. It is quite possible that the information passed to our adversary by these spies might have given the Soviets the capability to bypass us, so the United States might have been defeated in a war."

Never having been prosecuted, Mlad has been able to devote his life to science. In his own small sphere of biophysics, Mlad has come to be regarded as nothing short of brilliant. By 1997, Mlad had retired from the laboratory to his pleasant little row house in England. These days, he has a lot of time to ponder what he did in the Manhattan Project five decades ago. Over the years, it has made Mlad and his wife more comfortable to discover that he was not alone in helping the Soviets break the American monopoly. There was the physicist Klaus Fuchs, the machinist David Greenglass, other Soviet assets he had never heard of.

"A whole bunch of other people broke the monopoly too," Mlad said. "So if I hadn't existed, it wouldn't have changed the outcome. The same could be said of all those other individuals. I don't know, five, ten—five at least. If any one of us had not existed, it would have made no difference because the others were there.

"But collectively, the fact that they were there—that at least one was there—I think may have had quite a lot of significance."

Joseph Albright and Marcia Kunstel
Moscow, April 1997

BOMBSHELL

CHAPTER 1

Babes in the Woods

It was a steamy June day in 1950 when Yuri Sokolov set out on a short, risk-riddled trip.

He was going only the few blocks from his office at the Soviet United Nations mission to an apartment on East Seventy-first Street, but he was entering hazardous terrain for a spy. He had to make a face-to-face, unplanned visit to the home of two principal agents, and to do that he would violate some cardinal rules of espionage: Never go unannounced. Never meet in homes. Make contacts in public places. That was basic spycraft.

But the FBI was closing in. Sokolov had to deliver a message from Moscow Centre that was calculated to save its spy network from even deeper collapse.

Just months after the Soviets aroused a worldwide shudder by exploding their first atomic bomb, the FBI and British MI-5 began bearing down on the intelligence agents who helped make it happen. Spy rings had been penetrated, people arrested. Klaus Fuchs was the first to crack. The German Quaker, a naturalized British citizen who had helped create the American bomb in Los Alamos, admitted in January that he had divulged its details to the Soviets. New York headlines said Fuchs had fingered scores of agents. As it turned out, he helped identify only one other person, his courier Harry Gold, but Gold would prove to be a critical link to others.

Authorities had not been able to prevent the secret of the century from seeping through what they had thought was a sound wall of security around Los Alamos, the desert laboratory in New Mexico where America clandestinely built the world's most devastating weapon. Now they were intent on uncovering the people who had betrayed its existence and its workings to Soviet intelligence.

The *rezidentura* in New York, the Soviets' spy headquarters, saw it coming. The atom network the *rezidentura* had assembled strand by strand was jeopardized when Fuchs broke. The couple Sokolov was en route to visit—Morris Cohen and his wife and spymate, Lona—already had been ordered to sever contact with their most recent controller, Colonel Rudolf Abel. The Soviets had begun to fear that discovery of any more of its agents might lead American spy-catchers to the entire ring. In fact, the FBI was about to get a lead on Lona Cohen from Gold, whom they had arrested in May. He would tell them later that summer about a key spy courier, a young woman he had heard about but never met, who lived in Manhattan somewhere around Sixty-eighth and Lexington. But Moscow had acted too fast for the FBI to track Lona. Moscow had not simply ordered its troops into low profile; it had shut them down.

Now the clandestine cadres needed even more protection. That was Sokolov's task when he left his UN office and his cover as chief of the Soviet mission's press operation. It was chancy. If the Cohens already were under surveillance, how could he explain why a Soviet diplomat had come calling in the middle of a torrid summer day? His cover would be blown. Furthermore, if he was being watched, his visit would reveal that Morris and Lona were more than merely a likable grade school teacher and his scrappy wife. But Sokolov had no choice.

When he walked out of the Soviet mission, the elegant old Percy Pyne mansion sitting across from Hunter College at Park Avenue and Sixty-eighth Street, Sokolov did not head for the Cohens' apartment, just a ten-minute stroll away. First he traveled around the city, then meandered up and down East Side streets to check for a tail. It wasn't hard for Sokolov to blend into the mélange of New York, although his pronounced accent made it clear he wasn't native-born. He was a vigorous man of thirty but seemed younger. This was no Soviet thug. With curly black hair and wire-rimmed glasses he looked like a European intellectual. As he walked his unplanned maze, Sokolov glanced at reflections in shop windows, doubled back on his route, and finally ended up at 178 East Seventy-first Street.

When Sokolov knocked on the door of apartment 3B in the homely brownstone, he surprised Morris and Lona Cohen relaxing in shorts. Morris, thirty-nine, was tall and lean, an athlete who had lost his beefy build when he was wounded fighting as a volunteer in the Spanish Civil War. He was the thinker of the pair, a history teacher prone to philosophical discourse on anything from baseball to American education. His leftist ideology had been grounded in reading and long contemplation before he put it into action. Lona, an irreverent bundle of verve at thirty-seven, always had been the doer. She lived, then figured out what it meant.

Luckily for the Cohens no friends had stopped by that day. Despite being alone, they were professional enough not to ask questions when the Soviet agent they knew as "George" appeared at their door. Sokolov had been their controller and still considered himself their friend, so it was easy to make innocuous, affable conversation with them as a cover, just in case authorities were onto the couple and had wired their third-floor walk-up.

Soon Sokolov dropped the chitchat. He pulled out a notepad and started writing—another precautionary bit of "over-insurance" in those tense times, he said.

"We knew the situation in general, that there was a witch-hunt and so on. And we didn't know exactly their position. How safe they are," Sokolov recalled. They would converse silently with paper and pen.

Moscow Centre had decided that the Cohens knew too much, especially about how Soviet intelligence had ferreted atomic bomb secrets out of Los Alamos. Lona had been the courier to Mlad, the special young scientist known to no more than half a handful of officers in the Soviet intelligence hierarchy. Morris and Lona had been in contact with Mlad even after the war; evidently that was reason enough for the Cohens to flee.

"I said, the situation has changed. And it's better for you both to leave the country," Sokolov recalled.

"They said, 'Why?'

"I said, 'Well, you know the situation. You know that some people are arrested, that probably the FBI will know about yourselves. So it is better not to wait until it happens.'

"I emphasized that it might be dangerous. It wasn't my aim to frighten them. I tried to be delicate," Sokolov recounted in describing their conversation-by-notepad.

Morris wrote in reply, strongly supported by Lona: "If it only MIGHT be dangerous, we have a possibility to work yet."

Not possible, Sokolov had to insist.

"Why is it necessary? We're fighters. We'll become illegals and fight on," Morris wrote.

"I had different orders," remembered Sokolov. "I was very slow in answering his proposal, and he guessed that probably I have some serious reasons.

"And he asked me, 'But you tell me. Is it an order?' *Eto prikaz?* 'Or an advice?' *Ili sovyet?*

"I told him, *prikaz*. 'An order . . .'

"He wrote, 'Well, that's that then.' "

When Sokolov looked up from the notepad, he saw smoke billowing out of the bathroom. Lona had taken away each page as the Soviet and her husband finished writing and was burning them over the sink. The tension broke as Sokolov laughed at Lona's disaster. The younger man had always looked at the Cohens as strong, experienced agents, forgetting they had almost no training in spycraft.

"I said, 'You don't know how to burn paper.' So I showed her how you do it." The method is to roll the sheet of paper into a cylinder, then light it at the top so it burns downward, he later recalled. "You light it up here. Then there is no smoke, and all that is left is a little white ash."

Conversation ended there, with a pile of white ash and an admonition to flee their country.

NINE MONTHS LATER a frightened young couple in Chicago tried to reach the Cohens. There had been a sudden knock on another door, this time the FBI showing up at a University of Chicago laboratory in the early spring of 1951. Agents were in pursuit of Mlad, the very young scientist the Soviets had been so intent on shielding.

He was Theodore Alvin Hall.

At only eighteen, Hall had finished Harvard undergraduate work and become the youngest physicist at Los Alamos when the first atomic bomb was being contrived. He was at the center of the scientific pioneering that made the bomb happen: He handled implosion experiments for Fat Man, the plutonium bomb dropped on Nagasaki, and helped determine the critical mass of uranium for the Hiroshima bomb.

And Ted Hall was one of a scattering of dedicated critics inside Los Alamos who believed any atomic monopoly menaced the world. Intellectually advanced and more politically motivated than most Americans—of his age or any other—Hall also was driven by the romanticism that leads young men to fancy their lives in heroic vistas. He had become so convinced of the dangers of nuclear monopoly that he decided to take steps himself to make sure the American lock on the bomb would be broken. Soon after this decision, the Cohens entered his life as agents for the Soviet people he wanted to help.

By 1951, Ted Hall thought his espionage and clandestine contacts were a chapter closed. He had gone from Los Alamos to Chicago graduate studies, fallen in love, and started a family. Encouraged by his wife, who insisted political work outweighed any additional covert contribution Hall could make, he told the Soviets he had finished what he saw as his duty. Ted and Joan Hall proceeded to combine academia with political activism, a route that in those days was not uncommon for intellectuals in the crackling political atmosphere of the University of Chicago. Henry Wallace's Progressive Party wasn't mainstream politics, but it was nothing you'd get arrested for joining. They had let themselves believe the ominous knock on the door never would sound.

But it did, that March in 1951 when the FBI came calling. And now the happy niche the Halls had carved themselves was on the verge of crumbling. Ted knew there was supposed to be a way to get back in touch with his old contacts in an emergency. This surely qualified. They had the home address of Lona and Morris in Manhattan, though they had met only a few times, and never at anybody's apartment.

Ted Hall remembered some sketchy procedure for sending a red alert with a postcard, but he wasn't quite certain how to set details for a meeting. And he had entirely forgotten the parole—the recognition code he was supposed to use. Joan practiced ways to camouflage her handwriting, and the two concocted their own coded message they thought would raise an alarm without endangering anybody, even if intercepted. They settled on JERRY IS MAKING A LOT OF TROUBLE, employing the old British term for Germans. The association of words was supposed to lead the Cohens to think of Nazis, to realize that the FBI or some other unwelcome somebody was putting them on the spot. The Halls included a veiled reference to a day and a place for meeting—right off South Michigan Avenue, inside the Art Institute of Chicago.

Hall's strangely charismatic friend Saville Sax was also on the spot that March of 1951. Sax had been Ted's Harvard roommate, political collaborator, and sometime espionage courier, and after the war he followed Hall to the University of Chicago to study. The FBI had grilled him on the same day agents interrogated Hall, indeed, at the very same moment. That's why both the Hall and Sax families, babies in tow, showed up on the appointed day at the Art Institute. They had hopes of spotting a familiar figure lingering at Ivan Meštrović's statue of Moses Receiving the Ten Commandments. No Cohens appeared. Nor any

Soviets. The Halls and Saxes knew it had been a half-baked plan, with a dozen potential pitfalls.

No help arrived, but at least three bewildered-looking guys suspiciously resembling G-men were hanging around within sight of the imposing Moses. Hall feared their postcard had been intercepted and the Cohens compromised. He or Savy simply may have been followed and didn't notice the tail until they had settled into the museum. But they had no way of knowing where the plan had fallen through.

Joan, Ted, Savy, and his wife, Susan, became more anxious. What if the FBI got ugly? What if these young couples needed to get themselves and their kids out of harm's way? It was no idle fear. All sorts of people, from renowned scientists to anonymous technicians, already had been caught up in the dragnet. Ethel and Julius Rosenberg, the parents of two small boys, had been convicted that spring of conspiracy to commit espionage. There was talk that they might face the unthinkable—execution. Hall and Sax knew their actions had been more consequential than anything the prosecution had used against the Rosenbergs.

The Halls and Saxes devised another scheme: Ted or Savy could dress up as a woman and simply walk into the Soviet Consulate in New York—the place where all this atomic espionage had started seven years earlier. Surely the Soviets would help them with a plan that would keep them out of jail. Sax thought it was inspired. He charged ahead plotting the details of how and when and where, envisioning one of them walking toward freedom in a wig, a dress, and a pair of pumps.

It was Joan Hall who dashed the plan, asking how either of these men could possibly walk five yards in high heels, much less outwit the certain U.S. surveillance at the Soviet Consulate. And why would the Soviets ever grant entry to a bizarre-looking "woman" who claimed to be on their side?

"That was a really flea-brained notion," Joan would later remark to one of the few friends she would trust with the story. "It goes to show how really immature we were. What babes in the woods we were."

PERHAPS THEY WERE babes, but they surely had violated the law— Hall and Sax and the Cohens too. Ultimately, they had done it because they believed they were surrounded by circumstances in which the greater good of society was incompatible with the laws governing them. They were a rare lot. Many ardent socialists went to fight in the Spanish Civil War as did Morris Cohen, but few volunteers let themselves be recruited into Soviet espionage. Like Ted Hall, many gifted scientists opposed American exclusivity of atomic weapons as an inherently unstable monopoly. But Hall is one of a half dozen Americans who passed information on the U.S. bomb program to the Soviets, and the only American scientist known to have given the Soviet Union details on the design of an atomic bomb.

Yet these volunteer informants were not hired hands like Aldrich Ames, the American who spied on his country for millions of dollars, giving information that he knew would lead to the deaths of CIA agents. These were young idealists who paid their taxes, voted because they believed in democracy, and didn't even consciously break traffic laws. They were first-generation Americans from families that had fled Russian repression to breathe the freedom and live the opportunity that America promised.

Somehow they became actors in one of the biggest, best-kept conspiracies of the century. Now that the secret finally can be unraveled more than forty years later, some may consider what they did a national betrayal. Others may assess it as an act that helped cut the risk that nuclear weapons would ever again be used in war. Right or wrong, something led Ted Hall, Saville Sax, and Morris and Lona Cohen to engage in clandestine acts of a magnitude that transformed them from inheritors of America's dream to transgressors of its fundamental rule of law. Until now, no one has known quite what they did. And certainly not how they arrived at the decision to do it.

CHAPTER 2

Roots of Rebellion

The start of the Great Depression was not a convenient time to be a furrier.

Ted Hall's father, Barnett Holtzberg, had done fabulously well until then, especially for a poorly educated Jewish immigrant who had escaped bigotry and waning opportunities in Russia's Pale of Settlement. He had married, sired four children, and ensconced them all in a rambling three-story house—with servants' quarters and the workers to fill them—on the South Shore of Long Island. But the fur collars and muffs and even coats that people splurged on in the 1920s weren't in much demand after the crash closed the decade in 1929.

Holtzberg's bright youngest son was about five when the family had to move from the big house at 15 Oak Street in Far Rockaway, but Ted always remembered the shock of suddenly being cramped into a small Manhattan apartment at 725 West 172nd Street in Washington Heights. His father's fur workshop suffered like so many others under the economic disaster that would anger and politicize a nation submerged in hard times for years. Financing the turn-of-the-century house had become an impossible luxury, so Barney Holtzberg took his family back to his old Manhattan neighborhood.

The new apartment was uncomfortable, but far more congenial than the place the Holtzbergs had first landed in America. Barney's immigrant family of nine people had started out in the Lower East Side in a tenement at 386 Grand Street. Their block had become choked with immigrants, mostly poor Jews from Eastern Europe trying to transplant Old World skills and languages into a city that placed little value on either. The neighborhood where the Holtzbergs lived in 1900 was the most densely populated section of the city. At 700 people per acre it was a new ghetto in a new, unknown land. Bodies spilled from tene-

ments, sweatshops, schools, factories, and tiny storefronts, and the unpaved streets were congested with peddlers' carts. The Holtzbergs lived not far from the teeming "Pig Market," where Jews bought and sold everything from eggs to eyeglasses—everything but pigs. Seven families, mostly "Russian" émigrés like the Holtzbergs, had been stuffed into that same Grand Street address. Tailors, merchants, a gold-plater, they had brought their families and their hopes to America in the 1890s from a land that was crushing both.

Czar Alexander III had been a furious anti-Semite who ignited pogroms across southern Russia and then imposed new restrictions against the Jews who had been victimized. This oppression was set off by the assassination in March 1881 of Alexander II, who had permitted a period of relative liberalism. By early 1891 it was all but impossible for the more than five million Jews in the empire to live anywhere except the Pale of Settlement, the swatch of land from the Baltic to the Black Sea where nearly 95 percent of Russian Jewry had become corralled over the centuries. For the rest of that year, it scarcely rained, and Russia suffered its worst crop failure in more than forty years. Famine was inevitable.

A new wave of Jewish refugees rolled into the Pale of Settlement in early 1893 after the czar's Ministry of Internal Affairs expelled 20,000 artisans and merchants from Moscow. There followed a general Jewish exodus from Russia. Often it meant taking big losses, for people had to sell their shops and belongings cheap. Still, many of those who could, got out. Some headed for Palestine, some to Western Europe. Most sailed for America. The Russian Jews did not forget the conditions they left, and many were sympathetic to the revolution some twenty years later that brought down the hated Romanov dynasty.

Among the Jews who started life over in America in 1893 were eleven-year-old Barney Holtzberg and his family. The family patriarch, Jacob, declared himself "Austrian" by birth, and his wife, Terza Kutner Holtzberg, listed herself as "Russian." But they were from the Polish-speaking region then divided between Austria-Hungary and the Russian empire. Most of their children were born in that part of western Russia where Polish was the predominant tongue. Jacob may have brought with him techniques of the fur trade learned in Russia or Eastern Europe, where pelts from Siberia were coveted buffers against the cold winters. However it happened, he and his largely uneducated children found work and then prosperity. By 1900 Jacob and his four boys were running the J. Holtzberg & Sons fur company near New York's

Washington Square. Even his daughter Leah came into the business to keep the books.

Barney, the third of seven children, was the bright and ambitious boy in the family. When he was eighteen, he was the only Holtzberg besides his father, Jacob, who was listed in the 1900 census as possessing the valuable skills of reading and writing as well as the ability to speak English. He was remembered not only as the driving force behind the family company, but also as a warmhearted man with a thick Yiddish accent and flashes of whimsical humor. In 1908 Barney married a New Yorker, Rose Moskowitz, whose immigrant parents ran a Hungarian restaurant.

The clan did well enough that at least two of the sons split off into separate fur businesses and escaped the Lower East Side by moving to apartments in Washington Heights. Barnett got even further from the inner-city moil when he took his young family to Far Rockaway. They managed to weather struggles with furriers' unions run first by criminal gangs and then by even more strident Communist Party factions, whose violent 1926 strike won their workers the first forty-hour week in the garment trades.

But their success was dwarfed by that of America's new corporate leaders, who saw profits jump by 43 percent in the six years leading to 1929, while workers' wages had gone up a mere 8 percent. It was the Pierre du Ponts and Andrew Mellons who profited so handsomely under President Calvin Coolidge's business-first administration. Indeed Mellon, the Republican secretary of the Treasury, pushed through a tax reform in 1926 that reduced the income tax for an American earning $1 million a year from 60 percent to less than 20 percent. The Holtzbergs hadn't rocketed into such riches, but neither would they be caught so viciously in the downward spiral when the bottom fell out, when construction and investment dropped in the wake of the stock market plunge, and unemployment and poverty bounced up in counterpoint. J. Holtzberg & Sons did go under when it couldn't meet its obligations and the bank foreclosed.

Barney Holtzberg's family wasn't happy to move back to an uncomfortable Washington Heights apartment in the same neighborhood where Barney and Rose first lived when they were married in 1908. But it was the Depression, and at least they were clothed and eating. Americans everywhere, even educated people, were hunting frantically for jobs. Those reduced to menial labor were still better off than the millions who were stunned into joblessness, hunger, and homelessness. By 1933, investment had fallen by 98 percent and unemployment stood at

24.9 percent. Barney Holtzberg managed to start over with a new partnership called HMJ Fur Company that polished fur and made pelts into fur coats and collars. And his wife, who had a high school education, got work as a secretary sometimes.

The conditions weren't terrible enough to spoil the boyhood and education of the favored youngest child, Ted. He was a latecomer born October 20, 1925, when his mother was thirty-nine and his father already forty-four. Rose adored and hovered about the boy until her death when Ted was seventeen. He was all the more cherished because Rose had been sure her third child would be her last. Childbirth had been complicated when Ted's brother, Edward, was born in 1914—a fraternal twin had been lost—and after surgery the doctors told Rose she never would conceive again. Eleven years later Theodore happened.

Ted still could summon decades later an early childhood memory of crawling into bed with his parents on Sunday mornings. It was a time for stroking and stories when nobody had to rush off early to work. Barney had an unending series of tales for Teddy, complex fables of good guys and bad spun from a timely political context of economic voracity and plunder. His forces of Good and Evil were the little butchers and big butchers. "The big butchers were always trying to wipe out the little butchers, but the clever little butchers had countermeasures," Ted remembered. "The big butchers would send troops, and the little butchers would be trapped on an island or something. And the little butchers would somehow get across them and escape from the island." He always wondered if these stories came spontaneously to his father, or if he conjured them during the week as he fought to keep his own small shop from being overwhelmed.

Barney Holtzberg was no political activist. But he knew what he believed. People needed protection. The world needed some rules, moneygrubbing some limits. The Depression pulled the Holtzberg family more firmly to the left, as happened to the majority of Americans angry at the swamp in which they felt the titans of capitalism had mired them. The concept of state intervention grabbed hold. The butcher stories, the move to a tiny apartment, the whole ravaged economic habitat his family was trying to negotiate—along with the rest of the world— got through to Ted at a remarkably young age.

It was quickly obvious that his mind was special. His brother, Ed, eleven years older and headed for a career in rocket engineering for the U.S. Air Force, took command of Ted's education. Perhaps Ed recognized that a gap was there to be filled, saw that their father was older now and tired and anyway not equipped to tutor an intellectually precocious young boy in modern math or science. "I had a much better background for bringing up a kid," Ed remembered. "I simply had the intention of keeping a clear mind in the boy."

To Ted, his brother's role was pivotal. "I worshiped my brother, and my brother decided I was really his child, not my parents'. When he was bringing me up, he taught me all kinds of things," Ted recalled years later. "He would find out what was going on in the math class and he would do it much better. . . . He would teach me the next step. I would be doing things way ahead of the other kids. He loved teaching me and I loved sopping up all that stuff," Hall said. After school Ted applied his mathematical gift to playing curb ball. When he was about eight, he was the ringleader of a team of kids from around 173rd Street called the Underdogs. What you had to do to control the bounce was to understand that the "angle of incidence equals the angle of reflection," Hall remembered telling his bemused teammates.

Being a favored child seems to have nourished a streak of willfulness that could propel Ted into defiance and later into real rebellion. Something as simple as being required to accompany his mother to Macy's, which he found boring and stupid, could turn him into a terror. On one of those trips when Ted was five or six, he became so angry that he managed to jam his body in the revolving door as they left the Macy's store on Herald Square. A crew of managers and building workers had to rescue this angel-faced, iron-willed child as his exasperated mother fumed on the sidelines of the spectacle.

Most of the time, Rose Holtzberg would smother Ted with love, which only enhanced the ego of the boy who was convinced he could best his mother intellectually in any conflict. He would get infuriated when Rose ended arguments the way mothers eternally have, with the command: "Just do it this way BECAUSE." It wasn't good enough. "I knew that 'because' was not a permissible way to win a logical discussion. I was always defeating her in arguments, at least logically I defeated her." His father was another story. He may have been retiring, but Ted found him logical. He would turn to his father to arbitrate arguments with Rose, probably because Barney often declared the boy in the right. One time when Barney did side with Rose, it so enraged Ted that he punched his father in the stomach.

Such an argumentative nature should not have been unexpected from a boy of nine or ten who already was beginning to outgrow the household encyclopedia called *The Book of Knowledge*. Ted passionately engaged his brother over its conundrum about the tree falling in the woods. Would this crashing tree make a sound if there was no one around to hear it? The book "distinctly took the idealistic position that if nobody heard the tree, then there wasn't any sound," Ted remembered. "It was obnoxious and outrageous to Ed, and he made it obnoxious and outrageous to me." To Ted's mind, a classical physicist would never dream of questioning whether the physical changes of density and pressure occurred. Of course there would be a sound, no matter whether anyone heard it. "But this was a very central point of argumentation, and this did affect me, taking the realistic position rather than the philosophical idealist position."

These kinds of discussions at home refined Ted's own considerable intellect and led him to make quick work of P.S. 173, the local public school on West 173rd Street and Fort Washington Avenue. By junior high school he not only had skipped three grades but was a teacher's helper in some classes. There was the unwieldy algebra class where Miss Lilienthal was trying to force formulas into the heads of disparately capable students. Ted would be dispatched to a quiet corner to tutor the slower kids, although he was three years younger than the classmates he was instructing.

It was not only schoolbook lessons that Ted absorbed at home. The Depression also was a teacher. His older brother was having trouble, looking for a night job while he studied at the City College of New York. Ted shared the frustration Ed felt at trying to sell shoes to people who barely could afford to keep bread on the table. When Franklin D. Roosevelt took office in 1933, this furrier's family was among the millions of Americans heartened. "They loved Roosevelt. My father did, my mother did. To them Roosevelt was the savior of capitalism," Ted remembered. Yet he also was exposed to the notion that the people must do more to capture control of capitalism and turn it to benefit the masses. "Everyone was for Roosevelt, but of course people who were communists considered that Roosevelt wasn't the be-all and end-all."

Ed Hall brought home radical publications from CCNY, where left-wing sentiment was strong. As early as 1932, Ed said, students at CCNY were politicized by the swelling fascist tide in Europe. When the college allowed three young Italian fascists to speak in the school's Great Hall, the Americans in the audience had no tolerance for their spiel. They bodily ejected the Italians—out the window. Ideological lines dividing the left started blurring with the appearance of this new enemy. From the Comintern had come a call in 1935 for a Popular Front against fascism. The Moscow headquarters of the world's communist parties told all its parties abroad to join with any willing left or liberal group. In America, that meant communists reversed course and started extolling the New Deal. And for many liberal intellectuals outside the party, the idea of making common cause with communists against the fascists sounded utterly sensible. "Our country and our government were stumbling, stumbling badly," Ed said in recapturing the spirit of that era. "So we all considered the ideas of socialism, the ideas of communism."

The writings of the muckraking radical Lincoln Steffens left an imprint on Ted's developing political mind before he was even a teenager. So did *The Communist Manifesto,* which Ed brought home from CCNY. These and other iconoclastic works not only challenged the economic order, but even warned that other fundamentals of American democracy were tainted. Ted read about conspiratorial groups hidden in the U.S. military, headed by generals prepared to organize concentration camps for dissenters and take over the government if need be. "They were fairly well documented, with evidence of existing plots," Ted said many years later. "They were not to be activated tomorrow, of course, but plots which might be activated if the time came, if there was no alternative for these people to remain in rule."

By the time he was twelve, Ted was focused as much on world events as on the basic principles of science. This child was worrying not just about economic dislocation at home, but about British and French appeasement of Hitler. "There was a lot of argumentation in the literature. There were books written which seemed to show very convincingly that the Allied nations actually encouraged the development of German fascism. They were very widely read," Ted Hall remembered. "The books were around the house and I remember discussing them." Seeds of doubts about the capitalist system were strewn already at this early age. They later would grow into a fear that American capitalism, too, could turn down the path of economic stagnation—witness the Depression—and then into fascism.

The rise of fascism was particularly troubling to Jews, religious or not. Like the majority of Jewish émigrés who left Eastern Europe and Russia in the early waves of the 1890s, the Holtzbergs were not an Orthodox family. They observed the major religious holidays, but not much more. But families like the Holtzbergs remembered why they or their parents had felt compelled to leave Russia, how Jews were singled out as the source of all sorts of evils. Now as the world Depression lumbered on, fascists already were blaming Jews for these new troubles. In

America, voices like that of the Catholic Father Charles Coughlin were spreading a proto-fascism that attracted millions. Coughlin's nationwide radio show in the mid-1930s, tuned in to by the Holtzbergs, kept finding new bogey-men to blame for wreaking such social injustice on the country. Coughlin did not become openly anti-Semitic immediately, but the direction was clear and feared by many.

When the Holtzberg boys decided to change their names it provoked a family controversy. But Barney and Rose finally acquiesced out of fear their sons' futures could be stunted by anti-Semitism. The parents did not like the anti-religious sentiment prevalent in their family's younger generation, so influenced by secularist radical politics. Yet they felt there was something to the argument that their careers or even their lives one day could be jeopardized, in a world where anti-Semitism periodically blew like a scalding geyser. Ed was the initiator of the name change. "I went to college, had two degrees, and couldn't get a job. I would go to employment agencies and register, and my name was never reached. So I finally realized I'm lost before I begin," he explained. He was convinced a simple, unobtrusive last name would ease his life. He chose Hall, and Ted followed suit. As for the name they gave up, they felt they were not after all abandoning something the family had cherished over generations. The family that left Russia in 1893 had been named Holtzenbecker, which somehow got shortened once they reached America, as did so many names processed on Ellis Island.

In the fall of 1936, petitions were filed on behalf of the two Holtzberg brothers to shorten their surnames some more. The name Holtzberg was "unnecessarily long, not easy to spell or to pronounce or remember and not at all euphonious," said one of Ed's court documents. It told the judge that having a shorter surname "will be of inestimable benefit."

Ted was close to his eleventh birthday when the petitions were granted. For the rest of his life his name would be Theodore Alvin Hall.

CHAPTER 3

A Revolutionary Young Girl

Lona Petka was older than Ted Hall when the Depression sank America to its knees. Though she was still a teenager, she was weathered enough to be outraged. By the time the stock market crashed in 1929, she had lived on her own for three years and was already a convert to socialism.

Lona was twelve or thirteen when she left her home on a Connecticut farm to look for work in New York City. "We lived in the country, it was far away from everything and there were no opportunities there," remembered Lona's younger sister Ginger. It was in the mid-1920s and Lona came to the city to join her older sister Gladys, who was making a living as a governess. This was the age when young women were shattering molds—smoking cigarettes, drinking in public, and wearing lipstick and scandalously short skirts, at least in the cities. Lona picked up some high heels in New York, but this headstrong mill hand's daughter didn't get them to go dancing at speakeasies. She was a kid who needed to look old enough to talk her way into a sweatshop. "She was only twelve years old. And she got a job in a women's clothing factory," her closest friend in later life, her husband Morris, would relate years afterward.

Even before finding her way into the netherworld of child labor, Lona had seen hardship. She didn't spend her early childhood in the pretty Connecticut countryside, but in the mill town of Adams, Massachusetts, where both her parents had worked as cotton weavers. Lona was born there January 11, 1913, the fifth of ten children. By then her mother had quit working the looms to deliver and rear Lona's four older siblings, three sisters and a brother who ranged from one to six years old.

Her father would work for more than twenty years as a weaver for the Berkshire Cotton Manufacturing Company, until Lona was ten

years old. The company was described rather quaintly in a town directory as "Mfrs. sateens, foulards, fine print goods and lawns." But Adams
was an iron-fisted company town, and the company in charge was Berkshire Cotton. Its owner, William B. Plunkett, was not only the dominant political figure in Adams but also a mover in national Republican
circles. President William McKinley was a personal friend and stayed
with Plunkett on visits to Adams until his conservative presidency was
ended by an anarchist's bullet in 1901.

The Petkas had started working at Berkshire Cotton around the
turn of the century, back when the nation didn't have labor laws or a
minimum wage. Most mill hands had immigrated from Eastern Europe
or crossed over from French Canada in search of work. Despite the conditions, many were happy enough to be in America and holding jobs.

Ladislaus "Walter" Petka had arrived in America in 1896, when he
was only sixteen or seventeen, probably without his parents. Records
indicate some of his sisters or cousins also ended up in the Adams mills.
Mary Czupryna came on her own in 1898—she was fourteen—to join
a sister who was running a grocery store in Adams and had enough
money to pay her little sister's passage. At that time it wasn't odd to dispatch even very young family members one or two at a time from Eastern Europe into new lives. It was a simple question of money. Perhaps
the knowledge that her mother, Mary, had undertaken such a huge adventure as a girl made it seem natural to Lona to make a similar departure in the 1920s.

For all their lives Polish would be the favored language of Mary and
Walter, who came from the part of the Russian empire that is now western Belarus. Although Czar Alexander III had died in 1894, his legacy
of Russification lived on in those lands where he had tried to erase di-
versity. Not only Jews had been targeted, but also Catholics like Lona's
parents. There was one church for the empire, the Russian Orthodox
Church, and no room for much else. In Adams, there were no obstacles
to Lona's parents being married by a Roman Catholic priest in 1901,
when Mary was a girl of seventeen and Walter was twenty-two.

Lona's political education was grounded in watching her parents
scrape to feed and clothe ten children on a mill worker's pay. And there
were clues that the daily grind abraded the fabric of the family. In the
spring of 1915, when Lona was two, the Petkas managed a $280 down
payment to buy a home after the former owner defaulted on the mort-
gage. It was the custom of the time in western Massachusetts for the
man of the family to put his name on the deed. Oddly, Walter Petka did

not appear in the records as the purchaser. The deed was signed instead by Lona's mother, Mary, who suffered from the double disadvantage of being a woman and speaking English even less fluently than her husband. Records suggest that at the time of the house purchase Mary was about three months pregnant. And yet for some unknown reason, this most important financial paper of their lives was executed without Walter. Whatever may have happened between them, the matter seems to have been put aside not long after Mary Petka gave birth to her sixth child that summer. The following spring, Lona's mother signed over the house to Walter for a nominal fee of $1.

An event that would resonate strangely in Lona's consciousness happened when she was a child during World War I. A neighbor had gone off to fight and didn't come back. "I was only four years old and I remember how my little friends cried because their father was killed in the war," Lona recalled much later. Lona always would consider herself a pacifist, often citing that childhood memory as one motivation for her politics. Not long after the death of her friends' father, Lona began doubting the religion pounded into her at her Polish Catholic grade school. Morris later would say Lona ran away from home "because she questioned God."

Lona was still living with her parents when the whole family managed to escape the gloom of Adams. Their house at 9 Albert Street was the springboard. When Mary and Walter jointly remortgaged the house in the early twenties—this time for the grand sum of $2,500—the rising property values handed them a nest egg. They decided to pack up and leave. In the summer of 1923, Mary and Walter sold the house and moved 100 miles southeast to a small farm they bought near Taftsville, Connecticut. It wasn't much of a farm, but it got them away from the cotton dust that Walter Petka had sucked for twenty years.

"All we had, we had a couple cows, some vegetables, and some hay. That's all I remember," Lona's sister Ginger said years later. "He really wasn't farming to make it a business. It was so he could have his own fresh milk and fresh vegetables." Walter started repairing shoes, and Mary went back to work in a textile factory.

Lona left no reminiscences that explain why she left her family a couple of years after the move to eastern Connecticut. But it was clear that besides being tired of Catholic school, she was fed up with her father. Friends in Lona's later life got the impression that her childhood "wasn't particularly happy"—and that she blamed it on Walter Petka. Many years later in Moscow, the wife of one of Lona's Soviet intelligence colleagues said she understood Lona's mother had been "cruelly" treated by Walter. Another friend got the sense from Lona that her father drank a lot. Whether or not drinking was a pattern with Walter Petka, a judge in North Adams did convict him in 1921 of driving an automobile "under the influence of intoxicating liquor." Who owned the car is a puzzle since Ginger said her family could not afford one. It was a time when automobiles were still novelties—when a mill worker would have drawn attention just driving a car, let alone driving it intoxicated. When that embarrassment hit the family, Lona was eight.

Lona's leftist instincts started to be defined very soon after she reached Manhattan and became an underage factory hand. "She was always talking about injustice and inequality, about the Negroes and people living in the ghetto," said Ginger. "She wanted to change the world." Lona quickly got hooked on politics as a way to make those changes happen. And she kept moving left in search of the best vehicle. At the same time, life apparently was not an unrelieved drudge. Once Lona left home, she got an apartment in Greenwich Village and "had a hell of a good time," one of Lona's New York neighbors later told the FBI.

Lona sampled different ideologies on her political odyssey. About 1928, two years after she left home, Lona thought she'd found the answer. "I was a revolutionary from a young girl," Lona later said. "I joined the Socialist Party when I was fifteen years old. But I left the Socialist Party because they were all old men and they all wanted to paw me. I was a nice young girl at that time. And I thought, 'What kind of socialists are they?' " How long Lona stayed with the socialists and where she encountered the objectionable passes is impossible to sort out so many decades later. She may have been referring to the time she tried out a political experiment called the single-tax movement and lived in its commune in Delaware. The timing of her sojourn with the single-taxers cannot be fixed precisely, but this intriguing community would help mold Lona through the coming decades as she grew more radical and free-wheeling.

The single-tax movement was the brainchild of Henry George, a journalist and visionary who wondered in the 1880s why poverty in America was so widespread when wealth was growing. Land ownership was the culprit, he decided. Landowners created nothing, just kept raising rents or land prices whenever land use gained in value. The land itself did not change if a factory was built on it, but its price went up. George thought all land should be nationalized, but realizing that was unlikely he devised a tax proposal instead. The tax should equal the full rental value of the land, so there would be little profit in landholding. The tax would not only go to the common good, but produce so much revenue that no other taxes would be needed. Hence, the single tax. George's book *Progress and Poverty* was a sensation in a dozen languages. It sold two million copies in America.

In the early 1900s advocates of the single tax set up a commune in rural Delaware to carry out on at least one plot of land the idea that had failed to win converts in positions of power. The commune still exists today, and Lona was one of the free-spirited alumnae who lived in this exotic mix without leaving any written traces. After spending a few years in New York, she must have linked up with the single-taxers sometime in the late twenties or early thirties. Lona's sister remembered an episode that leaves no doubt Lona spent time in the mid-1930s in Arden. Ginger recalled paying a visit to Lona when her sister was working as a room clerk at the Mary Bruce Inn, a house with a huge fireplace that was one of the landmarks of the Arden commune. Built by the author and socialist Upton Sinclair in 1911, the house had briefly served as a brothel in the 1920s before an Arden character named Mary Bruce took over and made it a cozy lodging place for visitors.

Arden, named after the enchanted forest in Shakespeare's *As You Like It,* was home to a jumble of ideologies and lifestyles. The communalists tended to the left, although no one political course was mandated. Arden developed a reputation in some respects more titillating than real. Socialists and anarchists and proponents of free love did live there at times. But art and craftmaking were also a focus at Arden, not just politics and sex, and elaborate Shakespearean pageants were enacted in the commune's lush woodland and timbered cottages. But the Depression also hit the commune, when the market for its crafts and art dried up. It would have been logical for a young woman like Lona to end a brief social experiment and find a paying job again. Before the end of the decade, Lona was back working as a governess in New York.

The Depression and continuing hard times in the 1930s seemed to further radicalize Lona, just as they piqued the political instincts of young Ted Hall. What she didn't see firsthand was widely reported in newspapers and radio broadcasts linking far corners of the nation that not so long before had been island communities. Most Americans today can scarcely conceive of what life was like then. Banks where average people kept their money declared "bank holidays" so all the funds would not be drained by panicked savers. But of course that meant depositers couldn't retrieve their money. In some rural areas—places not unlike Arden or Lona's family farm in Connecticut—people resorted to eating weeds. In New York the hungry groped through garbage bins in search of cast-off food. Groups of dozens of unemployed men would barge into food stores and demand something to eat. As early as March 1930, a breadline of more than 1,000 people awaiting food from the New York City Salvation Army broke down into chaos, when the frustrated people assaulted two bakery trucks making deliveries to a hotel.

One of the bloodiest cases of class conflict erupted when protesters marched on Henry Ford's River Rouge auto plant in Dearborn, Michigan, to be met first by tear gas and later by live rounds of fire from police who killed four demonstrators and wounded fifty more. At the mass funeral days later, the face of Vladimir Lenin gazed down at the caskets from a red banner, and 40,000 people listened to the "Internationale" as the bodies sank into the earth.

It was not only the poor or working class who turned to socialism as a cure for the disaster. Although his New Deal solutions were too modest for the most radicalized Americans, President Roosevelt did shift American government policy into unprecedented activism in an effort to bandage some of the worst economic wounds. One of his advisers, Rexford Guy Tugwell of Columbia University, was so intent on central planning that he was convinced the Soviet Union he visited in 1927 exemplified the way of the future. Prominent intellectuals endorsed Marxism. Before the 1932 election a group of fifty-two writers, critics, and professors—people as well known as Sherwood Anderson, John Dos Passos, and Theodore Dreiser—published an open letter on behalf of the Communist Party presidential candidate William Z. Foster.

By 1935, when she was twenty-two, Lona Petka was so convinced by Marxism that she had joined the American Communist Party. Coming sometime after her run-in with the socialists, the Communist Party became one of the few planks of stability in her life. Clearly opinionated and non-conformist at this early age, she wasn't the type to have cheered when the Comintern called on the comrades to reverse their denunciations of liberals and to come out in support of FDR. But her rebellion against family discipline didn't apply to her politics, now or in the future. She was loyal enough to accept the need for a Popular Front against fascism. She was a good communist cadre who went to meetings, raised money, and got evaluations recommending her for higher party school.

It was fitting that Petka, working woman and young radical, bumped into communist organizer Morris Cohen on July 19, 1937, at

Madison Square Garden. It was a breathlessly invigorating evening when 20,000 people came out to declare solidarity with Spanish loyalists fighting the fascist tide of General Francisco Franco. The American left was refocusing its fixation from the economic threat at home to the even more frightening threat of totalitarianism abroad. The Spanish loyalist cause seemed so compelling that the two most imposing lions of the left, the Socialist Party chairman Norman Thomas and the Communist Party leader Earl Browder, put aside their rivalry and spoke at the same Madison Square Garden rally.

This was one of the biggest anti-fascist rallies held in New York since the beginning of the Spanish Civil War a year earlier. Lona was there with party workers Morris knew, and the knot of young people found a cafeteria after the speeches for coffee and more heady talk about confronting the ominous times.

Morris Cohen was twenty-seven, finished with the university, and already a serious communist organizer. Within days he would put his convictions to the test by embarking on a trans-Atlantic journey to fight in Spain. Lona had wanted to go, too, but the party brass told her this was only for men. The few women whose journey the party would sanction were nurses who went to wield bandages and syringes, not guns.

On this day the burly athlete cum journalist cum radical was focusing on something besides war: the feisty young woman comrade at his table. "That was the first time I met her," Morris recounted years later. "She looked like a picture in her suit. She wore a suit I remember. And a hat, like a little bit . . ." Tilted, perhaps? Lona, short and shapely and stylish at twenty-four, did have a penchant for berets. And Morris acquired a penchant for her. "Her only disadvantage was that she was too pretty, like a bride attractive to too many people," he said. "And though by character I was absolutely opposite to her—too modest and indecisive—I decided firmly to make her fall in love with me by all means."

Petka would have been surprised to know his reaction at the first meeting, for she remembered fuming at his seeming indifference to her. "Until that time, I had read only delight in the eyes of every man. My woman's pride was hurt and I got angry with him," she recalled. "But I have to confess that I liked Morris at the first meeting. He had a very pleasant appearance. Brown eyes and very, very kind." He managed to get her phone number. But by the time Petka would see those brown eyes again, more than two years would pass. And Cohen would have found a new life, both intriguing and illicit.

CHAPTER 4

Illegals

Morris Cohen was not among the first wave of American volunteers to set out for Spain, a shortcoming he acknowledged with some discomfort on a soldiers' questionnaire. But he got there in time to be tapped for a life of service in Soviet intelligence.

For a year the Spanish cause had been a feverish topic in book stores and coffee shops and anywhere else American leftists got together. Morris was seized from the beginning by the need to stand with Spain's elected Popular Front government of communists and socialists against a military revolt led by the right-wing nationalist General Francisco Franco. "It was principally a question of leaving my parents," he wrote to explain his delay in reaching Spain. But an impassioned speech at a Bronx County party meeting had convinced him he could wait no longer. "I decided that my duty lay where liberty was in the greatest danger, in Spain."

The decision probably pleased his parents as much as it worried them. His father, Harry Cohen, may have been a produce peddler in New York, but his roots were in revolution. As an eighteen-year-old back in the Ukrainian town of Tarashcha, Harry had been an agitator for Lenin's Russian Social Democratic Labor Party. He had chosen not to leave despite the czarist repression and pogroms that continued to convulse this part of the empire in the early years of the twentieth century. He chose instead to join the increasing numbers who were fighting back. On August 9, 1905, Harry Cohen was arrested carrying leaflets to farmers in the surrounding Ukrainian towns. "Reform or Revolution" was the title of one pamphlet. "What Rights the Workers Want" was another.

Dissent had spread from St. Petersburg, the very heart of the empire, where it had crackled months earlier. Then summer got politically hot in Kiev and in towns like Tarashcha, about sixty miles to the south. Teachers were organizing. Farmers were striking. Often Jews led the protests. The response—or was it a cause of rebellion?—was typical. From February to mid-October of 1905, the militant, reactionary Black Hundreds inspired fifty-seven anti-Jewish pogroms against the perceived enemies of the czar. Sometime that year, Harry Cohen got away.

Harry toned down once he got to America, concentrating on making a living and a family. But he and his wife, Sonya, were real believers. She had arrived in New York from Vilnius a year later than Harry. The young émigrés met, married, and followed the fate of the revolutionary movement they had left behind. Friends recalled the driven, dark-haired woman as a fiery communist. At their apartment at 40 East 100th Street, their sons, Morris and Abner, learned the songs and dances of the old country, basics of the Jewish faith, and hatred of the inequities that drove his family into exile.

"Moishe got communism as his mother's milk," said one family member, using Morris's Yiddish name. "The real question isn't why Moishe became a communist. The real question is why Abner did not." While Ted Hall would learn about John Reed as a historical figure, Morris always remembered hearing one of the radical's speeches when he was seven years old. His parents took him to Tompkins Square Park on the Lower East Side to hear Reed inveigh against the United States' intervention in the Russian revolution. Seventy years later, Morris still told stories about meetings in support of the revolution that so excited his parents.

Born July 2, 1910, Morris got through school during the free-form days of the Roaring Twenties. He started out at a Talmudic school, but the whole family gradually moved away from religion as their communism deepened. Morris went on to a new laboratory school in the Bronx for bright kids, where he was remembered as a big, likable guy who got along with everybody. He combined his father's amiability with his mother's drive, and he eagerly adopted his parents' shared political values. Perhaps that unquestioning acceptance is the reason Morris—like Ted Hall—always would be the favored child whose mother felt "the sun rose and set with him."

But politics wasn't Morris Cohen's first love. Football was. At James Monroe High School, he played right guard on the 1927 team that amazed New York City by taking the Bronx championship in only the second year that Monroe fielded a team. Cohen rubbed shoulders with another athlete in his class, a boy who starred in just about everything except football. Hank Greenberg was a Monroe sportsman who would go on to become a baseball Hall of Famer for the Detroit Tigers. Sports eventually would drop in priority to second or third in Cohen's life, but he always maintained his interest, as a coach himself or just following a new sport—cricket—when he started a new life in Britain more than two decades later.

Cohen was a so-so student at James Monroe. Then after high school he spent two years at the New York University Washington Square branch, where he registered to study journalism. But the Depression was eating into the nation, and at the end of the summer of 1929 or 1930, Moishe and his brother, Abner, came back from their upstate resort jobs to find their father couldn't pay all the bills at his fruit store. Naturally Morris had worked for years at odd jobs—since he was nine years old, in fact—but now he helped by getting an athletic scholarship to Mississippi A & M College (later renamed Mississippi State University).

The Deep South was an alien world in 1931 for a New Yorker who was both radical and Jewish. One of the most shocking things for Morris when he got to Starkville, Mississippi, was not the mandatory military drills. It was that in the end this New York City boy didn't have the stuff to make a southern football team. The campus newspaper reported that "M. Cohen" suited up for the freshman team, the Baby Maroons, in their first game in 1931 against Eastern Mississippi Junior College. Not long after, Morris said, he hurt his knee and never made the varsity. But the Mississippi A & M coaches liked him and decided his sports and journalistic background qualified him to be a team trainer and publicist. "He got good recognition for the team," said former coach D. W. Aiken. A good football image always helped attract funds. And Mississippi A & M needed any help it could get then. It sat on the cusp of bankruptcy due to the Depression and political tampering by Governor Theodore Bilbo that temporarily cost A & M and three other state schools their academic accreditation.

Despite being both a football trainer and a member of the drama club, Morris was a loner in Mississippi, considered a little strange and a lot liberal for southern taste. "He was very evasive. He didn't socialize with people very much," recalled "Buddy" Richmond, who was a halfback when Morris was there. "It looked like he was what we called leaning to the left. Very liberal, you know. . . . It was most unusual to have anyone like that on the campus." Besides, Richmond said, the New Yorker was "too soft" to make varsity. The charm that would make Morris welcome in left-wing and intellectual circles later didn't have much cachet in a provincial pocket like Starkville, especially not in somebody who spoke openly about the merits of the Communist Party.

And what could Cohen possibly have thought about Mississippi A & M? It was a campus where "secret political societies" not only still existed, but were strong enough that critiques by the student newspaper brought its editor threatening letters. It was a campus where the black scientist Dr. George Washington Carver was enthusiastically received for a speech, then described in the campus newspaper as proving "that there are members of his race that are capable of being worthwhile if only given a chance." It was a college with no black students and few women, where the only jobs blacks held were menial. It was the 1930s South, and there wasn't a glimmer of agitation to integrate anything. Morris never spoke much about the political climate in Mississippi. But his actions afterward were a clear response to the racist conservatism he found there.

During college Morris Cohen worked as a stringer for the *Memphis Press-Scimitar,* and in the summers he hustled back north to work in the Catskills. He didn't just wait tables at those summer resorts upstate. He also organized waiters' strikes. "At that time everybody was talking politics," Morris later told a Russian interviewer. "There was unemployment—twenty million people. Farmers were throwing their milk away. They didn't want to sell it for two cents, or watermelons for five cents a pound. So they threw it into the river."

It wasn't long after he left Mississippi in 1935 that Morris Cohen became a Communist Party member. By that fall he was in graduate school at the University of Illinois at Urbana receiving *The Daily Worker,* working with a communist front called the American Student Union, and constantly tying up the phone with his "activities" at the house where he lived in Champaign at 104 East John Street. He worked in the University of Illinois locker room as a football trainer and traveled with the team. But what made him especially proud was his role in "building a cooperative restaurant for Negro and white students," a project he led after joining the Young Communist League. Students and a few professors got hold of a bankrupt café on the campus, renovated it themselves, and turned it into an integrated cooperative. The project nourished Cohen's political growth at the same time it kept him fed.

Cohen was stirred not only by the flawed conditions he saw around him in America, but also by the absolutely opposite tide of events he was convinced was washing over the Soviet Union. "Russia in fact did not look like any other country. It was the model of a new just society," he wrote later. "How could it not attract attention if the whole West had fallen in deep economic depression? And young Russia was developing and implementing the Herculean first five-year plan. The Soviet Union was attractive for me also because everyone had a job there, and here in America vice versa—unemployment was flourishing. That's why, like many thinking people in the West, I was overwhelmed by ideas of socialism, which were embodied in active construction of the most just society." Not until the 1950s would Cohen get the first inkling that life wasn't quite so just in Stalin's Soviet Union.

His brand of leftist activism turned out to be unwelcome in Illinois. Morris and fellow radicals printed revolutionary leaflets at night and distributed them at dawn, quickly drawing the campus cops, who plucked down the offensive fliers as fast as they were pinned up on the walls. He and another activist were called into the president's office. The president, trustees, fraternity leaders, all had gathered to warn these guys to straighten up or get out. "We were considered, you might say, the two devils in the pie," Morris remembered. They didn't stop. Morris was kicked out of the university by the end of the school year.

Back in New York in late 1935, Morris made the leap from student dabbling. He joined the Communist Party and quickly became a branch organizer in the Bronx, where he lived with his parents at 1244 Grand Concourse. He went back to New York University for more graduate studies, at the same time coaching back at James Monroe and working as an energetic young cadre of the party. While joining the Communist Party was far more acceptable in the hard times of the mid-1930s than it would be later, most members still used pseudonyms. In some cases even members didn't know each other's real identities. Thus Lona Petka may well have met someone who called himself Comrade Bruce Pickett that July in 1937, not Morris Cohen.

Cohen already had gotten a false passport in February 1937, when the first American blood began spilling in Spain. News that the American detachment lost 120 men in its first battle was no deterrent. Six days after meeting Lona Petka he was on a ship sailing for France, leading a group of seventeen American volunteers. He carried a passport in the name of Israel Altman. Many volunteers took fake documents to keep their personal records clean after the U.S. government had declared travel to Spain illegal on American passports. Washington maintained it was keeping neutral in the war. Even with false passports, sailing directly to embattled Spain wasn't possible. Most went to France, then infiltrated over the mountains.

One of Cohen's salient memories was the young French girl who met his train from Paris and led this band of foreigners silently to a farmhouse at the foot of the Pyrenees, motioning with her eyes what to do and where to go. From there they went by bus and by foot. "We walked up into the mountains all night long. We climbed, climbed, climbed. All we could see was darkness," he later recounted. "Finally we came to a plateau and there we suddenly saw sunlight shining over the Mediterranean. It was shimmering. We looked into it and everybody burst into singing 'The Internationale.' Just spontaneously, everybody started singing 'The Internationale.' "

Throughout the Spanish war Morris displayed devotion if not naïveté in his acceptance of the communist cause. Many years later he would speak about problems of competition and ego, the political infighting that eroded efforts on behalf of the loyalists. But at the time his commitment was absolute. Elected as one of nineteen low-level battalion political officers within two weeks of his arrival in Spain, Cohen was awed by the level of politicization he saw in the countryside. In a battalion questionnaire asking what had impressed him, he praised the farm workers who showed up at 3 A.M. for a political meeting before heading into the fields. Morris never wondered whether the farmers were coerced into starting their already arduous work day with political education. He described with approval how they met in "a former church, shorn of every ecclesiastical vestige, transformed into a House of the People."

In answering another question about future plans, Cohen showed not only his ideological correctness, but also a commitment that he had no way of knowing then would be so deeply tapped. "When the war is finished, I would like to return to activity in the American Labor movement. However, if circumstances require my presence elsewhere, similar to the Spanish struggle against fascism, then I would go there," he promised.

Morris was willing, but he didn't last long as a soldier. Machine-gun bullets tore through both his legs on October 14, 1937, at the battle of Fuentes del Ebro, where eighty International Brigade members died and another 150 were wounded. He spent the next four months in hospitals and even there managed to maintain his cheery nature and single-minded promotion of communist ideals. An old friend from New York, Edward Lending, found the attitude maddening when he ran into Cohen. "The first wounded casualties from the carnage of the battle of

Fuentes del Ebro were being carted in. I scouted the rooms for pals. Found Morris. A chunk of his thigh was gone. The blood had seeped through his bandages, soaked the bedding, and was still oozing. 'How are you doing, Moishe?' He responded with the beatific look of pure sainthood. 'Just *great!*'" Lending described. He rebandaged Morris's thigh and beat a fast exit. "Throughout the war, Morris remained a pre-eminent member of the widely disdained political 'Boy Scout' faction," Lending remembered.

Party functionaries thought better of Morris. Hospital political commissar Oscar Hunter, for example, credited him with "a fine sense of what the comrades want and how to develop the work around these needs." Morris was organizing while he recuperated there. By the end of January, Cohen had been elected the agitprop (agitation-propaganda) leader of the hospital's communist cell.

By February 1938 he had been chosen for the "special school" outside Barcelona, where a select group was trained in techniques of infiltration and sabotage. But in the columned, two-story villa near the hospital—a picture of it much, much later would hang on the wall of Morris and Lona's apartment—an even more select nucleus of soldier-students also was schooled in the related techniques of intelligence. General Alexander Orlov of the Soviet NKVD, who would become one of the most famous Soviet defectors, turned this branch of the special school into Stalin's first spy training ground outside the borders of the Soviet Union. Orlov set its curriculum along the lines of the Central Military School in Moscow and chose the trainees. His training center was so secret that even the Spanish authorities whom the Soviets had come to aid didn't know of its existence. In one message to his superiors Orlov boasted of his success simply in keeping the place running, "taking into consideration that the whole school is illegal." One war account said the unit's underground training in guerrilla tactics and espionage was so secret that Spanish militia "once mistakenly arrested the entire group, requiring direct intervention of André Marty [the International Brigade commandant] to obtain its release."

Morris Cohen became one of the elitest of the elite at the special school. One day he was invited outside the villa for a discussion about radio techniques. The discussion was cover for an invitation to become an intelligence operative when he got back to America. He thought he was being asked to work for the Comintern but it was for the Soviet NKVD.

"At that time the fascists were trying to cut through the front and they were nearing the sea, the Mediterranean," Cohen remembered. "It was a very difficult moment. And then the comrades at that time—the Soviet comrades—suggested that fighting against fascism could be advanced by going into [their] Service." General Orlov's NKVD file credited him with personally recruiting and training Cohen. Why Orlov never told American authorities about Cohen after the general received asylum in the United States in mid-1938 remained Orlov's secret; perhaps he forgot Israel Altman's real name. In any event, Cohen required no coercion or brainwashing. Working for international communism seemed a logical step in his ideological journey. "So I said to the comrades: 'Yes.'"

Even these high-performance comrades of the special school got a few breaks from their training. Jack Bjoze, a recruit from New York who remained a lifelong friend of Morris Cohen, recalled: "He wasn't much of a drinker. One drink and he giggled the rest of the night. We went at night bar hopping, sometimes looking for girls." Then there was the miscalculated soccer challenge to the German team. "They slaughtered us," remembered Bjoze, "but Morris was the best player on our team." Bjoze said Cohen wasn't there the day he met Ernest Hemingway at the Ritz Hotel in Barcelona. But in a letter years later Cohen said he too at some time had bumped into the writer who gave the world a passionate and critical glimpse of the Spanish war in *For Whom the Bell Tolls*.

After a few months of intelligence training, Cohen was assigned in April 1938 to the International Brigade headquarters in Albacete as a "special guard." For the last six months of the war, Cohen served in an NKVD-run intelligence unit whose functions remain unknown. Judging from the reminiscences of Cohen's wartime comrades, the unit was mainly held in reserve and took no part in investigations and executions of Trotskyist "traitors," the manhunts that would become a target for the American Communist Party's critics after the war. Morris's buddy Jack Bjoze would remember that the intelligence unit did little more than hang around waiting for orders.

Cohen sailed on the *Ansonia* for New York in December 1938, leaving Spain just before Barcelona fell to Franco. In January the remaining foreigners fled with a panicked flood of refugees into France, to be followed shortly by 220,000 loyalist soldiers of the Spanish Republican army. By March, the left-wing Republican government had fallen. Vet-

CHAPTER 5

Quirky Talent

In that summer of 1939, Ted Hall was a chubby-cheeked boy of thirteen who couldn't decide whether he wanted to become a comedian, a journalist, or a physicist. Ever since he was six, Ted could race through math problems faster than a Yehudi Menuhin cadenza. In English and every other subject, he was also far above average. After skipping three grades, he sat for the city-wide examinations and won one of about eighty precious places in Townsend Harris High School, the city's free training ground for intellectually gifted boys.

During his first weeks at Townsend Harris in the fall of 1937, his mother asked Ted what he wanted for his twelfth birthday. He named a book by the visionary British physicist Sir James Jeans. *The Mysterious Universe* was a sophisticated primer on the burgeoning field of physics with chapters on cosmic rays, Einstein's theories of relativity, and even the daunting subject of quantum theory. Even to a family of furriers in the trough of the Depression, Ted's musings about growing up to be a physicist somehow didn't sound far-fetched. Rose found the book and added an inscription. On the flyleaf she wrote: "To My Son Theodore, On His 12th Birthday. As you say, perhaps with this book, 'You have started your career.' Many, many happy returns of the day, son. And good luck. Mother."

The James Jeans book "fired my imagination," Ted would recollect. He and his older brother, Ed, plowed through it together page by page. To his delight, Ted came to realize that there were riddles in physics and advanced math that he could grasp faster than Ed. One was matrix multiplication, an algorithm for multiplying sets of numbers that is used today as a benchmark for comparing the speeds of computer chips. "I was very intrigued at the time. There were times when A × B does not equal B × A—what the hell is that all about?" Ted recalled. "I really wanted to get to the bottom of it." Ted idolized his brother, who was eleven years older and already had a B.S. degree in engineering and a second in chemical engineering from City College of New York. His brother, Ed, was the kind of person who could make anything work, the kid who built radios for fun and ran special effects for the high school drama club. Ted was put off by Ed's impatience with his boyhood clumsiness whenever Ted built something with his hands. "I had the feeling that the whole engineering side of things had been preempted by my brother," he recalled. "I didn't want to enter that field because it would be completely dominated by him. He was not a theoretical physicist by any means. So I thought, okay, I'll be a theoretical physicist."

There wasn't a school in New York that could have done more in 1937 to challenge Ted than Townsend Harris. A year later, the new experimental Bronx High School of Science opened at Crestwood Avenue and 184th Street. But through the rest of the decade, Townsend Harris was just about as good as Bronx High in the sciences and superior in everything else. Townsend Harris was an intellectual sibling of City College of New York, where three fourths of Harris graduates went on to study. Harris occupied the ninth through thirteenth floors of the City College business school building on Twenty-third Street in Manhattan, a ten-minute walk from Greenwich Village. The high school was named after a self-taught New York merchant of chinaware who became American ambassador to Japan and returned to found CCNY. As the city's school for the intellectually gifted, Townsend Harris tended to draw immigrants' sons who were smart enough to have skipped several grades. About 80 percent of the school was Jewish. "You could always tell the Harris students from CCNY students because the ones from Harris wore short pants—they were a collection of very young people," remembered Ted's classmate Gilbert Steiner, who was to become a Brookings Institution scholar on social policy. Ted joined the science, German, and French clubs and played on the class baseball team. In his spare time, he memorized the batting averages of his Major League favorites, played Ping-Pong, and read books about Newton and Einstein.

As an adolescent Ted Hall manifested the same puckish, non-conformist streak that would follow him to Los Alamos and beyond. Ted grew up with parents who believed in Judaism and an elder brother who was agnostic. As Ted neared his thirteenth birthday, he developed his own antipathy to religion. "How can I have a bar mitzvah if I am an atheist?" Ted remembered asking the rabbi. Barney and Rose pressured

Ted to go through with his bar mitzvah, and Ted finally stopped his protests rather than provoke a family crisis. But when he did go to shul on Saturday, he chanted a parody he and Ed composed of the Hebrew ritual song "Adon Olam": "I don't know Lum, he don't know me. I don't know Lum, and his whole family. Who is this Lum, a gol-darn bum, Lum, Oh Lum, a bum by gum." Either the rabbi didn't hear Ted above the chants of the other kids, or he pretended not to.

When it came to preparing his bar mitzvah speech, Ted decided that he wasn't going to recite the set formula. With the rabbi's permission he drafted a jeremiad on the dangers of fascism in America, but the rabbi rejected it as too polemical for a bar mitzvah. Ted produced a second draft and a third, until in the end he felt the speech was no longer his. Ted complained to his brother, and together they concocted a joke. It involved one of the hottest secular topics in the neighborhood, the proposed destruction of the Sixth Avenue El. Especially in Forest Hills, the suburb on Long Island where the Holtzbergs had moved, a lot of people didn't want the screeching old elevated line abandoned. But others in the congregation thought the city would be better off with the new Eighth Avenue subway that Mayor Fiorello La Guardia had promised. It was a subject on which every New Yorker had an opinion. So when Ted finally stood up in the synagogue with the rabbi beside him and his family in the front row, the little cherub wound up his memorized speech with a flourish the rabbi hadn't vetted: "We must eliminate from the world: poverty, greed, intolerance . . . and the Sixth Avenue El!" The congregation was outraged. But according to Holtzberg family lore, the rabbi not only pronounced Ted a man but told the congregation that the Jewish community needed fearless individuals like Ted. His brother, Ed, scarcely expecting him to carry through with the stunt they had cooked up, buried his face in his lap. "It was just something that I thought would be absolutely irrelevant and would spark off something," Ed remembered long afterward.

Three weeks after Hall's thirteenth birthday, his school and the rest of world had to react to a much deadlier outrage, the Kristallnacht pogrom in which ninety-one Jews died in Nazi Germany. It didn't take long for the wrath of activist students, Ted among them, to turn against Herr Miermann, the German teacher at Townsend Harris. "There was one episode where Miermann made some anti-Semitic remarks and the whole class got up and walked out," said Ted. Another time, he and some other pupils trooped to the principal's office after Miermann and a student named Wolinsky had a classroom set-to that they felt had anti-

Semitic overtones. Ted seems to have taken the Miermann issue a good deal more seriously than some of his classmates. "I am not sure the sentiment against Miermann was widely felt, even though a very substantial portion of the class was Jewish," said classmate Steiner, who also took German from Miermann. By Steiner's account, most Townsend Harris students "were so preoccupied with their schooling that concern for the outside world and political affairs was virtually nonexistent." But another classmate, Bob Bleiberg, who would go on to become publisher of *Barron's Financial Weekly,* recalled that the mindset of most of his teachers and fellow students was left-wing. "The radical thing was just taken for granted," remembered Bleiberg. "Given the climate of the times, what else could one have been in New York City?"

Ted had been reading his brother's left-wing literature since he was ten or eleven. He was about thirteen when he joined the American Student Union (ASU), the same communist-orchestrated student organization that Morris Cohen had joined three years earlier at the University of Illinois. It was an affiliation of student socialists whose beliefs on American domestic politics roughly paralleled those of the most liberal flank of Franklin D. Roosevelt's New Deal coalition. It steered well to the left of the Roosevelt administration on foreign policy. When Ted joined the ASU in around 1938, the Spanish Civil War was the glowing issue. With the Soviet-backed loyalists suffering defeat after defeat, the ASU thundered condemnations against the Roosevelt administration for imposing an arms embargo on the Spanish loyalist forces. Ted was only thirteen, but he was to remember the Spanish Civil War as an event that influenced his outlook for the rest of his life.

Though Ted had no reason to know it when he joined, many ASU chapters were led by people involved with the Young Communist League or the Communist Party. The student who founded the ASU chapter at City College in 1936 was an undergraduate in electrical engineering who would make a big name for himself: Julius Rosenberg. Ted, who was seven years younger than Julius Rosenberg, never met him. After a year or so, Ted decided that he didn't belong in what he had come to regard as a knee-jerk "communist front." Julius stayed in the communist movement, but Ted drifted away from the ASU around the time of Stalin's decision in August 1939 to sign a nonaggression treaty with Hitler.

That winter of 1939–1940, Ted's gift for piercing the most complex algebraic equations and his incessant reading yielded very high marks on the New York State Regents examination. The fourteen-year-old senior may have scored even higher on Columbia University's entrance test, recording what his mother would claim were among the highest marks ever. Ted was tentatively admitted to Columbia. But when his mother brought him in for an interview, Ted's youth was against him. "We don't think he should be entering Columbia at this time," an admissions officer told his mother in the spring of 1940. "Academically, obviously he is up to it. But why don't you send him around the world for two or three years?"

Even if they could have afforded it, world travel didn't strike Rose and Barney Holtzberg as the best idea for their fourteen-year-old Townsend Harris graduate—certainly not when France was falling and Britain was evacuating its army from Dunkirk. Besides, Ted was going through a difficult stage. One sign was his growing rebelliousness against organized religion. Not long after his bar mitzvah, Ted started refusing to attend synagogue, even on Yom Kippur. On one high holy day, Barney gave Ted a direct order: Get dressed for services. Ted, who was wearing his only dress shirt, responded by grabbing the shirt and pulling until he ripped off all the buttons. "I hated this commitment to a religion that was part of my parents," Ted remembered. "I thought it was utterly irrational and couldn't be justified. I launched a one-man sabotage campaign." The best way to handle Ted, the Holtzbergs decided, was to keep him close to Forest Hills. Instead of sending him along the expected path to the Manhattan campus of CCNY, Ted's parents entered him at Queens College, the local branch of the city university, where he would be close to home and distractions would be fewer.

Ted started Queens College in the fall of 1940, two months before his fifteenth birthday. Once again, he soared ahead of his classmates, especially in mathematics. "Calculus was a delightful subject," remembered Ted. Sociology interested him also, but what he really wanted was to become a mathematical physicist. "I remember thinking that what I would like to do was to have really two careers," Ted said. "I would like one career that would be sort of in an ivory tower, where you could just enjoy theoretical physics abstractly, not on a utilitarian basis, but just for the pleasure of doing this work. I also felt that I had a social debt, that people should do things which would benefit humanity. So I felt I would try to balance my career. If I did enough work that was useful to humanity, then that would earn me enough time to do the academic work that had no apparent use." It was this vision of repaying his "social debt" that would soon lead Ted Hall to take the law into his own hands, confident that he knew how to make the world a safer place.

Just as his quirky talent for math was surfacing, the world was being transformed by a revolutionary discovery that would nudge Ted further down the physics track. In January 1939, an Austrian Jewish émigré in Copenhagen was experimenting with a source of neutrons that was nothing but a vial of radium salts mixed with beryllium powder. When physicist Otto Frisch put the neutron "source" up close to a bit of uranium, he found that his oscilloscope went crazy. Every time Frisch repeated the experiment, the oscilloscope measured an unexplained "spike" of energy. Other more eminent physicists in Rome, Paris, and Berlin had tried the same experiment but failed to grasp the meaning. Frisch consulted by phone with his physicist aunt, Lise Meitner, in Stockholm. Together they decided the pulses must mean that uranium atoms were splitting when assaulted by neutrons.

Frisch was the first to call the splitting of the atom "fission." The phenomenon reminded him of watching through a microscope as a one-celled paramecium divides. Frisch and Meitner published a momentous monograph in the British journal *Nature* entitled "Disintegration of Uranium by Neutrons: A New Type of Nuclear Reaction." Enrico Fermi, already a Nobel Prize winner and now a refugee from Mussolini's fascist Italy at Columbia University, knew instantly what their discovery meant. As Fermi looked out the window at Manhattan stretching below his office, he curved his hands into the shape of a large ball. A bomb no bigger than this and it would all disappear, he told his Dutch colleague George Uhlenbeck.

In the next year and a half, as Ted was finishing Townsend Harris, revelations about the innards of the atom spilled out in a synergystic stream from physicists around the world: from Otto Hahn in Berlin to the Joliot-Curies in Paris to Louis Turner at Princeton. At first, their findings didn't resonate beyond professional journals. But a few weeks before Ted's graduation from Townsend Harris, *The New York Times'* science correspondent William L. Laurence published a front-page story headlined: VAST POWER SOURCE IN ATOMIC ENERGY OPENED BY SCIENCE. Laurence wrote of fresh experiments by Columbia Professor John Dunning toward extracting a new, magical-sounding isotope that could not only serve as a fuel but also explode with enormous power. "A chunk of five to ten pounds of the new substance, a close relative of uranium and known as U-235, would drive an ocean liner or an ocean-going submarine for an indefinite period around the oceans of the world," Laurence reported. The discovery of this strange uranium 235 isotope bore tremendous implications for the outcome of the European war, Laurence wrote. "Every German scientist in this field, physicists, chemists and engineers, it was learned, has been ordered to drop all other researches and devote themselves to this work alone."

California Institute of Technology physicist R. M. Langer wrote that summer in *Collier's* about a coming atomic Garden of Eden in which energy would be so abundant that it would cost nothing and people would scoot around in uranium-powered cars. "War itself will become obsolete because of the disappearance of the economic stresses that immemorially have caused it," Langer predicted. The only problem, he wrote, was that citizens of the future would have to keep uranium 235 out of the hands of "eccentrics and criminals." Just one ton of the magic isotope "might well be made to destroy every creature for hundreds of miles."

More than half a century later, Ted remembered the grip that nuclear physics exerted on him. "I read that there was this tremendous potentiality for atomic energy—that you would be able to drive the *Queen Mary* across the ocean on the energy locked up in the atoms of a cup of tea," said Ted. "That captured my imagination." But he could also see darker possibilities. One day, most likely as a Queens College freshman, he handed in a composition in which he described an imaginary episode that would remain in his memory for the rest of his life. It told how he woke up one morning and "there was this glow in the sky and it turned out to be the result of a nuclear chain reaction," Ted remembered.

During the summer after Ted's freshman year at Queens College, the war in Europe took an abrupt turn that would alter everyone's life. In a surprise attack on the night of June 21–22, 1941, the Nazis struck the Soviet Union along an 1,800-mile front. Thus ended the two-year-old Nazi-Soviet nonaggression pact during which Stalin had supplied Hitler with food and raw materials. Hitler's "Operation Barbarossa" instigated the most violent battle in the history of warfare, involving a German force of 3.2 million troops in the largest invasion army of any war. Before the war on the Eastern Front ended three years later, it would consume over 35 million victims in the Soviet Union, Germany, and the lands caught in the middle.

For all the devastation the Nazis caused to the Soviet homeland, Hitler's invasion brought shivers of excitement to many idealistic young Americans like Ted. Now that even President Roosevelt was on the side of the Soviets, the 1939 Nazi-Soviet nonaggression pact was forgiven or forgotten. As the Red Army absorbed blow after blow from the Wehrmacht, a broad band of the American left began pulling for Stalin to prevail. About the only ones who wished Stalin ill were the Trotsky-ists, who wanted to see another revolution that would purify the Soviet Union of Stalin's errors. Ted had some Trotskyist friends and they used to spend afternoons together doing volunteer work at the Henry Street Settlement House on the Lower East Side of Manhattan. Along with some passionate debates on the "crimes" of Stalin, these teenagers spent a lot of the time at Henry Street listening to the Victrola playing anti-fascist working-class songs like "United Front," a melody from pre-Hitler Germany written by Hanns Eisler with verses by Bertolt Brecht. One of the songs Ted found most rousing was "Meadowland," which became a sort of unofficial Soviet theme song to many Americans on the left. "Oh, working folks, peasant folks, Keep on building, keep on till-ing," the song exhorted, promising Soviets new "fruits of revolution."

For Ted, the war on the Eastern Front became a preoccupation. From Queens College he would hurry home after classes to read the battle dispatches in the *New York World-Telegraph.* "There were these enormous maps showing the movements of the armed forces and battles that were taking place. And I felt tremendously taken up and involved in the reports of these battles. I was following the developments on the other fronts too, of course, but the front that was of greatest interest for some reason was the Nazi-Soviet battle front. I felt a tremendous con-cern whether this city would fall or whether there was a counterattack in that city."

He felt more of a "response on a human level" when he read about the Red Army than he did, say, about the Battle of Britain or the 1942 American landings in North Africa. It wasn't that he considered himself a communist. But like many East Coast college students of his genera-tion, he was intrigued by the potential of the Soviet social system. And he came to feel that the American government was manipulating the war to crush this promising experiment. Ted was enraged when he heard that Missouri's Senator Harry Truman had remarked on the day after the Nazi invasion: "If we see that Germany is winning we ought to help Russia, and if Russia is winning we ought to help Germany, and that way let them kill as many as possible."

When Ted began his second year of commuting to Queens College, the Soviet cause seemed hopeless. Even if he had wanted to help, what could Ted do as a sophomore in an academic backwater? Soviet resis-tance was cracking. "For all military purposes Soviet Russia is done with," Hitler's press chief, Otto Dietrich, exulted on October 8, 1941. German panzers had captured Minsk and Kiev, encircled Leningrad, and broken through the road to Moscow. So grim were Stalin's prospects that he was ordering most of his government to evacuate from Moscow to the Urals. When Ted marked his sixteenth birthday on October 20, 1941, the Soviet Union seemed finished.

Then came the first blast of Russian winter, catching most of the Germans without warm uniforms. "If they want a war of extermination, they shall have one," Stalin said November 6 in a ceremony deep inside Moscow's Mayakovskaya metro station. After that came a surprise Soviet counterattack, spearheaded by fresh Red Army units rushed from the Far East by the Trans-Siberian Railroad. The German offensive was blunted just twelve miles short of Moscow. Now there was time after all to send aid to Stalin, and both Franklin D. Roosevelt and Winston Churchill hastened to do just that.

What Stalin wanted was guns, guns, and more guns. He wanted all the capitalist countries would give through official channels—and all his spies could get through stealth.

CHAPTER 6

Comrades

N ow Stalin's intelligence service enlisted a new clandestine operative in New York. Though no one could have imagined it from her dossier, this latest agent would begin helping the Soviet war effort almost immediately.

By the opening of the 1940s, Lona Petka was anything but a Mata Hari. She had her hands full with a Manhattan project of her own: bringing up a rich kid on Park Avenue. For several years Lona had worked as a governess for the Winstons, a prosperous family with two small children, a son and a daughter. The way Lona understood it, the Winston wealth came from a bedsheet-manufacturing business. Her main job was rearing Alan Winston, who was about ten and liked to play in Central Park. During her off-hours Lona devoted her energy to the American Communist Party. But up to then she had been involved in nothing more underhanded than teaching Alan to play catch. "She was a tremendous tomboy," said Robert Beatson, an FBI agent who investigated Lona long afterward. "She was the kind of person who could throw a baseball and skate." Even after Alan Winston went on to Columbia University, he would talk fondly about how important Lona was to him growing up.

Lona was fated for a plunge into espionage, and it started a fortnight after Hitler's June 1941 invasion. That is when she ran off to Connecticut to marry Morris Cohen. Morris had been infatuated with Lona for months, and he was not the only one. No one would mistake her for Garbo, but she did have what it takes to make heads turn. Flippant, blond, and five-foot-five, she exuded a throaty sexiness that not everyone found attractive. "She was kind of flighty and drank a lot," said fellow Communist Party member Jack Bjoze. Jack had been one of Morris's buddies in the Soviet intelligence school in Barcelona and met

Lona after the two men returned to New York. Jack, who never really liked Lona, considered her "sexy" but scarcely "pretty."

Morris's parents liked Lona even less. Part of it was that their Moishe was the first-born, the favorite, the college boy, the wounded Spanish war vet. Morris's mother, Sonya, felt that her son was too good for a woman with so little schooling—not to mention the fact that Lona wasn't Jewish. Marxist to the core, Sonya Cohen had long since rejected Judaism as a faith. But that didn't mean she welcomed their Moishe marrying a woman who grew up Catholic. "On the surface Lona was accepted as a good communist," said one of Morris's relatives. "But there was also a level on which she was considered a hardnosed Polish shiksa."

Morris had courted Lona since early in 1940. Tuesday was her day off from the Winstons', and Morris would take her to the Cameo Theater on West Forty-second Street, which specialized in Soviet-made movies. For months, Lona had her doubts about him. For such a smart and well-educated man, she found him unbelievably reserved. "Once I told him, 'That's my advice to you, Morris. Be yourself. Be reserved, but not too much,'" Lona recounted. "Because people who are too much closed up inside themselves attract attention."

Ostensibly, Morris was working two jobs. One was as a kitchen helper in the cafeteria of the Amtorg general offices at 210 Madison Avenue. It was an impressive building at the corner of Thirty-sixth Street with polished brass mail chutes and tiled Art Deco wall mosaics in a high-ceilinged lobby. His second job was substitute teaching at a Manhattan public elementary school. The school was in a poor neighborhood—or so his old high school coach Joseph "Doc" Weidman figured, "because he called me and asked if I could lend him some baseballs, footballs, and bats."

What only the Soviets knew was that Morris had a third occupation as a full-fledged agent of Soviet intelligence, assigned to Semyon "Sam" Semyonov's spy ring that operated out of Amtorg. Cohen was Semyonov's main and perhaps only American espionage assistant inside Amtorg. Morris didn't tell a word to Lona about this, but she sensed that he was up to something. Why else would he sometimes vanish from New York without explanation?

Morris's initial assignment for Soviet intelligence was finding out what German Nazi supporters might be up to there in New York. But given the breadth of what Semyonov was trying to pull off, it was only natural that Morris gradually became Semyonov's link to various spies, either those the Soviet had recruited or those Morris developed on his own. In the early forties Semyonov was running an industrial espionage ring that was harvesting technologies from labs and factories throughout the Northeast. One of Semyonov's agents, Alfred Slack, was giving him details of the manufacture of film from his job at Eastman Kodak in Rochester. Another agent, Harry Gold, was helping Semyonov obtain an operating manual from the DuPont plant in Belle, West Virginia, for making nylon. Semyonov also was credited with obtaining equipment to make the 1940s wonder drug penicillin.

Being a disciplined Red with her own contacts in the American Communist Party leadership, Lona took her quandary about Morris to headquarters. "I couldn't make up my mind," Lona explained. "I had a different boyfriend. He was a lawyer, he had a lot of money. And I knew the party always needed money. So I went to one of the high officials in the party and I said to him: 'Look, what in the devil shall I do?' "

"What are you talking about?" the communist official asked Lona. She replied that if she married the lawyer, she was sure she could wind up sending more money to the party treasury. "Look, you'll get married, you'll get a wealthy husband, you'll have servants, you'll have everything you want," said the American Communist Party functionary. "You'll forget about communism."

"No," Lona answered. "Never."

"Well, then marry a poor man and you'll do your work together," she remembered the communist leader saying.

By the summer of 1941 Lona was still wavering. "I thought about it and I thought about it," she said. Her doubts dissipated a few days after Hitler launched "Operation Barbarossa." On July 3, Stalin spoke to the Soviet people over the radio, and the speech was the lead story in *The New York Times.* "Our country is in serious danger," Stalin said as the panzer columns rolled toward Moscow. Admitting that Latvia, Byelorussia, and much of the Ukraine had fallen, Stalin called on the Soviet people to retreat if necessary after destroying everything. Five days after Stalin's speech, Lona walked into the county registrar's office five miles from her mother's farm in Taftsville, Connecticut. She filled out the marriage license application, listing herself as Lona Terese Petka, a twenty-eight-year-old governess. She described Morris as a thirty-one-year-old "steward," probably a reference to his work in the Amtorg kitchen. They were married on July 13, 1941, by Albert J. Bailer, the justice of the peace in Norwich.

"It wasn't really a wedding," remembered her sister Ginger. "It was just a family gathering. It was a very, very small affair." So small, in fact, that not a single one of Morris's relatives was there. Ever afterwards, the Cohens blamed Lona for ensnaring Morris with sex. The wife of Morris's brother, Abner, recalled Abner telling her in later years: "Moishe was a very sexy guy and Lona lured him. They started living together and she gave him all the sex he wanted, that's why they got together. Because a mental genius I don't think she was. But she was a good-looking woman. And a sexy woman. And my husband said his brother fell for it." To one of the men in the family Abner sometimes put it more crudely: "Moishe was a good man, but Lona always led him around by the dick."

Raw physical attraction was certainly part of it, but there was also an ideological passion between Morris and Lona that Abner couldn't ever grasp as a Joe American patriot with his own vegetable business in Trenton, New Jersey. Morris and Lona started seeing each other while the Hitler-Stalin nonaggression pact was in effect, and that meant they were clinging to the same ideological lifeboat. Thousands were quitting the New York branch of the party. Those who stayed in were pummeled with criticism from old friends. "It was really awful, because everyone jumped on us, on the people who were sympathetic to the Soviet Union," remembered Lona. Morris was the target of similar taunts. Just a few years earlier, Morris had worked with the head of Waiters Union Local No. 1, Benny Gottesman, when they were both campaigning to organize New York's waiters and waitresses. Gottesman was the kind of man whom idealists in food unions admired, a man who stood up to racketeers like Arthur (Dutch Schultz) Flagenheimer when they had tried to take over Local No. 1. Now even Benny Gottesman told him, "Why, you dirty Red, what about the nonaggression pact the Russians have signed with the Nazis?" Morris and Lona came to feel that they were sharing adversity and he admired her because she wasn't the sort of woman to back away from an argument. The pact was not nearly as bad as it sounded, Lona kept saying: Stalin was simply buying time to build up the Red Army. Morris used the same line. "My Uncle Joe is very smart," he told Gottesman. "He'll smoke his pipe and he'll watch."

Only as a newlywed did Lona learn that her husband's real job was espionage. Morris sprung this little surprise on his bride within weeks of their marriage. "One day he came with a bouquet of red roses and put them in the hallway," Lona remembered. "I could see that he wanted to tell me something but he could not." Finally he got up the courage. And in the same conversation he went on to suggest that his superiors wanted her to work as an intelligence agent too. Lona reacted as if she had been stung by a hornet. "When I told her about my mystery, all at once she accused me of something like treason," Morris recounted. "I had to explain to her that if I betrayed America for money, or if I had betrayed the party or my convictions, that would have been a different thing since I would have betrayed the ideas which made up my credo."

After fulminating about Morris's "treason," Lona calmed down. Whether it was because of her passion for communism, or hunger for adventure, or dedication to her new husband, Lona came to the conclusion that spying might not be so bad. She agreed to try it and sometime later she was instructed to use the pseudonym "Helen" in dealings with her American contacts, a cover name she would use the rest of her life. Soviet intelligence also assigned her an internal code name—"Lesli"—which was to be Lona's secret designation in enciphered Soviet intelligence communications with Moscow.

The newlyweds pulled off a minor sensation within her first few months in the Soviet secret service, according to a veiled disclosure fifty years later by the KGB. Lona was said to have wormed her way into the confidence of an American engineer working in a fighter-plane factory near New York. The KGB said Lona convinced the man to tell her about an American experimental project to develop a new aerial machine gun that could increase the killing power of fighter planes. Once her information reached Moscow, Soviet aircraft experts asked the Soviet intelligence *rezidentura* in New York if it was possible to obtain a sample.

Lona was then assigned to a second phase of the job. She was told to "explain" to her American friend that he had already violated the law—an unsubtle threat that if the man didn't go along, his original leak might be disclosed to the FBI. Lona's contact was induced to walk out of the airplane factory with the machine-gun barrel strapped to his back inside a heavy coat. Somewhere outside the factory, the man rendezvoused with Morris, who had brought along a carrier. It was a musician's case for transporting a double bass, the only container anyone could think of that was large enough for a machine-gun barrel.

"The problems with receiving the barrel did not end there," the KGB account said. "The barrel had to be sent to the Soviet consulate, but anyone trying to get onto the grounds was likely to be searched at the gates by the American police." Nor could Morris simply deliver the barrel to Amtorg, which was by then under FBI surveillance. So Morris arranged to hire a cutout: an "unemployed Negro" who is said to have taken the double-bass case to a flea market in Harlem. The unsuspecting courier was instructed to look for "a man in purple trousers and a long checkered coat." Sure enough, the man turned up and the "double bass" was loaded into a Soviet diplomatic car. The barrel was in the next diplomatic shipment to Moscow.

The machine-gun caper was Lona's first triumph. But the KGB-approved version omitted one key detail: the name of a young American communist who allegedly covered Morris as a backup agent while he was transporting the machine-gun. That backup agent—or so one KGB veteran has claimed—was Julius Rosenberg, a CCNY engineering graduate who supposedly worked in tandem with Morris more than once before the war.

Soon there was no need to steal machine guns. In January 1942, the American Lend-Lease program began shipping Stalin billions of dollars' worth of fighter planes, tanks, guns, blankets, and radios. Relieved of the need to steal ordinary weapons, Soviet intelligence began to focus its attention on obtaining technological secrets. One of them was the new science of tracking distant objects with electronic pulses by measuring the echo. It was so new that the U.S. Navy had just assigned it a code name: radar.

Thanks in considerable part to Morris Cohen, radar didn't stay secret from the Soviets. In the spring of 1942, someone in an American war plant gave Soviet intelligence an initial clump of documents on radar and agreed to give more later. For the next three years, that's what the "radar source" did. "He passed many secret documents to us," recounted the retired Soviet intelligence officer Alexander Feklisov. "They were a matter of great interest to our scientific research institute. Every year he transmitted to us two or three thousand pages of photographs of secret materials, the majority of which were appraised as either 'valuable' or 'extremely valuable.'" Feklisov devoted a long section of his memoirs to describing his World War II dealings with the radar source, who still remains unidentified. The Feklisov book included a vague but intriguing account of how the radar source was first recruited: Some unnamed Soviet agent, who was about to be called into the army, signed him up and then turned him over to another Soviet agent to supervise. It was only in 1995, over a cup of tea in his Moscow apartment, that the eighty-one-year-old Feklisov finally disclosed that the recruiter of the radar source had been Morris Cohen.

Cohen didn't have long to savor his deed. "He already had received a letter telling him he was to be drafted into the American Army," Feklisov said. On July 8, 1942, five days before his first wedding anniversary, Morris Cohen got a notice that he was inducted. Two weeks later he reported to Fort Jay, New York, to join the river of young draftees called by Roosevelt to fight Germany and Japan. Most veterans of the Spanish Civil War got the worst assignments the U.S. Army had to pass out, and Morris was no exception. He was sent to the Quartermaster Corps' 241st Service Battalion, trained as a cook, and then shipped out. Private First Class Morris Cohen would spend the next two years at an American transit base at Dawson Creek in northern Canada, near the Alaska border.

"I went into the Army and Helen took over," Morris would remember. "We had been building up a group until there were about seven comrades in the group. And she took over this work."

For a while, managing these seven agents was all Lona Cohen did for Soviet intelligence. But it wouldn't be long before the New York *rezidentura* appraised her performance highly enough to assign her several more agents. One of her new charges would be a young scientist inside a secret War Department weapons base in New Mexico nicknamed "the Hill."

CHAPTER 7

Harvard Egg Roast

If Ted Hall hadn't decided to transfer to Harvard, he would never have been recruited for the Hill, let alone been diverted into a rendezvous with Lona Cohen.

It was Ted's older brother who introduced the idea of transferring to Harvard. Not long after Pearl Harbor, Lieutenant Ed Hall came home on furlough to Forest Hills from the U.S. Army Air Corps. With all the overbearing persuasiveness of an older brother who had just been made an officer, Ed denigrated Queens College as a "high school" and said sixteen-year-old Ted was wasting his brain. If Ted was ever going to amount to anything, he had to find the best university in the country.

Harvard's deadline had passed, but Ted applied anyway and the university sent back an acceptance almost by return mail. In the spring of 1942, that really wasn't remarkable. Spurred on by President James B. Conant, Harvard was fast transforming itself into an extension of the war effort. Eager to attract more students with a bent for chemistry, physics, and mathematics, Harvard was losing its Groton accent and admitting the raw cream of public high schools that might not have passed through the strainer in the thirties. Now students should concentrate on one objective, Conant told the freshmen who appeared in Cambridge for a special summer term. That was to "frame their college career with an eye to winning the war."

By the fall of 1942, when Ted Hall arrived, Harvard was starting to look like an offshoot of Annapolis. "A flag pole rose in front of Hollis, and nightly retreat ceremonies were in order," wrote the freshman class historian. "Bells were installed in Navy dorms, and loudspeakers blared orders of the day through the yard to add to the general confusion. Even Holden Chapel was turned over to the military for the first time in its long history since Revolutionary War days. The martial air invaded Soldiers Field where the ROTC held their own daily ceremony." For the first time Harvard offered a course in the science of military camouflage. Physical training classes were compulsory four days a week. Students competed to see who could sell the most war bonds, and rooms were scavenged for scrap rubber, old clothes, and metal for the war effort. And from atop its new perch on Widener Library, an air-raid siren interrupted classes with its mournful practice wails. Harvard had to absorb still another innovation in 1942: women. An account by a Harvard class historian said: "The formerly cloistered walks of the Yard now swarmed with women students, of all types, from the traditional Midwestern high school teachers to the sweater girls of the big Eastern culture factories." There were also hundreds of Navy wives. The Navy took over the dormitories in the north end of Harvard Yard for its V-12 officer trainee program. The Yard's walkways were widened to accommodate four-abreast marching columns, and bicycle riding was banned to avoid collisions with Navy wives pushing baby carriages.

Of the sixteen-year-old whiz kids who entered Harvard in 1942, Ted Hall was granted the most advanced placement. Instead of starting him in the freshman class, Harvard decided his Queens College transcript was strong enough to make him a junior. Fortunately for Hall, he had matured early. Slender as a fence post, he stood five feet eleven and a half inches tall and was rather handsome. Especially after he bought his new tweed sport coat, he didn't look like the prototypical grind. And though physics was clearly his specialty, he had a curiosity that reached far beyond the laboratory. "Have you seen any Italian prisoners & how are they?" Ted wrote to Ed on September 6, 1942, a few days before he was to leave Forest Hills for Harvard. His brother was now an Army Air Force engineering officer for the advance U.S. contingent at a Royal Air Force base near Oxford, England. "How does the India situation seem from England?" inquired Ted's neat script. "What kind of a guy is Cripps (ditto Churchill, Bevin & Co.); how does British industry compare with American; how does the average Britisher stand politically, etc.?"

One of the formative accidents on Ted Hall's path toward espionage was that Harvard assigned him to room with two of the leading campus Reds. It happened because Ted drew a room in Leverett House. Since the 1930s, the brick residential hall overlooking the river had a reputation as a magnet for leftist intellectuals, hence its nickname "Moscow-on-the-Charles." The name originated after Leverett students founded the John Reed Club in 1932 to honor the 1910 Harvard grad and Communist Party member who wrote *Ten Days That Shook The World*. The John Reed Club, said to be Harvard's first pro-communist organization, was an intellectual society for studying Marxism. Later in the thirties, interest in left-wing ideas grew strong enough that Leverett chose one of the only communists on the faculty as the house's "counsellor on American history." The professor picked for this novel assignment was Granville Hicks, who had become the toast of East Coast radical circles when he published a glamorous biography of John Reed in 1936 subtitled "Making of a Revolutionary."

Toward the end of the thirties, the club was still going strong at Leverett under a new name—the John Reed Society. But by the time Ted arrived, the John Reed cult seemed an odd relic to many. Granville Hicks had left Harvard, the Stalin-Hitler nonaggression pact had made communism less chic, and besides there was a war on. "I heard of something called the John Reed Society, but I never understood whether it existed, or was defunct, or what," remembered Roy Glauber, another physics student who lived a few corridors away in Leverett. And judging from accounts in the Harvard archives, Leverett dwellers were far more interested in the house sport of pitching coins in the Common Room, a game called Shove-Ha'Penny, or in performing bawdy skits whose authorship was attributed to a creature of "infinite wit and sagacity" named Joshua, the canine mascot of Leverett House.

Among the 3,494 undergraduates at Harvard in the fall of 1942, there were no more than a dozen active participants in the John Reed Society. It was only by chance that Ted Hall was assigned to room with two of its leaders. Both were so witty and articulate that their influence on Ted was instantaneous. "My roommates as a matter of fact are quite brilliant," Ted wrote to his brother less than a month into his first term. A few months later he wrote Ed that they "are tops—absolutely exceptional." As Ted Hall remembered, his roommate Jake Bean was the campus chairman of the John Reed Society, and the other, Barney Emmart, was one of its more active members. Emmart, the son of A. D. Emmart, the *Baltimore Evening Sun*'s acclaimed editorial page editor, alternated among a hundred preoccupations, from eastern religions to calypso music. Jake Bean, a Minnesotan, was so brilliant in art history that he was invited into Paul Sachs's celebrated "Museum Course" for graduate students at the Fogg Museum. Bean never finished college but he would go on to become one of the world's foremost connoisseurs of Italian and French drawings and the curator of drawings at New York's Metropolitan Museum of Art.

These were intriguing sorts compared to the students he had known at Queens College, and it wasn't long before Ted decided to join them in the John Reed Society. Neither of his roommates was convinced the John Reed Society offered the ultimate answer to politics. "They regarded it as sort of a joke," Ted remembered. "Certainly they had no training in Marxism and they were without any passionate devotion." Sometimes it seemed to him that Barney and Jake applied the same clever cynicism to communism that they did when their cat fouled Emmart's music box. That's when the three composed a takeoff of the official Leverett House fight song, giving Ted Hall a chance to test his teenage talent in parody writing. The least bawdy of their lyrics went:

> *Pepsi-Cola, pig's asshole-a*
> *Somebody shat in my Victrola . . .*
> *Leverett House, Leverett House, rah, rah, rah.*

DESPITE TED'S INITIAL impression that Harvard offered him "incalculably more than Queens," his first term at Harvard was almost his last. He began by filling his plate with courses in physics and math, including optics, electricity and magnetism, and mechanics. Then, to satisfy the registrar's distribution requirements, he added German and a philosophy course called "Fundamental Issues at Stake in the War." Once the courses began, Hall was dismayed to find himself thrown into a succession of big lecture courses that met only an hour or two a week, leaving no room for interchange with professors. The trouble with Harvard, Ted wrote his brother, was that "there is no laughing in classes . . . no appreciation of the lusty beauty of effective learning that is to be applied to world-building." He recognized that his professors and fellow students were a cut above those at Queens College, but he complained that a Harvard education consisted of listening while "an authority is dumping his irrefutable facts into the heads of good students who will learn it all." Increasingly, Ted devoted his energy to extracurriculars. He signed up for guerrilla training and attended lectures on how to parachute behind enemy lines. He also joined the math club, played tennis, and learned how to row a shell on the Charles. To satisfy his "war service" requirement, Ted became an air-raid warden and spent evenings monitoring a switchboard at an Air Raid Precaution Unit office in Boston. He was on duty November 26, 1942, when a call came about a fire out in the suburb of Quincy. This wasn't the Nazi air raid the city had been dreading, but almost as bad: The Cocoanut Grove nightclub fire killed 491 people, including fourteen affiliated with Harvard.

There were gloomy stretches during those first four months when Ted doubted whether Harvard was right for him. "I was full of angst at the time," he remembered. "It is what happens to lots and lots of college students, maybe most. 'What is this for? Is it really relevant? Is this what I want to do? What good is it?' So I used to spend a lot of time playing table tennis when I should have put more time in on my studies." When the grades for the term came out in December, Ted found that he was not even close to the the the top. "I was used to being way, way ahead of my class," Ted Hall would recall years later. "And here was a bunch of people who were equally bright, at least. The material being taught was deeper and more difficult. It sort of threw me, getting used to the different standard." The pangs of what amounted to first-time failure for Ted were so acute that he had a hard time controlling his nerves over Christmas break. "Personally I have been suffering psychological violence," he wrote to Ed in early 1943. "I almost quit college last December—I had absolutely no interest in work in any field. I decided to leave but Mom and Dad got me back against my will. That was lucky—now for the first time I am going steadily and securely in several fields under my own power—and know I shall continue that way."

After barely surviving his first semester, Hall experienced a kind of awakening in the spring of 1943. It was partly because he was taking Physics 41, a course in "Kinetic Theory and Statistical Mechanics" taught by Professor Wendell Furry, who was also his college adviser. "Mathematical physics is surprisingly remote from physics—you seem to get results from nothing," he marveled in a letter to his brother.

The deeper Ted dug into the curriculum of advanced math and physics, the more captivated he became—and the more his precocious talent became evident to his professors. Einstein's work mesmerized this seventeen-year-old junior, and he wrote to Ed about his encounters with the theories of special and general relativity. "The special is astonishingly simple and elementary—it could be fully appreciated by a bright student who has had no more than an elementary calculus course. The general takes a lot more sophistication mathematically, is an unbelievably ingenious and imaginative hunk of analysis and is correspondingly beautiful." Ted was equally enthralled by quantum mechanics. "The old or 'classical' quantum theory is a nice enough piece of work as far as it goes," Ted wrote. "It seems to open the way—to strengthen and prepare the mental muscles—for the bold and sweeping quantum mechanics or wave mechanics just as [Einstein's] special theory did for the general. The old quantum theory is just a simple little hypothesis or set of hypotheses. The new is hot stuff, but it introduces few new mathematical tools. It is conceptually bold but easy to follow—not like the general theory of relativity." In fact, Ted found quantum mechanics so engrossing that everything else in his field paled by comparison. "Simple atomic physics is pedestrian stuff," he wrote Ed dismissively. "It's lots of fun, but hardly dazzling."

Aside from science, what absorbed Hall most in that spring of 1943 was Marxism. Trying to develop his own alternative to Marxist analysis, Ted began to ponder how to reduce any economic system to a set of equations, using the kinds of dependent and independent variables he studied in math class. Perhaps political forces, not Marx's economic imperatives, were the impulses that really governed society, Ted speculated. "I even gave a talk on that to the John Reed Society—to about ten people," Ted was to recall. To him it seemed an outrage that the Communist Party had strayed so far from its Marxist origins. His first year at Harvard coincided with a period when Stalin was downplaying Marxism as a goodwill gesture to the Allies. Ted was ruffled because the American Communist Party was sounding like a pale version of the New Deal. "I remember once remarking to Jake Bean that John Reed was lucky to have died when he did," Ted remembered, "because if he had lived another ten years, he would have turned into a cynical anticommunist." Despite Hall's disapproval of the latest party line, he spent a good deal of time in bull sessions about communism as a philosophy. That April Ted typed a two-page account for his brother about what he had been doing at Harvard. The only thing Ted mentioned besides physics was in the final paragraph: "As to other activities, if you are interested, I have been very active politically."

During the war-imposed summer term, Harvard became a grimmer and less frivolous place, especially for Ted. Washington had lowered the draft age to eighteen. Campus social life had turned into a round of alcohol-sodden farewell dinners for classmates en route to the front. "Our youth is spent, our fling is flung," said a couplet in the *Harvard Lampoon* addressed to President Conant. "So shoot the sheepskin to us, Jim, we're off to war." Ted's summer semester started well enough when on the strength of his spring grades Harvard awarded him a $200 scholarship, an honor that was rarely given to transfer students. Still only seventeen, he was also asked by the Physics Department to fill in as an instructor to teach elementary physics to Army trainees who were now filling Leverett House. But just before summer classes started, a personal blow knocked him off his trajectory. In mid-June, Ted's mother, Rose, went into a coma and died after eleven days, a victim of cancer. Until much later Ted did not realize how hard this hit him. This woman who had irritated him all through high school by telling him "Do this BE-CAUSE" was gone at the age of fifty-seven. After that, there was no-body like her to tell him what he should or shouldn't do. "Superficially this had very little effect on me, but looking back, I think it made me a little more lost," Ted said. The bleak moods of the previous fall once again intruded that summer, and he again let his grades slip below A's. To recoup his top standing in Professor George David Birkhoff's rela-tivity course, Ted had to work forty-nine straight hours around Labor Day to write a term paper exploring the mathematical nexus between atomic physics and Einstein's theories of relativity. "I cite the thing [his term paper for Birkhoff] as evidence that all spark is not dead," Ted replied defensively after Ed had sent a worried letter about why he wasn't working to his capacity.

When the fall term started in October, seventeen-year-old Ted Hall was one of the rare seniors not yet in uniform. Leverett House had been commandeered as a military barracks, and Bean and Emmart had found their own quarters. Ted had moved next door to Lowell House. He also acquired two new roommates—who would both play puzzling roles in Ted's later life.

Initially, Hall roomed only with Roy Glauber, the physics student he'd known from Leverett. Glauber, just one month older than Hall, had come to Harvard as a sixteen-year-old freshman out of the first graduating class of Bronx High School of Science. At this point he was only a junior, but the department also made him into a part-time in-structor. Given their common interest in physics, it wasn't surprising that Glauber and Hall had decided to room together in the two-man suite. The surprise was that another student, Saville Sax, appeared to join them in Lowell House during the fall.

Hall was out of town the day Glauber came back to the room to find Sax crouched over the fireplace. "He was burning some paper," Glauber remembered. "I asked him what he was doing, and he said, in a kind of husky voice, 'I'm roasting eggs.' Somehow the dining halls weren't open, and he had a couple of eggs that he had put into the fire, and of course they burst, and scattered egg about. And I thought this was one of the strangest people I had ever met." Sax moved in with Ted and Roy Glauber and began sleeping on the couch in the living room.

Dark, wiry, and bohemian, "Savy" Sax was a lost soul at Harvard. He had arrived as an eighteen-year-old freshman in September 1942 intending to become a writer or a poet. He had come from De Witt Clinton High School in New York, where one of his closest friends had been another boy with literary ambitions, James Baldwin, the black writer whose searing commentary was to arouse a generation. Sax came from a family of poor Russian Jewish immigrants who escaped to America in 1914 after pogroms struck their ghetto town of Vinnitsa in the Ukraine. His father, Boris Sax, had gotten in trouble for publicly criticizing the czar and would remain a lifelong devotee of the Russian revolution. Like Ted Hall's father, Boris Sax grew prosperous in America. In the 1920s and 1930s he ran a New York upholstery business, making money on the side importing Russian embroidered altar cloths, samovars, and other artifacts that had been confiscated from aristocratic Russian estates by Lenin's followers. Unlike Ted Hall's family, the Saxes had made little effort to assimilate into American society. "Not only were all the people that they knew Russian and Jewish and communist, but they were all from the same village," said Sax's eldest son, Boria Sax. "Quite a number of the people from the village came with them, and they all lived together in one big building in New York."

Saville Sax was a child of double handicaps. He was born with a deformed left hand, the result of a tangled umbilical cord while he was in the womb. Then when he was twelve, he was psychologically wounded by his role in the death of his father. His mother, Bluma, who was going into the hospital for surgery, had detailed Savy to sleep in the same room with his father and give him his heart medicine when it was needed. One morning Savy woke up to find that Boris Sax was dead. "Apparently he slept through his father's heart attack," said Savy's future wife, Susan. "And from then on, Bluma would sometimes in moments of rage accuse him of causing his father's death." From a childhood as the bright, charming, and over-indulged son, Savy grew into an adolescence darkened by Bluma's rejection and possessiveness.

At Harvard, Sax could not focus his talents. "He had wild and interesting ideas, but no intellectual rigor," explained a friend who came to know him after the war. "He found it difficult to find his way." As it turned out, what mattered most about Saville Sax was not his poetry but the politics he absorbed from his parents. By the time he roomed with Hall and Glauber, Saville Sax was a believer in Soviet communism and a participant in the John Reed Society. Despite their different academic interests, Hall and Sax became close friends on the basis of their political proximity.

By the start of his senior year, Ted had crunched through the whole catalog of undergraduate physics courses. Now, along with Glauber and a few others, he was pushing deeper into post-graduate territory. Only one course they took really mattered to Hall's future, and that was Professor John H. Van Vleck's class in quantum mechanics. Van Vleck was one of the two or three leading American experts in this abstractly fascinating area of modern physics; he would go on to win a Nobel Prize in 1977 for his work in the thirties on magnetism. But there at Harvard, Ted Hall considered Van Vleck's course superficial. In Ted's view, Van Vleck "did absolutely nothing about shedding any kind of light on all the usual paradoxes of quantum physics: such as how can a particle be somewhere and you can't determine where it is."

Though Professor Van Vleck didn't satisfy Hall's curiosity, Ted demonstrated an uncanny intuition for imagining how infinitesimally small chunks of matter are interconnected. "Oddly enough, I was pretty much at home with it," Ted remembered about Van Vleck's course. "Somehow I managed to guess at the right answers to some rather confusing questions. I felt that I didn't fully grasp the subject and yet I could guess at how you perform little tricks of calculation." In any event, Van Vleck noticed Ted—and that made an irrevocable difference. Ted didn't know it, but Van Vleck was one of the half-dozen luminaries of American theoretical physics whom J. Robert Oppenheimer had assembled in the summer of 1942 in Berkeley, California, to start designing an atomic bomb. Most of the participants, including Edward Teller and Hans Bethe, had gone on to join Oppenheimer at the War Department's atomic research laboratory in Los Alamos, New Mexico, that opened in March 1943. Van Vleck, who was five years older than Oppenheimer, had spent several weeks at Los Alamos that spring as part of a top-level advisory committee sent by the War Department. But Van Vleck decided not to join the Manhattan Project and instead returned to teach at Harvard. Even so, he stayed on good terms with another New England Brahmin, Vannevar Bush, who was now Roosevelt's wartime chief of research and development.

Thus, when Bush needed some bright physics students to work under Bethe's theoretical physics group at Los Alamos, he naturally turned to Van Vleck. He and Physics Department Chairman Edwin Kemble selected at least four candidates. Soon a civilian recruiter from

Washington arrived at Harvard's red brick Research Laboratory of Physics, a fifteen-minute walk from Lowell House. The man was in his late forties, wore a dark suit, and had been a physics professor at the University of Pittsburgh before the war. His name was Merrill Hardwick Trytten, and he was Bush's chief of personnel.

Poison gas had made World War I into a war of chemists, but what the United States needed now was physicists. One 1943 report showed that between the Army and Navy and Bush's Office of Scientific Research and Development, the nation was seeking 315 physicists for high-priority projects. Bush had grabbed up fully two thirds of all the physicists in the United States for his projects, draining every top university of physics professors, instructors, even graduate students. "Almost overnight, physicists have been promoted from semi-obscurity to membership of that select group of rarities that included rubber, sugar, and coffee," scientist J. Hammon McMillen observed.

It was Trytten's job to find physicists for the three secret crash projects considered vital by the Joint Chiefs of Staff: radar, under the Radiation Lab at MIT; solid-fuel rockets, at the California Institute of Technology; and the proximity fuse, assigned to Johns Hopkins. But what had brought Trytten to Cambridge that day was a far more speculative project, one that Roosevelt had approved as a hedge against a Nazi breakthrough despite the skepticism of the military. It was the idea Enrico Fermi visualized from his window at Columbia in the spring of 1939: the chain-reacting bomb that could destroy everything in sight.

Roy Glauber kept the clearest memory of what happened after Trytten arrived. Glauber remembered Trytten calling him into a dimly lit faculty meeting room that had been unused for many months. "That room had the mustiest smells," said Glauber. "The shades were drawn in there. But we went in there and sat at the table. And he sat and told me in the most earnest terms that there was some war work in which he thought I might be qualified to take part, but he couldn't tell me a thing about it." Before they left the room, Glauber filled out a security questionnaire. It asked him to list every organization he had ever joined, every place he'd ever lived.

Ted Hall met Trytten separately about the same time. It was within a few weeks of Ted's eighteenth birthday on October 20, the date he became draft-eligible. Ted recalled sitting in a room somewhere in Cambridge with a middle-aged man from Washington who told him "that there was this project, that it was doing quite important work, and they needed some more hands." When Hall asked about the project, all the man would say was that it was very secret and very important to the war effort. Though Hall didn't know it yet, he was on his way to becoming a junior physicist on the Hill—insiders' jargon for J. Robert Oppenheimer's atomic bomb lab.

AFTER THE RECRUITER left for Washington, Ted walked back to Lowell House. In a room upstairs Ted soon got into a discussion about the mysterious interview. It was a "light-hearted" conversation with one of the other three Harvard undergraduates whom Trytten had summoned. It turned out that neither student had even been told the location of this secret site where they might be working, so all they could do was "trade speculation" about what kind of a strange project this might be.

Saville Sax, Ted's leftist, literary-minded roommate, overheard the conversation. When Savy realized that Ted might be sent off to do secret military research, he murmured something in Ted's direction. As best those words of Saville Sax can be reconstructed, they went like this: "If this turns out to be a weapon that is really awful, what you should do about it is tell the Russians."

Ted Hall wasn't outraged at the suggestion of passing secrets to the Soviet Union; actually, his mind was already turning over that same possibility. What really startled Ted that day was that the idea had occurred to Savy. Ted took him aside. Never, never talk to anyone else about this, Ted said. Not even as a joke.

CHAPTER 8

Awful Magic

All Ted Hall knew when he stepped off the train in the high desert of New Mexico was that he had been offered a secret job that involved physics. He had finished his course work at Harvard, so wouldn't miss much by being off campus for the six months before the Class of 1944 was due to graduate. Despite his speculation about the nature of the project, this gifted, moody teenager hadn't come close to guessing that he was on his way to the most important secret scientific enterprise of the twentieth century.

It was January 27, 1944, six months before the Allied landing at Normandy. Ted had ridden the Santa Fe Super Chief from Chicago with Roy Glauber. The two physics students from New York were about to join a Noah's Ark of other science prodigies at a military base that hadn't existed one year earlier. At eighteen, Hall and Glauber were the youngest scientists ever recruited for what Oppenheimer called "this somewhat Buck Rogers project."

A tall man in blue jeans and cowboy boots hailed them on the platform at a desolate crossroads town called Lamy, New Mexico. Glauber thought the greeter must be a touch of local color supplied by the Fred Harvey hotel chain, which had enlivened earlier whistle stops by sending Indians through the passenger cars selling Navajo blankets. "A Fred Harvey cowboy," Glauber remembered thinking.

The "cowboy" turned out to be a mathematician working for Oppenheimer who had come down to pick up them and a third passenger getting off at Lamy. A stocky dark-haired man of about forty, this older passenger introduced himself as "Mr. Newman." The three arrivals piled into the car for the eighteen-mile drive north to Santa Fe. Once in the drowsy state capital, the man in cowboy boots led them to an unmarked door at 109 East Palace Avenue, right on the main square.

They moved through a courtyard, past a shabby screen door, and into the Army Corps of Engineers reception center. When Roy Glauber signed the log book, he felt a click of recognition. "Mr. Newman" had just signed his name as "John von Neumann." Here was the same Hungarian-born mathematician from Princeton whose insights into quantum mechanics had become a topic of wonderment among American theoretical physicists in the late thirties. What Hall and Glauber didn't know was that Oppenheimer had invited von Neumann to Los Alamos to solve the mathematics of creating an "implosion," which seemed an outlandishly difficult problem to the rest of Oppenheimer's staff.

After picking up their temporary passes, Hall, Glauber, and von Neumann climbed back into the car. From Santa Fe they drove twenty-five miles north on the Taos Highway, then turned west at the Indian trading post called Pojoaque to cross the rickety one-lane Otowi Bridge over the Rio Grande. Then west up a steep, unmarked road cut through the red rocky hills toward the Jemez Mountains. Finally, they reached the top of a broad mesa riven by canyons left over from the collapse of an ancient volcano.

On Pajarito Plateau, 7,200 feet above sea level, they found the cabins, barns, and ice house of the old Los Alamos Ranch School, which had been a prep school for fifty boys. At Oppenheimer's suggestion the Manhattan Project commandeered the school in late 1942 as site for a new laboratory that would centralize research on fast-neutron physics, the scientific thruway to the atomic bomb. The lab's name and location were military secrets because of the risk of Nazi sabotage. To the Army Corps of Engineers, the 54,000-acre site was "Project Y," "Zia Project," or "Area L." Those who worked there referred to it by an even vaguer circumlocution: the Hill. Only in internal documents was the place ever referred to as the Los Alamos laboratory.

Once inside the fence, von Neumann parted company with the neophyte physicists. No sooner had he left than Hall startled the admissions staff with a remark that implied he already knew what was going on at Los Alamos. "When we were assigned our room numbers in the dormitory, I made some crack, some silly little crack," Hall remembered. "My room was number T-236. And I said lightheartedly, 'Oh, that's just next door to U-235.' The others could see that I had said something I shouldn't have. I didn't know anything. It was a pure spontaneous joke. I knew absolutely nothing." The next day they understood the alarmed reaction. At an orientation, Ted Hall and Roy

Glauber rejoined their Harvard schoolmates Kenneth Case and Frederic de Hoffmann, who had arrived on the Super Chief three days ahead of them. Now the four Harvard men learned they really would be working on a secret weapon—just as Hall and his other roommate, Saville Sax, had suspected back at Lowell House. There were two substances that might serve as "active ingredients" in the chain-reacting bomb the lab was designing, they were told. One was U-235, a difficult-to-separate isotope that made up one part in 140 of natural uranium. The other was referred to only by its code name, "49." It was the artificial element plutonium, which had to be manufactured atom by atom in a cyclotron or nuclear reactor.

Their briefer, the Cornell physicist Robert Bacher, made clear that Los Alamos scientists worked in an exotic atmosphere of utter candor mixed with absolute secrecy. Bacher was the dour, straitlaced chief of Oppenheimer's experimental physics division. Outside the lab's two-story wooden work buildings called the technical area, scientists were forbidden to say anything, he said. But inside the nine-and-a-half-foot barbed-wire fence, there would be no limits on what they would be allowed to know. Oppenheimer and others would hold wide-ranging colloquia to share what was known and what wasn't. The weekly colloquia and all the laboratory's classified scientific reports would be open to anyone with a white badge, which denoted a member of the scientific staff. Months earlier at Harvard, the four students had filled out their security questionnaires and had received their War Department clearances with no delay. That was all. Once at Los Alamos, they got their white badges automatically.

Over the next few days they completed their white-badge initiation by reading "The Los Alamos Primer," the secret booklet prepared in April 1943 to bring new scientists up to speed on the theory of bomb making. In the first seven paragraphs the primer laid down an eye-catching hypothesis: one kilogram of U-235 $\cong$ 20,000 tons of TNT. Marshaling a phalanx of formulas, diagrams, and logarithmic charts, the twenty-four-page mimeographed primer drove relentlessly toward the conclusion that an atomic bomb was not hard to achieve, once enough "active material" was available. All one had to do was to figure out a way to "shoot" together a "critical mass" of the magic isotope U-235. The simplest way, the primer said, might be to adapt the barrel of a U.S. Army cannon—a scheme that came to be called the "gun-type bomb."

Behind all the formulas, the theory of bomb making was plain. With its 92 protons and 143 neutrons, an atom of U-235 was so huge and cranky that it needed just one little tap before it split: Simply ping it with a high-speed neutron to start a chain reaction. This fast neutron was likely to get "absorbed" into the uranium nucleus, instantly rendering the nucleus so unstable that it would fly into pieces. What would be left over after such a U-235 fission would be a pair of new smaller atoms, each with roughly half the original atomic weight of uranium. The split would also yield at least two "fast" neutrons whizzing out with enough energy to collide with other nearby U-235 atoms. That could keep a chain reaction going through new generations of neutron multiplication. The awful magic of fission was that the particles created by splitting one atom would weigh a smidgen less than the atom that disappeared. If the chain reaction ran fast enough, the neutrons would multiply through about eighty generations before the bomb core flew apart, and the missing smidgens would be transmogrified into a monstrous surge of energy. The same kind of a chain reaction should work if plutonium 239 were substituted for U-235, except it ought to take less plutonium to make the bang.

By the time Ted Hall checked in, Los Alamos had been functioning ten months and some of the initial optimism reflected in the primer was wearing off. Oppenheimer had assembled a staff of 600, from physicists and radiochemists to cooks and medics, and recruits were arriving every week. A sizable minority of the senior staff were eminent European Jewish émigrés, including Hans Bethe, Emilio Segrè, and Edward Teller, who had been driven into exile by the "Aryanization" of European universities inspired by Hitler and Mussolini. The rest were mostly unknown American assistant professors or graduate students from Berkeley, Princeton, Columbia, the University of Wisconsin, and the few other campuses that taught advanced physics before the war. The average age of the scientists was about twenty-nine, and it wasn't unusual to find graduate students in their early twenties entrusted with important work. It was a galaxy of talent with ideas whirling in all directions.

By wartime standards they lived a constricted but relatively comfortable life behind their barbed-wire fence. Everyone worked long hours six days a week, and in the spring it got muddy because there had been no time to build sidewalks. But few griped about the locale and the lack of creature comforts. It was only the regime of wartime security that bothered Laura Fermi, who would settle in during the summer with her husband, Enrico. "We were too many of one kind, all packed together," she remembered. "None of us [European scientists] had lived in such conditions, conditions so similar to those of a concentration camp. . . . It was not only the barbed-wire fence, the passes and the badges, the inspections of the cars going in and out of town. It was also the Army running the town uncontested and on a socialist basis. The apartments, for instance, were assigned to us according to the number of people in the family. We had no voice in choosing them and we paid rent according to salaries!" As the juniormost civilian scientist, Ted Hall had his own room in one of the two-story wooden dormitories for bachelors built on patches of land a mile or more beyond the log cabins of the ranch school. There were soldiers to haul coal and stoke the stoves. Hall ate most of his meals in North Mess, the common eating hall run by an Army mess sergeant. With the country on food rationing the fare was monotonous. But as a civilian with a white badge, Hall didn't pull KP.

The big problem at Los Alamos in early 1944 was that the Manhattan Project's much larger sites at Oak Ridge, Tennessee, and Hanford, Washington, had not yet started producing active material. Los Alamos had scrounged all the paraphernalia it needed for radiation tests, including a cyclotron trucked in from Harvard, a Cockcroft-Walton accelerator from the University of Illinois, and two Van de Graaff particle generators from Wisconsin. But without samples of real factory-made plutonium and enriched uranium from Oak Ridge and Hanford, the experimental physicists on Oppenheimer's staff could not measure the physical properties of these strange and virtually untested substances that the laboratory was supposed to make into bombs.

Major General Leslie Groves, the chief of the Manhattan Project in Washington, was getting impatient. On February 4, 1944, Groves informed President Roosevelt that an efficient bomb would require somewhere between eight and eighty kilograms of U-235. Groves had to acknowledge that the amount of active material needed for a single bomb was unknown and would remain so until Los Alamos received the test samples from the other Manhattan Project sites. With that range of uncertainty, Groves couldn't know whether the first bomb would be finished in a year or a decade.

Of the four Harvard recruits, Ted Hall fell into the most important job: directly measuring uranium's most crucial properties. De Hoffmann, Hall's suave and aristocratic classmate from Austria, was sent to the lab's experimental nuclear reactor, the "water boiler," and assigned to apply fireproof paint to the inside of a thermostat box. Case was put in Hans Bethe's more prestigious T-division, the theoretical physics division, and given routine work churning out calculations on the likely distribution of neutrons in a gun-type bomb. Initially Ted, too, was sent to T-division. But within a few days he heard that Glauber was unhappy with his assignment to the experimental physics division. "That was all right with me, I wasn't particular," Hall remembered. "And so I swapped. And that is how I got into Bruno Rossi's lab."

Bruno Benedetto Rossi, Ted's boss for the next eighteen months, was one of Oppenheimer's established luminaries. A thirty-nine-year-old Italian émigré physicist with a world reputation in measuring cosmic rays, he came to Los Alamos from Cornell in the summer of 1943. Oppenheimer assigned Rossi to design and build electronic counters for the rest of the lab. Rossi was one of the six group leaders in Bacher's experimental physics division, or P-division. That autumn Rossi and Philip Koontz, a younger cosmic-ray physicist from the University of Colorado, began developing an ingenious new fast-acting radiation counter. Packaged in the one instrument were a fission counter and an electron-collection chamber filled with the inert gas argon. It was called a "double ionization chamber" because it was supposed to allow simultaneous measurements that would match the known physical properties of hydrogen against the unknown properties of uranium or other potential bomb ingredients.

When Ted turned up as Rossi's new junior scientist in early February, he was just in time to help finish building the double chamber. Within a few weeks, a courier finally arrived in Los Alamos with the first few grams of enriched uranium from Alpha II, an electromagnetic separation plant at Oak Ridge. Rossi had said he needed two grams of enriched uranium for his measurement, but Bacher put him off. Instead he parceled out the first Oak Ridge sample to other scientists in P-division for tests using cruder equipment, since stray vibrations were interfering with Rossi's double chamber. Rossi planned to fix the device by hanging the whole chamber inside a soundproof metallic shield; helping to do this was Ted's first job.

It was only in mid-March 1944, after the second courier shipment from Oak Ridge, that Phil Koontz and Ted Hall were allocated a strip of metal foil plated with a layer of enriched uranium. They carried the strip into Technical Building W, a peaked-roof clapboard structure close to the lip of one of the canyons. There, on March 29, Koontz and Hall inserted the strip inside the double chamber and bombarded it with a beam of high-energy neutrons from the "long tank," as one of the Van de Graaff particle generators was nicknamed. A week later they ran a second test on the long tank and the results matched perfectly. "The results of these tests seem most encouraging," Rossi wrote in a report that reached Oppenheimer.

Ted's job was to insert the uranium-plated foil into the double chamber while Koontz, Rossi, and others watched. "It wasn't the easiest gadget to work with," Hall remembered about his first attempt. "Just mechanically, it was a little bit fiddly getting the specimen in place. . . . As I mounted the specimen, I remember my hands were shaking. I don't know whether they were shaking enough for anyone else to see. But they all sort of looked the other way."

What seemed more worrisome than contamination was that the dab of uranium might be lost and the tests could be delayed for weeks. But Hall didn't drop it. Rossi's progress report of April 15, 1944, said Koontz and Hall had produced a first set of measurements on the "cross section of fission" of U-235 under the impact of high-energy neutrons. Fission cross section simply meant the probability a given atom would split when its space was impinged upon by an approaching neutron. The higher the fission cross section, the lower the critical mass of uranium needed for a chain reaction—that was something every Los Alamos white-badger realized. The Manhattan Project's Metallurgical Laboratory at the University of Chicago had already determined uranium's fission cross section for slower-moving "thermal" neutrons, the variety of neutrons that Enrico Fermi had harnessed there in 1942 inside the first atomic reactor under Stagg Field. But the only way to detonate an atomic bomb was to employ fast neutrons, and no one really knew the likelihood that an onrushing fast neutron would succeed in splitting a uranium atom. The Koontz-Hall experiment was the first in the world where uranium's fission cross section had been so precisely measured in relation to these bomb-type fast neutrons. Now it would be straightforward arithmetic for the Theoretical Division to plug the new physical constants into an equation and calculate the critical mass of uranium.

Rossi stripped away the qualifiers in his report for the lab's senior staff on May 15. Koontz and Hall had succeeded in measuring the cross section of fission of U-235 in six separate experimental runs, Rossi said. The only problem was that the cross section they measured was nearly 20 percent lower than Oppenheimer had been anticipating. This signaled that each uranium bomb might require 20 percent more uranium than had been calculated in the Los Alamos primer. Another team at Los Alamos confirmed the new measurements using an entirely different method. However, it was a relief for Groves, who was expecting worse and had added a big cushion in the uranium estimates he submitted to the military. After a trip to Los Alamos in June 1944, the general reported to the War Department's military policy committee that the maximum amount of uranium needed for one bomb could now be considerably reduced.

Within the confines of Los Alamos, Ted Hall was given ample credit. That summer the experimental physics division circulated a report informing others in the lab of the absolute values of the U-235 fission cross section and how they were calculated. "Hall, Koontz, and Rossi" were listed as having performed the work, with Koontz and Rossi named as its writers. Perhaps Rossi modestly decided to list all three collaborators in alphabetical order, a practice that was far from universal even in the democratic milieu of wartime Los Alamos. Or perhaps Rossi was impressed enough with the work of his youngest collaborator to toss him some recognition. Whatever the reason, Rossi put Hall's name in the most prominent position on the title page of a document that circulated to Oppenheimer and all the laboratory's division chiefs. It was like a copy boy getting a byline on the front page of *The New York Times*.

Half a dozen other groups at Los Alamos were still competing to define the fission cross section for use in a uranium bomb. But in the fall of 1944 a follow-up report by another Los Alamos group leader, Professor John Williams of the University of Minnesota, acknowledged that the Hall, Koontz, and Rossi measurements had been accepted "as a standard of cross sections for fast neutrons in this laboratory." These first readings, which Ted Hall helped Koontz and Rossi take, would remain the standard until well after World War II. Fifty years later, when a team of Los Alamos officials compiled the definitive technical history of the wartime laboratory, they cited "Theodore Hall, Philip Koontz, and Rossi" as having not only constructed the counter, but also run the experiments that defined U-235's fission cross section for fast neutrons.

In June 1944, Ted graduated cum laude from Harvard in absentia. Not yet nineteen, he had experimented on the frontiers of atomic physics and played a bit part in determining the critical mass of the uranium in the gun-type Hiroshima bomb. Now, no more than a few weeks after his graduation, Ted was promoted by Rossi into a new, more sensitive position as a team leader on a project involving the actual mechanism of the bomb. Rossi's July 1 progress report specified that Ted and two older scientists, Hans Staub and David Nicodemus, were assigned to make and test "detecting equipment for [the] Ra-La implosion experiment." In other words, Hall, Staub, and Nicodemus were supposed to help check out the same far-fetched idea of an atomic implosion that had drawn von Neumann to Los Alamos back in January.

The discovery of one of the nasty properties of plutonium caused a crisis at Los Alamos that summer. Though Ted had nothing to do with the discovery, it would make his work on the Ra-La implosion experiment far more important. Until then everyone from Oppenheimer down had assumed that plutonium would be no trickier to fashion into a bomb than uranium. But in April 1944, Los Alamos had received the first samples of plutonium made in a nuclear reactor at Oak Ridge. Using fission counters set up in a U.S. Forest Service cabin in the Pajarito Canyon, physicist Emilio Segrè discovered that this production-grade plutonium showed an unexpectedly high rate of spontaneous fission. The Oak Ridge plutonium turned out to contain an unstable impurity, the isotope Pu-240. This hadn't shown up in the first specks of plutonium made in the Berkeley cyclotron. But cyclotrons couldn't make enough plutonium for a bomb; the only way to create enough had been to build exorbitantly costly nuclear reactors. Now, after the reactors had been built and paid for, Segrè was finding that one gram of this impurity produced an ominous 1,600,000 spontaneous fissions every hour. And no one knew how to scrub out the impurity. Oppenheimer realized almost overnight that "Thin Man"—a plutonium bomb based on the gun-type design—was condemned to "predetonate." The muzzle velocity of a "gun" was limited to 1,000 meters per second, and that was far too slow for slamming together a critical mass of plutonium. At the instant before detonation the plutonium components would melt and Thin Man would fizzle.

Oppenheimer, devastated, considered resigning as director of Los Alamos. He broke the news about Segrè's readings to the lab staff at a colloquium on July 4, 1944. Now there was only one hope for salvaging the Manhattan Project's massive investment in making plutonium reactors. It looked like a long shot but Oppenheimer could see no alternative. As the Los Alamos technical history put it, "It was decided to attack the problems of implosion with every means available, to 'throw the book at it.' "

All of a sudden, the best experimental route for testing whether any kind of plutonium bomb was salvageable was the Ra-La implosion experiment to which Ted Hall had just been assigned.

CHAPTER 9

Clues to Enormoz

The first tip said the secret Anglo-American atomic bomb lab was "somewhere in Mexico." Two months later, a second version mentioned an unknown "Laboratory V" where uranium research was under way. Neither clue pinned down the place as Los Alamos, but no matter how slim and deceptive the information, it was enough to tantalize Leonid Kvasnikov.

Stalin's lieutenant Vyacheslav Molotov had sent the thirty-nine-year-old intelligence operative to New York in early 1943 for one reason—to check out rumors about a uranium bomb project. But now in September 1944, the deputy station chief of the New York *rezidentura* had little to work with. His most reliable informant, Klaus Fuchs, had gone missing in August. Kvasnikov had no reason to foresee that Fuchs's tip about a secret Mexican lab would evolve into a mission for Lona Cohen—much less that Lona would come back with a design that would remind him of a layered *matryoshka* doll.

That same September, Lona had been placed in cold storage, Soviet intelligence vernacular for deactivated agents. No one at the *rezidentura* thought to contact Lona after her old controller, "Sam" Semyonov, was recalled to Moscow at the end of September. Moscow Centre had decided to bring Major Semyonov home because the FBI had penetrated his cover; after her last meeting in August with Semyonov, Lona heard nothing. Her internal code name, Lesli, didn't even show up in the two rosters of active agents the *rezidentura* cabled to Moscow Centre on Lubyanka Square. But the experience she had gained and the enterprise she had shown under Semyonov's tutelage would be put to use before long.

The 1941 bombing of Pearl Harbor had begun a harrowing period in the life of the twenty-eight-year-old Lona Cohen. In addition to occasional covert jobs for Soviet intelligence, she worked on the assembly line as a Rosie the Riveter with a husband off at the front. For more than a year after Morris got drafted in July 1942, Lona lived with his parents in their apartment on the Grand Concourse. Lona's first war-plant job was working with taps and dies at Publix Metal, a machine shop at 100 Sixth Avenue in Manhattan. By November 1943 she had moved to Aircraft Screw Products Company in Long Island City, Queens. That month she also moved out of the Cohens' apartment in the Bronx and sublet a one-bedroom apartment in a brownstone at 178 East Seventy-first Street, just off Third Avenue on the Upper East Side of Manhattan. Though Morris Cohen's parents were communists, they didn't know about Lona's covert activities and couldn't understand why she needed her own apartment just to work for the Communist Party. "My in-laws were furious because they said that she was chasing around with men," said Claire Cohen, the wife of Morris's brother, Abner.

Moving out of the Bronx wasn't the only complication in Lona's life. One day at Aircraft Screw, her hair got caught in a machine. The gears kept crunching until part of her scalp was torn. The injury was serious enough to win Lona a damage award, but to get it she had to carry the case all the way to the Workmen's Compensation Board in Albany. In the meantime Lona's new neighbors formed suspicions about her lifestyle. "Lona Cohen definitely believed in free love and had very loose morals," a neighbor in her building would later inform the FBI. Whether Lona was acting on that belief or simply spouting doctrine from her days at the Arden commune to give her staid neighbors a jolt wasn't documented in the FBI report. Someone else in the neighborhood said Lona dressed in "mannish attire," while others were struck by the fact that Lona wore a beret and sunglasses and "regularly wore slacks the year round."

What the people on Seventy-first Street didn't know was that Lona the Riveter had been leading a parallel life as a clandestine operative for Semyonov, who ran the biggest and most prolific of four Soviet networks operating in the United States during the first years of the war. Semyonov was accumulating thousands of pages of technical intelligence from "dozens" of pro-Soviet moles in American war plants throughout the Northeast, and Lona Cohen was one of his two or three most active couriers. Couriers were the mules of espionage. The Soviet slang for courier was *svyaznik,* which meant an agent who made connections. Lona's job was to make clandestine pickups of blueprints and weapons components that Semyonov's agents had managed to smuggle out from the war plants. "I was in touch with someone who worked in

Amtorg," Lona Cohen recalled. "I was his contact, and many times I had to go to Baltimore, Rochester, different towns where they [the sources] worked. Military factories. And we got certain information and I used to turn it over to our comrades."

At least two of her missions involved night-time encounters on the New York waterfront. The *rezidentura* was using American Communist Party members working on merchant ships to carry messages from Soviet intelligence agents in Cuba, Mexico, and South America, even in North Africa. Lona was assigned to monitor the shipping columns in the New York newspapers. When certain ships docked in New York harbor, it was Lona's job to talk her way through the port security. "There was a seaman who worked in the merchant marines during the war," Lona said. "And I had to go along the seacoast in New York in the dark." The seaman had been told how Lona would be dressed and what she would be carrying in her hand. But the problem was that she had to get past the checkpoint at the entrance to the docks. "Listen, young girl, none of this," she remembered the dock guard telling her. "Look, just five minutes," she pleaded, "let him see me, and maybe then I'll meet him outside." She got the guard to relent. "All right, just two minutes, because I'll get in trouble," the guard said as he allowed Lona to approach the ship. "So the seaman saw me there, swinging, like, turning like, you know, and he came out and gave me a roll, a film," Lona remembered. "Well, I passed it to my contact that worked in Amtorg. He was very pleased, he said, 'That's wonderful.'"

After a while Lona was given a more important assignment. She was made the courier to a Soviet agent who, as she understood it, worked inside the U.S. Office of Strategic Services, the wartime predecessor of the CIA. As Lona remembered the story, the OSS man would write her coded letters and mail them to his brother's address. Lona's job was to pick up the letters from the brother without raising his suspicions. Once, she said, the brother pressed her: "Who are you? Why doesn't my brother write to you directly? What's this all about?" Lona asked him, "Do you want to help your brother?" Lona must have made it seem that she was the agent's girlfriend, because at one point the brother asked her, "Are you going to marry him?" Lona answered: "Who knows?" American codebreakers later found an echo of Lona's anecdote in a fragment of a Soviet intelligence cable from August 1944. The partially decrypted cable talked of some unspecified information which "Volunteer's wife" (i.e., Lona Cohen) had obtained from the brother of an agent code-named "Zveno." But since the Americans never learned that Volunteer was the code name of Morris Cohen, they didn't realize that Lona was the spy courier.

While Lona Cohen was ferrying information on weapons and other secrets around the East Coast in those early days of the war, she was kept in the dark about the new project the *rezidentura* was trying to develop. The controllers still were trying to find espionage sources for "Project Enormoz," Moscow's code name for the uranium bomb. At the time Semyonov left and Lona was put on hold, they hadn't gotten very far.

The NKVD had been alerted to the prospect of an atomic bomb in 1940 by Leonid Kvasnikov. In 1938 the head of the NKVD, Lavrenti Beria, had assigned Kvasnikov, the son of a railroad worker from the Russian arsenal town of Tula, to a three-member scientific and technical intelligence section. By 1940 Kvasnikov had already advanced to deputy chief of the section when he noticed a spurt of articles in Western scientific journals about uranium research. At his instigation, the NKVD sent a directive late in 1940 to its station chiefs in the United States, Britain, and Germany. The three *rezidenturas* were ordered to assemble "evidence on possible work in those countries on the creation of atomic weapons."

The London *rezidentura* responded with a breakthrough soon after Hitler changed course and invaded the USSR. In October 1941 one of Kim Philby's "Cambridge Five" spy ring filched a voluminous British Cabinet document called the "Report of the M.A.U.D. Committee on the Use of Uranium for a Bomb." The document said a uranium bomb "is possible" and would make "a very powerful weapon of war." The most likely leaker was John Cairncross, who was private secretary to Churchill's scientific adviser, Lord Hankey. By the time this first British data reached intelligence headquarters on Lubyanka Square, the Wehrmacht had driven to within thirty miles of Moscow; within days Stalin would order the capital evacuated. It was only six months later, after the winter had paralyzed the Nazi offensive, that Beria had time to brief Stalin about the M.A.U.D. report.

"In a number of capitalist countries . . . research has been launched into the utilization of the nuclear energy of uranium for military purposes," Beria finally wrote Stalin in an April 1942 memo summing up atomic research in France, Britain, the United States, and Germany. Kvasnikov's signature appeared on the only draft of Beria's memo that has survived in Soviet archives, a sign that he was among those who prepared it. Three years before Hiroshima, the memo foresaw the rudiments of how an atomic bomb would work: "In designing the bomb, its core should consist of two halves, whose sum total should exceed the critical mass."

Stalin put Foreign Minister Vyacheslav Molotov in charge of determining what to do to catch up. The wily old Bolshevik with the pince-nez had been Stalin's closest confidant since before 1917. In October 1942, Molotov called in the people's commissar of the chemical industry and ordered the resumption of pre-war investigations of radioactive elements. But with both Stalingrad and Leningrad under siege, Molotov put off deciding whether the Soviet Union needed a futuristic uranium weapon. Kvasnikov, the Moscow Centre specialist on foreign atomic research, was allowed that October to meet with two of the foremost Soviet physicists, Abram Ioffe, who had studied in Wilhelm Roentgen's X-ray laboratory in Munich, and Pyotr Kapitsa, who had spent thirteen years at the Cavendish Laboratory in Cambridge, England. Two months later Molotov summoned Kvasnikov and told him he was being shifted from headquarters research to the "active staff" of the Soviet intelligence. Molotov told Kvasnikov to leave quickly for New York to pursue all leads about the atomic bomb as deputy chief of the New York *rezidentura* in charge of an expanded branch for scientific and technical intelligence.

In New York, the job of fulfilling Moscow's renewed demand for information on Enormoz research had already fallen to Semyonov. Because of wartime transportation delays, it took Kvasnikov, his intended replacement as scientific branch chief, three months to reach New York via Vladivostok and Japan. In the meantime Semyonov made inquiries of his own. "One evening in New York City, about October–November 1942, Semyonov asked me if I had heard anything about a military weapon involving a 'pressure wave' of hitherto unknown power," remembered Harry Gold, who was a chemist from Philadelphia and one of Semyonov's best couriers. "I was puzzled," remembered Gold. "Pressure wave? I had a mental picture of some kind of advancing front, as a storm foundation. So Semyonov asked me to watch the technical literature very closely and also to see if any even small bit of information was let drop at scientific meetings or by one of my professional acquaintances."

Gold knew nothing, but Semyonov had other sources. A few months later one of his contacts came through in spectacular fashion. As one of Stalin's wartime associates, General Pavel Sudoplatov, would disclose in his memoirs, Moscow obtained through Semyonov "a full report" on the first nuclear chain reaction in Chicago on December 2,

1942. The report on Fermi's experiment arrived in Moscow "at the end of January 1943," Sudoplatov recalled.

Sudoplatov's memory was accurate on this point, for it is now clear that a Soviet intelligence report on Fermi's reactor must have been among the briefing documents that Molotov turned over to the Leningrad nuclear physicist Igor Kurchatov, whom Molotov had picked to lead a small-scale Soviet uranium project on February 11, 1943. Three weeks later, Kurchatov wrote a fourteen-page top secret review of the stacks of atomic data that Soviet intelligence had been accumulating since 1941. Kurchatov said he was fascinated most of all by a Western technological advance called the "uranium pile"—a term for a reactor used only by Fermi and his associates. The pile could be used to form "an element with the mass number 239," Kurchatov wrote. There was a possibility that this new element 239—i.e., plutonium—could be used "as the material for a bomb," Kurchatov noted with an air of enthusiasm on March 7, 1943.

After a delay over his transit visa through Japan, Kvasnikov finally arrived that March to set up the new atomic intelligence branch in New York. Like Semyonov, he began work under the cover of an engineer at Amtorg. Kvasnikov also set up shop in a metal-shuttered room on the fourth floor of the town house at Sixty-first Street and Fifth Avenue that served not only as the Soviet Consulate, but also as the Soviet *rezidentura*. "At first he was like a vacuum cleaner," said his granddaughter who tape-recorded his memoirs. "He was the only one in his branch." Later he took on as his assistants two young NKVD officers, Anatoly Yatskov and Alexander Feklisov. By summer Moscow Centre was able to put together a dossier on American progress on Enormoz, along with what had been reported earlier on Britain, Germany, and Canada. In the resulting summary report, the chief of foreign intelligence of the NKGB (the new name for the NKVD) displayed an uncanny familiarity not only with the new American uranium pile, but with other aspects of developing research on the American bomb. The foreign intelligence chief, Gaik Ovakamian, included the hitherto secret fact that Fermi was leading "major works in America" related to the atomic bomb. Ovakamian didn't specifically say that the pile was Fermi's work, nor did he specify that it was located in Chicago. But his report called "About Works on a New Source of Energy—Uranium" makes it indisputable that the Soviets had glimpsed the outlines of the Manhattan Project by the summer of 1943.

At the beginning of this year the Americans put into operation
the first "uranium boiler" (American terminology "pile"). . . .
The work of this very powerful machine gives the possibility: a)
to have an electric station of enormous power (on the order of
100,000 to 1 million kilowatts) . . . b) to produce materials
needed for the preparation of an atomic superbomb (uranium 235
and element 94), c) to receive experience and materials for the
production of radioactive means of warfare in the near future.

Simultaneously a production-strength facility is also planned,
and the manufacture of necessary raw materials and accessory materials—metallic uranium, uranium fluoride and oxide, graphite,
and heavy water. The means of obtaining heavy water in a production quantity is of special interest, inasmuch as several years
ago (3–5 years) the quantity of it in the whole world was measured in grams. In the near future the production of 250 kilograms of heavy water a month will begin.

By the time the Ovakamian memo was written, the New York *rezidentura* was already in touch with at least one scientist who had worked
in the early stages of American nuclear research, someone to whom the
Soviets had assigned the code name "Kvant." One Soviet intelligence
cable told of a meeting with Kvant on June 14, 1943, at the Soviet Embassy in Washington. It said Kvant was given $300 after he had men-
tioned that he expects "recompense for his labor," as the cable delicately
put it. The next day, the New York *rezidentura* cabled Moscow a lengthy
summary of the scientific formulas allegedly provided by Kvant about
separation of uranium isotopes through "vaporization." A few months
later, Kvant vanished from Soviet cable traffic. What happened to Kvant
remains a mystery, but there is no question that his or her absence had a
telling impact on the *rezidentura*'s performance. The seven-month gap
after Kvant's disappearance would be the only interruption in the cas-
cade of intelligence that Moscow Centre obtained from inside the Manhattan Project from early in 1943 until late in 1945.

If Kvasnikov was going to satisfy Lubyanka's appetite, he desperately
needed new atomic sources. Near the end of 1943 his luck changed.
Word came that a high-level Soviet atomic spy in Britain was being
transferred to work in New York. Harry Gold, the only courier in the
rezidentura's stable conversant with scientific terminology, was told by
Semyonov to break his previous links with other sources. Semyonov

told him "the mission was far more important than anything I had ever done before," Gold remembered.

And so late in January 1944, Gold met a slender, ascetic-looking man with glasses outside the Henry Street Settlement House on the Lower East Side of Manhattan. This was where Ted Hall used to hang out with his Trotskyist friends before he transferred to Harvard, but that was a coincidence. Gold's contact was Klaus Fuchs. A physicist from Germany with a fertile brain, Fuchs had been hired in the spring of 1941 in England to calculate the hydrodynamics of gaseous diffusion for the British atomic project code-named "Tube Alloys." Hitler's rise to power in 1933 had transformed Fuchs from a German student socialist into an underground communist and then into a refugee in England.

Hitler's invasion of the Soviet Union had changed everything for the thirty-year-old Fuchs. He was just as passionately stirred by the event as another introverted intellectual named Ted Hall, then a fifteen-year-old freshman at Queens College. In the summer of 1941, Fuchs approached Jurgen Kuczynski, a German communist leader he knew in London, asking how he could assist the Soviet war effort. Contact the Soviet Embassy, Kuczynski said. And for the next two years Fuchs passed everything he knew about Tube Alloys to Jurgen's sister Ursula Kuczynski, who was an agent of Soviet military intelligence in London. Fuchs didn't have much. Tube Alloys had become a sideshow to the burgeoning U.S. Manhattan Project.

When Fuchs arrived in Manhattan as part of the British mission sent to work with the American atomic project, the New York *rezidentura*'s productivity jumped overnight. To Gold's surprise, he heard after his first meeting with Fuchs that he no longer would report to Semyonov, that he would deal from now on with "John." Gold's new control officer was Anatoly Yatskov, the thirty-year-old intelligence officer who was one of Kvasnikov's assistants. The material Fuchs passed to Yatskov through Harry Gold in the first half of 1944 wasn't of crucial importance, but Fuchs did disclose engineering details about the new K-25 uranium separation plant at Oak Ridge, including the use of sintered nickel powder to make gaseous diffusion membranes. On July 25, 1944, the *rezidentura* cabled Moscow for permission to award Fuchs a $500 bonus.

By now the *rezidentura* was also running a second agent at Oak Ridge, someone whose Soviet code name was "Fogel" and who had access to plant blueprints. And from the latest Fogel report, it was obvious that the information from Fuchs was real. "The materials . . . are very interesting and important because they indicate that at least part of the factory is already working," commented Isaak Kikoin, the Soviet nuclear physicist in Moscow assigned to evaluate the intelligence from Fogel. "The text and chart (especially the latter) are extremely important because they give some idea of the size of the buildings. Any elaboration would be extremely important and a big help."

Late in July Fuchs met Harry Gold near an art museum on the West Side. For an hour and a half they walked through the winding paths and small roads of Central Park. During their stroll, Fuchs gave the *residentura* the first clue about the existence of Los Alamos. Fuchs was certain that he told Gold he might be transferred to "New Mexico." But as Gold heard Fuchs, the German said the place was "somewhere in Mexico." In any case, Fuchs and Gold agreed to meet again on August 5, 1944 in front of the Bell Cinema in Brooklyn, near Eastern Parkway. But when Harry Gold showed up at the Bell Cinema, there was no Klaus Fuchs. Two weeks later Fuchs again failed to appear for a control meeting. Then, from the superintendent at Fuchs's apartment building, Gold heard that the physicist had gone back to England. It was too late to give Fuchs the bonus that Moscow had approved—he had disappeared.

Just then Soviet intelligence picked up another clue about a secret research laboratory. Someone had managed to procure a classified paper called "A Review on the Uranium Problem," perhaps a summary written for British or American political decision-makers rather than an internal paper for scientists. The Soviets have never disclosed how they obtained it, but decrypted Soviet cables show that Vladimir Pravdin, a TASS correspondent in New York who worked with the NKGB, had already set up a mechanism for clandestine contacts with Moscow's newest atomic spy in the United States, British diplomat Donald Maclean. "A Review on the Uranium Problem" could well have been one of the first documents that Maclean was able to steal in his new position as the British Embassy's staffer on a committee coordinating U.S., British, and Canadian atomic research.

When Soviet intelligence later passed the "Review" to Kurchatov for appraisal, he made a note for the Moscow headquarters of the NKGB about "the extremely curious remark on page 9." It described a place Kurchatov had never heard of called "Laboratory V," a place where scientists were measuring the physical properties of uranium 235 and plutonium "in connection with manufacturing a bomb."

The information may well have passed through the NKGB station in New York, giving Kvasnikov his second morsel to savor. Could "Laboratory V" be identical to that mysterious place "somewhere in Mexico" that Gold had heard about from Fuchs? Could Fuchs be there now? Or had he been arrested? These had to be the most vivid questions facing Kvasnikov while Ted Hall was beginning work on the Ra-La implosion experiment and confronting his own questions about what was happening at the laboratory on the mesa.

CHAPTER 10

Impact of the Gadget

On Sundays Ted Hall lounged on his bed and ruminated while classical 78s revolved on his Victrola. He was enthralled by the work at Los Alamos, but could he limit himself to the complexities of atomic physics? Other dimensions of his life seemed just as important.

What if capitalist America got the atomic bomb and then collapsed into an economic depression? For someone who had been attracted enough to Marxism to join the John Reed Society at Harvard, this question did not seem far-fetched. Nor did the follow-up: What if post-war depression dragged a nuclear America so far down that the country fell into the hands of fascist leaders, as had happened in Weimar Germany? Could that lead to another world war? Over the next three or four months Hall's questions became more radical. Shouldn't someone take steps now to break America's monopoly on atomic research before it was too late?

The same quandary was occurring almost simultaneously in the summer of 1944 to a good many of his elders on the Hill. One was Niels Bohr, the patriarch of nuclear physics and winner of the 1922 Nobel Prize, who had escaped from his home in Nazi-dominated Denmark and was now working at Los Alamos. He would try to convince world leaders that secrecy was both wrong and counterproductive. But no one became more stirred by the idea than Ted Hall. As he lay on his bed in Los Alamos, Hall chewed over a concept that had intrigued him since Queens College. To be really fulfilled, he must pursue two careers in parallel. One would be an ivory tower existence in which he enjoyed theoretical physics for the sheer pleasure of it. The other somehow would pay back what he liked to think was his social debt to humanity.

Could this be Ted Hall's time to repay his social debt? Was it his moral duty to inform the Soviets about the bomb?

As Hall's mind churned, his dormitory room would vibrate with his favorite piece, Strauss's opus 20, *Ein Heldenleben* (*A Hero's Life*). Classical music had been Ted's passion from the days his first-term Harvard roommates filled their suite with Mahler. At Los Alamos he began building a collection of 78s that soon would occupy an oblong packing crate in his room. A month before his arrival, Los Alamos had started its own low-powered radio station to broadcast classical records from the collections of other aficionados including another Harvard alumnus, J. Robert Oppenheimer. While many of Ted's generation were listening to Glenn Miller's "String of Pearls" and Count Basie's "One O'Clock Jump," Hall's tastes centered on Mahler, Prokofiev, and the overripe romanticism of Richard Strauss. Strauss's *Ein Heldenleben* was not just a nice piece with some glorious passages, Hall felt. He identified with Strauss as the heroic composer whose brawny fortissimos fended off the "sniveling winds and pompous tubas" that represented his musical critics.

There were times in 1944 when Hall couldn't help imagining himself as a romantic hero taking on an evil world. His other Strauss favorite at Los Alamos was the rollicking symphonic poem *Till Eulenspiegel's Merry Pranks*. The music celebrated the folk tales of the irrepressible German prankster Till, who made kings and peasants smile at his cunning tricks at the very moment he was duping them.

Sunday was scientists' day off. When Ted wasn't brooding in his room, he played Ping-Pong on the veranda of Fuller Lodge, hiked in the foothills of the Jemez Range, or caught a ride into Santa Fe. Often he hung around with Glauber, Case, and de Hoffmann. The four came to be viewed by some on the Hill as a clique of boy brains from Harvard. "People had a feeling that if you were from Harvard, you must be a snob, so we'll look for signs of that," remembered Glauber. "And on top of that, you must be a genius—an arrogant genius. It took a long time to work that off."

Ted Hall did manage to widen his circle of acquaintances, especially after his group leader, Bruno Rossi, put him to work on instruments for the Ra-La implosion experiment. "Luis Alvarez used to kill me on the billiards table," Hall remembered of the thirty-three-year-old Berkeley physicist who initially was in charge of the experiment. Hall also got to know the Swiss physicist Hans Staub, with whom he worked in designing Ra-La test instruments. Staub was a fanatical worker, always caught up in his job, who was known to his Los Alamos neighbors for his often-stated philosophical opposition to the lab's regime of secrecy. Recalled one neighbor, "Hans Staub . . . went around asking in emphatic tones of prophecy, 'Are these big tough MPs with their guns here to keep us in or to keep the rest of the world out?' "

One of Hall's closest friends was Sam Cohen, a twenty-three-year-old physicist who came to Los Alamos as a soldier in the Army's Special Engineering Detachment (SED) and would go on to become the inventor of the neutron bomb. Hall regarded Sam Cohen as a practical joker with an odd sense of humor. One of the times Cohen succeeded in flummoxing his friend was when Hall was learning to drive at Los Alamos. Cohen reached over and turned the key, killing the engine and leaving Hall in the middle of the road momentarily unable to restart it. To Cohen, Hall was a brilliant eccentric and a free spirit. "I think he always had a secret ambition to be a modern day Till Eulenspiegel," said Cohen a half century later. "He was interested in tweaking the system— he was a natural-born rebel." Once in 1944, Cohen recalled, he went into Hall's workplace late in the evening to ask him out for a cup of coffee. Cohen found Hall sitting cross-legged on top of a ten-foot-tall stack of wooden crates, lost in thought. Like a Buddhist monk in a trance, Cohen thought, walking out without ever capturing Hall's attention.

The best contemporary snapshot of the psychological state of Ted Hall in the months before he began his clandestine dealings with Soviet intelligence is a letter he wrote to his sister-in-law, Edith Hall, in Britain. Edith had written Ted a few weeks earlier to announce the birth of their first child. Edith was a war bride. An English ambulance driver who had been a tennis player at university, she had married Ted's brother, Ed, in the summer of 1943 while he was serving as a junior engineering officer with the U.S. Army Air Corps at an RAF base near Oxford, England. Ted's letter started with pleasantries about the infant nephew and then moved on to advice.

Saturday, May 20, 44
Dear Edith,

. . . .

If Ed is to have a good-sized share in this upbringing, I should like to offer a precaution, if I may. . . . When he had finished building a good foundation in me, he had no way of standing aside to let me grow. The moral is that your kid should be permitted more mistakes and sketchier assistance. More accurately, he should not have the good ideas and potent machines of this earth served up to him on a platter like a well-planned meal; this food should rather first be encountered on the hoof and on the stalk, with assistance rendered when wrong or feeble technique is used for making it digestible. Please pardon my interference in this matter, but Ed is a real menace in this respect, and I do think the previous experience can be pondered to advantage.

Living conditions are still poor here and will remain so, but I would be willing to live on whale blubber alone in an igloo at the South Pole for a crack at the same job. It is not perfect: I have been doing less theoretical work than I would like to recently. (Those books I requested are not as urgent now as I would like them to be.) But for my own case I have suspended for the duration my edict about one-sided absorption in a job.

The question of drafting 18-year-olds or fathers is splendid political fodder and Congress recently whipped itself into quite a frenzy about it, resulting in the drafting of very nearly every physically-fit person under 22. (I suppose younger people are physically and mentally better soldiers, though I do wonder why our army is being made so big.) However, I am still a civilian, and am now fairly sure that I will remain so.

Yours,

Ted

The writer was someone extraordinarily sure of his own judgment. So self-confident was he that he could write lengthy instructions to a new relative in another country—someone he'd never met—about how she should avoid mistakes in rearing her infant son. Ed had been a "real menace" raising him, Ted wrote, reflecting his complicated feelings toward his loving, but domineering, older sibling.

From Hall's description of the "poor" living conditions, it sounds as though his contrarian streak from high school was still with him at Los Alamos. Here it was Hall's first spring in New Mexico, and the mesa would have been painted with wildflowers. He wasn't living in a foxhole but rather in an intellectual colony where General Groves went out of his way to provide extra comforts so that "his prima donnas [would] be happy." Yet to Hall the living conditions were poor and destined to remain so. Like Hans Staub and Laura Fermi, Ted Hall hated to be regimented.

Not that he disliked the work at Los Alamos: As he wrote, he would willingly "live on whale blubber" to keep his first job in what had to be the most provocative scientific atmosphere in the world. Who wouldn't? This was the week when Hall was recognized in Bruno Rossi's progress report for having wrapped up the uranium cross section measurements. Ted felt so engrossed by experimental physics that he was going to abandon his earlier edict against burying himself in physics to the exclusion of social concerns—at least that is what he thought when he was writing Edith. But over the next few months the idea of pursuing a double life reemerged like a plant that has been cut back only to flourish with stronger shoots.

There was a rarefied, fast-metabolism atmosphere about Los Alamos that helped speed the maturation of Ted's ideas. The intellectual climate at Los Alamos was far more conducive to Soviet sympathy and globalist musings than the leaders of the Los Alamos laboratory would acknowledge, either then or later. In 1946, Oppenheimer's secretary Priscilla Duffield would articulate what had come to be the official line: There were never any discussions at Los Alamos about the "social implications" of the bomb. If there were any, she said, she would have known about them. But as time passed it became more and more evident that wartime Los Alamos was spiked with discussions on the politics of the bomb. Often these conversations revolved around the same question bothering Ted: Would the postwar world be more stable if the bomb were shared with the Soviets? Ted Hall was aware of some ferment, but he was a very junior scientist and would not be remembered as a vocal participant in those talks.

"There was considerable discussion among the scientists" in 1944 and 1945 about the need to inform the Soviets about atomic bomb research, recalled Martin Deutsch, the Austrian-born physicist from MIT who worked near Ted's office in the experimental physics division. By Deutsch's confidential account to the FBI in 1950, a great many wartime Los Alamos scientists believed the atomic bomb must be placed under permanent international controls. "The conclusion was therefore reached," Deutsch was quoted in a top secret FBI report, "that the Russians should know of the atomic research, and that in an effort to engender good will, it was much preferred that they be told before the task was completed than afterward."

Half a century later, Deutsch sat in his garden in Cambridge, Massachusetts, and confirmed that most of what the two FBI agents quoted him as saying was right. But when he finally got a chance to read the FBI report, Deutsch was dismayed. Deutsch, who had retired after a career as an MIT physicist and occasional CIA consultant, was sure the two FBI men must have misunderstood him when they paraphrased him as saying that a number of scientists "expressed the opinion that if the proper officials in Washington were not wise enough to see this situation, then in the interest of humanity, it was incumbent on someone of them to advise the Russians without further consultation with Washington authorities."

One of those most distressed by the exclusion of the Soviets from the Manhattan Project was a thirty-five-year-old Polish-born physicist who five decades later would become the only former Los Alamos scientist to win the Nobel Prize for Peace. Joseph Rotblat, the co-founder of the postwar Pugwash Conferences, which produced the first international movement for nuclear disarmament, came to Los Alamos as part of a team of British physicists early in 1944. In March, Rotblat began his circuitous path to the 1995 peace prize when he was invited to dinner along with General Groves at the cabin of James Chadwick, head of the British mission at Los Alamos. After dinner, Groves and Chadwick sat back and talked about the postwar world. It was at a time when the Grand Alliance of Churchill, Roosevelt, and Stalin was in disarray over future spheres of influence in Eastern Europe. Rotblat, too junior to take part, remembered being stunned at hearing Groves suggest that the atomic bomb was not really intended for the war against Germany. "I know what he [Groves] said exactly, because of the great shock it produced in me," Rotblat said. "He said, 'You realize, of course, that the whole purpose of the project is to subdue the Russians.' "

Later that year Rotblat became part of a revolving group of about twenty established scientists, many of them group leaders, who would gather to talk about once a month. "It used to be in the evenings, usually at somebody's house like the Tellers, someone who had fairly large rooms," Rotblat remembered. "People would meet to discuss the future of Europe, the future of the world." One question was whether Europe could be made more stable by dividing postwar Germany into several countries. Another issue the scientists talked about, according to Rotblat's recollection, was whether it was wise to exclude Soviet scientists from knowledge about atomic research.

Oppenheimer gave mixed signals, never saying much about politics but letting others talk. Rotblat remembered that Oppenheimer came to at least one of the 1944 meetings. "I always thought he was a soul mate in the sense that we had the same humanitarian approach to problems," remembered Rotblat. But another time in 1944, Oppenheimer sent word to Robert R. Wilson, the leader of the cyclotron group, that it was inappropriate to indulge in political talkfests until the job was finished. Wilson and twenty-five others, mostly from the cyclotron group, had held what he called an informal meeting in the X Building on "the impact of the gadget." Glauber, who knew about the Wilson meeting, said the consensus was to send Wilson as an emissary to seek Oppenheimer's permission for a more formal discussion. "The word came back from Oppenheimer that he really took a very dim view of that sort of thing, and he was certain that General Groves wouldn't like it at all," Glauber recalled.

By all accounts, in 1944 the most fervent advocate of sharing the secrets of the Manhattan Project with Moscow was Bohr, then in his fifties and living at Los Alamos part-time. In his Delphic phrases and nearly inaudible voice, he poured out to Oppenheimer and others his compelling sense that there must be international control of nuclear energy. "He made the enterprise, which often looked so macabre, seem hopeful," Oppenheimer would remember. While he was at Los Alamos in early 1944, Bohr decided that it was up to him to persuade Churchill and Roosevelt to communicate right away with Stalin about the atomic bomb and make a generous proposal to share control over it.

That summer, near the time of the Normandy landings, the Danish physicist would sometimes come to Rotblat's room in the Long Cabin. Rotblat had a shortwave radio receiver, and he and Bohr would listen to the 8 A.M. bulletin on the BBC World Service. When it was over Bohr and Rotblat would talk about the future. "It was there," remembered Rotblat, "that we talked of this idea that we should share the knowledge with the Russians, to bring them in before the bomb was made." As Bohr described in a roundabout way to Rotblat, he had traveled to London in May and wangled a private meeting with Churchill. Bohr and his physicist son had tried to convince the prime minister of the need for atomic collaboration with Stalin, but Churchill told him: "I cannot see what you are talking about. After all this new bomb is just going to be bigger than our present bombs."

Churchill had "scolded us like two schoolboys," Bohr said later, but he wasn't prepared to give up. In July, not long after his conversations at Long Cabin with Rotblat, Bohr composed an anguished memo to Roosevelt warning that it was best to inform Stalin straightaway because the Soviets would eventually get the bomb anyway. Bohr met the president, and he left the White House believing he might be sent on "an exploratory mission to the Soviet Union." But when Roosevelt met Churchill at Hyde Park, New York, on September 19, 1944, they agreed to have Bohr investigated as a security risk. "The President and I are seriously concerned about Professor Bohr," Churchill wrote the next day, adding, "It seems to me Bohr ought to be confined, or at any rate made to see that he is very near the edge of mortal crimes."

Just as the Bohr initiative was collapsing, Ted Hall was getting ready to make his own exploratory mission, this one into the clandestine world of Soviet espionage. As far as can be established, Ted's decision had nothing to do with the failure of Bohr's efforts. Ted Hall had met him only once, when they happened to sit at the same table during dinner at the Fuller Lodge. Nor did the decision to contact a Soviet agent grow out of some low depressive period in Hall's life. It matured in his mind at a time when his work at Los Alamos was flourishing and when it looked as though Germany was about to capitulate. The Normandy landing and the capture of Paris touched off a period of rampant optimism in the United States. When the American 82d and 101st Airborne Divisions crossed the Rhine and penetrated into Germany in mid-September, hopes soared that the Nazis would surrender by Christmas. For the first time, it was possible to visualize a real end to the fighting and a post-war world in which America would be a dominant force, while Europe struggled to put together the pieces.

As the news reached Los Alamos that General Dwight D. Eisenhower's forces had captured the French port of Cherbourg, Ted Hall was getting ready for the first preliminary test shot of the Ra-La implosion experiment. Luis Alvarez had obtained two Army tanks from Dugway Proving Grounds to serve as mobile bunkers. When Ted heard about how the test went, he must have realized he was involved with something important—and risky. "I was sitting in the tank when the first explosion went off," Alvarez would remember of the July 25 test. "George Kistiakowski was in one tank and I was in the other. We were looking through the periscopes and all that happened was that it blew a lot of dust in our eyes. And then—we hadn't thought about this possibility at all—the whole forest around us caught fire. These pieces of white-hot metal flying off into the wild blue yonder setting trees on fire. We were almost surrounded."

Radioactive lanthanum, Ra-La for short, was an intensely radioactive tracer isotope. The idea was to implant a tiny canister of Ra-La in the center of a spherical shell and then try to crush it with an external blanket of explosives. The intensity of gamma rays from the lanthanum would reveal whether the explosives had achieved a smooth implosion. And it was the job of the instruments team, nominally under Ted Hall's leadership, to make the fast ionization chambers to detect the gamma rays. After the practice explosion without Ra-La inside the canister, a second shot using real lanthanum was fired on September 22, only a few days after the first U.S. airborne troops crossed the Rhine. The September shot was inconclusive but Ted Hall's ionization chambers worked perfectly. Two more shots followed on October 3 and October 14. Again his instruments functioned, but the implosion wave turned out to be asymmetrical.

On October 15, the day after the third shot, Ted Hall left Los Alamos for two weeks of annual leave. Ostensibly he was going home to celebrate his nineteenth birthday with his parents in New York. However, by the time he departed, Ted Hall had all but decided he would try to inform the Soviets about the existence of the secret bomb project.

What finally provoked Hall to go beyond ruminating and approach the point of no return? The best approximation of his thought processes is the draft of a statement that he began to write half a century later. He started preparing it late in 1995, when his name first came up in declassified Soviet cables and he thought he might need to explain his rationale to the public. His draft—which he finally finished and gave to the authors more than a year later—frankly acknowledged that he considered talking to the Soviets but drew a line just short of admitting he actually passed any information to them:

> I have occasionally been asked to explain what motivated me in 1944. Thinking back to the rather arrogant 19-year-old I then was, I can recall quite well what was in my mind at the time.
>
> My decision about contacting the Soviets was a gradual one, and it was entirely my own. It was entirely voluntary, not influenced by any other individual or by any organization such as the Communist Party or the Young Communist League. I was never "recruited" by anyone. Nor was I prompted by any personal problems. I had grown up in a very loving family and had a successful and happy life.
>
> During World War II, I shared the general sympathy for our allies, the Soviet Union. After they were attacked, everybody knew that they were bearing the main load in the fight against Nazi Germany. Their propaganda was characterized by a craving for peace

far deeper than was apparent in the Western countries. I think this came about partly because the Soviet Union suffered devastation far greater than anything experienced in the West.

My political views had been shaped by the economic depression of the 1930s. With the New Deal Roosevelt had tried to restore prosperity, but this was only partly successful and it was not until the war that the depression really ended. What would happen when the war was over?

At nineteen I shared a common belief that the horrors of war would bring our various leaders to their senses and usher in a period of peace and harmony. But I had been thinking and reading about politics since an early age, and had seen that in a capitalist society economic depression could lead to fascism, aggression and war—as actually happened in Italy and Germany. So as I worked at Los Alamos and understood the destructive power of the atomic bomb, I asked myself what <u>might</u> happen if World War II was followed by a depression in the United States while it had an atomic monopoly?

In fact I was very optimistic. I didn't believe that there would necessarily be a depression or that a depression would necessarily lead to war. But it seemed to me that an American monopoly was dangerous and should be prevented. I was not the only scientist to take that view: for example Einstein and Bohr both felt keenly that the best political policy was to reach an understanding—the opposite of the Cold War. I remember reading that Bohr tried to persuade Roosevelt to send him to Stalin to work out a peace-directed alliance and policy.

I did not have an uncritical view of the Soviet Union. I believed the Soviet Union was a mixture of good and bad things, and hoped it would evolve favourably. But in any case there was no question of the Soviet Union ever having an atomic monopoly.

Of course the situation was far more complicated than I understood at the time, and if confronted with the same problem today I would respond quite differently.

Long before Ted Hall became aware of such complications, the seed of espionage had been planted with an exchange of quips at Lowell House in the fall of 1943. Now the idea had germinated on the Hill, and the spy in him was about to blossom.

CHAPTER 11

Advent of Mlad and Star

S triding into Midtown Manhattan, Ted Hall moved like a man with a purpose. Fast. Determined. He weaved around the less energetic or less focused who didn't match his pace, which meant just about everyone else on the pavement. That was how he often walked, in silent competition with the rest of the world. He would catch a side glance at potential rivals traveling at a good clip, then move faster, pushing past the unwitting losers left trailing in his dust. It was part of his style, picking his own private targets for achievement.

On this mid-October day in 1944 Hall had a clear and pressing objective as he walked south past uptown apartment houses with their scattering of apothecaries and groceries, then cruised into the frenetic high-rise center. He was en route to the Soviet trade company Amtorg, where he hoped to find a way to tell the Soviets how the wizards of American science were rushing into existence the world's most devastating weapon.

His faith in the principles of democracy had made him question whether he had the right to take this unilateral step and share American technology with another country, even an allied country. But he had worried for some years now that what was going on in America wasn't quite democracy. This decision to build the atom bomb, for example: Neither the American people nor their Congress even knew about it, much less approved it. He found Congress itself to be a skewed version of democratic government. "The U.S. Congress was controlled by the various committees, and the chairmen of the committees were all southern Democrats who were not by any means democratic representatives of a democratic country," he said in a discussion years later. "They were usurpers who were in their position because half or more of their people couldn't vote." How would American power grow and what would be its shape if there were no counterbalance anywhere on earth? He thought it was too great a chance to take, especially when potential disaster could be so easily checked. What he wanted to do might not fully clear what Hall considered his social debt to the world. But he thought it would be a goodly down payment.

Not long before this walk downtown Hall had been at Saville Sax's apartment at 15 West Seventy-fifth Street, a red brick building not quite up to the standards of the neighborhood's stately brownstones or the nearby Museum of Natural History. Sax and Hall met several times during Ted's two-week breather from Los Alamos, but none of these meetings was a simple social get-together. His loyal friend Savy was the one person Hall could rely upon to understand and help him clandestinely guarantee a global balance of power after the war. Most Americans would have been scandalized at Hall's plan to give top secret defense data to a communist regime, even an allied one; he was right to assume Savy would not disapprove. Sax the undisciplined dreamer was different from the probing scientist Hall, but politically they shared a world view. It was right, they thought, and the danger added a romantic edge that appealed to both young men.

Savy's mother, Bluma, an excitable Old World matriarch most comfortable speaking Yiddish, was ironing in one of the apartment's two living rooms and seemed preoccupied the day her son brought Ted to visit. That was fortunate for the two young men, because Bluma's bossy, loving nosiness would have been hard to circumvent. Had her mind not been elsewhere—possibly on her work as a volunteer with Russian War Relief getting bandages and food and clothes to her war-torn former countrymen—she probably would have pounced on Hall with a string of demanding questions: Why had he left Harvard in the middle of a term? How come such an able-bodied young man wasn't in uniform, anyway?

Hall wasn't even supposed to mention where he was working, and certainly not to say anything about what he did there. And now he and Savy were trying to plot the touchy logistics of getting exactly that information into the hands of Soviet intelligence operatives. Bluma, who supported the communist revolution till the end of her life, might not have objected to the plan in principle, but she surely would have objected to a risk like this. Decades later, she still refused to talk openly about what Savy had done because she feared that the law might yet catch up with him.

Savy's older sister was hanging around the apartment, too, so Ted and Savy may have gone outside to talk. The two identified several places with the potential to handle Hall's proposition, according to information pieced together from decrypted Soviet cables and other sources. Both young men were familiar with leftist publications such as *The Daily Worker* that chronicled the doings of Soviet-related organizations, so they easily could compile a list of places to approach. The hard part was figuring out what to say.

Trying to connect with a receptive Soviet spy, Sax embarked on a Woody Allen adventure. He began at Artkino, the branch of Soviet cultural propaganda that produced Soviet films and distributed them in the West. It was a risky bet, going to a place with an obvious political aura that was likely to attract American counterespionage attention. Nonetheless, that was Sax's starting point.

Nicola Napoli, the president and manager of Artkino in New York, didn't bite. A sloppy kid shows up at his office on Times Square with a tale about his buddy the teenaged super-scientist who was building a super-bomb—his buddy who wanted to share this top secret information with the Soviets. Could this be anything other than an FBI provocation? According to a Soviet intelligence telegram, Napoli, "not wanting to listen to him," sent the boy packing. But not entirely empty-handed. Stranger stories were recorded in the annals of espionage, and, after all, the Soviet Union was gliding on a tide of popularity in America. It was a comrade in arms, suffering but still standing up against Nazi tyranny. So maybe there really was a whiz kid who wanted to help. Napoli nervously suggested Savy look up Sergei Kurnakov. It was certainly legitimate to send such a story to a Soviet author and journalist well known as a "military analyst" for communist newspapers in New York. Napoli couldn't lose. If Sax was a plant, he had done nothing wrong by sending him to a journalist. If it looked like he was a legitimate source, then Kurnakov would take it from there. A White Russian cavalry officer who had emigrated to America in the 1920s and then become enamored of the revolution back home, Kurnakov was now an agent of Soviet intelligence. He was trained to make decisions about guys like Sax.

Sax apparently wasn't satisfied that some journalist was the proper vessel for the hot disclosures Hall was ready to deliver. From Artkino Savy went to knock on the door of Earl Browder, the head of the American communists. He fared even worse there than he had with Napoli.

He couldn't get past Browder's secretary with his tale of secret U.S. weapons. This shouldn't have been surprising: Browder's people had been under intense FBI surveillance just a few years earlier that had resulted in Browder's imprisonment for using a false passport. Relations were better now that the Soviets and Americans were fighting on the same side, but the party still was wary of potential traps.

Possibly at the same time Sax was knocking on doors that fall day, Hall was hiking down to the purchasing office of Amtorg at 238 West Twenty-eighth Street near Seventh Avenue. Few Americans knew or even suspected that Amtorg's $1.5 billion in import/export activities covered clandestine contacts by a network of Soviet spies and their American agents. Hall figured only that he'd have a better chance talking to some "nice businessmen" than to propagandists at the film company, who were sure to be edgy about surveillance. Little did he know that paranoia was rampant at Amtorg—work had been paralyzed one day at the head office when two Dominican nuns innocently tried to solicit contributions and were taken for provocateurs. Yet when Hall wandered in, he got spectacularly lucky. He simply walked up to an American employee he found stacking boxes in some corner of the Amtorg warehouse and started talking. Whatever veiled version of his mission Hall gave, it made the guy nervous. The workman seemed to think this earnest young man was balmy, but before he shooed him out he gave Ted a name and a phone number for a fellow named Kurnakov. It was the same contact suggested to Sax at Artkino.

Hall had only a few days left in his fourteen-day leave, which ended October 29. He needed at least a couple of days to ride the train back to New Mexico. Hall quickly managed to set a meeting.

How could Sergei Kurnakov believe his good fortune when Ted Hall walked into the Soviet agent's lower Manhattan apartment and started talking? He immediately realized that the nineteen-year-old scientist "has an exceptionally keen mind and a broad outlook, and is politically developed." Himself the son of a famous scientist, Kurnakov understood the import of what Hall was doing when he described the installation at Los Alamos and his work there and then offered to keep the Soviets informed of developments in the classified lab.

Today's Russian intelligence services do not acknowledge that Hall and Kurnakov were the principals, but KGB veterans have circulated variously disguised versions of the "recruitment" of a Los Alamos scientist in the 1940s. There are common threads to these KGB-approved accounts: The young American volunteered his service; he acted out of idealism that included belief in socialist goals and fear and hatred of fascism; he wanted to assure a post-war strategic balance in the world; he was indignant at any hint that the Soviets might pay him for his trouble.

One of the lesser-known elements of the real conversation is that Kurnakov kept pressing Hall to gulp down shots of vodka as they talked in the dim Manhattan apartment. True, it is a Russian custom. Also true that Soviet *razvyedchiki,* like spies the world over, hope the liberating influence of alcohol may flush out inconsistencies or mistakes and uncover a source as a double agent. The liquor slowed down Hall, who wasn't much of a drinker and may never have tasted vodka before that day. But there wasn't much to reveal that he hadn't already laid out for the agent.

At one point Kurnakov openly challenged this self-recruit to convince him that he both was serious and had some goods to deliver. Hall was prepared for exactly that tactic. He handed over a file folder containing a report he had written on Los Alamos and a list of the scientists there working on the atomic bomb.

Kurnakov may have been anxious to open a permanent channel to Ted Hall, but he didn't have the authority. He was a low-level officer without diplomatic cover and thus forbidden even to acknowledge that the Soviets fielded an intelligence network of which he was one strand. NKGB policy dictated that he couldn't accept Hall's offer of services, but he decided to stretch a point and accept Hall's allegedly secret data. And the journalist snapped a photograph of Hall, telling him this would be a critical source of identification for anyone wanting to get in contact with him again.

Kurnakov could only promise to check into the situation despite Hall's warning that after he left New York he would be virtually incommunicado on the New Mexico mesa. Trying to facilitate the link-up that Kurnakov wasn't empowered to make, Hall also let the Soviet agent know that he came equipped with his own courier. Saville Sax was willing to play the role.

After the Kurnakov meeting Ted and Savy were in a bind. Who ever would have suspected it would be so difficult to give people something they so clearly needed? How could it be so hard to hand over such a gem—no charge, free of strings? Hall and Sax had to find a quiet place to talk where they could be alone, out of earshot of anyone who might try to stop them. Sax would later remember that twice they went rowing on the lake in Central Park, renting a rowboat for an hour or so from the boat house in the Ramble off East Park Drive in the middle of the park. An hour on the lake was easy, inconspicuous, and private in an obversely public way. That may have been where they decided Sax would have to take another stab at getting to a high-placed Soviet, someone more competent than Kurnakov seemed to be. He would do it the next day.

The Soviet Consulate was in Manhattan's most expensive neighborhood at 7 East Sixty-first Street, near the corner of Fifth Avenue. The Pierre Hotel was on one corner, Central Park across Fifth Avenue, and a string of fine homes spread down East Sixty-first. Perhaps not wanting to advertise the fancy neighborhood to their colleagues back in Moscow, the Soviets code-named the consulate *zavod,* or "the factory," in their secret cables, conjuring up a much drearier vision than East Side elegance and greenery. When the inelegant Saville Sax arrived at the guarded door, he needed a cover story ready to guarantee passage. The tale he later told the FBI was that he visited the consulate to inquire about the fate of his mother's relatives left behind in the German-occupied western Soviet Union. (In fact, the Sax family eventually would find that no one had survived the Holocaust. Many were probably among the 100,000 Jews who perished in their former Ukrainian home province of Vinnitsa, which was the site of the Nazis' Pechora concentration camp.) But that day his real mission was getting Hall's Los Alamos file into the hands of somebody who would know what to do with it. He succeeded.

Sax managed to meet with Anatoly Yatskov, then a clerk at the Soviet Consulate. He was also a spy who would focus almost exclusively on developing atomic espionage sources, the man who was Klaus Fuchs's control officer. Sax and Hall posed a dilemma for Yatskov. Potential sources had to be vetted before they could be recruited for real spy work. It was unthinkable to accept overtures like this from guys walking in off the street. Yet Hall came to the Soviets at the very moment they were hungering to find a sympathetic scientist in America's most secret weapons project. Yatskov made no greater commitment to Sax right then than Kurnakov had made a day earlier to Hall. But he did accept a second copy of the paper on Los Alamos that Ted had pressed on Kurnakov the day before. Yatskov had little time to act. Hall was catching a train in two days.

Based on his conversation with Sax and what he learned about Kurnakov's talk with Hall, the credentials of both young men looked good. Sax's mother, Bluma, had contacts with the Communist Party, besides working for Russian War Relief. Both young men were considered "gymnasts," evidently the Soviet code name for associates of a communist youth organization. Both had belonged to the John Reed Society, and Sax may have been in other groups. Hall had been a member of the American Student Union in high school, although he may not have been aware that it was a communist front. Both were smart enough to attend Harvard.

That day Kvasnikov, Yatskov's boss and the deputy station chief in charge of scientific intelligence, was unavailable to consult. Instead, Yatskov talked with his NKGB station chief, Stepan Apresyan, who also wore the official hat of a Soviet vice consul. They decided the consequences of losing Hall and Sax if they were legitimate were worse than the consequences of accepting them if the two were American undercover agents. Yatskov and Apresyan told Kurnakov "to feel out H., to assure him that everything was in order and to arrange liaison with him." Initially they would let Sax be the contact, keeping the scientist a healthy step away from any Soviet controller.

The day Hall was to leave New York, his father and stepmother took him out for a send-off lunch. They had a leisurely meal at Bonat's Café, a French restaurant on West Thirty-first Street, two blocks from Penn Station. Then they all walked over to the station. As they stood talking in the main booking hall, waiting for the train to Chicago, Ted got a shock. There was Kurnakov, standing not far away and beckoning him to come over. His family also saw the man, so Hall couldn't simply ignore his insistent gesturing. Mumbling an excuse to his family about some acquaintance he really ought to greet, the astonished Hall went over to the Russian. Kurnakov assured him that he and Sax had been accepted into the club. Hall was anxious that this bumbling fellow—who had, after all, waylaid him in a public place with his relatives around—might not actually have talked to Sax. So he quizzed him on his friend's appearance to make sure Kurnakov had met a young man with a deformed left hand. The Soviet confirmed it. Then Kurnakov indulged in another bit of behavior that left Hall mortified. Apparently moved at the thought that a brilliant young man would risk his career and even his life to supply the Soviet Union this critical information, Kurnakov drew himself up tall and saluted Ted.

The first Moscow heard of Hall and Sax was in a November 12, 1944, cable from the New York *rezidentura*, two weeks after Ted Hall left New York for the atom bomb laboratory. It named the two young men from New York (code-named "Tyre") and told how they offered to work for the Soviets. It noted that Hall (code-named "Mlad") turned over to Kurnakov (code-named "Bek") the same report on

Los Alamos (code-named "Camp-2") that Sax (code-named "Star") gave Yatskov (code-named "Aleksej"). And it reported that Yatskov and Apresyan (code-named "May") authorized Kurnakov to arrange liaison.*

From: NEW YORK
To: MOSCOW
NO: 1585   12 Nov. 44

To VIKTOR.

BEK visited Theodore HALL [Teodor KhOLL], 19 years old, the son of a furrier. He is a graduate of HARVARD University. As a talented physicist he was taken on for government work. . . . At the present time H. is in charge of a group at "CAMP-2" (SANTA-FE). H. handed over to BEK a report about the CAMP and named the key personnel employed on ENORMOZ. He decided to do this on the advice of his colleague Saville SAX [SAVIL SAKS], a GYMNAST living in TYRE. . . . With the aim of hastening a meeting with a competent person, H. on the following day sent a copy of the report by S. to the PLANT [ZAVOD]. ALEKSEJ received S. H. had to leave for CAMP-2 in two days' time. He was compelled to make a decision quickly. Jointly with MAY [MAJ] he gave BEK consent to feel out H., to assure him that everything was in order and to arrange liaison with him. . . . We consider it expedient to maintain liaison with H. [1 word or letter unrecovered] through S. and not to bring in anybody else.

When Ted Hall was asked about this cable early in 1997, he didn't try to dispute that he had met Kurnakov on that furlough years earlier. The only thing that he condemned in the Venona decryption as "simply wrong" was the implication by the Soviet *rezidentura* that he had to be talked into passing atomic information by Sax or anyone else. As he put it in his statement printed in Chapter 10, "I was never 'recruited' by anyone." Whether or not the contemporary Soviet cable was more ac-

---

*To minimize confusion, we have spelled Russian names and code names in accordance with a widely used modern Cyrillic-to-English transliteration system. Fifty years ago, U.S. government code-breakers alternated among several other transliteration systems, so their translations of decrypted Soviet cables spelled names slightly differently. When quoting from the decrypted cables, we have replicated the spellings and punctuation used by the U.S. codebreakers.

curate than Hall's memory, this was the last time Hall and Sax were mentioned by name in a decrypted cable. In subsequent references they would be called by their new code names, "Mlad" and "Star." Hall would be known as Mlad, from the Old Slavonic adjective *mladoi,* which means "young." Sax, who was one year and not quite three months the elder, was code-named "Star," the short form of the adjective *starii* or "old."

Mlad and Star—Young and Old—were in active service.

CHAPTER 12

Mole Hunt

In the waning months of 1944, the Los Alamos security network was certain it had snagged something big. It had a dossier filled with reports that one of the scientists had been off the compound and talking to unauthorized people about what was going on in the secret laboratories on the mesa.

The U.S. Army Counter Intelligence Corps was watching the suspect. CIC agents were convinced he was a communist partisan discussing the importance of the Soviets getting the bomb, and they believed he already had a plan to help the Soviets. To a young woman friend living in Santa Fe, the suspect had mapped out a plan to go to Britain and join the Royal Air Force. The way the CIC was getting the story, this scientist intended to parachute into Poland or the Soviet Union, someplace where he could reach local communists and "tell them all he knew about the formula and the Los Alamos project." The scientist's name: Joseph Rotblat, the future Nobel Peace Prize laureate.

The CIC case against Rotblat shows the reach of Manhattan Project security as well as its ineffectiveness. Three others inside Los Alamos were being activated as Soviet moles in those very weeks that attention focused on Rotblat. They were undetected.

Rotblat always believed that Los Alamos security forces fixated on him because he was an exception. He had come to Britain from his native Poland in 1939 to work and study; then the German blitzkrieg closed his country. He joined British physicists dispatched to work on the bomb in America, but he was refused a visa to enter the United States because he had not accepted British citizenship, a condition the Americans had imposed on the British mission. Rotblat's wife remained trapped in Poland, and he expected to go home after the war. He had no wish to be a British citizen. It took the intervention of James Chadwick, head of the British mission, to win General Groves's assent for Rotblat to join his colleagues already in America in early 1944. "Of course this marked me straightaway as not going with the crowd. I'm sure it must have put some question mark on me," Rotblat said decades later.

Rotblat said he learned he was suspected of espionage late in 1944, when he decided he must stop working on the bomb. Chadwick had told him about an Allied intelligence report at the end of November confirming what had been a growing suspicion: The Germans weren't close to creating an atomic bomb and were in fact no longer even working on it. The fear that the Germans would win the atomic race was what had compelled Rotblat to join the Los Alamos scientists. When that threat disappeared, he could no longer justify to himself the creation of the atomic bomb by any country—or at least his participation in it. He already had been dismayed at hearing Groves say at the Chadwicks' dinner that the bomb was being created as a hedge against the Soviets in the future as much as against the Germans in the present. But when Chadwick told the Americans running Los Alamos that Rotblat wanted out, security chief Major Peer de Silva gave a startling response: They must settle the issues in Rotblat's inch-thick security dossier.

"I was accused of all sorts of things. This was a terrible shock to me," Rotblat said. "Chadwick of course never believed it, because he knew me sufficiently well to know that I wouldn't have engaged in this sort of activity. 'But still,' he [Chadwick] said, 'this all is written down.' "

When Rotblat and Chadwick met with de Silva, the security head read out page after page documenting the Polish physicist's alleged meetings not only with the young woman in Santa Fe, but with a number of other people outside of Los Alamos whom he had never reported contacting. Dates, places, and times were supplied. "They were people I've never heard of. It was pure imagination. Fortunately for me I could show straightaway that at the times I was supposed to be there [in unreported meetings], many people knew where I was." After their discussion, Rotblat said, de Silva agreed he had unreliable information and apologized. He promised to destroy the dossier.

There was, however, one transgression. Rotblat had to acknowledge he had visited a civilian outside the project without authorization from the Americans. She was twenty-two-year-old Elsbeth Grant, a British native whom he had met while he was a professor and she a student at the University of Liverpool. Her family had moved to the United States in 1942, and she had come to New Mexico seeking treatment for a hearing disorder. After receiving a letter from a friend who mentioned Miss Grant was living not far away in Santa Fe, Rotblat wrote her a note. She invited him to visit. Los Alamos censors reported on their letters. He did visit her in June 1944, and he continued to see her periodically. After Rotblat's visit on December 3, Miss Grant dropped by the home of an older woman who had befriended her in Santa Fe, Aileen O'Bryan, the mother-in-law of a close friend of Grant's back in Britain. It was Aileen O'Bryan who told CIC that Rotblat had the strange idea of parachuting to the aid of the Soviets, a plan that she said Grant had described to her. The CIC must have tied the story to the fact that Rotblat had been taking flying lessons in Santa Fe. O'Bryan, whom the CIC had asked to pump Grant for information, also reported that Rotblat asked Grant to mail letters for him, and that the two discussed communism.

"Although most of the story was untrue, 99 percent untrue, nevertheless they had something on me," Rotblat later explained. "One thing is, I was always all my life sort of a rebel. Particularly I dislike unnecessary bureaucracy." He added he always would go out of his way to "avoid" bureaucratic restrictions. While Rotblat said he had told his mission leader, Chadwick, about the trips to see Grant, he had "avoided" Los Alamos regulations by not informing the American authorities. Rather than face a lengthy inquiry that would have involved Grant and delayed his departure, Rotblat agreed to de Silva's conditions: He was not to make later contact with his Los Alamos associates or tell anyone he was leaving out of disaffection over the atom bomb program. Instead, Rotblat told friends he was too anxious over the fate of his wife in Poland to continue work on the bomb in America. He left on December 8, 1944, having secured permission to stop in Santa Fe to tell Elsbeth Grant that he was departing.

The CIC investigation did not stop with his departure from Los Alamos. "That they didn't trust me is clear in that they robbed me of all my belongings, my intellectual belongings," Rotblat charged. He said he had packed a wooden crate, specially made for him by the Special Engineering Detachment soldiers, with all of his old scientific notes and papers brought from England, a collection of books he had purchased that were unavailable abroad, and other possessions. The crate got as far as Washington, D.C., where he spent several days with the Chadwick family. The crate was put on the train he took from Union Station, but it didn't arrive in New York. Rotblat never saw it again. "I feel that because of me, they diverted attention from the real spies, that Klaus Fuchs would have been more suspect if they hadn't decided to watch me," he said many years later.

Rotblat and Grant maintained that the CIC's account of their meeting was at best fanciful. At worst, it was intended to harm or discredit the Polish scientist. The FBI, which in the 1950s investigated Rotblat in the course of a broader espionage inquiry, minimized the significance of the CIC case. It did not find evidence to pursue Rotblat.

The Rotblat story exemplifies the strange and spotty nature of security at Los Alamos. From the start, the Americans faced a daunting job. They wanted to create an entire town with the world's most sophisticated scientific facilities and at the same time keep the whole place hidden. They also were trying to corral some of the most brilliant and eccentric scientists in the world, along with their families and hundreds of auxiliary personnel who weren't supposed to be let in on the secrets of the laboratories.

The initial fear of German or Japanese sabotage was fairly easily laid to rest. The first line of defense had been the selection of a remote site easily guarded against a physical assault. On another level, the key minds of the project got the special attention of personal bodyguards. A handful of scientists, like Fermi and Oppenheimer, couldn't leave the compound without a bulky, gun-wielding companion. And some of the world's best-known physicists arrived under pseudonyms. Fermi was Mr. Farmer. Old friends of Niels Bohr found it ludicrous to call him by his registered name, Nicholas Baker, but settled on "Uncle Nick."

General Groves was frightened not only by the idea that Germany might infiltrate the Manhattan Project, but also by the possibility that other countries—even the Allies—might learn how to build the bomb. The military was so nervous that for the first half of 1943 even the British were kept in the dark about Manhattan Project atomic developments, until Churchill got FDR to lift the ban. The Soviets never were sufficiently trusted to be let in on atomic secrets. In a book written after the war, General Groves listed his three security aims. The first was keeping the Germans unaware of what was happening, and the second was ensuring complete surprise about when the bomb would be used in combat. The third, he wrote, was "to keep the Russians from learning of our discoveries and the details of our designs and processes." Groves didn't come close to realizing the extent to which his secret factories were penetrated by Soviet intelligence.

Hints began to reach the general and his scientific adviser, James B. Conant, in early 1943 that the Soviet Union was getting serious about uranium research. At the end of January—almost exactly when the first Soviet intelligence reports reached Moscow about the new American chain-reacting pile—Stalin's government openly asked the U.S. Lend-Lease Administration to send 10 kilograms of uranium metal and 100 kilograms of uranium oxide and uranium nitrate to Moscow. Rather than exhibit an excessive interest in uranium, Groves approved the export licenses for the uranium compounds to be flown to the Soviet Union in early April but rejected Moscow's request for uranium metal.

While the Russian shipment was in the works, a squad of Groves's Army counterintelligence agents in northern California spotted a man who called himself "Joe" entering the home of Steve Nelson, a leader of the American Communist Party. Counterintelligence agents identified Joe as Joseph W. Weinberg, a former student of Oppenheimer and a physicist at the Manhattan Project's Radiation Laboratory at the University of California in Berkeley. Based on informants' reports and hidden microphones, the FBI believed Nelson gave information from Weinberg to Soviet vice consul Pyotr Ivanov. Groves later told Congress that Weinberg passed on "the object and progress of the project, materials and means used, and the location of other installations engaged."

A week after Groves's agents saw Ivanov receiving atomic information in the spring of 1943, Conant got a letter from Aristid V. Grosse, an émigré chemist from Germany who had begun working on uranium fission at Columbia University in 1940. Grosse, who had left nuclear research after Pearl Harbor to work on synthetic rubber for the U.S. War Production Board, told Conant that he had traveled to Moscow in January 1943 to lecture on rubber chemistry at the Soviet Academy of Sciences. When his lecture was over, Soviet academicians surrounded him on the podium. They pressed him about his work at Columbia on fission, which had been mentioned in a page-one article in The New York Times three years before. One of the Soviets, Abram Ioffe, asked Grosse for one milligram of the radioactive element proactinium. Ioffe said he wanted it so Soviet scientists could work on spontaneous fission, one of the key nuclear processes Groves's scientists were also studying. If there was any doubt in Washington that the Soviet Union was getting serious about nuclear research, the Aristid Grosse letter should have put it to rest.

These early traces of Soviet espionage crossed Groves's desk in the spring of 1943, just as he was opening Los Alamos. And the effect of the general's security worries was unmistakable at the new laboratory. Every person, everyone except the babies, was fingerprinted and issued a pass. Off the compound, no one was supposed to speak to any outsider without permission. Starting late in 1943, all mail going into and out of Los Alamos was censored, and the perimeter fence was patrolled to keep strangers from coming in and the inhabitants from leaving without notice. Less known was the radio intercept system designed to catch any unauthorized transmissions. Nor were most Manhattan Project participants aware of the undercover agents posing both inside the lab as co-workers and at nearby towns as hotel clerks, electricians, and even gamblers.

But it was still America, and the scientists and families and other personnel at Los Alamos couldn't be kept prisoner. Family members and other non-working personnel could hop on board the twice-daily bus to Santa Fe and post a letter there, though they would risk a run-in with undercover security if spotted. Holes in the fence were well known to Los Alamos children who couldn't be bothered to walk to the gate. One section even was left loose so residents of the surrounding Indian pueblos could sneak in to see the evening movies. Practical jokers like the twenty-six-year-old physicist Richard Feynman exulted in baffling security officers. To protest against mail censorship, Feynman inserted meaningless codes in his letters. Another of his stunts was signing out at the main gate, then slipping back in through a hole in the fence. Repeatedly. John von Neumann once bet security chief de Silva that he could sneak a scientist onto the grounds undetected. De Silva took the challenge, but, after contemplating the security conditions of the compound and the intellect of his charges, he withdrew from the wager. In retrospect, the former Soviet intelligence station chief in New York, Colonel Vladimir Barkovsky, who was intimately familiar with the development of atomic espionage, said the biggest fault of Los Alamos security was the failure to do body searches of people leaving the place.

To guard fully against espionage would have meant clamping a security vise over the entire country. There were too many potential leaks in a program as geographically scattered as the Manhattan Project. As it was, security precautions were extraordinary for a country as open and unrestricted as the United States boasted of being. In the Soviet Union body searches might have been an accepted standard of security for civilian scientists and their families. In America it was not.

Yet some things could have been done differently, especially given Groves's worries about Soviet penetration—and the signs that it was actually happening. The most effective step would have been stronger and more public retribution against those found passing technical secrets. Joseph Weinberg, for example, was quietly drafted and dispatched to Alaska. The same thing happened in April 1944, after an FBI surveillance team in Chicago watched physicist Clarence Hiskey of the Metallurgical Laboratory meet with Arthur Alexandrovich Adams, a known Soviet spy. Hiskey was drafted and spent the rest of the war at a base near the Arctic Circle at Mineral Wells, Alaska. Weinberg and Hiskey had their security clearances revoked and were forbidden to work on nuclear projects, but news about their ruined careers was not circulated to other scientists. Even the case of Rotblat was entirely silenced. Even now the question lingers: Would Ted Hall have risked the trip to Amtorg had he known about the travails of Weinberg and Hiskey?

During the war the Manhattan Project's unit of the Army Counter Intelligence Corps handled 100 cases of "probable" wartime espionage and 200 cases of possible sabotage. Not one resulted in a prosecution for a major crime. Had there been any obvious effect of the security precautions—had anybody been caught and publicly punished—Manhattan Project personnel might have better understood both the threat and the need for security. The military did not even conduct effective background checks before passing out top-secret clearances. All three known spies at Los Alamos had been members of the Communist Party or offshoots of it, yet the CIC wasn't aware of any of their connections.

One of the most vexing breaches of security in Groves's view was Oppenheimer's refusal to compartmentalize work. Groves had wanted to limit the exchange of information within Los Alamos so each scientist and technician would know only what was absolutely necessary to carry out his or her own small bit of research and experimentation. Oppenheimer refused, arguing that he needed an exchange of ideas if he were to build this new weapon quickly. He held weekly colloquia in which the leading scientists talked about their work, because he was convinced it was good for morale when people knew how their job fit into the overall picture. It worked. Oppenheimer produced a bomb in a remarkably short time. But Groves also was right: The lack of compartmentalization made life much easier for the spies of Los Alamos.

At the very time agents were following and then confronting Rotblat in the summer and fall of 1944, the Soviets were snaking their way into Los Alamos through other means. Out of contact for months, Fuchs finally was found by his Soviet handlers. Whether or not he intended to, Fuchs had left a hint about where he was. Before disappearing in August, Fuchs had told his spy contact Harry Gold about his sister Kristel in Cambridge, Massachusetts, and had spoken fondly of her. Gold told his controller, Anatoly Yatskov, about Kristel in September, and the Soviet immediately realized she was their best chance of learning what had happened to Fuchs. At their next meeting, Gold recalled that Yatskov informed him "with great glee" that he had discovered the full name of Fuchs's sister in Cambridge. Late that fall Gold came calling. He learned the scientist had contacted Kristel from Chicago, probably while he was en route to Los Alamos. It was a smart move, since Fuchs would find only two closely guarded telephones in all of Los Alamos when he arrived, one in the custody of Oppenheimer and the other in the military headquarters. He told her he would be working in New Mexico and would try to come visit around the holidays. Gold left a telephone number for Fuchs to call when he got back to the East Coast.

The message the New York *rezidentura* sent to Moscow on November 16, 1944, must have been heartening. Fuchs had been found and was expected to give the Soviets news within months, maybe weeks, about what was happening at "Camp No. 2," the code for Los Alamos, the heart of the bomb project.

It now is known from American decryptions of Soviet spy cables that at the same time a second spy was being activated at Camp No. 2. Just before Thanksgiving Ruth Greenglass was about to leave New York to visit her husband, David, a machinist who had been drafted and assigned to work at Los Alamos. She had agreed to ask him to divulge information to the Soviets. David Greenglass was the brother of Ethel Rosenberg, and Ethel's husband, Julius Rosenberg, had convinced Ruth to cooperate. By mid-December Ruth came home with good news for the Soviets. Her husband already had been thinking about passing information to the Soviet allies. Technical Sergeant Greenglass was ready to help, and he would be home on leave in January. The December 16, 1944, cable to Moscow announcing the Greenglass recruitment also carried a note of caution. Greenglass had warned that "authorities of the Camp were openly taking all precautionary measures to prevent information about Enormoz falling into Russian hands."

The third source of information for the Soviets was Ted Hall. He had arrived at Los Alamos months before Fuchs and Greenglass, and he was the first to supply details about it. The first known information from Los Alamos came to Moscow in the November 12, 1944, cable that said Hall had handed to Kurnakov "a report about the CAMP and named key personnel employed on ENORMOZ." The New York *rezidentura* promised to send details by post, but within weeks sent another cable listing the scientists working on "the problem." Cable was the fastest way to communicate, since letters and reports tucked into the black diplomatic suitcases were transported on Lend-Lease airplanes based in Montana, which traveled through Alaska and then on to Moscow Centre.

The American decoders who intercepted the December 2 cable attributed the information it contained to Mlad. It fit the brief description in the November 12 cable of what Ted Hall had turned over to Kurnakov: It was a lineup of the world's stellar physicists, including Hans Bethe, Niels Bohr, Enrico Fermi, John von Neumann, Bruno Rossi, George Kistiakowski, Emilio Segrè, Geoffrey Taylor, William Penney, Arthur Compton, Ernest Lawrence, Harold Urey, Edward Teller, and Percy Bridgman. The inclusion of Bridgman was interesting, since few knew that he was working in virtual seclusion on bomb-related research at Harvard, Hall's alma mater. Even stranger was the inclusion of two Germans who were pioneers in nuclear research. As written in the cable, they were identified as "Werner Eisenberg" and "Strassenman." The reference probably was to Werner Heisenberg and Fritz Strassman, who were believed to be working on the bomb for the Nazis at the Kaiser Wilhelm Institute for Physics.

On December 25, Igor Kurchatov was handed another bundle of Manhattan Project documents that had been pouched to Moscow from the NKGB in the United States. Judging from Kurchatov's notes, one of the more intriguing bits was a "group of reviews" that summarized research "from March 1943 to June 1944" in a certain foreign nuclear laboratory. "This group of reviews is interesting because it covers methods of studying physical aspects of the problem of uranium, and it covers some of the works which are used now abroad and about which we did not have information before," Kurchatov wrote.

The laboratory was not named in Kurchatov's evaluation, but the contents of his report suggest that the lab was the Experimental Physics Division at Los Alamos. That was where Ted Hall had worked until the summer of 1944. The most revealing clue about the source of the group of reviews that reached Kurchatov was the reference to an obscure piece of detection apparatus called an electron multiplier. The electron multiplier was a device developed in the Experimental Physics Division at Los Alamos in the summer of 1943. As far as can be determined, no other laboratory in the world used an electron multiplier in cyclotron experiments during the 1943–44 period. Kurchatov said the work with the electron multiplier interested him because it indicated that an atomic bomb was feasible.

The report from the unnamed laboratory "from March 1943 to June 1944" may well have been what Ted Hall passed to Kurnakov in Manhattan. In view of the timing, Fuchs could not have been the source. Greenglass's narrow focus on machining lens molds meant that he had no access to results of obscure experiments on uranium. Thus Ted Hall is the most plausible suspect for having passed the document, but this suspicion cannot be confirmed from archival records. The remaining possibility, of course, is that the Soviets had yet another "friend" in Los Alamos who has never been discovered.

Whether Kurchatov was soberly assessing the prospect that the American program would complete its atom bomb soon, or expressing optimism that the Soviets would be able to succeed, he gave the NKGB a positive analysis. "On the basis of theoretical data, there are no grounds to believe that in this respect there will be any difficulties in implementing the bomb," he wrote.

Whatever Ted Hall's contribution to Soviet atomic data was in 1944, he had gotten enough out of high-security Los Alamos to whet the appetite of Russian physicists.

What Hall had not yet provided were concrete details on how to build a bomb.

CHAPTER 13

Savy's Rendezvous

A few phrases, a few passages of poetry, that's all it took to fool the censors. Ted Hall and Saville Sax had perfected the Walt Whitman code during Ted's October furlough, perhaps while they were in the rowboat in Central Park. Each owned the same edition of *Leaves of Grass,* and they decided to make certain pages of it their codebook. Their cipher system was really quite primitive. All it could communicate was a time and date for a clandestine meeting in New Mexico.

Now that Ted Hall had the codebook near his bed at Los Alamos, he had to face whether he really wanted to get in deeper with the Soviets. Hall was still irritated at Kurnakov's blatant indiscretion in turning up at Penn Station. Was this whole scheme too risky? What he had given Kurnakov was scarcely more than a peek at the work of Los Alamos. A few names and some interesting data on secondary neutrons, perhaps. But nothing approaching the actual design of a bomb. Would he now convey a fuller, more current picture? Or should he simply not activate the Walt Whitman code?

Not many weeks after Ted's furlough, he and Sax began to exchange letters. Through the Walt Whitman code they arranged a meeting in Albuquerque. It was to take place on a certain day, a day "a few months" after Hall's furlough, said someone who knew the truth. And as things turned out, *Leaves of Grass* was the ideal codebook for fixing dates. Whitman had attached to each of his verses a number from one to thirty-one and beyond, and each verse had a dozen lines or more. The *Leaves of Grass* method was something that Hall and Sax invented without help from Kurnakov; in the whole history of Soviet intelligence this was the only known instance when secret information was ever transmitted by the ancient cryptography system known to cipher experts as a "book code." Had the Manhattan Project censors caught on, chances are Hall would have been drafted and sent off to the Arctic. His career in nuclear physics would have been ruined, but the odds were he would not have been prosecuted. Back then, the priority for the Manhattan Project was to isolate the risk and move on.

Once the Los Alamos censors let through one of his Walt Whitman letters, the next step was up to Sax. Like Ted, Savy now faced another choice in the incremental progression into espionage. Had this whole thing gone too far? Or was he prepared to become Hall's messenger? Sax had to decide this while he was going through what he later would call a "state of depression" whose triggering event had been his failure to pass his draft physical while at Harvard in 1943 or early 1944. Savy's sense of rejection, originally due to his deformed hand, deepened after his best friend, Ted, left for secret war work. Sax's grades nose-dived in 1944 and he would later explain that he felt Ted Hall was "the only person he could rely on to get him out of his state of depression."

Harvard was swollen with temporary students and it wasn't easy for a regular member of the class of 1946 to flunk out. But Savy found a way: He cut classes, then exams. After he was expelled for failing grades around the middle of 1944, Sax took one manual job after another. Distressed that he wasn't in uniform, Sax resolved to find work in a war plant. For a while Savy worked as a punch-press operator at two New York steel companies, World Steel Products and Atlantic Metal Products. For a time he worked in a silk-screening shop, F & D Textile Printing. While in New York Savy lived with his widowed mother, Bluma.

Why Sax decided to go forward into espionage after receiving Hall's coded signal is a question he never chose to answer. In later years even Savy's ex-wife Susan insisted he had never really told her about the encounters he had with the Soviets. She knew he was in contact with them after they got married in 1948, but it took some time for her to realize what he and Hall had done during the war. "It just came out by osmosis," said Susan. Although she didn't know the whole story, Susan did finally get the picture. Her cumulative impression, she said in 1996, was "that Ted had been at Los Alamos and Savy had acted as a courier." The Saxes' son Boria came to believe that his father had been driven by a mixture of motivations, including an attraction to Soviet communism. "I believe he probably felt a lot more loyalty to Russia than to the United States, but both were on the same side," he ventured. However, Boria's view of his father's loyalties did not ring true to Ted Hall. Based on what Hall insisted were "extensive discussions" he had with Savy before they left Harvard, Hall said, "Given his awareness of the purges in

Russia, I am sure he felt no 'loyalty' to the Soviet government. His concern was for humanity—for ideals and principles, rather than for states."

Another puzzle is why the New York *rezidentura* ever decided to trust Sax to be Hall's courier. By then, the *rezidentura* was operating a stable of at least three seasoned couriers—Harry Gold, Julius Rosenberg, and a Spanish Civil War veteran named Michael Sidorovich. Yet it chose Sax for the trip to New Mexico even though he had no training in spycraft. Sax hadn't even been accorded the normal vetting the NKGB required of all new clandestine workers. The only explanation is that Ted Hall must have insisted on working through Savy, and there is good reason to believe this is exactly what happened. Even so, it must have occurred to Kurnakov that Sax was likely to have great trouble blending in during a trip to the wartime Southwest. "Savy was a very unlikely spy," said Susan Sax, who was his wife for twenty years. "First of all, he was not inconspicuous. He was very untidy and dressed unconventionally. He talked to himself. He'd sort of stride down the street talking to himself and making hand gestures. So people would notice him. He was conspicuous. Very much so."

Whether it was Sax, Hall, or the Soviets, someone came up with an admirable cover story. Savy's legend would be that he was visiting Albuquerque to check out the University of New Mexico, which interested him because he wanted to shift to a new field, anthropology. Savy took at least one step to buttress this scenario. He visited a library in New York where he found a course catalogue for the University of New Mexico. He also took some time to read up on the anthropology of American Indians.

Sax bought a bus ticket and left for New Mexico "a few months" after Ted Hall's October furlough. From clues that would later turn up in intercepted Soviet intelligence cables, Savy may well have left New York between Thanksgiving and mid-December of 1944. This deduction is based on a spurt of cables relating to Mlad between December 2 and December 16. Three New York–to–Moscow cables clearly referred to Mlad (which had just become Ted Hall's code name) and two other Moscow-to-New York cables seem to have been related.

One cable warned Moscow Centre that Gold could not possibly serve as the only courier to all the *rezidentura*'s atomic sources. "We consider it risky to concentrate all contacts relating to ENORMOUS [ENORMOZ] on ARNO alone," the cable said. "This is good in that it limits the circles . . . but it is dangerous to disrupt . . . work on

ENORMOUS." This cable may well have been the *rezidentura*'s justification to Moscow for sending Sax instead of the seasoned Gold to visit Hall, but this inference cannot be proven because the U.S. decoders were unable to break a subsequent paragraph discussing how the Soviets planned to maintain liaison with their atomic spies.

As the day for the rendezvous with Savy approached, Ted Hall also had to decide how much he really wanted to pass to the Soviets—something that had become a much more important question since he had met Kurnakov. Before his October furlough, the laboratory had been running into one obstacle after another, making it unclear whether a bomb could be ready before the end of the war. But now the summer's setbacks were being overcome and Los Alamos was closing in on the designs for two bombs—the gun-type uranium bomb code-named Little Boy and the implosion-type bomb code-named Fat Man, which was to be made of plutonium.

Working in the Ra-La group in the thick of the most dramatic developments, Hall would have known almost as much as Oppenheimer about the design of Fat Man. Only three months earlier, Robert Christy of the Theoretical Physics Division had proposed changing the core of the bomb from a hollow shell of plutonium to a solid sphere. In September Hall's boss, Rossi, heard of the solid-core design and persuaded Oppenheimer to authorize a Ra-La test shot using Christy's idea.

As a white-badger, Hall also knew a good deal about advances by the Gadget Division on the uranium bomb, quite likely even including its oddball variant that was being called the "uranium hydride bomb." On November 28, Otto Frisch's G-1 group achieved the first "critical assembly" when it piled together hundreds of cubes of uranium hydride inside a "tamper" made of beryllium oxide. Their critical assembly experiment was a test to measure how neutrons would multiply inside an actual bomb made of pure uranium 235, or perhaps of one of U-235's chemical compounds. A half century later, Ted Hall didn't recall knowing anything about the uranium hydride option, but at the time he probably did know of it. Hall knew Otto Frisch slightly, and he was good friends with one of Frisch's assistants, Freddie de Hoffmann. On December 7, Oppenheimer ordered a final push to settle the design of the uranium gun. The uranium hydride idea had been the brainchild of Edward Teller, who had already developed a reputation in the lab as an erratic genius. As far back as 1943, Teller had sketched out a low-budget bomb that he thought would explode using one twentieth as much uranium 235 as would be required by a bomb made of pure metallic uranium. His idea was to convert the uranium into a chemical compound called uranium hydride and let the hydrogen atoms in the hydride contribute by slowing down the neutrons. Twice in 1944, Teller's uranium hydride bomb had been discarded as unworkable. But now, after the hydride cubes had been used so successfully in the critical assembly experiment, Teller's idea couldn't entirely be dismissed. Both the implosion bomb and uranium hydride experiments were live topics when Ted Hall embarked on the three-hour rocky ride to Albuquerque.

TED'S RENDEZVOUS WITH Saville Sax was so amateurish it would have made Kurnakov cringe if he had known. Instead of converging on the meeting place, Ted and Savy approached on foot from the same direction. They "bumped into each other in the street" some distance from their pre-planned meeting spot, something that would have appalled any NKGB trainer.

Hall had taken a room in a hotel near the Albuquerque train station and Savy was already checked in at another Albuquerque hotel. After reaching a private spot for their meeting, Savy took out a single piece of paper that he had brought inside his shoe all the way from New York. On the paper was a question typed in English given to Sax by a Soviet intelligence officer. The question was "some specific technical little thing" involving the use of sulfur dioxide—or so Ted Hall would tell a few friends in England in the 1990s. Sulfur dioxide for what? There was no answer. But the mere fact that Soviet intelligence was asking at the end of 1944 about a sulfur compound was intriguing: One of the chemicals used at Los Alamos in the summer of 1944 was uranium 235 sulfate. In fact, it was the key ingredient in one of the first Los Alamos experiments to calibrate the critical mass of uranium. If Ted ever told Savy anything about sulfur dioxide, neither of them has talked about it. Sax and Hall spent only that one evening together in Albuquerque before Ted had to hurry north to Los Alamos.

Sax carried back to New York a piece of paper far more important than a response on sulfur dioxide. It was only a page or two, something Hall had written by hand during one of his breaks from work in the Gadget Division. What Ted Hall gave his Harvard roommate that day was a bold new concept for assembling a critical mass so rapidly that all risk of a fizzle could be eliminated. The idea would become the key to the invention of the plutonium bomb.

. . .

SAVY'S RUN WAS scarcely finished when Ted Hall was abruptly drafted into the U.S. Army. On December 28, 1944, he was inducted and dispatched the same day to Santa Fe to begin immediate active service. Hall was put up for the night at the La Fonda Hotel in Santa Fe, then given orders the next day to report forthwith to Fort Bliss, Texas, for Army basic training.

"Wait a minute, this isn't right," Hall remembered telling the recruiting officer. "I am supposed to be staying on the Hill. You ring such and such a number and you'll find out." And, as it turned out, Ted was not being exiled to Alaska like Clarence Hiskey. Rather, he had been caught in the nationwide manpower shortage. Under pressure to fill quotas for the final push on Germany, Selective Service was inducting thousands of middle-aged men with children. Complaints multiplied when rumors reached Congress about single young college boys who weren't being drafted just because they happened to be scientists. General Groves tried to head off the Selective Service back in 1943 by setting up an Army board to review the cases of each draft-deferred scientist in the Manhattan Project. Oppenheimer appealed to keep all his junior scientists in civilian clothes. But in 1944 he compromised with Groves, who shared the sentiment in Congress and the Pentagon that all draft-age males should be in uniform. Scientists with advanced degrees would keep their draft deferments, they decided. Those in their early twenties with no more than B.S. degrees would go into a draft pool and return to Los Alamos after minimal training, wearing the uniform of the Army's Special Engineering Detachment. The SED was a unit of five hundred young scientists, machinists, welders, and other technical workers who were already at work at Los Alamos.

When the recruiting officer in Santa Fe checked into Ted Hall's claim, he found that Los Alamos did indeed want him back on the Hill as fast as possible. A roomful of other draftees shipped out, but Ted was held in Santa Fe. "I was then sent down to Fort Bliss in a hell of a hurry. And I went through the whole induction procedure myself, which meant sitting in a projection room and watching the films where the draftees were warned about the consequences of fooling around and getting VD." About two days later, Hall was back in his old job on the Hill, this time wearing the uniform of a U.S. Army private. Hall never even went through basic training. Of the four junior physicists from Harvard, Ted was the only one drafted. At the end of the war, only 19 of the 2,600 Los Alamos staffers were SEDs who had been civilians on the laboratory staff.

As the story filtered down to Ted Hall, his draft notice was the consequence of cynical log-rolling between Groves and Oppenheimer. "I don't know how accurate this is, but I heard I was traded for a sidewalk," Hall said. "I think Leslie Groves was sympathetic with the view that you shouldn't have these able-bodied civilians who weren't in uniform. At the same time, there was another issue hanging fire. When you walked along the main street where the labs were, your trousers got very muddy. Oppenheimer was agitating to get sidewalks. And Groves was agitating to have people drafted. They reached a consensus: I was drafted and the sidewalks appeared."

EXACTLY HOW SAX returned to Manhattan is a mystery, but long afterward, Sax's children heard an intriguing tale from their father. After swearing them to secrecy, Savy told them about the time he once delivered a parcel of atomic documents to the Soviet consulate in New York. "This was something I heard only once, and it was at a pretty young age," recalled his eldest son, Boria, after Saville Sax's death. "I just couldn't grasp that this was significant, but maybe on some level it did register, because I remember it. What I remember is that he'd somehow participated in smuggling the atom bomb to the Russians with Ted Hall." One thing that stuck in Boria Sax's memory was that his father left a suitcase at the Soviet Consulate containing documents about the bomb. However, the way his sister Sarah heard the story from their father, the documents were in a briefcase, not a suitcase.

Insofar as it affects Ted Hall, this is all distant hearsay, and Hall has said he knows nothing about a briefcase or suitcase of documents. But contemporary records show that in the second half of December 1944, the New York *rezidentura* did suddenly order full background checks on Ted Hall as well as Saville Sax and his mother, Bluma. The *rezidentura* assigned this inquiry to a trusted Soviet contact inside the American Communist Party, Bernard Schuster (code-named "Ekho," or, in English, "Echo"), who had access to the party's secret personnel records. Even before receiving Schuster's report, however, the *rezidentura* dispatched at least one cable to Moscow Centre relating to Ted Hall; this one evoked two return messages whose contents are unknown. This blip of Soviet cable activity seems to substantiate indications from other sources that it was around mid-December that Sax checked in with the Soviets in New York following his return from Albuquerque.

A message in early January 1945 brought Moscow a further surprise about Mlad. He had been drafted, but instead of being sent off to dig ditches, he was returned to work at "the camp" (i.e., Los Alamos). The same message included revealing news about Star: He was about to resume his course of study at Harvard University. It also disclosed that Mlad's data was now being handled by the *rezidentura*'s agent handler in charge of atomic spies, Yatskov. Yet despite two years of experience in sifting all kinds of atomic information, Yatskov (code-named "Aleksej") was clearly puzzled about whether the data from Mlad was reliable. Ted Hall's original handler, Sergei Kurnakov (code-named "Bek," or "Beck"), had lost control of the agent he had recruited, and Kurnakov was obviously irate about it. Such bureaucratic squabbling almost never spilled over into the *rezidentura*'s cable traffic to Moscow. The fact that it did this time could suggest that Mlad had reported something important—so important that two senior intelligence officers would risk an embarrassing fight that Moscow would have to arbitrate. Following is the decrypted Soviet cable. Its text—prepared in 1953 by the NSA's code-breaking staff—is not easy to follow, since the American drafters unfortunately intermixed Hall's actual code name in Russian (Mlad) with the name Young, the English translation of Mlad. Similarly, the text interspersed Sax's code name in Russian (Star) with the English translation of Star (Old).

From:	NEW YORK	
To:	MOSCOW	
No.:	94	23 Jan 1945

To VICTOR

Your nos. 316 and 121. The checking of OLD [STAR] and YOUNG [MLAD] we entrusted to ECHO [EKhO] a month ago, the result of the check we have not yet had. We are checking OLD's mother also.

　　BECK [BEK] is extremely displeased over the handing over of OLD to ALEKSEJ. He gives a favorable report on him. ALEKSEJ has met OLD twice [but] cannot yet give a final judgment. YOUNG has been seen by no-one except BECK. [On the

8th of January] YOUNG sent a letter but never [made arrangements] for calling a meeting. He has been called up into the army and left to work in the camp.

OLD intends to renew his studies at the Harvard University at the end of February.

Once some initial confusion about translated code names is overcome, the significance of the decryption is obvious: Mlad's military history at the end of 1944 fits Hall's known movements like a pair of shrunken Levi's. And the detail about Star returning to study at Harvard in early 1945 coincides perfectly with Sax's return to Harvard. Without meaning to reveal anything, the *rezidentura* had included enough checkable details in this one cable that American counterintelligence agents would later have little trouble making a firm deduction of the identities of Mlad and Star. In a classified note circulated in the U.S. intelligence community in the early 1950s, the agents spelled out their conclusions with no "ifs," "buts," or "maybes":

> STAR: Saville Savoy SAX.
> MLAD: Theodore Alvin HALL.

The *rezidentura*'s cable not only pointed at the identities of the two Harvard roommates. It also conveyed a strong impression that whatever Sax had brought back from Albuquerque wasn't trivial. It had been important enough to grab Kurnakov's attention. And Yatskov's attention. And Moscow's attention, too.

CHAPTER 14

Passing the Implosion Principle

Ted Hall was just one minute cog in the Manhattan Project. As part of Bruno Rossi's Ra-La group, he did have a hand in settling the final design of the implosion bomb, but so did dozens of other junior white-badgers of the Los Alamos Gadget Division. Yet in Moscow, Hall's alter ego, Mlad, was causing a very important wheel to start rolling. Mlad's new report had evoked "great interest," read the cable Lubyanka sent to the NKGB *rezidentura* in New York. It was a report card from Lieutenant General Pavel Fitin, who was the closest thing Stalin had to General William "Wild Bill" Donovan of the OSS.

After Savy's visit, Ted Hall's main task was tinkering with the dummy bomb cores that Bruno Rossi was imploding in the Bayo Canyon. Before long it had reached Oppenheimer that Private Hall was one of the most capable technicians at Los Alamos in the intricacies of creating a test implosion. To simulate a plutonium core, a shop would make a sphere of heavy metal about five inches in diameter. Rossi's group started with iron and copper cores, then moved to cadmium when the metallurgists said it would compress just like a real core made out of plutonium. Each of Rossi's metallic mock-ups had to be fitted with an instrument package, usually four ionization chambers and some amplifiers. Building the ionization chambers was the job of a group of technicians led by Ted Hall. Hall was also in charge of the calibration tests that Rossi wanted before each dummy bomb was imploded.

When a simulated bomb core was ready for calibration, it would be delivered to a little cabin that had been assigned to Hall for his "static measurement" tests. The simulated core consisted of two matching hemispheres that were fitted with interlocks. In the center of the two hemispheres was a cavity to hold a tiny pellet of radioactive lanthanum 140, or Ra-La, the fission product that had been "milked" out of other hot wastes of an Oak Ridge production reactor. Ted's job was to insert a pellet containing a relatively weak shot of Ra-La into the slot, then to connect the two hemispheres. The result was a metal sphere about a foot in diameter whose outer layer was made of aluminum. Once he had assembled the ball with the Ra-La inside, he would suspend it from the cabin's rafters for ten minutes. To take his baseline radiation readings with the least possible interference, he had to hang the device from the smallest possible wires. To minimize his own exposure to gamma rays, he had to work fast, Hall remembered. Occasionally there were accidents, but Rossi kept him at it. "Twice I dropped the damn object on my toe," Ted Hall remembered. "I did it once and everyone was very sympathetic, and then I did it again."

After Hall's calibration tests were finished, someone would haul the metal sphere down into Bayo Canyon, which was two miles from the lab headquarter buildings. The sphere was fitted with instruments and wrapped with between 200 and 750 pounds of high explosives until the dummy bomb looked like a beach ball. Then, just before the detonation, someone would truck a heavy lead box out to the canyon test site. Inside was a small cone, this time containing a full-strength pellet of Ra-La. The trickiest part was inserting the Ra-La cone into the little slot in the center of the bomb mock-up. Each cone contained up to 240 curies of Ra-La, the equivalent of a half pound of pure radium. Nowhere in the world had scientists run experiments with such intense radiation sources. One of Hall's colleagues would place the Ra-La cone into the center of the dummy bomb, wielding a ten-foot rod "like a fishing pole."

When everything was ready, one of Rossi's helpers would set off the high explosives while the others, including Ted Hall, watched from a blast shelter. An instant before the mock bomb core was crushed, they would watch the telltale pulses relayed from Ted's ionization chambers. As the implosion crushed the bomb's inner core and the density of the metal increased, some of the Ra-La's gamma rays would be retarded inside. The more the gamma-ray count diminished during the test, the more effectively the central sphere of metal had been squeezed. "We were turning out ionization chambers like sausages," Hall remembered. "It made me feel funny to blow up all those ionization chambers we had built so carefully. We would just destroy them and build some more."

A set of three Ra-La test shots between February 7 and 18, 1945, gave Rossi's group the results everyone at Los Alamos was pulling for. Finally the oscilloscopes registered a nice smooth shock, thanks to Luis

Alvarez's invention of electric detonators that allowed the thick outer shell made of high explosives to detonate simultaneously. On February 20, the leaders of the Ra-La Group, Bruno Rossi and Hans Staub, met with Samuel K. Allison, one of Oppenheimer's deputies. The group leaders proposed setting up a second Ra-La test site in Bayo Canyon and they named four "capable people" who should be assigned to the crew. They had to be "good men with critical judgment on experimental set-ups" or else the quality of the work might fall off, they warned Allison. One of the four capable people they named was Ted Hall.

On February 24, Rossi's original crew set off another Ra-La shot, and once again it was an almost perfectly smooth implosion. On February 28, 1945, Oppenheimer, Groves, Conant, Kistiakowski, and three others met in Oppenheimer's office and settled on a design for the bomb that would be tried at Alamogordo. Pending confirmation from further Ra-La tests, they decided to go with Robert Christy's solid core and Alvarez's detonators. At another meeting about the same time, Rossi heard Oppenheimer say, "Now we have our bomb."

FEBRUARY 28, 1945, was just as crucial a day in Stalin's quest for the bomb. That was the day the NKGB finished its first comprehensive report on atomic intelligence in two years for Lavrenti Beria, the people's commissar for internal affairs. For the first time, Moscow Centre could report that the American War Department was close to building an atomic bomb—one that could destroy "everything within a radius of 1 km." The report would rank among the more remarkable intelligence feats of World War II. Despite all the resources of Nazi intelligence, Reichsführer Heinrich Himmler never came close to piercing General Groves's security, nor did Japanese Prime Minister Koiso Kuniaki. Yet the Soviets knew all the main elements of America's secret weapon five months before it was tried out at Alamogordo—thanks in no small measure to Theodore Hall's decision to volunteer.

"NKGB USSR presents intelligence information herein on the progress of work toward the creation of an atomic bomb of great destructive power," the NKGB's February 28 report to Beria began. It was signed by Vsevolod Merkulov, whose wartime job was akin to that of FBI director J. Edgar Hoover, except that Merkulov's department also included the NKGB's first directorate for foreign intelligence.

The most sensational particulars involved "Camp 2, or Camp Y" in Los Alamos Township, New Mexico. Moscow Centre had heard only the faintest rumors about this site before Hall and Greenglass material-ized in the fall of 1944. But now Beria's information was rich in detail and presented with an assurance that could have come only from solid inside sources: "Camp 2 is isolated from the outside world. It is located in the desert area on the top of the flat 'table' mountain. On the terri-tory of the camp, fenced off by barbed wire, and guarded by special se-curity, live about 2,000 people. Good living conditions are created for them: comfortable apartments, sport grounds, a swimming pool, a club, etc. Mail with outside world is controlled. Departure of the workers from the camp is allowed only by special permission of military author-ities. There are several test ranges around the camp. The nearest of them is Anchor Ranch, located 5 miles from Los Alamos."

The crux of Report No. 1103/M was a capsule description of how the bomb would work, and when:

> Two methods of the producing of the explosion of the atomic bomb are being developed:
> 1. ballistic, and
> 2. "explosion to the inside" method.
> There is not any definite schedule for producing the first bomb because so far the design and research works haven't been finished. It is thought that a minimum of one year and maximum five years will be required to produce the first such bomb.
> As for bombs of somewhat smaller capacity, it is reported that already within several weeks one can expect the manufacture of one or two bombs, for which the Americans already have avail-able the necessary quantity of active substance. This bomb will not be so effective, but all the same it will have practical meaning as a new kind of weapon by far superior in its effectiveness to all the currently existing kinds of weapons. The first actual battlefield explosion is expected in two or three months.

From decrypted Soviet cables it is now clear that very little if any of this information had come from Klaus Fuchs. Indeed, report 1103/M was well into the drafting stage before Moscow Centre had anything from Fuchs. One day before the intelligence report was turned in to Beria, NKGB headquarters dispatched a peremptory cable to the New York *rezidentura* demanding to know what had happened to agent Charl'z (Fuchs). All Lubyanka knew was that Charl'z had finally sur-faced in Massachusetts, but the Soviet Union's spy headquarters did not know what he had told Harry Gold. The cable from Moscow Centre on February 27 read: "Advise forthwith: exactly where and in what capacity Charl'z is working in the Zapovednik; the object of his trip to Chicago and whom he met there; what he has been doing since August; why the meeting with him has been arranged only in June . . . how in detail their meeting went off; what materials were received from Charl'z."

The wording was plain: Just one day before the report was sent to Beria, Fuchs's overseers in Moscow didn't have a clue about what he knew. All the Centre knew was that their errant spy was working in the American atomic center that the Soviets had code-named "Zapovednik," a Russian word that meant "the reservation." Judging from other decoded cable traffic, Zapovednik was probably another code word for Los Alamos. Wherever Fuchs had been, he had remained out of touch from July 1944 until mid-February 1945, when he finally checked in from his sister's house near Boston. About three days after Fuchs's phone call, Fuchs met with his courier, Harry Gold, on February 16 in Kristel Heineman's upstairs guest room. As Fuchs would later confess, he gave Gold everything he knew about Los Alamos: "the principle of A-bomb construction," the critical mass of plutonium, the "principle of the method of detonation," and also Emilio Segrè's discovery of the high rate of spontaneous fission in plutonium. Fuchs's information was two months fresher and considerably more complete than anything Moscow had from Hall and Greenglass. But it hadn't yet reached Moscow when the NKGB began drafting the February 28 report to Beria.

Because of the lengthy logistics of sending secret messages, it was too late for New York to respond in detail to Moscow's query before the final draft went to Beria. Conceivably, the *rezidentura* did rush off some short summary of Fuchs's data, but no such cable has ever surfaced. Even sending a few paragraphs overnight would have been a tribulation for the code clerk. Each intelligence cable had to be manually enciphered. Because only one or two code clerks in the *rezidentura* were entrusted with this sensitive labor, it normally took New York three days or more to answer a Moscow cable. Once New York cables arrived in Moscow, several more days were required to decipher them, then to paraphrase the cable into a *spravka,* or intelligence summary.

If anything did reach Moscow from Fuchs before the report to Beria was finished on February 28, it was so late that its only value would have been as confirmation of information already in hand. In other words, the report to Beria had to be written from reports from Private Ted Hall and Technical Sergeant David Greenglass, the two Soviet spies serving in the Army's SED unit at Los Alamos, who have insisted that they never knew each other.

From clues in declassified documents, it appears that both Greenglass and Hall contributed something to report No. 1103/M—and that Hall's information was far more important. Appraisal of overseas technical intelligence was one of the main duties of Igor Kurchatov's secret Laboratory No. 2, where several dozen Soviet physicists in Moscow were trying to keep pace with the whole Manhattan Project. The NKGB used Kurchatov's reactions to the latest raw intelligence documents as the basis for cabling feedback to the New York *rezidentura* on the technological value of materials obtained from spies inside U.S. bases and war plants. On March 5 Kurchatov was allowed to read one such raw document, a paper that contained the scientific background for several crucial points in Merkulov's earlier briefing document for Beria. It was from this document that Kurchatov heard for the first time about the Americans' implosion method of detonating an atomic bomb. Kurchatov was astonished. "The materials are of great interest," he wrote in an evaluation he turned in to NKGB headquarters on March 16. "Great interest" was a high accolade that Kurchatov had not employed in his three earlier secret commentaries on nuclear materials obtained by the NKGB's foreign spy network. To emphasize his enthusiasm, he underlined the whole sentence.

In his assessment for NKGB headquarters, Kurchatov said he was greatly intrigued by two ideas he had not thought of. "They are 1) The use of uranium hydride 235 instead of metallic uranium 235 as the explosive substance in the atomic bomb; 2) The use of 'explosion toward the inside' for activating the bomb." Kurchatov was forced to use the cumbersome phrase "explosion toward the inside" because there was no single word for implosion in the Russian language. "The 'explosion toward the inside' method makes use of the immense pressures and velocities that develop during the explosion," Kurchatov wrote. "It is mentioned in the materials that this method opens the possibility of increasing the relative velocity of the components up to 10,000 meters per second if symmetrical pressures will be achieved, and if so, this method should be given preference over the 'shooting' method."

Within two weeks of Kurchatov's report, someone at NKGB headquarters decided it was time to send one of its periodic report cards to New York relaying the appraisals of Moscow scientific experts. Kurchatov's appraisal hadn't indicated where this intelligence originated; as a scientific consultant Kurchatov had no need to know. But the NKGB officer in Lubyanka who prepared the report card to New York did have access to sources' code names.

"Mlad's report about work . . . great interest," said the resulting NKGB cable that went out on March 31 over the signature of foreign intelligence directorate chief Fitin. "Great interest" was the same phrase Kurchatov had used two weeks earlier when commenting on the raw document describing the implosion principle. The duplicated phrase was very likely not a coincidence but rather the result of bureaucratic caution within the Soviet intelligence agency. To avoid being criticized, the drafters of Moscow Centre's periodic feedback reports tended to adhere to the exact wording of the appraisals from outside scientific consultants. Thus the phrase in the cable referring to Mlad's report was almost certainly a paraphrase of Kurchatov's glowing review just two weeks earlier about the prospect of an implosion bomb.

As a white-badger, especially one working on the Ra-La project, Ted Hall was thoroughly versed in the implosion principle. He had to know such details as the relative velocity at which an implosion is supposed to crush the critical mass. After all, his job was preparing instruments to measure the efficiency of a practice implosion. But it was the kind of technical data for which a machinist like David Greenglass had no clearance.

A second clue pointing in Ted Hall's direction was that the raw document that so interested Kurchatov stressed the possibility of making a bomb of uranium hydride. Because of the odd history of the uranium hydride bomb, it is possible to triangulate a sixty-day period during which that information most likely passed into the hands of the NKGB. That window lasted from late November 1944 to late January 1945—a period that contained Hall's meeting with Sax in Albuquerque. It was only in this one brief span, Los Alamos records show, that the laboratory possessed enough U-235 in the form of uranium hydride to make a critical mass. Starting in November 1944, metallurgists had converted twelve kilograms of U-235 into 1,350 small cubes of uranium hydride. The cubes were for the critical assembly experiments carried out by Otto Frisch's G-1 group. Twice in those two months Frisch and his assistants did stack together enough hydride cubes to reach a chain-reacting critical mass. Very likely it was this same pile of uranium hydride cubes that Merkulov had in mind when he wrote to Beria on February 28: "The Americans already have the necessary amount of active substance for two or three bombs of lesser effectiveness."

By the time Sax met Hall in Albuquerque, Oppenheimer and his division leaders were indeed toying with the option of trying to make several "bombs of lesser effectiveness" out of uranium hydride. Edward Teller's hydride-gun idea had gone into and out of fashion, but it remained a live possibility until the end of December 1944. But after Sax's visit, the picture changed overnight, making the hydride bomb a dead letter. On January 1 Oppenheimer froze the design of Little Boy, a bomb that needed all of the Manhattan Project's stock of U-235 in the form of pure uranium metal. Oppenheimer's metallurgists were immediately ordered to convert all 1,350 hydride cubes into metallic uranium. By early February 1945, the uranium hydride cubes were gone and the option of making several small bombs "of lesser effectiveness" had disappeared.

Klaus Fuchs's far more detailed report on implosion reached Igor Kurchatov on April 6, a full six weeks after Fuchs's meeting with Gold in Cambridge. When he read the report, Kurchatov was lyrical in his praise of Fuchs's intelligence on the implosion method. Yet the implosion principle was no longer a new idea to Kurchatov, as his commentary to the NKGB made clear. Kurchatov referred to the implosion method as something that "we found out about only recently and are just starting to work on." It had been only five weeks since Kurchatov had been allowed to read the first report on implosion. But his memo showed that he had become a believer. "We have already realized all of its advantages," Kurchatov wrote in his evaluation of Fuchs's description of the implosion principle.

"The materials are of great value," Kurchatov wrote after he had read the Fuchs report, underlining the phrase "of great value." On April 10, three days after Kurchatov signed his evaluation, NKGB headquarters dispatched a second report card to New York, along with Kurchatov's follow-up questions. The NKGB cable said Fuchs's material was "of great value," once again repeating the exact words that Kurchatov had underlined in his evaluation. It was the second time within a two-week period that a NKGB report card lifted the precise phrase from an evaluation of its scientific consultants. This is one more grain of documentary evidence suggesting that when General Fitin wrote "Mlad's report about work . . . great interest," he was referring to what Mlad had reported about implosion and the hydride bomb.

So the crosshatched clues in the Soviet documents virtually rule out Fuchs—and strongly point to Hall—as Moscow's first source on the implosion principle. Beyond these archival indicators, there is also the persuasive account of a source who has confirmed Hall's involvement but has asked not to be identified. What Hall gave to Sax in Albuquerque, this source said, was a short summary of the early results of the Ra-La implosion experiments. Hall's handwritten paper included a description "in the form of equations" of how an implosion was supposed to work. It also contained a capsule explanation of why this new technique for rapid assembly of the critical mass was seen on the Hill as promising.

This was the germ of one of the seminal inventions of the twentieth century, and the idea was so counterintuitive that Soviet physicists might have taken a decade to come up with it on their own. Without the implosion principle, it seems likely that the Soviets would have failed in their first desperate attempts to catch up to the Americans on the bomb. Not realizing the pitfalls of plutonium, the USSR might well have rushed blindly into building a bomb based on the older, cruder concept of a gun-type design. A gun-type bomb would have worked only if the Soviets had enough time and money to separate large quantities of U-235. Yet during the summer of 1945, plutonium would have looked like a far quicker and cheaper route than uranium. Logic would have pushed Kurchatov and Beria toward building a gun-type bomb out of plutonium—the same technical mistake that nearly ensnared Oppenheimer's laboratory in 1944. Unless Soviet physicists somehow managed to duplicate Segrè's discovery of the high rate of spontaneous fission in plutonium, they would not have realized the need for the extremely rapid compression of a plutonium bomb's fissile core. As a result, the first Soviet atomic bomb would have been the fizzle of the century. "What we did was something a little adventurous," Edward Teller remembered about the early Los Alamos implosion work. "I believe it [implosion] was the best way to do things. But it was by no means obvious."

Hall was probably not only the first conveyor of the implosion principle to Moscow, but also the source of the concept of the uranium hydride bomb. If so, he was doing the Soviets no favor because the hydride bomb turned out to be a dead end. In Los Alamos, it took nearly two years to establish that the hydride option was not as technically alluring as it had first sounded to Edward Teller. Toward the end of 1944 theoretical physicist Richard Feynman finally demonstrated to Oppenheimer that the efficiency of neutron multiplication inside a hydride bomb would be "neglible or less," as Feynman put it. How the early Soviet bomb designers managed to steer past the blind alley of the low-budget hydride bomb remains unknown. If someone from Los Alamos later managed to tell the Soviets that the American hydride project had been abandoned, no trace of the warning has been uncovered.

BY LATE MARCH 1945, when the New York *rezidentura* received General Fitin's cable about Moscow's great interest in Mlad's report, Private Ted Hall was getting much less complimentary assessments— from the U.S. Army.

Hall wasn't in trouble about espionage. It was about his open warfare against military discipline at Los Alamos. "Here was a guy who was obviously brilliant and obviously a rebel," said Arnold Kramish, a junior physicist sent to Los Alamos as an SED in the spring of 1945. "He was the most ridiculous soldier you ever saw," remembered Kenneth Case, a junior physicist from Harvard who did not get drafted. "He didn't dress right. He didn't shave. He was disreputable. He acted as if he was completely annoyed by the Army."

Ted's war against Army discipline came several months after his entry into the world of espionage, but both developments reflected the same inner streak of rebelliousness. It wasn't only that Ted never learned how to salute, or that he would forget to say "sir." It was also that Private Hall didn't like living in the barracks and would sometimes move back to his old room in the civilian dormitory. Once Ted was accused of going AWOL for ten days when he was simply with his civilian friends in the dormitory. Then there was the time he accidentally ran into a car when he was learning how to drive. The car he dented belonged to the commanding officer of the Los Alamos SEDs, Major T. A. Palmer.

Ted, who hated wearing hats of any kind, took especial umbrage at his Army cap. Once he set out to destroy it with a band saw in his laboratory's shop, but the cap was too tough for the blade. Another time he was reported by the MPs for walking around on a Friday night without his regulation hat. For one of the few times since his bar mitzvah, Hall had decided to begin wearing a yarmulke, and the base legal officer decided he was within his rights not to wear his regulation cap. "He was the least religious Jew you can imagine, but he found a way to tweak them at every opportunity," remembered his physicist colleague Sam Cohen, who was also a soldier in the SED.

"It was a strange situation," said Hall of his time in the Army. "I had this protected existence. It was a little like Richard Feynman's idiosyncrasies, I guess. It was just accepted that I was doing work that the group leaders would not want interfered with, that they wanted the work done. It was basically civilian-type work. It wasn't the kind of thing where Army discipline had any relevance. And I never had any Army training.

"I found out fairly soon that I had enough protection from the people in high places in the project—well, in moderately high places—I had enough protection so that if I broke the Army rules it wouldn't make any difference. We got these automatic promotions and I'd be promoted, then I'd get into some kind of scrape and I'd be demoted again. I went up and down a few times. It was recognized that the Army had no business in what I was doing anyhow."

All spring, the Ra-La implosion test project was going full tilt. As the final design for the plutonium bomb was being perfected, Rossi's group hurried through five Ra-La implosion test shots in April 1945, another three shots at the end of May, and seven more in June. For most of these fifteen test shots, the static implosion calculations came from Hall, who worked alone with each new dummy bomb core in his cabin on the mesa. Rossi needed more than a technician to take raw measurements of radiation and density. He also needed a scientist who could quickly perform integral calculus to interpret what the changes in density showed about the smoothness of the implosion. In the run-up to Trinity, Ted Hall doubled as technician and scientist, performing admirably in both roles.

As Hall remembered, his calculations went roughly like this: "You take a sphere of known materials with such-and-such a density, and then you measure the density in the exploded case, and turn the explosion around backwards." Of course, to do his static calculations, Ted had to know the outer dimensions of the dummy bomb core. He also had to have at least a rough idea about the inner configuration of the metal mock-up. After all, it was Hall working in his solitary workspace who had to disassemble the dummy core of the mock-up, insert the Ra-La canister into the center, and then re-assemble the concentric layers. Hall would have surely known the dimensions of the inner core made of simulated plutonium. He would have surely known about the heavy tamper around the central core, and also about the layer of aluminum around the tamper. The one thing he had no reason to know the details of was the initiator; that was about the only part of an atomic bomb that wasn't pre-tested by Hall and the dozen other key staffers in Rossi's Ra-La implosion group. The Soviets could not have hoped to find a junior scientist in a more sensitive position than Ted Hall.

CHAPTER 15

An Inkling About Alamogordo

It was cold that day but it was not winter. "Very gloomy. Clouds. And it was early morning too. A nasty day," Alexander Feklisov would remember. The NKGB officer was on backup duty, standing twenty yards outside a coffee shop in Manhattan. Inside, Anatoly Yatskov was meeting Lona Cohen after her first courier mission to New Mexico in the spring of 1945. "It was somewhere uptown, you know, about Eighty-seventh street," Feklisov said. "Or maybe Seventy-ninth street."

This same Alexander Feklisov would climb the ladder of espionage to become the KGB station chief in Washington during the 1962 Cuban missile crisis. When someone in Moscow wanted to send a back-channel message to Secretary of State Dean Rusk, Feklisov carried the proposal. It said Khrushchev was willing to remove the missiles from Cuba, provided Kennedy pledged not to invade Castro's island. Feklisov conveyed this to ABC News correspondent John Scali over lunch at the Occidental Restaurant. That evening, Scali said yes, Rusk was interested, and that was one of the reasons the crisis de-escalated. The Occidental hung a plaque commemorating a nuclear war that didn't happen.

Nobody ever put up a plaque at the New York coffee shop where Alexander Feklisov waited that morning in 1945 for Yatskov to connect with Lona Cohen. Fifty years later Feklisov couldn't remember the name of the restaurant. All he knew was that it was overcoat weather . . . sometime before Hiroshima . . . sometime near the end of the war . . . somewhere uptown from the center of Manhattan.

Back then Feklisov was a junior spy-handler in the *rezidentura*'s scientific and technological unit and Yatskov was his best friend in New York. In 1939 and 1940, Yatskov had been Feklisov's messmate at the School of Special Assignment in Balashikha, the spy-training compound twelve miles northeast of the Kremlin. He and Yatskov had been posted together in 1941 to the New York *rezidentura*. When Kvasnikov came from Moscow to start the *rezidentura*'s scientific and technical unit in March of 1943, he picked out the two messmates from Balashikha to be his assistants. Yatskov became the atomic specialist; Feklisov concentrated on electronics and ran a stable of war-plant spies that, by his account, included Julius Rosenberg.

Feklisov would not have been needed outside the coffee shop that day except for one thing. "Yatskov had a slight defect," Feklisov remembered. "He could not recognize the difference between red and green. When Anatoly was driving, he wasn't sure sometimes whether or not he was being followed by the FBI. So a couple of times when he had a meeting with an important agent, he asked me to cover him to see whether he was being followed." It was hard for Yatskov to give his attention both to the street lights and to a potential tail, especially at a moment when he couldn't afford to make mistakes, when he was meeting a courier loaded with goods. That spring, the *rezidentura* was being forced into all sorts of extra tricks to avoid surveillance. In those closing weeks of the war, Hoover's men seemed to be everywhere. There were only about fifty or sixty agents on the FBI's Soviet espionage squad in New York. But Hoover knew that Soviet agents were trying to infiltrate the Manhattan Project, and he was trying to make it as hard as possible.

The FBI had a name for Hoover's quiet harrassment: "physical surveillance." Agents would sit in bureau cars and stand in doorways, trying to follow every suspected Soviet intelligence officer round the clock. Feklisov and Yatskov were small fry to the FBI compared to identified spies like Semyon Semyonov and Arthur Alexandrovich Adams. But even they were sometimes trailed when they left the Soviet Consulate. Once, Feklisov remembered, he and Yatskov went to the Manhattan Bureau of Motor Vehicles to get driver's licenses. When they finished the paperwork, they stopped in a little restaurant that was partitioned into two sections by a curtain. The two NKGB officers decided to check behind the curtain. "We saw all the drivers of the FBI watch cars playing cards," said Feklisov. "When they saw us, they all rushed out. We didn't know we were being followed, but when they rushed out, we understood."

As one of only three officers permanently working on scientific and technical espionage in New York, Feklisov had come to know many of Yatskov's secrets. But their chief, Leonid Kvasnikov, had put such a tight hold on this New Mexico case that Feklisov wasn't told exactly what Lona Cohen's mission had been. All he really knew on that nasty day was that Lona Cohen was coming back from New Mexico. He knew better than to ask the identity of Lona's contact. "Yatskov and Kvasnikov, they guarded that agent—that source—very carefully," Feklisov would remember.

Technically, it was on Kvasnikov's recommendation that Lona Cohen had been called back from cold storage a few months earlier. He cabled Moscow Centre for permission on January 11, 1945, but his message sounded as if it were a response to an earlier suggestion from an officer at Lubyanka. In any case, that was when Kvasnikov cabled saying he had checked on the availability of Lona Cohen and her husband, Morris, by putting a question to a certain agent code-named Serb, who lived in Philadelphia.

Whoever Serb was, his news on Morris was so dismal that Kvasnikov obviously thought he needed to check with Moscow before actually recalling Lona to duty. "Serb has advised that Volunteer has died at the front in Europe," read Kvasnikov's cable to Moscow Centre. "The last meeting with Lesli was had by Tven about six months ago. Do you consider it advisable to establish liaison with Lesli to render her assistance and activate her in the future as a courier. . . ." Volunteer was Morris Cohen's code name; Lesli was Lona's code name; and Tven was her former controller, Semyonov.

Happily for Lesli, Serb had gotten it wrong. Volunteer never quite made it to the front, though he had come close to it a few weeks earlier when the American front lines were contracting during the Battle of the Bulge. In spite of what Serb had heard, Morris Cohen was not among the 70,000 American troops killed, wounded, or missing in this climactic Nazi counterattack. His 241st Service Battalion was a typical Quartermaster Corps labor battalion in U.S. General Courtney Hodges's 1st Army. As a rear-echelon unit, the 241st had landed on Normandy's Utah Beach six days after D-Day and gradually leapfrogged forward, keeping well behind the front lines. The job of a labor battalion was to dig graves, put up fences, and work in supply depots; the Army's records show no indication that Cohen's sub-unit—the 3233rd Service Company—did anything different. When Kvasnikov's cable declared Morris dead, he was stationed at Perwez, Belgium, about forty-five miles from the Bastogne road junction where the 101st Airborne had held back the Nazi counteroffensive.

Lona had been far too busy to turn up at the *rezidentura* asking for spy work. Her fellow workers at Aircraft Screw Products had elected her union shop chairman. There were 800 workers in the factory and it was "quite unusual" for them to elect a woman, as Morris would fondly tell a KGB historian. "The workers had confidence in her," Morris said. "She felt it was her moral duty to protect their interests."

Not surprisingly, the bosses at Aircraft Screw considered Lona a troublemaker. "She displayed anti-management attitude and followed the Communist line," one would later tell the FBI. She was such a thorn to management that her superior blamed her "indirectly" for damage to a shipment of machine tools ordered by the Army Air Corps. Water was "carelessly" thrown on the shipment by members of the night shift, her boss claimed. An FBI report later quoted the man: "He stated that the careless attitude on the part of night employees in the plant may be caused indirectly by Lontina Betka [*sic*], who was a union shop steward and who is in [short FBI deletion] opinion, a Communist." Coming home on the subway one day from a union meeting, Lona had a fiery encounter with two women wearing fox fur and bragging about their husbands. "Oh, you know, my husband is making so much money that I hope the war will last for a long time," Lona remembered hearing one woman say. Lona was sitting right next to them. "I got up, eyes shimmering. . . . I said: 'Damn you! People are dying, our boys are dying, and you want the war to continue.' And there were three other people sitting there. 'Good for you,' they yelled. 'Good for you.' "

After the war Cohen told one acquaintance that dropping her trade union activities had been a personal sacrifice when she was called into active Soviet espionage. Whether it was quitting as shop chairman or just assuming a less confrontational demeanor, Lona always felt she had to give up something when she returned to espionage. But she also felt it was her duty as a communist, and she accepted. Sometime in the first chilly months of 1945 Lona took her initial out-of-town run for Kvasnikov. The destination, in all likelihood, was Canada. The New York deputy station chief preferred to send bulky documents, especially those lifted from the Manhattan Project, through Canada rather than rely on the Soviet diplomatic pouch. "Part of the materials was sent with couriers, more often through the Canadian border," Kvasnikov remembered. "Even my wife, Tonya, several times went to see Niagara Falls in such a way." Their granddaughter Yelena Stuken added: "My babushka would

go on excursion and a person would come to her. A package was transferred to that person, and he would go through the Canadian border
with the information."

Lona's Canada connection probably started with simple runs to Niagara Falls just like those of Tonya Kvasnikova. By the end of the war,
however, Lona had gotten in deeper. Her contacts with Soviet intelligence networks in Canada were close enough to convince her that she
was in danger of arrest following the September 1945 defection of the
Soviet GRU code clerk Igor Gouzenko, who blew most of the Soviet
apparatus in Canada when he fled into asylum from the Soviet Embassy
in Ottawa. "Remember the Canadian case?" Lona once remarked to
her husband. "And we are connected."

Only in 1995 did the Russian Foreign Intelligence Service finally
acknowledge that Lona Cohen was doing more than just running pack-
ages to Niagara Falls. "By orders of the Centre she obtained a sample of
uranium from Canada," said her official intelligence biography. Vladimir
N. Karpov, the Russian intelligence official who wrote the biography,
said the uranium sample arrived in New York in late 1944 or 1945. Once
Kvasnikov also made reference to having received uranium while he was
deputy chief of the New York *rezidentura*. "I was interested not only in
the bomb, but also in ores," Kvasnikov reminisced. "We contacted people on this issue. In my safebox in New York there was an envelope with
powdered uranium ore for a while, before it was sent to our scientists."
Kvasnikov didn't mention which courier brought the envelope or what
source provided it. But the only uranium sample known to have reached
the New York *rezidentura* is the one Russian intelligence now credits to
Lona Cohen.

Yatskov, Lona's new controller, toyed with the notion of making
Lona Cohen a backup agent for Harry Gold. But in the end, Yatskov
never introduced the two couriers, and the reason now seems obvious:
Yatskov needed a good courier like Lona to replace Sax as Hall's contact. For by early spring, Sax had reapplied to Harvard. "His mother
and sister went to Harvard and pleaded that he be given a second
chance," recounted Susan Sax, his future wife. "They said he was upset about the war and being 4-F. And they succeeded." Sax had flunked
out in 1944 after taking liberal arts courses—including Ancient and
Medieval Philosophy, Survey of French Literature, and Social Psychology. After his jaunt to Albuquerque, Sax was back at Harvard in early
1945 with a whole new course of studies—one that meant changing

fields so he could follow in Ted Hall's footsteps. He started signing up for physics and chemistry courses, along with two in astronomy and one in engineering. Sax's latest brainstorm was to become a physicist.

IT IS LIKELY Sax never heard about that nasty day when Lona came back to New York to meet Yakskov after her first run as his replacement. It was probably in April or early May 1945. What Feklisov remembered most about the day is that he and Yatskov managed to reach the street outside the coffee shop without an FBI tail. "We looked that everything was quiet. There was no danger signal, no suspicious person. When I gave him a signal that he was not being followed, then and only then did he go inside to meet Lona." Though he couldn't remember exactly when it happened, Lona's appearance as she walked out of the coffee shop did stick in Feklisov's mind. She was blond, maybe bleached blond, he remembered five decades later. "She had some kind of a hat. And an overcoat, you know."

Yatskov's meeting with Lona may not have been long enough to finish a cup of coffee. Swift hand-offs were de rigueur whenever there were documents to pass: When Gold was couriering Fuchs's documents in the spring of 1944, he remembered that his first turnover to Yatskov took "possibly a minute or so." The first rule of security was to meet for "as brief a period as was necessary" to complete your business. Once the documents were passed, a follow-up meeting would be set up a few weeks later so Yatskov could get chapter and verse on everything a courier could remember. But since Lona had brought back espionage materials from New Mexico, the conversation would have been held to a few curt words.

After that day, it took Kvasnikov at least a fortnight to send Moscow Centre his preliminary report. First he needed to check and recheck, testing whether his sources corroborated each other. Kvasnikov finally cabled his first appraisal to NKGB General Pavel Fitin on Saturday, May 26, 1945. It was cautious in the extreme, telling Lubyanka little more than Fitin knew already. The main addition to what Fuchs and Hall had disclosed over the prior six months was that the Manhattan Project was now setting up a "base in the area of Carlsbad, State of New Mexico" to test an atomic bomb. Moscow's first inkling about Alamogordo read as follows:

From: NEW YORK
To: MOSCOW
No.:   799   26th May 1945

TO: VIKTOR

Reference your No. 3367.

MLAD's material contains:

(a) A list of places where work on ENORMOUS [ENORMOZ] is being carried out:

1. HANFORD [KhEMFORD], State of WASHINGTON, production of 49.

2. State of NEW JERSEY, production of 25 by the diffusion method. Director UREY [UREJ].

3. BERKELEY, State of CALIFORNIA, production of 25 by the electromagnetic method. Director LAWRENCE [LOURENS].

4. "NOVOSTROJ", administrative centre for ENORMOUS; also production of 25 by the spectrographic method. Director COMPTON.

5. CHICAGO, ARGONNE [ARGONSKIJ] Laboratories—nuclear research. At present work there has almost ceased. Director COMPTON.

6. "The RESERVATION [ZAPOVEDNIK]", the main practical research work on ENORMOUS. Director "VEKSEL".

7. Camp [2 words or letters unrecovered] base in the area of CARLSBAD, State of NEW MEXICO, the place for the practical testing of the ENORMOUS bomb.

8. MONTREAL, CANADA—theoretical research.

(b) A brief description of the four methods of production of 25—the diffusion, thermal diffusion, electromagnetic and spectrographic methods.

The material has not been fully worked over. We shall let you know the contents of the rest later.

ANTON

Kvasnikov had an extra reason to be cautious about the way he reported Mlad's materials. There was something strange about the way Lona Cohen had obtained the information; she had not even met Ted Hall and yet had somehow come back from New Mexico with these documents. Kvasnikov had blandly cabled Moscow that materials had been received "from Mlad," omitting the fact that Lona had not managed to meet Hall. Just how Lona Cohen got her hands on Mlad's materials remains a puzzle with many pieces still hidden. Possibly Mlad left the documents for Lona in some prearranged "dead drop" outside Los Alamos. A more plausible explanation is that Major Palmer unexpectedly refused to give Ted Hall a pass to leave the Hill on the appointed day. Perhaps Hall convinced some friend to deliver an envelope to Lona. Would you mind taking this letter to my "girlfriend" in town? Ted might have asked. His friend might have agreed, never realizing the implications. It is also conceivable that Hall handed an envelope to some unidentified friend who knew perfectly well it was spy material.

What isn't speculation is that Kvasnikov remembered Lona Cohen making two trips to New Mexico and returning both times with espionage materials. The materials came from a Los Alamos physicist—a physicist other than Fuchs, Kvasnikov insisted at the end of his life. If anyone knew the whole story of Lona Cohen's contacts, Kvasnikov should have; but he wasn't the only one with a clear memory. Lona, her husband, Morris, and her controller, Yatskov, all remembered that she made two trips to New Mexico. In contrast to Kvasnikov, however, Yatskov said one trip "wasn't successful" because Lona hadn't met the source she had been sent to see. If Lona came back twice from New Mexico with materials but met her intended contact only once, how did she obtain them on both journeys? The answer to that question is the biggest of the missing pieces.

On the same day Kvasnikov cabled Moscow about Mlad's materials, Yatskov met Gold at Volk's Bar on Third Avenue to brief him for his upcoming trip to Santa Fe. It was May 26, 1945. After a drink at the bar, Yatskov led Gold to a table in the back because they had a lot of business to settle. Not only did Yatskov want Gold to keep his long-standing date with Fuchs on June 2, he also ordered Gold to rendezvous with a second person, a man who also worked on the "atomic energy project." Yatskov gave Gold a recognition signal for this second contact, who would turn out to be Sergeant David Greenglass. Gold was allegedly supposed to tell him, "I come from Julius." Gold immediately objected that it was counter to all of his espionage training to contact both Fuchs and some second spy on the same mission. But Yatskov insisted. Gold would never forget Yatskov's next outburst: "I have been guiding you idiots every step. You don't realize how important this mission to Albuquerque is."

Once toward the end of his life, Yatskov gave a revealing glimpse of why he had been in such a rush on that May 26 to pick up every shred of information from Los Alamos. "Already in May and June of 1945, my couriers, one in May and the other in June, brought me information which contained a description of the atomic bomb, its composition, its size, its form, the full construction of the nuclear bomb—the plutonium bomb." From Yatskov's words it is evident that by the end of May, he had already received one set of atomic bomb plans from Los Alamos. They were almost surely the same Los Alamos documents that Lona Cohen had handed him in the restaurant. Thus when Yatskov made his outburst at Gold in Volk's Bar a month or so after Lona's trip, it was almost certainly an indication of the need he felt to help Kvasnikov double-check the authenticity of documents Lona had already obtained.

Especially in light of Lona's failure to meet Mlad directly, Kvasnikov was under considerable pressure to ensure he didn't cable Moscow about a secret weapon that was a hoax. "His task included making sure that there was no disinformation," said his granddaughter Yelena Stuken, who would tape his reminiscences. Though she never knew exactly what information her grandfather was after and when he obtained it, Stuken did come to sense the stress he was under: "He understood that his own neck was at risk. He had to use his own mental faculties to understand the problem, and only when he was personally convinced that it was not disinformation could he send information of such importance." The cautious Kvasnikov must have known the *rezidentura* was breaking all the rules of compartmentalization by sending Gold to New Mexico to meet both Fuchs and Greenglass. By far the likeliest explanation is that either Kvasnikov or his overseers in Moscow felt it was worth any risk to confirm the Mlad materials.

Fuchs was a few minutes late for his meeting with Gold on June 2, 1945, in Santa Fe. Gold was waiting "on Alameda Street, where it lies along the river . . . where there are trees and benches adjacent to the street," Fuchs remembered. Gold got into Fuchs's gray Buick and they drove across the Castillo Street Bridge to a "deserted spot" near a gate at the end of a dead-end lane. Fuchs handed over what Gold remembered as "a considerable packet of information." Fuchs recalled that his report in longhand included "a description of the plutonium bomb"; "a sketch of the bomb and its components, with important dimensions indicated"; "as much up-to-date information about the bomb as he then knew"; "additional information concerning ignition—although this research was not yet finished"; "a description of the initiator"; "the type of core"; and "the intention to use the bomb against Japan." Fuchs recalled that it was only during a discussion in the car that he told Gold that the atomic bomb would soon be tested.

The following morning Harry Gold stopped at an apartment at 209 North High Street in Albuquerque. It had been rented by Ruth Greenglass; her husband, David, just happened to be there because it was a Sunday, his only day off from Los Alamos. Greenglass remembered turning over to Gold a list of those "whom I thought might be ideologically suited for recruitment." Greenglass also recalled giving Gold "a sketch of a high explosive lens mold which was an experiment to study implosion effects." By now Greenglass had evidently heard of the Ra-La implosion experiment, but he had only the dimmest understanding of it. Betraying his confusion, he erroneously told Harry Gold the purpose of the implosion experiment was to determine the critical mass of uranium.

After seeing Greenglass, Gold caught the overnight train to Chicago, then a plane to Washington, followed by a train to New York. Around 10 P.M. on June 4, Gold met Yatskov on Metropolitan Avenue in Brooklyn. The meeting "lasted about a minute, that was all," remembered Gold. Yatskov wanted to know if he had seen both "the doctor and the man," and Gold said yes. "Then I gave [Yatskov] the two manila envelopes." About two weeks later Gold met Yatskov in Flushing, this time to give him a two-and-a-half-hour report on everything he had learned in his two meetings in New Mexico.

Even without what Fuchs told Gold orally, the documents in Fuchs's manila envelope were enough to give Kvasnikov the second version of the bomb he was awaiting. In fact, Fuchs had produced a good many details on the bomb that Mlad hadn't included in his earlier report. Within the next few days someone in the *rezidentura*—probably Kvasnikov—began drafting cable number 18956/568. When it went out to Moscow on June 13, it not only contained a description of the atomic bomb, but also a prediction of when the Americans would set off the first explosion.

It was as important a cable as the *rezidentura* had ever sent. When it reached Moscow, someone inside Lubyanka begin drafting a summary. When that summary was ready for Beria, it would list just two sources for some of the most dramatic intelligence of the century.

CHAPTER 16

The Grauber Incident

natoly Yatskov and his superiors in the New York *rezidentura* were shaken by a scorching reprimand from Moscow. A July 5 cable had accused New York of permitting "a compromise of Mlad," the young scientist who in just eight months had proven himself so valuable. The cause of this was Aleksei's (Yatskov's) "completely unsatisfactory work" with the agents on ENORMOZ, Moscow charged. But while Lubyanka was spitting fire over the possibility that Mlad had been compromised, the fruits of atomic espionage the New York agents had sent home over the last month were in the final stages of being digested in Moscow. The results would save Yatskov and his network from disgrace.

On June 13 the New York *rezidentura* had cabled the first of two crucial messages, giving the latest data that two scientists had reported independently from Los Alamos. Between them the spies had produced the most detailed description of the plutonium implosion bomb that Soviet physicists had ever seen. And not only that. New York also was able to relate that the weapon, which could blast with a force equivalent to 5,000 tons of TNT, was nearly ready for a test detonation.

In Moscow a compilation of this remarkable material was presented to Igor Kurchatov, the physicist directing the Soviets' atomic research. The report outlined construction down to the thickness in centimeters of the aluminum envelope. He received the summary on July 2, 1945, according to the date hand-written on the briefing paper. This is the information he received:

TOP SECRET
    Bomb of the type "HE" (High Explosive)
    The first atomic bomb explosion is expected in July of this year.

Construction of the bomb. The active material of this bomb consists of element 94 without uranium 235. In the center of a sphere of plutonium weighing 5 kilograms is housed a so-called initiator—a source of alpha particles made of beryllium-polonium. The plutonium is surrounded by 50 pounds of tube-alloy,★ which acts as a "tamper." All this is lodged in a shell of aluminum of the thickness of 11 centimeters. This aluminum sheath is surrounded, in its turn, by a coating of explosive material called "Pentolite" or "Composition C" (according to other information "Composition B") with a casing 46 centimeters thick. The casing of the bomb in which this active material is lodged has an interior diameter of 140 centimeters. The overall weight of the bomb, including the Pentolite, the body and so forth, is about 3 tons.

It is expected that the force of the explosion will be equivalent to the power of an explosion of 5,000 tons of TNT. (The coefficient of usable force is 5–6 percent.) The amount of fission is equal to 75×10^{24}.

Stock of active material.

a) Uranium 235. In April of this year there were 25 kilograms of uranium 235. Present production is at the rate of 7.5 kilograms per month.

b) Plutonium (element 94). In camp-2 there are 6.5 kilograms of plutonium. Its production set up, the plan of output is being exceeded.

★Tube-alloy—the code name of uranium.

The explosion is expected on roughly 10 July of this year.

Two days later another cable arrived from New York with still more information on the bomb, quite likely the result of the debriefing session Yatskov held with Harry Gold in late June to hear extra tidbits Gold had picked up from Fuchs in Santa Fe. The disclosures in the June 13 and July 4 cables were hot enough that Vsevolod Merkulov, the head of wartime intelligence, presented them to his demanding boss, Lavrenti Beria, in a July 10 update on atomic espionage. Stalin's security chief was not a man to whom one addressed frivolous or faulty material. Merkulov felt confident enough to write: "From several trusted agent sources NKGB USSR is received intelligence that in the USA, in July of this year, is scheduled the carrying out of the first experimental explosion of the atomic bomb." He went on to outline basic technical characteristics of the weapon that would be tested.

The letter was typed, but in the upper left-hand corner was written by hand: "Sources 'Mlad,' 'Charl'z.' " Just below the code names, also written by hand, were the numbers and the dates of the June 13 and July 4 messages from New York. Soviet intelligence has acknowledged that Charl'z was Klaus Fuchs. There is every reason to believe that the Soviet intelligence officer who listed Mlad as a source was referring to the same Mlad whom Sergei Kurnakov recruited in New York: Theodore Alvin Hall. It is the clearest documentation that has ever come from Soviet archives connecting Ted Hall's code name with the receipt of crucial information on the design of the bomb itself.

The letter to Beria said the test explosion was expected "around July 10." The date would be slightly off, since last-minute glitches delayed the desert test. But that was the most profound inaccuracy.

The handwritten note on Merkulov's letter was not the only evidence that the bomb design data was based on at least two sources. The Russian NKGB officer who compiled the earlier document for Kurchatov's briefing also indicated that more than one source had supplied the information. He cited a difference of opinion in respect to the "coating of explosive material." To be safe the NKGB officer included both versions. One source had designated it as either "Composition C" or "Pentolite," while he noted in parentheses that another source thought the explosive material would be "Composition B." According to Fuchs's confession of espionage four and a half years later, it was he who had described the explosives components as "Composition B." Fuchs was right. One can only speculate on the reasons why Mlad was listed first as a source, and why Fuchs's information on "Composition B" was added only parenthetically. It is quite conceivable that Kvasnikov and Yatskov began drafting their June 13 cable on the basis of Mlad's material, since it arrived at the *rezidentura* first. When Harry Gold got back from New Mexico after seeing Klaus Fuchs, they probably wove Fuchs's detailed material into the early draft of their cable.

In all likelihood, the information from Mlad was the report that New York had promised in late May. The May 26 cable had included the list of places where research was ongoing, and said additional information from Mlad "has not been fully worked over" but would be messaged later. The information from Fuchs, as his confession later made clear, had come from his meeting with Gold in Santa Fe. A strange twist is that the Merkulov letter did not even mention David Greenglass as a source of anything. Ironically, the sketches he handed to Harry Gold in Albuquerque would help place Julius and Ethel Rosenberg in the electric chair. But the New York *rezidentura* apparently didn't think his material was urgent enough to highlight in the June 12 and July 4 cables to Moscow.

The *rezidentura*'s intelligence breakthrough may have saved Yatskov's neck after he was denounced for "completely unsatisfactory work." But there was no escaping the fact that Soviet intelligence would suffer if Mlad really was exposed to suspicion. The July 5 cable connected the compromise to an "incident involving Grauber." American decoders later concluded that "Grauber" was a misspelling for an actual person, and FBI teams were subsequently sent to question Roy Glauber, Ted Hall's friend at Harvard and Los Alamos. Glauber was quizzed twice by the FBI, in 1951 and again in the mid-1960s.

When interviewed years later in his office at the Harvard University physics department, Glauber said he never suspected Hall of delivering information to the Soviets and that he hadn't a clue as to what the "Grauber incident" might entail. "It is very bizarre. Because I cannot associate anything at all with that period of time. That doesn't ring true," Glauber said. He recalled neither any fumbled attempt to attract him into espionage, nor any unusual contacts involving Hall. Once they got to Los Alamos, Glauber said, he didn't see much of Hall. That was especially true after Hall was drafted and lived in the military barracks. He acknowledged the FBI questioned him about his relations with Hall and Sax in 1951 and again later, in the mid-1960s. Neither time was Glauber accused of anything, and he went on to teach for four decades at Harvard, winding up as the Mallinckrodt Professor of Physics.

The unusually long July 5 message from Moscow, only bits of which have been deciphered, accused the New York *rezidentura* of being haphazard in observing the Centre's instructions regarding the handling of Enormoz sources. The New York agents must "immediately inform us by telegraph about each meeting," must send "the most precise reports" as follow-ups, and must find "safe houses" around Manhattan Project installations. It further gave some specific directions for handling Mlad, an indication that, despite their fears, the decision-makers of Soviet intelligence were going to take a chance that Mlad had not been exposed to American counterespionage forces. They would continue contact with him.

The sudden infusion of knowledge represented in the Mlad/Charl'z document gave Kurchatov support for his proposal to devote more Soviet resources to bomb development. His program still was progressing sluggishly. In May he and Mikhail Pervukhin, the deputy premier responsible for the project, had written Stalin and the Politburo a memorandum urging special measures to speed up their research and the creation of a nuclear industrial network. They apparently received no response, despite the fact that the end of the war in Europe had eased the drain on resources. The Soviet political leadership and even some scientists still doubted the atomic bomb would succeed.

If not quite skeptical, their American counterparts in many cases were similarly cautious. One example was the Interim Committee of Cabinet officials and scientific consultants set up to advise the White House on decisions related to the bomb—now advising President Harry Truman after Roosevelt's death on April 12. It turned down proposals merely to threaten the Japanese with this new American mega-weapon, fearing that a demonstration explosion might fail. If it did, it could embolden the Japanese and intensify the war. Nor did the committee even wish to invite Soviet scientists to observe the test, another proposal tabled at its May 31 meeting. James Byrnes, Truman's secretary of state–designate, nixed the idea with his protest that even informing the Soviets at this stage would prompt Stalin to seek full partnership in the project. There also was the potential embarrassment of a failure.

By then, Washington's calculations about postwar relations with Moscow had become entwined with the last stages of building the atomic bomb. That was one reason for the pressure to hold to the schedule of Trinity, the test explosion of the Fat Man implosion bomb. The original July 4 test date had to be pushed back because things simply weren't ready. Even the target of July 16 began to look too optimistic. There were repeated problems molding lenses out of Composition B. Then, just days before, a magnetic test experiment at Los Alamos led the physicists to believe their theories were wrong, that the implosion bomb they designed would not explode. Even the weather forecast was bad. But General Groves was adamant that the scientists and military technicians must continue trying. President Truman was scheduled to meet Churchill and Stalin in Potsdam on July 15. The White House wanted to have some news for Mr. Stalin. It well might affect any definition of territorial influence that would be discussed there. They held to the July 16 target. Scientists who had been uneasy over the true intent of the Manhattan Project had increasing justification for concern, but most of them were too preoccupied with making Fat Man work to worry about it.

If any shadow had fallen over Ted Hall as a result of the "Grauber incident," it was quickly dispersed. The nineteen-year-old SED was among those assigned to work in the desert scrub near Alamogordo, 210 miles south of Los Alamos, where the first implosion bomb would be tested. Surely no one suspected of passing information to the Soviet Union would have been permitted to witness this critical event. Hall wasn't mingling with the project's leading figures, men like Oppenheimer and Teller and Segrè, who were posted at various sites five, ten, or twenty miles from the heart of the explosion; he was assigned to a covered truck as part of a group of 160 young soldiers sent as a rescue team should anything go wrong. Their job would be to evacuate local farms and Indian villages if winds shifted and fallout began encroaching.

Like everyone else, they arrived early and sat out the thunderstorm that lashed base camp with thirty-mile-per-hour winds, delaying the detonation an hour and a half, till near dawn at 5:30 A.M. "The guys discussed all sorts of things, like marriage, divorce, the high divorce rate among Hollywood stars," Hall recalled.

Rockets flashed up signaling five minutes, then two minutes, then one minute and the soldiers turned their backs, closed their eyes, and covered them with their arms as they had been told. Even so, the explosion blasted light through their cocooned eyelids. "I do remember the cloud and the glowing, and the thing coming up and making this tremendous light," Hall said decades later. He also remembered not being surprised at the success. "I had rather expected that it would work. I certainly didn't get any feeling of a heroic achievement or Promethean accomplishments," he said in retrospect. Most of the scientists who saw the test of the implosion bomb at the time expressed greater awe at the power they had released on the world. But even then, and more so later, many had feelings mixing the pride of their scientific accomplishment with guilt and fear over how this power would be used.

What weighed on Hall's mind long after that event at Los Alamos was not the visual experience of seeing the desert darkness replaced by the ominous flash and ascending swirls of flame. It was the reaction of some of his fellow scientists. As Hall remembered, there was a seminar not long after the detonation where the luminaries of the atom project spoke. He remembered Oppenheimer, "who spoke in a very trembly and shaking way, and made quotations from the Hindu scriptures, the Bhagavad-Gita, impressing everybody." But he said the greatest impact on him was carried in the comment of another scientist, he thought

Arthur Compton, "who concluded his talk with the stirring cry of 'It may not make us happy, but it will make us great.' I thought, 'Ugh.' "

Years later, Hall further explained his feelings about Trinity: "Things happen. It's a piece of mechanics or physics or whatever you want to say. This thing had been worked out. It looked as if it probably would work and the explosion would give the expected yield, and it did. Okay. But what people said the next week was part of human history and human development and that's a different category. And I guess underneath maybe I'm more interested in societies than nuclear weapons."

The volatile mixture of technology and humanity that would preoccupy the world quickly began to effervesce after Trinity. Truman already was at the Potsdam Conference when he got word that the implosion bomb had been born kicking. It was exactly what the U.S. side had wanted to hear. It meant there need be no pleading or deals to convince the Soviet Union to enter the Pacific war. In fact, it would be much better if America could use this new weapon to end the war with Japan before the Soviets could join. Then they would have no stake in the victory. Truman waited until July 24 to mention to Stalin that America "had a new weapon of unusual destructive force." Stalin's muted response—just a "thank-you" and a nod—perplexed the Westerners, who wondered if he had understood Truman's message.

What the other Allies did not know is that Stalin was ready for this news. It would have been an extraordinary lapse on the part of Beria not to have prepared Stalin for just such an eventuality at Potsdam, having been alerted two weeks earlier by the memorandum from Merkulov about the upcoming implosion test. Vadim Kirpichenko, the retired first deputy chief of the KGB who in the 1990s was in charge of compiling an eight-volume official history of the Soviet intelligence service, was convinced Stalin knew. "It was the beginning of the Cold War. They wanted to put Stalin in his place," Kirpichenko said. "But Stalin was informed completely and he made no reaction. And the advisers of Churchill and Truman thought, 'Oh, Joe Stalin didn't understand.' "

It is another question whether Stalin and his circle fully understood the import of this weapon, not just for ending the war, but for the future balance of East and West. Returning to his quarters after that chat with Truman, the Soviet leader did tell Molotov: "We shall have to have a discussion with Kurchatov about speeding up our work." It took the actual use of the bomb, however, to produce much speed in Moscow.

Hiroshima was the Americans' first target, on August 6, 1945. The gun-type uranium 235 bomb with the power of 13,000 tons of TNT caused the deaths of at least 140,000 people. The Soviet Union declared war on Japan three days later, and Stalin's troops immediately advanced so that the war would not end before he established a right to the eastern lands he so desperately wanted. On the same day, the plutonium implosion bomb exploded over Nagasaki with the force of 21,000 tons of TNT. Deaths there exceeded 70,000. Five days after Nagasaki, on August 15, the Japanese surrendered.

Simply getting intelligence from Mlad and Charl'z on the Americans' progress in creating an atomic weapon had produced a stir in Moscow but not enough urgency to mobilize much force behind a Soviet nuclear project. The August lessons on the ground in Japan were absolutely clear. And they were absolutely compelling.

Bomb in a Kleenex Box

It certainly wouldn't do as a "safe house" for holding clandestine meetings, as the Centre had advised would be prudent. But Lona Cohen had at least managed to find herself a cheap, comfortable room—one flight up on the second floor—to stage her act as an easterner afflicted with tuberculosis. To all appearances she had come to Las Vegas, New Mexico, for a cure of dry air and mineral hot springs. At least that was the prescription written out by some New York doctor, just in case anybody got too curious about a young woman who suddenly showed up in a small western town without job or friend or family. Her real task in New Mexico that August was atomic espionage.

What an incredible piece of timing it would turn out to be. While Lona Cohen idled away her days at a spa-town boarding house, nervously waiting to connect with Ted Hall, the Soviet leadership was making the building of an atomic bomb the nation's number one priority. It was a decision of Stalin himself.

Finding an obscure place to stay had been a challenge to Cohen's skills. The *rezidentura* was still edgy over the notorious "Grauber incident," so she had to be even more careful about attracting attention than she had been on her first trip out West. A regular hotel in Santa Fe or Albuquerque might have been under the eyes of undercover agents keeping up with strangers anywhere near the top secret bomb lab. Now, of course, the place wasn't top secret any more. She had arrived after Hiroshima, after the mysteries of Los Alamos had begun to unravel. Locals in Santa Fe who had been so suspicious of what was happening up on the Hill suddenly had themselves a new crop of heroes. Prominent Santa Fe families soon would be trying to snag a scientist or two to spice up parties. The scientists had helped end the war, and they and their families quickly noticed friendlier treatment in Santa Fe shops and bars.

Of course, that meant strangers attracted more attention. Out of either intuition or happenstance, Cohen found lodging distant from both Santa Fe and Albuquerque.

Gregarious Lona, a working-class woman who well knew how to banter with other workers, found out from someone in the train crew about Las Vegas. She'd had plenty of time for talking on the long trip, first New York to Chicago and then through to New Mexico on a train that took at minimum one overnight. She may have talked a little too much to one guy, a fellow passenger who found the thirty-two-year-old with a throaty voice attractive enough to make a pass. Lona gave him the brush-off, she later told her husband, making it clear she'd rather look at the majestic scenery. In more congenial conversations with train attendants, she found out that Las Vegas was a popular town with railway workers, a place where the shift would change and tired crew would get a day's rest. The boarding house they recommended there was just right: an inconspicuous room, breakfast included, in a pretty town whose hot springs made it a destination for people suffering kidney trouble, rheumatism, intestinal ailments. And tuberculosis.

It wasn't that Cohen expected to be there long. The arrangement was to meet her "young scientist" in Albuquerque on the following Sunday. If everything went as planned, she would be back on the train again soon, this time headed north and east. She took the bus to Albuquerque that Sunday morning, found the designated spot on the University of New Mexico campus, and waited. And waited. This wasn't a trained agent she was meeting, who would know that tradecraft dictated you make a meet on time or don't bother. Five minutes was the prescribed wait for the Soviet service, but how would the scientist know that? Cohen may have relaxed the rules, wandered around the university and the town, easing back past the site now and again in case he showed up. He didn't. Cohen had a three-hour bus ride 120 miles back to Las Vegas to think about how to occupy herself until the following Sunday. That was the fallback.

She could have been stuck in a worse place. There were tree-covered hillsides to hike, the Old Town plaza of adobe shops and Indian trinkets, the Montezuma hot springs on the edge of town where anybody could jump in for a soak. The next Sunday she rode back to Albuquerque. And then the next. Three Sundays in a row she went to Albuquerque and came back empty-handed. She was disappointed and also angry that her contact failed to show for the prearranged meeting. Trees and mineral baths had their limits.

"However, she thought she would go one more time, the fourth time. And then if he didn't show up, she would go home," her husband, Morris Cohen, told a Russian intelligence historian years later. "So she went the fourth time, by bus, regular public transport bus, from the town where she was staying to the university town where she was to meet him. And from his dress, the materials he carried, she understood that [he] was the one she wanted. They met. He spoke as if a mistake had been made by someone else, not by him. Well, they patched it up, and he gave her the material."

Hall would never publicly acknowledge that he met Cohen in Albuquerque. One of the few times he ever opened up with friends, he did remember a series of mishaps that almost scotched the whole thing. One touchy moment happened in his Los Alamos laboratory when he was assembling a paper for the Albuquerque rendezvous. It was on a Sunday and Hall expected to have the lab to himself, but suddenly Philip Koontz, the lab partner and supervisor who was supposed to be on an outing with his family, walked in on him. Hall had to cram into his desk the papers he couldn't possibly begin to explain. It was Hall's good fortune that Koontz seemed embarrassed about the encounter, too—there was his associate laboring on a Sunday while he was heading off for a day of fun—so Koontz quickly left. Then, Ted was three weeks late for the meeting with Lona. He didn't remember being that tardy, but he did know the linkup happened after Trinity, too late to give the Soviets the heads up he had hoped to supply about the American test. Once he arrived at that lonely encounter with Lona Cohen on the University of New Mexico campus, he was "horrified" that he couldn't precisely recall the recognition signal. It was something about a magazine poking out of a bag.

Nor did Lona have a great reputation for remembering signs and codes, but she had probably seen Hall's photograph from that first time he'd met Kurnakov in New York. The campus was almost empty on an August Sunday. There was this young guy who didn't seem to be doing anything, and this woman turned up at the same place and didn't seem to be doing much more. They sized each other up and made the connection.

Hall thought he and Lona must have talked for about half an hour while they wandered around the campus. Lona came across as not exactly sexy, but certainly attuned to the physical side of men and women. Earthy, perhaps. When a good-looking woman walked past, Cohen made her inexperienced young companion uncomfortable if not a little pink. Wouldn't he like to spend some time with that one? Cohen wondered out loud.

When they did get down to business, their conversation had little if anything to do with the technical details of making an atomic bomb. It was less than two months after Moscow's alert about the "compromise" of Mlad, and Lona Cohen was quick to assure Hall that the Soviets didn't forget their friends. The network had ways of taking their agents out of harm's way. They were up to some dangerous business, said Lona, whom Hall knew under her courier's name of Helen. She warned that "things might turn out to be pretty hot." Hall understood that. But he did not understand Cohen's blithe acceptance of the prospect of being rescued to a new life in the Soviet Union. She thought that would be great. Hall recalled thinking the prospect grim, and he told her as much. He suggested that things in Moscow "weren't as happy and wonderful as she thought" and that he "didn't really share her opinion of happiness." But they hadn't come to Albuquerque to debate the merits of life in the Soviet Union. They made their meet, talked as much as they needed, and Hall passed Cohen the papers he had prepared about the work at Los Alamos.

Lona hustled back to her boarding house, where she had already packed, having decided earlier that she would leave that day, regardless of her success in Albuquerque. But she had succeeded, and she had every reason to congratulate herself on her patience as she stuffed the papers from Hall under some tissues in a Kleenex box and headed for the train station.

She soon realized she was heading into trouble. Plainclothes agents were questioning and searching everyone getting on the train, two agents at every car. After President Truman had told the world about Hiroshima, *The Santa Fe New Mexican* had been released from censorship and had reported on the front page how the Los Alamos Ranch School had been transformed into a secret bomb laboratory under J. Robert Oppenheimer. Worry about the safety of Oppenheimer and other scientists was reason enough for the FBI and the Army CIC to tighten security.

Lona Cohen didn't care why the security net had been spread. She was worried only about how to breach it. Ever the disciplined spy courier, she stood in the station till almost time for departure, mentally building her new image as a bit of a ditsy doll, a woman innocent and silly and not a threat to a soul. The most detailed description of what happened next came from her controller, Yatskov, the man who met her when she returned to New York and who was the first to hear her tell the story. His melodramatic recounting in an internal KGB newspaper would become a classic in the genre of nostalgic espionage war stories:

> Judge for yourself. As luck would have it, [Lona Cohen's] ill-fated train ticket disappeared somewhere. For others, the ticket stays in its proper place. Others also arrive at the station well ahead of time. But she, as is certainly understood, does not belong to the category of "other" people. Does she really look like these thrifty, boring, harassed people? Nerves get rattled by petty things. Dismiss from your mind these trifles that turn you stale! On the order of non-petty things are a pimple suddenly popping out on the face. Or a button lost from the dress. . . . Her purse she deliberately hung on her arm, put a little suitcase on the ground, and only a box re-mained in her hands and deliberately hindered her search for the ticket. The woman was obviously marking time, which was press-ing in on her. A lot of stuff—a suitcase, a big bag, and a big box with Kleenex paper tissues. She could not open the zipper on the bag. It got stuck. They tried to help her, like servants. Nervously she tore at the zipper, and it jammed. And the time was running.
>
> Without hesitation, self-confident Helen handed the box with the tissues to one of the checkers, found the ill-fated ticket, at the same time answered the questions they posed, and was directed into the car with the ticket, the handbag, and little suitcase, as if she'd forgotten about her box. That's how she explained it later: "I felt in my bones that the gentleman himself must remind me about this box."

That is exactly what the gentleman did, recounted Yatskov. The guard on the platform hailed Lona and handed up to her the Kleenex box in which she had hidden the documents. Yatskov said the material she brought him could have put Lona Cohen into the electric chair, and yet she joked in New York that it "had been in the hands of the police."

There are sharply conflicting recollections about the papers Lona Cohen smuggled from New Mexico. There were only five or six hand-written sheets—that was what stuck in Hall's memory about his meet-ing with Lona. On one page he drew a rough sketch showing the concentric spheres of a mock bomb—just like the gadgets he had sus-pended from the ceiling of his little cabin dozens of times to take static measurements for the Ra-La experiments. Though the Ra-La tests used scale or full-size models of the actual plutonium bomb, Hall still had the feeling that he wasn't really giving the Soviets very much. He remembered a sense of anxiety that the material would seem "redundant" because it mostly updated what he had given already. By contrast, when Lona met Yatskov a day or two later in New York, he remembered receiving more: "a thick pile of documents covered with packed-together writing." How to explain the discrepancy? It is of course conceivable that Lona was ordered to make a second pickup from another source in New Mexico, a source nobody has ever mentioned. But in light of Moscow's alarm just weeks earlier that Mlad had been compromised through sloppy tradecraft, it seems extremely unlikely that the New York *rezidentura* would have taken that kind of risk. Memories can both fade and inflate over so many years. If Hall didn't quite recall the details of what he gave, Yatskov also may have exaggerated the volume of what he received. His "thick pile" of papers would have overweighted a lady's box of tissues and might have raised police suspicions.

Hall heard nothing about Cohen and the Kleenex box until the story was gleefully retold by Sax in 1946 or 1947 after Hall left Los Alamos. Fifty years later, Russian spies still marveled over Cohen's moxie. Five other KGB veterans would retell Yatskov's Kleenex box tale with slightly varying details, and the story would be made part of the official history of the Russian Foreign Intelligence Service.

Lona Cohen might have felt even more strain had she known how important the material she was carrying back to her Soviet controller had become. While she was brooding in sleepy Las Vegas that August, events pertinent to her mission were clipping along back in Moscow. After the Hiroshima bombing, Stalin understood he must make his own atomic weapon, and he must do it fast. At the head of his new initiative he appointed Beria, by some accounts as quickly as the day after Hiroshima exploded. Beria became chairman of the new Special Committee on the Atomic Bomb, which was created August 20, 1945, by the State Defense Committee to oversee the building of the bomb and of the national nuclear industry. They would need uranium mines, processing plants, reactors—the kind of infrastructure on which Ambassador Averell Harriman told Stalin the Americans had spent $2 billion. And of course they must have a design for the bomb itself. Stalin is reported to have called in Kurchatov, practically rebuking him for not getting atomic research a higher priority in the Soviet Union. "If the baby doesn't cry, the mother doesn't know what he needs. Ask for anything you need. There will be no refusals," Stalin told the scientist. The Soviet leader cogently summed up the reason for this new attitude: "Hiroshima has shaken the whole world. The balance has been destroyed."

While the defense and scientific establishments in Moscow were still pondering the swift series of atomic development—Trinity, Hiroshima, and Nagasaki—the Americans put out a publication on August 11 that by Soviet standards must have seemed extraordinary. In fact, it was extraordinary even by American standards. "Atomic Energy for Military Purposes," commonly known as the Smyth report after its author Henry DeWolf Smyth, outlined the development of the West's atomic project. After the years of zealous secrecy, this commentary told who had done what and where it had happened. In his foreword, General Groves said it was time to share with the public the history of the project and the scientific principles utilized. Groves sternly warned readers of the report not to bother asking anybody or any organization for more details about the atomic bomb, just as he warned the project employees to remain discreet. "Persons disclosing or securing additional information by any means whatsoever without authorization are subject to severe penalties under the Espionage Act," Groves wrote.

Was it possible now for Soviet atomic espionage to shut down? While the report offered a wealth of heretofore classified information, it was not nearly so detailed as to give anyone a blueprint for the bomb. Absent were most of the findings from Los Alamos—the details of implosion, spontaneous fission of plutonium, explosive lenses, initiators. Smyth revealed in a 1976 essay that the scientists of Los Alamos had been so unhappy with his version of their work that in July they proposed an alternative draft chapter. "It was far more interesting than my version, but unfortunately it violated the security rules that had been set up," he wrote. A secondary reason for publication, Smyth recalled, was to give the thousands of personnel involved in the Manhattan Project a means of explaining their wartime work, without explaining too much. They could hardly be expected to keep mum about everything. This report provided them a ceiling, a talking limit.

The Smyth report was one of the documents translated into Russian by the new Department S, the special unit Beria set up in the accelerated bomb program to translate, evaluate, and distribute the information Soviet intelligence agents were collecting. Another was the more revealing document Lona Cohen had brought from Los Alamos. Department S was named for its director, NKGB General Pavel Sudoplatov, who had guided clandestine work from the assassination of Leon Trotsky to guerrilla warfare behind German lines. "Of course there was a panic here. So everything began to spin very fast," remembered Arkady Rylov, one of two physicists assigned to work with Department S in late September 1945. "The Central Committee sent me to Sudoplatov. He made the paperwork go incredibly quickly." With six translators, two editors, two scientists, and a crew of helpers to copy, collate, and courier material, Rylov said Department S worked long hours inside Lubyanka spy headquarters every day until the Sudoplatov unit was disbanded ten months later. It worked always with copies, rarely with handwritten documents, and never with anything showing the names of the sources of information, he said. Diagrams, drawings, mathematical formulas, and texts—all these documents were securely held in iron safes and carefully signed out by whomever was working on them before submission to Kurchatov. "The intelligence service greatly diminished the time for progressing on this problem [the bomb]," said Rylov. "If we hadn't had any piece of information on this problem, it would have probably taken fourteen years instead of four years. Maybe twenty. Who knows."

While the Smyth report would be Beria's basic proliferation primer, once again it was Harry Gold and Lona Cohen who had produced the most crucial data on the design of the bomb. The versions they had delivered were what the Soviets ended up believing, despite a confusing hodgepodge of information and misinformation that filtered into the *rezidentura* almost simultaneously from a third agent, David Greenglass.

Lona Cohen was the first to report after Trinity, delivering her stuffed Kleenex box in August or early September. Whether she met only Ted Hall or may also have made contact with another sympathetic scientist during her month's stay in New Mexico is a question for the future. By early 1997, Hall said he had come to believe that Los Alamos probably did harbor yet another Soviet informant, a conviction based solely on the description of the extremely precise data the Russians said that they received. "I never had access to detailed data on the assembly of the bomb," Hall insisted, declaring with much emphasis that he did not "recognize himself" as having been in a position to supply the kind of precise bomb dimensions furnished to the Soviets. For their part, neither Yatskov or any other KGB veteran has ever hinted that Lona might have made clandestine pickups from two different agents that August. When Lona herself told the story to Svetlana Chervonnaya, a historian at the Russian Institute of the USA and Canada, she described having met only one informant on that visit to Albuquerque: a very young man, quite tall, and wearing "a large shirt with an open neck." Until Soviet archives are opened the possibility of another source cannot be excluded, especially since there remain at least two Soviet atomic agents—Kvant and Pers—whose activities have not been traced by U.S. investigators past 1944.

Based on everything now known, the likeliest scenario is that Hall came through first, filling the Kleenex box in August with at the very least a five-page conception of how a bomb works. David Greenglass, who had gotten an unexpected furlough because the war had ended, arrived back in New York in early September with his offering of bomb data. In his handwritten account passed through his brother-in-law Julius Rosenberg, he described the explosive lens molds he had worked on and offered a misinformed description of how both the tamper and the gold-plated beryllium initiator functioned. Also in September Harry Gold kept his appointment with Klaus Fuchs in Santa Fe, receiving from Charl'z another batch of papers describing how to duplicate the bomb that exploded at Alamogordo. Fuchs's precisely detailed report included an exact sketch of the initiator—the one crucial component on which Ted Hall had never worked.

During Gold's conversation with Fuchs in the German's dilapidated car, Fuchs for the first time expressed uneasiness about the bomb and the destruction it had brought to Japan. It was as though the scientist had never thought about the end result of what he had helped to create over nearly four years. Hall, to the contrary, had expected the bomb probably would be used and would cause terrible harm. But he believed that by sharing the technology with the Soviets, he was acting to prevent it from being used again. Both Fuchs and Hall thought the science fascinating as well as inevitable. The creation of an atomic weapon was going to happen, with their help or without, now or soon. They and Greenglass all believed that it must not be kept under the control of a single nation when it happened, but was something that belonged to the world. This was a rare phenomenon, unique in American history: Three individuals unknown to each other decided for reasons of political philosophy to commit espionage at the same time, in the same place, giving approximately the same kind of information to the same foreign government.

Leonid Kvasnikov, the Russian in charge of the New York network in 1945, was the person most concerned that disinformation might be handed to his agents. It was his head on the line if erroneous data telegraphed to Moscow wasted the money of the war-torn state or the time of its scientists. He wanted fast results, but good sourcing and sound material were more important. Long afterward, Kvasnikov finally acknowledged that his task was simplified by the fact that Fuchs was not the only scientist in Los Alamos working with the Soviets. "For example, information about the entire construction of the atomic bomb we received from another physicist, also from Los Alamos. His contact was Leontina Cohen," Kvasnikov said in a private oral memoir. Kvasnikov himself studied the intelligence his agents and couriers brought back, deciding if the reports seemed technically feasible before passing them along. He said he became so familiar with the construction that years later he still remembered it by heart. "I called the bomb *matryoshka,* because it had many layers," Kvasnikov said, referring to Russia's traditional wooden toy—a series of nested dolls. His final verdict: "Was it possible or not to build a bomb by the data we received then? When I was in New York and considered these materials, I made a conclusion that I myself, although I was not a very good craftsman, I could have built a bomb with this data, if I had certain materials, of course."

Lona Cohen's information "was so detailed that it allowed Kurchatov to build the plant immediately, bypassing the stage of experimental production," Yatskov, her controller, said in a 1992 Russian interview. At other times Yatskov called the documents she procured "priceless" and "urgently needed in Moscow." Yatskov's longtime friend KGB Colonel Vladimir Barkovsky, a clandestine agent who reviewed all of the Enormoz files in the 1960s as deputy chief of scientific intelligence, said the material obtained from Fuchs and Lona Cohen "matched page to page." As Barkovsky put it, "When you have two sources who aren't connected with each other and they bring information that intersects, then you can be certain they are reliable." For his part, Sudoplatov claimed in his memoirs that Lona Cohen obtained from Mlad a "thirty-three page design of the bomb" that was very similar to the design that came from Fuchs. Possibly trying to shield the real informant, Sudoplatov claimed Mlad was the Italian physicist Bruno Pontecorvo, who wasn't even at Los Alamos. In 1945 Pontecorvo was working at the isolated Anglo-Canadian nuclear research lab at Chalk River, Canada; he would defect to the Soviet Union five years later.

Sudoplatov said the September 1945 clandestine reports from Charl'z and Mlad were major components of a summary his Department S unit wrote for Beria and Stalin, though he did not delineate what each source contributed. "This document became the basis for our own program of work on the atomic project over the next three or four years," he wrote.

That bedrock for the Soviet bomb program was received by Beria in an October dispatch, a blow-by-blow account of how the plutonium implosion bomb was put together. One of the most important sections—probably from Fuchs—described how the "Urchin" initiator allowed a perfect stream of neutrons to reach and activate the plutonium. The summary was complete down to details showing the initiator grooves layered with 0.1 mm of gold and thirty curies of polonium. The summary also explained the importance of the tamper—the shell that surrounded the critical mass, reflecting and retarding the escape of fast neutrons so less plutonium is needed—and underscored the need for precise measurement of the air space (not to exceed one thirty-second of an inch) between the explosives and lenses. It was signed by Colonel Lev Vasilevsky, the deputy to Sudoplatov in Department S. Soviet intelligence director Merkulov added a cover letter explaining he was submitting a description of how to construct an atomic bomb, compiled "on the basis of agent materials received from the NKGB USSR."

That seven-page bomb design would become the basis for dividing the earth into two competing camps; for forty years of carving out spheres of influence, of staging regional wars, of distrust, tension, and the expenditure of multi-billions of dollars to keep two superpowers at a roughly equivalent threshold of strength. The atom bomb was not the only seed of the Cold War, but its possession by the United States and the Soviet Union nourished the competition into a flourishing worldwide struggle.

But had the United States retained its nuclear monopoly, precluding a bipolar world of balanced forces, Hall believed circumstances could well have led to a more calamitous scenario. As he expressed it many years later, "There's the other possibility that half the world would be cinders by now."

CHAPTER 18

Seeds of the Super

As soon as the atomic bomb crashed into the world's consciousness, Los Alamos became a different place. The scientists had succeeded; now what were they supposed to do?

Within months the exodus would begin, partly because many of the men and women who created this catastrophic weapon were no longer sure of the morality of their creation. There were exceptions such as Edward Teller, who agitated to continue developing what he knew could be an even more powerful force of destruction. Others who decided to stay on were simply relieved at the chance to mesh their minds with the best brains in physics. Work continued, but in a new, softer atmosphere. It was a time when Hall's instinctive gift for physics would propel him into one of his most prolific periods as a scientist. Just two or three weeks after the Kleenex box incident, Hall began the first in a chain of new assignments that would soon have him talking pure physics with Enrico Fermi, Hans Bethe, Victor Weisskopf, and even Klaus Fuchs. Hall was still just a nineteen-year-old who hadn't started graduate school, but his career was on a roll.

One of the first postwar tasks at Los Alamos was figuring out the radiological aftereffects of the atomic bomb. Ted's first foray beyond the Ra-La implosion group was as a human guinea pig. Shortly after Hiroshima, the director of the Trinity test site, Kenneth Bainbridge, ordered the formation of a team to take measurements of gamma-ray intensity at Alamogordo's Ground Zero. The order may well have come down from General Groves in Washington. Stunned by Hiroshima and Nagasaki, Japanese experts were saying that the two Japanese cities were permanently uninhabitable, and a good many American scientists were also alarmed. Anyone who visited Hiroshima for the next seventy years would be committing suicide, said physicist Harold Jacobsen of Columbia University. American military spokesmen were trying to portray all this as a myth, saying that almost all the radiation disappeared quickly from the test site. Toward the middle of August, Bainbridge's radiation monitoring specialist, Paul Aebersold, began scouting around Los Alamos for volunteers. He wanted junior scientists who wouldn't be terrified around radioactivity. Nobody knew how hot the site would be, but there was good reason for even the most hardened atomic veteran to be anxious. Immediately after Trinity, physicist Herbert L. Anderson entered the crater in a lead-lined Army T-4 tank and found the radiation far higher than predicted. He found readings of 700 roentgens per hour in some places, enough to be fatal to anyone who stood in the open for as long as ninety minutes. At the end of July, Bainbridge and five others returned to the crater to recover instruments and found that the radiation was still intense.

Now, in the middle of August, Bainbridge thought it prudent to send a fresh team. "I got volunteered for this little enterprise," Ted remembered. "They assigned me a jeep and I got loaded up with dosimeters. Tons and tons and tons of meters for checking radioactivity so I wouldn't get over-exposed. And I remember driving just about through the crater. I was very surprised—I had expected a very high level of radioactivity and there wasn't much."

Aebersold's team, which arrived twenty-seven days after Trinity, found the radiation had decayed so much that in some places it was now safe to walk around and take measurements. To Aebersold's surprise, the highest readings of fifteen roentgens weren't found directly in the center of the 500-foot-wide, six-foot-deep crater. They were in the strange ring of grayish debris 180 feet wide that lay inside the crater and partially encircled Ground Zero. When the news of the rapid radioactivity decline reached Washington, General Groves decided it was time to counter the growing impression that atomic weapons created a permanent poison. On September 9, Groves and Oppenheimer led thirty-one journalists through the fence at Trinity, letting them see the 2,400-foot-wide saucer littered with green globs of fused sand called Trinitite. *Life* magazine splashed the story across seven pages.

That fall, Ted Hall rose from guinea pig to full-fledged physicist, outgrowing his status as a junior scientist when he was barely twenty years old. Even before Trinity, Ted had begun puttering around the lab to find out what happens when liquid helium is bombarded by high-energy neutrons. Along with Phil Koontz, Ted irradiated helium in the same Van de Graaff generator that they had used in 1944 to measure uranium 235's fission cross section. Of course they knew helium wasn't fissionable, but if a high-speed neutron collided with a helium atom, it could bounce off at an angle. The probability of a neutron bouncing was something nobody had measured accurately. Their experiment to measure liquid helium's scattering cross section had nothing to do with the mission of building the Gadget from uranium and plutonium. Rather, it was a chance to probe the inner workings of one of the four mysterious light elements—hydrogen, helium, lithium, and beryllium. That is the angle of inquiry that propelled Ted Hall into the same intellectual orbit as Edward Teller. Teller, unlike most of his Los Alamos colleagues, thought the light elements were far more fascinating than uranium.

"There was an interim period when we were looking around for things to do and picking up our careers again," Hall remembered. "And I just continued fiddling in the lab on this and that. I wrote this paper on interpretation of some scattering data involving helium ions." Something in Ted's draft on the helium experiment caught the attention of Hans Bethe, the head of the Theoretical Division. Ted was called to present his data before Bethe, Fermi, and a handful of other theoretical physicists. "I disagreed vehemently with Fermi on some point of interpretation, when actually I didn't understand very well what I was saying," Ted remembered. "He was very tolerant."

Ted's helium paper had a tangential bearing on the feasibility of Teller's scheme of building a hydrogen bomb, which was why it caught the interest of the double domes of the Theoretical Division. During the first few weeks after Trinity, Teller had appealed to Fermi, Bethe, and others to help him perfect a far more devastating weapon based on fusion of hydrogen. On August 15, the day Japan surrendered, Oppenheimer came to Teller's office for a long talk. "The war is over," Oppenheimer told him. "We must stop work on the hydrogen bomb." Teller thought Oppenheimer was giving up too soon and spent the next three months trying to persuade his colleagues that Los Alamos must push on immediately toward a thermonuclear fusion weapon he called the Super. Teller was certain America had a new enemy: the Soviet Union.

Teller never could convince Oppenheimer, but he got Fermi interested enough to prepare a series of secret lectures in 1945 summing up how far Teller had come in two years of Super research. Notes on the Fermi lectures show that he had spotted "one disadvantage" in Teller's scheme for a superbomb made of deuterium (the rare isotope of hydrogen called heavy hydrogen). Fermi described the problem in the lingo of nuclear physicists: Deuterium's neutron cross section was an unknown quantity. "Neutron cross section" was a statistic predicting the likelihood that deuterium would interact with an onrushing neutron. Without having this cross section pinned down, Fermi felt, it was impossible to predict how high the temperature would have to rise inside the core of a hydrogen bomb before a thermonuclear burn would begin. Teller was certain he could make the Super ignite, but nobody else in a senior job at the lab supported him. Bethe recalled a gloomy conversation with Teller that fall as they discussed whether Teller should take over from him as head of the Theoretical Division. "For the first time in my recollection, he [Teller] expressed himself as terribly pessimistic about relations with Russia. He was terribly anti-communist, terribly anti-Russian. . . . The war was not over and Russia was as dangerous an enemy as Germany had been."

In his obsession about stopping the Soviets, Teller took on a new helper whose political leanings were diametrically opposed to his. In September 1945, Ted Hall was attached to Edward Teller's Super group and assigned to work on the problem Fermi had highlighted in the notes for his secret lectures: the neutron cross section of heavy hydrogen. Teamed up with Freddie de Hoffmann, Hall worked on and off for the next four months on defining deuterium's neutron cross section. Hall and de Hoffmann also undertook another research project for Teller's group, this one on a bit of physics esoterica that Teller began studying in 1937. It was an attempt to develop equations describing how neutrons scatter when a form of normal light hydrogen called parahydrogen is chilled close to absolute zero and irradiated in a cyclotron. Both Hall and Teller would remember fifty years later that the work wasn't directly related to the hydrogen bomb. Nevertheless, it got Hall back into theoretical physics and primed his mind for the studies on helium and beryllium that he would work on for the next five years.

Teller was one of several bosses for whom Tech Sergeant Hall was working simultaneously late in 1945. Oppenheimer and most of the civilian scientists were going home. Just before Oppenheimer departed, he signed a recommendation letter for Ted—one of hundreds that were drafted for the lab director's signature by the Los Alamos group leaders. Oppenheimer wrote to Hall: "According to your Group Leader, you are to be especially commended for work done as a scientific assistant. You have participated in the construction and testing of special detecting equipment and you have been responsible for carrying out a number of difficult measurements in the field of nuclear physics. You have performed your work with great intelligence and care. You have given proof of a sound scientific background, of experimental ability, and of keen interest in scientific research." He signed it with his official signature, "J. R. Oppenheimer," not using the informal signature "Robert" or the nickname "Opje," both of which Oppenheimer reserved for close colleagues or friends.

Oppenheimer urged Hall to use the letter "as a reference," but Hall wasn't quite ready to leave Los Alamos. "You know, the situation was fluid with respect to jobs and assignments," Hall reminisced. "People floated around from group to group, involved in this thing or that, one thing or another. I floated around too, maybe a little more than most. The space I was working in got switched to something else, and I ended up sharing office space with Victor Weisskopf. I sort of moved in on his office. He sort of gasped when he saw the size of my record collection." At the time, the Austrian émigré Weisskopf was head of a small staff in the Theoretical Division that was trying to explain the unexpectedly high efficiency of the Fat Man implosion bomb at Trinity and Nagasaki.

Another opportunity materialized in September 1945, when a memo was posted for everyone working in the Technical Area about the creation of "Los Alamos University." To keep the wartime staff from dissipating, Groves had decided to start an ambitious university physics department inside the fence at Los Alamos. The purpose, Groves said, was "to give the younger staff members a chance to learn some of the things that they had missed in the war years, about the actual development of the bomb at Los Alamos and recent scientific progress." The faculty consisted of the scientists who had made the bomb work: people like Weisskopf, Rossi, Kistiakowski, Fermi, and Bethe. Los Alamos University lasted only one term, but while it was going it offered seventy-seven undergraduate and graduate courses from organic chemistry to neutron physics.

Hall signed up for two courses, the most any student was allowed, and they were among the most advanced in the catalog. One was nuclear physics, taught by Weisskopf. The other was hydrodynamics—not just about the way fluids flow, but the fundamental science behind interpreting the damage wrought by a nuclear explosion. The course catalog said the lecturer would be Rudolph E. Peierls, the senior physicist in the British mission. When Hall met Peierls, he volunteered for an extra duty that was considered something of an honor: Hall became the official compiler of Peierls's lecture notes so they could be distributed to auditors and saved in the Los Alamos library.

Ted Hall didn't know that Peierls would later decide to delegate four of the most advanced lectures to the brilliant, reclusive German who worked for him: Klaus Fuchs. After classes in Room 47 of Sigma Building, Hall would reproduce the thicket of formulas Klaus Fuchs wrote on the blackboard. To make sure it was right, Hall would meet Fuchs between classes to check the formulas. Ten students registered for credit in hydrodynamics and another eighteen audited; Hall was one of only three who persevered to the end and got credit for hydrodynamics when Los Alamos University closed its doors in January 1946. As far as can be determined, neither Ted Hall nor Klaus Fuchs knew the other was a Soviet spy.

If Lavrenti Beria had known about these academic tête-à-têtes between Hall and Fuchs, he would have been all the more skeptical about the "atom secrets" his New York *rezidentura* had obtained. Maintaining several independent sources of information had been one of the *rezidentura*'s strongest selling points, and even that didn't convince Beria toward the end of 1945. "From the very beginning, Beria suspected that the materials contained disinformation," Yatskov remembered. "He thought that the enemy was trying to get us involved in huge expenses and efforts that had no future."

That October, when NKGB chief Merkulov sent Beria the bomb design in all its intricate detail, Beria thought it looked too good to be true. Beria's doubts probably ballooned three months later, when Merkulov sent him another raw document that had been pouched from New York. Entitled "Notes on the Construction of the Atomic Bomb," it was a third version of how to design an implosion weapon. It was almost certainly the same muddled atomic bomb drawings that Sergeant Greenglass had passed to Julius Rosenberg during his September furlough in New York. Greenglass's design was not quite the same as the design Beria had approved, the one based on matching intelligence from Fuchs and from Lona Cohen's source in Albuquerque. One difference even Beria could grasp: The Greenglass version had "36 pentagonal lenses" in the outer layer of high explosives; Beria's approved bomb design had only thirty-two such lenses.

"If this is disinformation, I'll send you off to the basement," Beria threatened Kvasnikov on one occasion when he came to report the latest atomic intelligence. When the head of the NKGB's overseas directorate proposed giving Kvasnikov a decoration, Beria reprimanded him, saying it wasn't clear yet whether Kvasnikov should be rewarded or punished.

Stalin undoubtedly knew about Beria's misgivings but decided there was no choice but to push ahead. On the evening of January 25, 1946, Stalin summoned Kurchatov and ordered the head of the Soviet atomic project to move "decisively" for the benefit of the motherland. Kurchatov's handwritten notes showed that they met for an hour in the presence of Beria and Molotov. Stalin told him: "It is not worth dealing with small-scale works, and it is necessary to carry out works widely, with Russian-type dimensions, and the broadest possible help will be provided." Stalin insisted that the scientists push as rapidly as possible for a "rough form" of the bomb, saying all great inventions, including the steam engine, had originally been made in rough form.

O N T H E D A Y Stalin gave the orders to Kurchatov, Teller was packing up his Steinway and preparing to leave Los Alamos. Blocked in his quest for the Super, Teller was on his way to the University of Chicago to teach physics. Teller never counted Ted Hall among his protégés on the superbomb as he did Hall's friend de Hoffmann. But Teller did think enough of Hall's talents to give him a recommendation letter to Chicago's graduate program in physics. A fortnight after Teller left Los Alamos, a report on the "neutron spectrum" of ultracooled parahydrogen was distributed within the lab. The cover sheet said: "WORK DONE BY: Ted Hall, F. de Hoffmann, Edward Teller, WRITTEN BY: Ted Hall, F. de Hoffmann."

Now twenty and still in uniform, Ted was among the old-timers at Los Alamos when he began his third year in February 1946. Oppenheimer and most of the other "first-teamers" were long gone. Of the Harvard Four, Case left in September, Glauber in December, and de Hoffmann in January. Only Ted Hall spent the winter working at Los Alamos. When Teller departed in late January, Hall returned to his work on helium with Koontz. In the third week in March they distributed two classified papers within the laboratory. The first, twelve pages long, described their improvement of Rossi's ionization chamber that they had developed to study neutron bombardment of liquid helium and nitrogen. The second, thirty-one pages, tried to explain theoretical oddities that had become evident in the helium cross-section measurements that Koontz and Hall had been working on for nearly a year.

The last event Hall would remember at Los Alamos began with alarm bells ringing. On May 21, 1946, his physicist acquaintance Louis Slotin and six others were irradiated at Pajarito Laboratory in a criticality accident. Hall and Slotin had sometimes swapped stories in the dormitory; Slotin was probably the only scientist at Los Alamos who had fought in the International Brigade in the Spanish Civil War, and he had told Ted about it. "There was a sort of a panic, people going around asking each other what was going on," Ted remembered. "Utterly by accident, I started a terrible rumor. I thought I had heard someone say that General Groves had been in the area of the accident and possibly exposed to radiation. Well, actually Groves wasn't there. It was a scientist named Al Graves, who was part of the same group with Slotin." Louis Slotin died nine days later while Al Graves survived.

Within two weeks came another shocker: Hall was called in by a Los Alamos legal officer, Major Ralph Carlisle Smith, and told that he had lost his clearance for atomic secrets. There was no explanation: Ted would simply have to pack up and leave Los Alamos within a few days. What seems most likely is that just when Ted's career as a nuclear physicist was on the upswing, the U.S. Army got around to reviewing his security file. He was on record for receiving anti-establishment publications through the mails, including George Seldes's iconoclastic weekly *In Fact*. Ted had also attracted the attention of the security office when he refused to accept his Army pay for a considerable stretch. But the most serious allegation involved a letter from his English sister-in-law, Edith Hall. The way the Los Alamos censors had read it, Edith's letter seemed to suggest that Ted Hall had told her about his work on the atomic bomb perhaps a year before the secret was disclosed to the world at Hiroshima.

"I hear you're working on something that goes up with a big bang. Can you send us one of them for Guy Fawkes Day?" That is how Edith remembered what she wrote in the letter that got Ted into trouble. It was probably in 1944, she recalled, the year after she married Ted's brother, Ed, who was serving as a U.S. Air Force engineering officer in England. "I asked Ed what Ted was working on. Ed said something to do with rockets, he thought." She said she didn't realize about the Los Alamos censorship. "I meant for it to be a joke," she remembered.

"Rockets, you see. I had no idea he was working on the atom bomb, because I didn't even know about the atom bomb or the Manhattan Project."

Around June 1, 1946, the Army revoked Hall's clearance, put him aboard a train, and transferred him to the Army SED unit in Oak Ridge. By now Hall assumed that Army investigators might know about his clandestine meetings with Saville Sax or Lona Cohen. When he got to Oak Ridge, he settled in his own room in an Army barracks, half expecting a court-martial. "You had your own room and it was quite nice and pleasant, an easygoing life," Hall remembered. He spent the warm Tennessee days as a laborer. "Once we drove someplace in a truck, where we had to unload a bunch of crates of Pepsi-Cola or Coca-Cola. I had sort of a work competition with an old black guy who just loved to work. He really went at it. We would see who could move the biggest number of bottles." Another time, Ted rode in a truck with another soldier to deliver a mound of dirty linen to a laundry depot. "I hung around in the sunshine all day while he waited for the laundry, and then we went back."

The Army must have quickly decided it had no case. After two weeks, Hall was shipped out from Oak Ridge, this time to a demobilization base at Fort Bragg, North Carolina. After a day or two, he left for home in Flushing with an honorable discharge dated June 24, 1946. He had lost his atomic clearance, along with one of his sergeant's stripes, but his Harvard classmates would later read that Hall had been awarded a decoration. It was a unit citation from President Truman for the achievements of the Special Engineering Detachment at Los Alamos.

CHAPTER 19

Destroy This Letter

By the fall of 1946, the University of Chicago had attracted a phalanx of Manhattan Project alumni still rebounding from the shock waves of the destructive creature they had produced. Samuel Allison was directing the new Institute for Nuclear Studies. Edward Teller had arrived in January. Enrico Fermi himself, for whom the institute later would be named, again was resident at the university where he had set off the world's first chain reaction.

Theodore Hall also ended up at Chicago. But after spending two years in Los Alamos rubbing shoulders and intellects with these giants of physical science, he arrived to confront the reality that he was a twenty-year-old with only a B.S. under his belt. For his age he had accrued exceptional credentials, including a cum laude degree from Harvard and cutting-edge work in nuclear physics, but his academic standing lagged behind his experience. As he set out to remedy that, Hall would be diverted from physics by other attractions—radical politics and love. He assumed this rush of activity in other directions would coincide with the end of espionage.

Settling in for Ted meant making a new roost in an attic office atop Eckhart Hall. It was the kind of stopgap space that had to do as existing offices filled with a corps of scientists, young and old, descending from the sites of the wartime government bomb project. The letters of recommendation from Oppenheimer and Teller obviously carried some weight with admissions personnel at Chicago, adding to Hall's attractiveness in a very competitive field. And he was especially drawn to Chicago. It offered not only academic excellence, but a roster of scientists who already had a reputation from Met Lab days as the most political in the Manhattan Project, the most rebellious against the dictates of the military and of Washington.

Besides going to classes in the master's program that first year, Hall devised his own collateral plan to cram in the knowledge he still lacked. He picked ten physics books that he considered important and decided to learn what was in them. It was the kind of independent approach to learning that distinguished the best minds in science or any other field. Back at Los Alamos, Hall had been one of the most prolific writers, and that reputation followed him to Chicago. When the government released the names of the first declassified research papers from the Manhattan Project, first-year graduate student Theodore A. Hall showed up as the co-author of four of the 124 titles. Other names on the list included one Nobel laureate, Fermi, and five more who would go on to win the Nobel Prize for physics. Three of Hall's Los Alamos papers would be updated and published in 1947 in *Physical Review* and *The Review of Scientific Instruments,* which rarely, if ever before, had printed the work of someone with only a bachelor's degree.

As Hall was starting to prepare for the master's examination, he joined about fifteen other young candidates in a study group whose members would include some of the leading minds of modern physics: Jeffrey Chew, Owen Chamberlain, Chen Nin Yang, Tsung-dao Lee, and Marvin Goldberger. Yang, Lee, and Chamberlain went on to win Nobel Prizes in the late fifties; the group's organizer, Goldberger, would become president of the California Institute of Technology and director of Princeton's Institute of Advanced Studies. At the same time Hall was studying, he began work on an assistantship the Physics Department awarded him. He was assigned to crunch numbers in a project run by Nicholas Metropolis, who had worked with Teller on the Hill on implosion theory and the hydrogen bomb. In the first months of 1947 Hall sat in the attic room amid the clanking and grinding, the whirring and buzzing of the early electromechanical calculators—the Frieden, Marchant, and Monroe. The aim was to pound out the answers to a set of algebraic equations that formed a model enabling physicists to predict the stability of the nucleus of a given atom. "This was a big subject of theoretical physics to explain and to be able to predict," Hall explained much later. The combination of intellectual curiosity and proven ability pointed to a potentially boundless future for Hall—provided his espionage remained a secret.

Although Edward Teller technically became Hall's supervisor, the match didn't last. Teller wasn't there much, because he was often scrambling off to give speeches or consult at Los Alamos. Teller's absences left an office for Hall to use while awaiting his own space, but the young scientist didn't recall getting much else from his association with Teller. "We just didn't share the same tastes or intentions or missions or anything," Hall said. Even their musical preferences clashed. "I remember once discussing music with him. Which composers really did things for us. He said Wagner. I said, 'If you like Wagner, then naturally you like Shostakovich, don't you?' And he said, 'Shostakovich, oihh!' " Within a year Hall switched advisers from Teller to Allison, the institute director. When Teller was in his late eighties, a half century later, he was quite apologetic that he remembered nothing about Ted Hall—not assigning him two projects at Los Alamos, not recommending him for the University of Chicago, and not serving as his adviser after Hall got there.

Their politics were even more at variance. It's true that in 1946 Teller was smack in the center of the scientists' emerging battle to keep science free and open, which included ending American military secrecy in favor of international controls over nuclear development. Teller gave his time to the new journal *The Bulletin of the Atomic Scientists of Chicago,* which was started at the university, and trudged off to gatherings like religious conferences in Cleveland to speak for the cause. The Hungarian, in fact, passionately advocated world government that would not only arbitrate issues of science, but the political and civil rights of all the citizens of the earth. World government was a popular concept of the time, something Teller believed was "inevitable, either by agreement or force." Teller also was a vehement anti-communist. One young scientist and student of Teller at Chicago said that as early as the end of 1945, before U.S.-Soviet relations were visibly fraying, Teller "expressed extreme apprehension about the Soviets and great concern over their growing military strength and their imperialistic tendencies." Communism could not thrive and continue to menace freedom under the kind of world federation he envisioned. But until that world government materialized, it was crucial for the United States to keep the nuclear lead in both defense and peaceful applications, Teller wrote. That sentiment increasingly would dictate his politics and the use to which he put his scientific skills. It was anathema to a young man like Hall, who would become more and more doubtful about the direction in which politics was moving in America.

Once Hall lost his clearance and left the scene of bomb development for academia, he figured his connection to the Soviets would wither away. But it wasn't formally broken. Finally getting his military discharge, Hall left Oak Ridge and spent some time with his family in

New York. He also saw Saville Sax that summer. Sax himself started contemplating a move to Chicago when he learned of his friend's plan. He was free to go because by the middle of 1946 he had flunked out of Harvard for the second time. And the University of Chicago attracted plenty of easterners as a stimulating, politically active campus. The friendship with Ted was no small factor in his reasoning. Their political affinity was strong, and they shared the passage into espionage that both viewed as a daring act of conviction. Friends later would say they sensed some emotional tie, that Sax seemed somehow dependent on Ted.

It is unlikely that Savy was ordered to Chicago by the New York *rezidentura* to be Ted's courier, especially since 1946 was a period when espionage rings were largely dormant. Yet the decision to follow Hall to Chicago would fit the Soviets' later plan of action. For as David Greenglass confessed, his Soviet contact Julius Rosenberg once told him the Soviets offered to pay him full expenses if he would go study at the University of Chicago "because several of the persons there previously worked on the Los Alamos atom bomb project." Whatever other bonds existed, Ted was Savy's link to a romantic underground world.

Sax arrived on campus in the fall of 1946 some weeks into the term and got a room at the same family home where Ted was staying. One shared interest was a group starting a cooperative housing project, an idea that had been catching on recently at larger universities with diverse collections of students. The notion was scandalous to the average American in the 1940s, that unchaperoned young people of both sexes, different races even, would set up housekeeping together.

At a Sunday morning co-op meeting sometime after the Christmas holidays, Hall and Sax ran into a bit of a complication in their friendship: seventeen-year-old Joan Krakover. A Chicago native whose grandparents were Russian Jewish immigrants, she showed glints of talent that didn't always produce good grades, but which had been enough to win acceptance at age fifteen to the University of Chicago, which had a special B.A. program for students with only two years of high school education. Now in her third year with challenging university classes and people, Joan had matured both socially and intellectually from a skinny kid in braces.

Sax was a strange breed of fellow, exotic-looking in a disarranged way, filled with unusual ideas, and keeping a schedule relaxed enough for lengthy musings over coffee or sodas. Joan Krakover hung out with him some after that first co-op meeting, but his friend Hall also made an early impact. It was not only that she thought him handsome. The second time she saw Ted, she was on the way into another co-op meeting. As she walked up the front stoop with a friend, Hall was waiting at the door and—splat!—he nailed them both with squirts from a plastic water pistol. A leavening agent definitely bubbled up to counteract Hall's serious scientific side. Joan began spending more time not just with Sax, but with both young men.

The weather got good enough for long walks and picnics, and for political meetings at a highly politicized campus beginning to respond to growing murmurings of anti-communism. Former British Prime Minister Churchill already had delivered his bellicose "iron curtain" speech the previous year, and now President Truman in March enunciated the policy for global struggle against communism called the "Truman Doctrine." To many leftists such as Hall and Sax, it sounded like an apologia for imperialism to come. Amid the opening salvos of Red-baiting, American liberal intellectuals distrusted claims that Stalin's agents were forcing Eastern Europe into submission. They wondered what was really behind reports of purges and arrests in Poland, Yugoslavia, Bulgaria, and the rest, unwilling to admit it might be Stalin's dictatorial grab for power. "That was the damned thing about that situation, a very unfortunate feature," Ted Hall would remember. "You were very aware that there was an awful lot of lying going on. A lot of the reports were fraudulent. If the other side, which took a negative view of the Soviet Union, had always restricted itself to the truth, then one's assessment might have been rather different. But any report that you read that took a very negative view of what was happening there, any report might well be fraudulent. You just had to exercise your judgment as well as you could." To the American left, the spread of communist governments in Eastern Europe looked more like a natural outpouring of sentiment by populations newly freed to act.

Ted and Savy were at a level of political conviction much beyond Joan's, although she clearly had inclinations toward leftist ideology rooted in early views of war and fascism in a household of strong Roosevelt Democrats. In high school she had discovered a micro-world of political activism working with a controversial, if admittedly amateurish, independent student newspaper. Her political thought had been refined in university classes. Now she was getting radicalized.

Hall was more solid, more focused than the mercurial Sax. Perhaps that was a part of it, but for whatever reason the chemistry between Ted and Joan quickly sparked into something stronger than friendship that

spring. Ted had seldom been on a date. Here he had found a bright, attractive young woman who not only had the same political instincts, but
had a dash of rebelliousness. He wanted to marry her. It was the kind of
impulsiveness that weaved throughout Hall's life. "It has been pointed
out to me that if you are totally inactive, that is a decision as well. You
make a decision just by crossing to the other side of the street or looking the other way," he said in later life. Failure to act might mean a one-
country monopoly over the atomic bomb. Or it might mean a young
woman would marry someone else.

Joan said yes. "I was madly in love, and I knew in my bones that I
would not meet his equal if I lived to be a hundred. He was twenty-one,
beautiful, brilliant, charming in a quiet modest way, with a unique sense
of humor and a mental lucidity I had never found in anyone else," she
would recollect many years later. "Our conversations—about politics,
music, anything at all—were exhilarating. Sometimes when Savy was
around, Ted and I would leave him behind, missing the point—not because we knew all that much, at least I didn't—but because of the way
we went at it, with a mutual passion for logic, precise expression, clear
definitions." The trio shrank to a duo, though Sax long would remain
involved in their lives in ways that Joan Krakover hadn't the slightest hint
of that May.

They quickly scrapped their early resolve to marry after six months.
They wanted to live together right away. Only their closest friends ever
would learn about one hurdle that remained before Hall felt free to ex-
tract a lifelong commitment from this young woman. He had to tell her
about what he had done at Los Alamos, about his connection with the
Soviets and Sax's involvement too. He had taken a risk that still could
come back to haunt him—now to haunt them—and she needed to
know. He plunged ahead one quiet moment before their wedding.

Joan was confused when her fiancé jokingly asked whether any microphones might be hidden in her bedroom. It was the opening to a
short monologue that surprised her in a way that wasn't entirely unwelcome. She was eighteen and profoundly in love. She also remembered
that at that time she was "naïvely convinced that the Soviet Union was
good and everything that was said about it, about purge trials and this,
that, and the other was a fabrication." It never entered her mind that
Hall had done something wrong—unlike Lona Cohen, who initially accused her husband, Morris, of being a traitor when he confessed to
being a spy. Joan felt she had discovered yet another heroic dimension to
Theodore Hall. Besides, Hall told her, his covert ties with Soviet intel-

ligence were all in the past. Of course she still wanted to marry him. They were wed on June 25, 1947, by Jacob Weinstein, a rabbi who lived in their Hyde Park neighborhood.

Family lore tells of one other occasion in 1947 when Joan grazed up against Ted's Soviet connection. Sometime before Ted's confession, their friends at the co-op had been dazzled to learn that Hall and Sax might come up with a loan for a down payment on a house. The two young men told Joan about "rich friends in New York" from whom they believed they could get some money for a good progressive cause like the co-op. Joan even ran into Savy unexpectedly on the street, arriving from the train station after a visit to his family and "the rich friends" back east. He said he had been successful. Some months later, Joan Hall was in her husband's attic office at Eckhart Hall killing time while he finished up work. They probably were listening to classical music, since he still had his unwieldy collection of 78s at the office, stacked in what looked like a coffin up under the eaves. Looking through some files, Joan uncovered a stack of twenty-dollar bills. It was the money Savy had brought from New York—$1,000, worth roughly $20,000 in 1990s dollars. She would learn that he had acquired it not from "rich friends" but from Soviet agents. Though neither Ted nor Savy cooperated with the Soviets for the venal motives of an Aldrich Ames, this was a substantial "honorarium" by Soviet intelligence standards. David Greenglass later would confess to receiving $500, and Klaus Fuchs accepted 100 English pounds (then worth about $400) after he returned to Britain. The $1,000 from the Soviets was in fact loaned to the co-op, but Hall never would accept repayment. He donated half the money to the housing co-op, deciding he wanted no personal benefit from the Soviets' money. He did convince Sax, who was in need of funds, to take $500 when the co-op was ready to pay off its debt.

One other thing Sax brought back from New York, probably from the same trip that produced the money, was a story that he related to the Halls with relish. Savy gave Ted and Joan a dramatic account of the brilliant dodge the courier they knew as Helen had performed at the New Mexico railway station, when she slipped his documents disguised as nose wipes through the hands of security agents. They, too, admired the woman's spunk.

The fall of 1947 was a time of unsettling transition for Joan Hall, and she decided not to go back to classes. Simply adjusting to marriage, especially at such a young age, was absorbing. She also increasingly felt compelled to join in some kind of political activism. "The Cold War period of witch-hunting and Red-baiting had begun, and the world situation looked disturbing and menacing," Joan would remember from the perspective of fifty years. While her husband continued preparing for the comprehensive master's examinations, Joan was beginning volunteer work with the *Chicago Star*, a left-wing weekly newspaper.

Soon the menace troubling Joan came very close to home. Ted Hall already had routed his activism into the committees that proliferated under the "scientists' movement." It was a broad collection of men and women dedicated to keeping control over their own research, their own scientific developments, upon which the government had been encroaching since it began the Manhattan Project. The impetus started with Niels Bohr, who unsuccessfully tried during the war years to convince American and British leaders to share atomic research with Soviet colleagues, and with Leo Szilard, who just as unproductively attempted to convince the White House that it first must threaten Japan with the new weapon before resorting to its use. Scientists' associations had formed at the different Manhattan Project venues as the war ended, and the people who created them finally demanded to be heard. Having seen the impact of their creation, they had strong opinions now: how and whether the bomb should be used again, how to prevent an arms race, the need for international control, the development of peacetime applications. Most such groups eventually coalesced into the Federation of American Scientists (FAS), which tried to shape the bedrock legislation being written in Washington.

The scientists in Chicago were among the most active anywhere in the country, springing from the driving spirit of Szilard and the Metallurgical Laboratory, which was being dismantled in 1946. Their most lasting contribution was *The Bulletin of the Atomic Scientists,* which would remain a progressive, investigative, and often controversial publication fifty years later. An early article by university Chancellor Robert Hutchins contended that treating atomic energy like a weapon to be kept under military control would be like declaring the airplane a weapon available only to military aviators. There is no "secret" of the bomb, he said, and other nations will make atomic weapons regardless of America's stance. Failure to be open with nuclear research now will result in a deadly arms race, he warned. Besides *The Bulletin,* there were committees to educate laymen, to liaise with the new United Nations, to promote international scientific relations, to keep track of the new Atomic Energy Commission.

Hall found himself attracted to one of the maverick offshoot committees led by Szilard. In fact, Hall started up a subcommittee of his own to look into the conditions of Soviet society and politics and to examine the prospects of forging good relations with the Soviet Union. It was an audacious move for someone who had been turning over secret documents to the Soviets, but points up how far removed Hall felt from that phase of his life once he stepped into graduate work in Chicago. He quickly learned how unwelcome the American authorities sometimes found the scientists' agitation. "It [the subcommittee] didn't exist for very long. After it had been going for a little while this guy Paxton from the FBI came around and said, 'What is going on here?' And I remember that he knocked on the door and I opened the door and he came in and I said to my wife, 'This is Mr. Paxton from the FBI, he is here investigating the atomic scientists,' " Hall later recalled. "It was quite a shock, naturally." Hall handed over to Special Agent W. Rulon Paxman (he misremembered the name as Paxton) copies of letters he had written on the subcommittee's behalf to the Soviet Embassy and Soviet Consulate in 1947 requesting literature for study. That seems to have been the end of Paxman's investigation, as well as the end of the subcommittee.

This was only one of the political and social developments disturbing Joan and Ted Hall in late 1947. It wasn't just the anti-Soviet attitude of the government and press, the rumblings that a new war might be brewing against the Soviets. The domestic scene didn't look too cheery to them, either. Jackie Robinson may have broken the color barrier in baseball that spring, but Chicago itself had plenty of examples of continuing racism. The black workers filling repulsive stockyard jobs for Depression wages were an example. The U.S. Congress was no comfort to liberal thinkers, passing legislation like the strike-curbing Taft-Hartley Labor Act that summer.

The answer seemed clear to this young couple: They would join the American Communist Party. "We found that you didn't just join the Communist Party. You had to be questioned and carefully vetted before you were accepted," Joan would recall. It was late 1947 or already 1948 when they began the requisite political education as fledgling party members. They studied revolutionary theory and learned about decision-making through "democratic centralism," which in fact was decision-making imposed top down. They had to read the official "short course" history of the Soviet party, which they discovered was "a dry and preachy book written entirely in jargon." Later there was the unsettling party meeting where members of Yugoslav descent were chastised for protesting against Moscow's denunciation of Marshal Tito in June 1948. Then the Soviet Union's blockade of Berlin had to be justified.

In retrospect the Halls acknowledged that they didn't apply their normally critical, analytical approach to politics to all these questions. "The connection we wanted to have with [the party] was as an American phenomenon," Ted Hall would explain from the vantage of retrospection. "I guess in many ways the Soviet Union for people like us was an embarrassment, because it was some sort of conundrum. We didn't know exactly what the present was—there was conflicting evidence on that. We certainly didn't know what the future would be." Joan again underscored the problem of believing that American officials and media simply weren't giving a straight story. "You made your choices on the basis of allegiances and on the basis of ideology, not on the basis of any objective ability to judge the correctness or accuracy of anything, because there just wasn't any possibility for judging," she said.

The Communist Party was more than international relations, and its approach to domestic problems made sense to them. Members got involved in the strike of the predominantly black Packing House Workers Union, helping distribute rent money and publicizing the issue. Joan worked with the neighborhood leftist bookstore. When the party got behind the 1948 Progressive Party presidential campaign of Henry Wallace, both Ted and Joan collected signatures to get the Progressives on the ballot. This was, after all, their own backyard, the life conditions that were more important than Tito's status in the Cominform.

For both Ted and Joan Hall joining the Communist Party was a step past a fail-safe point. This was clearly not the route scientists followed if they expected to be awarded the best jobs at the nation's prestige institutions. It was not the way to access labs doing the meatiest research. It may not have been obvious to them, but their decision also posed a threat to the job security of Ted's brother, Edward Hall, and to members of Joan's family. Ed had returned from wartime service in England to a new posting in Air Force technical intelligence at Wright-Patterson Air Force Base in Ohio and, still in the military, in 1947 and 1948 was working on his own advanced aeronautics degree at the California Institute of Technology. The government was getting stickier about allegiances. By executive order Truman had devised the Federal Employees Loyalty

Program, which mandated dismissal of federal workers who associated with any of a long list of organizations less radical than the Communist Party. The House Committee on Un-American Activities was deep into its hunt for "subversive" elements, already tackling Hollywood at the time the Halls were signing up for the party. Those developments that would endanger the Halls' future of course were the very developments that spurred them into action.

The common attitude toward radical politics was the one shown by de Hoffmann, who visited the Halls in Chicago and spotted Ted's copy of the Soviet publication *Novoye Vremya,* or *New Time.* "Freddie was scandalized when he saw a copy of *New Time* in English. He wanted to run ten miles away and said I should never subscribe again," Ted recollected.

Joining the party also meant something else to Joan and Ted. They knew they could end up under investigation simply by mingling with radicals—going to meetings, passing petitions, helping strikers, all the political activities that were important to them. They felt there was no way for Ted to maintain even the weakest ties with his Soviet contacts under those circumstances. It would endanger both sides. The time had come to terminate the relationship. In early April Saville Sax had married Susan Healy, a young university student from the north side of Chicago who had come out of the bohemian climate at Chicago's Francis Parker private school. The Saxes had gone back to New York to live. So sometime in the middle months of 1948 Ted wrote that Savy must "tell our friends" in New York that he and Joan had joined the Communist Party and suggest they "might not want to have anything more to do with us."

Just to be safe, Hall added a postscript that Savy should "Destroy this letter I guess."

CHAPTER 20

Paris and Back

Forced inaction had exasperated Lona Cohen, who, as one Soviet intelligence officer said, had gotten used to "walking on the edge of the knife" as a courier. Much of the New York network had been practically shut down for more than a year. Then suddenly Lona and Morris Cohen both were called back into service in the spring of 1947. Not only did they have to catch up with their sources—the young scientist Mlad among them—but they had to get passports, buy tickets, arrange travel plans. They were going to Paris to report to their old friends Anatoly "Johnny" Yatskov and Semyon "Sam" Semyonov.

The trouble that put them on hold for so long had started on September 5, 1945, when GRU code clerk Igor Gouzenko decided to defect in Ottawa. To gain asylum, Gouzenko turned over to the Canadians 109 top secret Soviet cables and other documents proving that Canadian and even American sites of the Manhattan Project were not nearly as secure as authorities believed. The barricades of secrecy had been breached by leaks from Alan Nunn May, a British pro-Soviet physicist who worked through the war in the Anglo-Canadian nuclear research project in Montreal. And Gouzenko knew because he had encrypted the fruits of Allied research to be cabled to the Moscow spy center. Soon after Gouzenko disappeared from the embassy, it became clear that the Soviets knew he had exposed them—they started pulling incriminated people out of Canada. The Soviet ambassador himself left on "a routine visit" and never reappeared. It was not until the arrests began early in 1946—including Nunn May, who already had returned home to Britain—that the extent of the damage began to show. There were too many connections between the Canadian and U.S. operations not to take precautions. It must have been especially grim for Moscow Centre to learn that the Canadians had arrested a minor suspect named Israel

Halperin. Halperin's confiscated address book happened to contain the name and address of Klaus Fuchs and of Fuchs's sister Kristel Heineman. (Halperin was a friend of a friend of Kristel Heineman.) That might well have led to Fuchs's arrest in 1946 if the FBI had investigated the lead with any vigor.

The Soviets might have taken more drastic action had they known that at about the same time Gouzenko defected, American Elizabeth Bentley turned herself in as an agent for the Soviets based in Washington. In November 1945, Bentley gave the FBI a 107-page statement detailing her intelligence contacts. She alleged widespread penetration in the nation's capital, but she had no supporting evidence and few arrests ever resulted. At the time, she at least raised an alert to make already suspicious law enforcement circles even more attentive to Soviet activities.

The Canadian disaster alone was enough to ice espionage operations in New York throughout most of 1946. "After the Canadian trial our work was interrupted for a short period," acknowledged Yuri Sokolov, the Russian who finally would come back to reactivate the network in 1947. "It was around a year. As far as the Cohens are concerned, about one year." Morris Cohen barely had gotten a taste of his old civilian life as Volunteer, the Soviet operative he had been before the war. He had been honorably discharged from the Quartermaster Corps in November 1945. By December he was put back into service by the New York *rezidentura*. "Although the Hitlerist Germany was defeated and the direct threat of the revival of fascism was not evident, M. Cohen without hesitation gave agreement to continue cooperation with Soviet intelligence," as his official biography put it. But in short order, both he and Lona were deactivated due to what his biography called a "campaign of spymania" in America. The controllers could not be certain that Lona's courier runs to the Canadian border had not been blown by Gouzenko. It was better to keep the Cohens out of action, to wait and see what would develop.

The waiting was easier for Morris Cohen. The war had taken a physical toll on him. Whether it was the lingering effects of frostbitten feet, snow blindness, or some other injury, he was eligible for Veterans Administration 10 percent disability payments for years afterward. But wartime service had only invigorated his ideological spirit. He had met communist underground leaders in Belgium and shared chocolate and cigarettes with Soviet soldiers who were in hiding after escaping German captors. He always would remember walking into the courtyard of the German death camp Buchenwald in April 1945, two weeks after it was liberated. "I saw what had happened, the ovens, the piles of dead, mountains of dead people. I saw all of this," he told KGB oral history project interviewers many years later. But that isn't all he found in the scene that would haunt the world for decades. "And there was this big portrait of Stalin, four floors high. He looked like a movie star. I looked at this and it seemed odd, strange to me. I couldn't explain it." Cohen said he found an emaciated prisoner, a member of the German communist underground, who told him the portrait had been made clandestinely under supervision of the communist prisoners who had been collected there from Germany, France, Belgium, Poland—all the places the Nazis overwhelmed. The picture was drawn square by square, each one in a different barracks that had been instructed which segment to draw and to hide. At the end, it was put together. The spirit that led these prisoners to undertake such an elaborate and dangerous game was the spirit that helped at least some of them survive, and Cohen believed it was based on a faith that communism would defeat the Nazis. "The feelings of the people were that the Soviet Union had saved the world from fascism," he said.

Morris had not been in front-line combat, but he had been in the midst of the struggle and the victory. Once he got back to New York, there were worse things than an unexpected rest before breaking headlong into the pressures of espionage again. Besides, he could take advantage of the GI Bill and go back to school. In February 1946, he enrolled in the master's program at Columbia University Teachers College.

Lona Cohen felt differently. Wartime production shut down and the Rosie the Riveters were relieved of their jobs so work could be given over to men getting out of uniform. Like thousands of other American women, Lona no longer was working. She and Morris started thinking about having children. Both were said to be very fond of children, and friends in later years would wonder why they never produced their own. "They wanted [children] very much. They wanted very much," said Yuri Sokolov, who would become their next controller and lifelong friend. "But unfortunately. . . . They got in touch with medicine, they did something. There were some hopes for them. Well, this was a rather delicate conversation. I didn't go into details. We didn't discuss it." No job. No kids. No spying. Lona had been embroiled in the most sensitive wartime espionage carried out in America, and now in the following year she couldn't even get her controller to talk to her. She did maintain some contacts with her sources and is said to have complained bitterly later that she was unable to deliver some "hot" information from one of them to Yatskov. He simply refused to meet her because he was sure he was under surveillance due to Gouzenko's revelations. He was right. On June 6, 1946, Hoover's Washington FBI headquarters had ordered its New York office to "institute active intensive investigation of contacts and activities of Anatoli Yakovlev [Yatskov]."

Things changed in the spring of 1947. By then Yatskov had left the country and resettled in Paris. The *rezidentura* contacted the Cohens and told them to get ready to go meet him. They were ordered to carry out a mission that was probably intended originally for Harry Gold. Following unusual precautions to avoid detection, Yatskov had held one final sour meeting with Gold on December 26, 1946, the day before Yatskov set sail for his new job in the Soviet Embassy in Paris. After telling Gold he would be directed to meet a physicist in France and take his intelligence materials to Britain the following March or April, Yatskov was incensed to learn that Gold had violated a crucial order. Gold had started working for the company of his old spy contact Abraham Brothman, who the Russians believed was under suspicion by the FBI. He had been told to stay away from Brothman. As soon as Yatskov heard of Gold's indiscretion, he stormed out of the meeting. The Cohens were tapped for Paris.

Both Morris and Lona were ready. They had seen what to them were uncomfortable changes in America. The opportunities that most Americans cherished were not at all admired by these two radicals. "In those years people began to fall away from the anti-fascist movement," Morris Cohen later explained. "The war was over. They felt what was necessary now was to live and get rich." It was remarkable to them that so many Americans were opening up businesses like beauty parlors or Laundromats, and so few were paying attention to politics. "How did people feel towards the Soviet Union? We ourselves felt that there was a change. You know that at that time the Cold War began. . . . Our position was much tougher than before." Despite the dearth of activism and growth of anti-communism in America, they had found while making catch-up contacts with their old sources that at least these allies were ready to resume their relations with the Soviets. The Cohens would be glad enough to see their old comrades in Paris and get new orders for work.

In the summer of 1947 Morris and Lona set off for the Continent, she on her first trip abroad. They got to France in time for the Bastille Day celebrations on July 14, where they were awed to see paraders led by top figures in the Communist Party, whom the crowds cheered and greeted by name. "I must say that we were thrilled by it," Morris recounted later, expressing surprise at "the informality, the close relations" between the party and the people. Later Morris and Lona sat with Parisians at sidewalk cafés and joined the drinking and dancing in the streets.

Their revolutionary fervor was fed, but their bodies didn't get the same caliber of sustenance. They spent several rather ascetic weeks waiting to make contact with their old Soviet "friends," behaving not at all like typical American travelers. As one informant later would tell the FBI, the Cohens "rented a house and lived like citizens, rather than as tourists." The couple was traveling on funds supplied by their Soviet contacts in New York, and they took pains to steward the money well. "We didn't want to waste the people's money so we used to go to cheap places, and we were so damned principled we didn't go to the black market," Lona recalled. When one of their comrades—probably Semyonov—finally met them after they had been in Paris three weeks, he was shocked that they were so skinny. "I said, 'Well, there's not much to eat,' " Lona would remember. "He said, 'Haven't you got any money?' I said, 'Yes, I've got money.' He said, 'Why don't you go to the black market?' I said, 'Listen, it's against my principles.' He said, 'You're gonna die of hunger. Look how you look like. You won't have any strength.' " After that, Lona acknowledged, they went to a black-market restaurant for a wonderful meal, though she still complained about the cost.

One such dinner saw the reunion of the Cohens with Yatskov and Semyonov. According to a version from a retired Soviet KGB officer, Mlad was a central topic of conversation. Lona handed the Russians an unpleasant surprise when she told them she had learned Mlad was involved in "a movement for peace and that he wanted the bomb to be stopped." The Cohens had probably received information about Ted Hall's work in the scientists' movement in Chicago from Savy Sax, who had traveled to New York that spring to see his Soviet liaison and retrieve the $1,000 for the housing co-op. Not only had Hall been working with the progressive scientists, but he and Sax had founded a short-lived political union of farmers, workers, and consumers, which never made it much beyond campus organization meetings. It is unclear whether Lona had summoned Sax to New York because she needed information for the upcoming Paris trip, or whether it was a coincidence that Savy arrived exactly when the *rezidentura* was starting to revitalize links again. In either case, the Soviet officers didn't welcome the news of Mlad's public activism. Semyonov reportedly told the Cohens that the climate of the Cold War made such efforts both ineffective and dangerous. Agent Mlad should get out of progressive organizations, keep clear of anyone who might be scrutinized by the FBI, and keep reporting anything he could find to his undercover contact. In these times, that was the only way to accomplish anything.

The good news for Lona and Morris was that they were back in business. Soon, they would be contacted by a new control agent who had just arrived in America, and they could get back to collecting intelligence. Lona reportedly told her Soviet friends in Paris that she might be in touch with Mlad again as early as November or December, which fit perfectly with the scheme to resuscitate the information artery. She and Mlad or Star had arranged a postcard signal to set a meeting. Little did she know that Ted Hall and his new wife, Joan, were becoming increasingly pulled toward the overt leftist politics that the Soviets wanted him to abandon. Rather than bailing out of American political life, Hall's inclination was to bail out of the Soviet network.

Yuri Sokolov had made a similar Paris stop just before the Cohens arrived, only he came from Moscow, en route to his first undercover job in America. The twenty-seven-year-old Soviet agent got stuck in Paris more than a month because of a French dockworkers strike, so he had plenty of time to be filled in by Yatskov on how to work the ropes in New York. "Anatoly Yatskov knew that I had to continue his ties with Morris and Lona. And he told me about them, some details, their characters and so on. Friendly, very friendly talk," he would recall. It would be late summer or fall when they finally connected, after the Cohens returned and he was sufficiently settled in the consulate to turn to his real mission in America.

Sokolov's first meeting with Lona Cohen gave him a taste of what to expect from his new charges. They were not sticklers for precision spycraft. Sokolov was supposed to meet Lona in the Bronx, he said, near Alexander's department store. He had seen her photograph so knew whom to expect; their identification code was some particular magazine held in a particular manner. When a woman who matched the photo approached, Sokolov started the verbal code by asking if she was waiting for Johnny, which had been the code name of Yatskov. "She said, 'I forget. I forgot everything. I just remember that I must call Johnny a stinker.' You know, 'stinker' was kind of the key word. So it was really Lona." Cautious young Sokolov didn't take chances. They started walking, and he engaged her in some general conversation. "Then we touched on some special questions which were known only to her and Johnny," he said. She understood, and she passed the test.

Lona thus returned to her role as a courier, a liaison who could distance the source of information from the foreign control agent. Morris worked as a student teacher at New York's Benjamin Franklin High School at the same time he resumed the job of finding and recruiting sources who could supply the technical and scientific data the Soviets still wanted. At some stage the Cohens' status as the hub of their own network was enhanced when their group acquired its own designation. Reflecting the nature of the participants, it assumed one of the code names Morris had used: the Volunteers.

One of the Cohens' priorities in the Volunteers would be Mlad and Star—especially now that Beria was avid to re-activate the wartime networks to learn everything that was going on in the West with nuclear weapons. Back in Britain that fall, Fuchs linked up with his new Soviet contact, Alexander Feklisov, the former New York NKGB officer who also had left America to serve in London. It was less than three years after he had stood backup on that nasty day and watched Yatskov meet Lona Cohen after her first trip to Albuquerque. Now Moscow had given Feklisov a new job. He had memorized ten questions to ask Fuchs, the most important of which was to find out what more he knew about the H-bomb. Fuchs had been out of touch with the Soviets since 1945 or 1946, and he didn't come prepared with anything in writing to that first meeting with Feklisov at London's Nags Head Pub on September 28, 1947. But Fuchs did relay a vital tidbit: that America's ongoing theoretical studies of the superbomb were happening at the University of Chicago under two men, Edward Teller and Enrico Fermi. "Fuchs described certain structural characteristics of the superbomb and its operating principles and mentioned the use of T [i.e., tritium] and D [i.e., deuterium]," wrote a Soviet physicist with access to classified files. "He verbally conveyed that, around the beginning of 1946, Fermi and Teller had proved, in effect, the workability of such a superbomb."

It didn't take Moscow Centre long to realize that the University of Chicago was a prime intelligence target, nor to devise plans to recontact its dormant sources there. It is almost certain that no Soviet agent made direct contact with Ted Hall. But there is reason to believe that someone—probably Lona Cohen—did get in touch with Saville Sax, roughly half a year after he had collected the $1,000 in New York. That fall, Sax was registered at the University of Chicago, taking courses in twentieth-century drama, German, and European philosophical thought through the French revolution. Sax lived within a few blocks of Ted and Joan Hall, and the three often got together on weekends. Like most of the physics students, Hall knew that Teller had spent the summer at Los Alamos and that he was trying to perfect the superbomb. Hall was repelled by the whole idea.

Within weeks after Fuchs's first tip-off that Chicago was a center of thermonuclear studies, Moscow received a remarkable intelligence report that sounded as if it came from someone very close to Teller. Nothing has emerged from Russian archives about which agent obtained the information—except that Fuchs was not the source. The report contained one supremely valuable nugget: that Teller had found a new thermonuclear ingredient, lithium, which would work as a starter fluid to help ignite a thermonuclear burn. The existence of this 1947 intelligence report was disclosed only in 1996 by Russian bomb designer German Goncharov, who was given exclusive access to nuclear archives in the Kremlin. Here is Goncharov's description:

> In October 1947 an intelligence report arrived in the USSR that
> related U.S. attempts to set off a chain reaction in a D-T-Li
> medium. It indicated that Teller intended to implement such a re-
> action to create a thermonuclear bomb that would carry his
> name. This communiqué was the first, and very likely the only,
> intelligence report of that time to mention lithium as a ther-
> monuclear fuel component (note that the isotopic composition of
> the Li was not indicated).

One of lithium's isotopes—Li-6—would turn out to be the stuff of dreams for theromonuclear alchemists in both the Soviet Union and the United States. If showered by neutrons in the instant of a nuclear explosion, Li-6 deuteride would give off copious quantities of the fusion fuel tritium, which was needed to complete the theromonuclear burn. Whether or not Sax and Hall knew it, Edward Teller began exploring fueling a bomb with lithium 6 deuteride during his 1947 summer consultancy at Los Alamos. As a specialist in the light elements, Ted Hall knew considerably more than the average physicist about lithium. Though he hadn't worked directly on lithium deuteride, he had conducted experiments at Los Alamos involving the bombardment of lithium targets in an accelerator in order to produce streams of neutrons. At Chicago, he published a report on why neutrons from lithium targets seemed to cause an odd pattern of "recoils" when encountering helium atoms. The intelligence report that reached Moscow in October left out a lot of crucial details. But the Soviets were quick to seize the importance of the idea and perfect it on their own. In December of the following year, Soviet physicist Vitaly Ginsburg proposed the use of lithium 6 deuteride as a source of tritium in a Soviet H-bomb. The chief designer of the Soviet H-bomb, Andrei Sakharov, called this suggestion by Ginsburg "The Second Idea" on the way to the Soviet thermonuclear weapon.

After March 13, 1948, when Fuchs held a second London meeting with Feklisov, greater angst began resonating in all directions from the Kremlin. The Russians still were struggling to put together the complex infrastructure to manufacture their first implosion bomb. It would be months yet before they even would get their reactors running smoothly enough to produce plutonium. And now at the March meeting Fuchs dropped into their laps the description of an even more powerful weapon with a destructive potential that defied imagination. In the sparest of terms, the document estimated a large Super would carry the following impact:

Blast—100 square miles. Flash burn to horizon or 10,000 square miles if detonated high up. Radioactive poison, produced by absorption of neutrons in suitable material, could be lethal over 100,000 square miles.

A weapon of this magnitude would devastate even a city the size of Moscow. Its radiation poisoning would infiltrate an area four times the size of Stalin's home republic of Georgia.

It is not that the Soviets had never heard of the Super. Soviet researchers, already alerted by Fuchs that the next-generation weapon was being investigated in America, had been working on the design for a hydrogen bomb at the Institute of Chemical Physics. But this new material from Fuchs—possibly the description of the effects—instilled a sense of urgency. On April 23, 1948, Beria ordered an evaluation of Fuchs's data by Kurchatov's team, which on May 5 proposed rush studies on the "theoretical and experimental verification of data" on the possibility of a hydrogen bomb. Beria's Special Committee on the Atomic Bomb agreed June 5, and the Soviet Council of Ministers followed suit on June 10 by setting up a secret new thermonuclear research team at a secret city 400 miles east of Moscow called Arzamas-16. Most of the job went to the Physics Institute of the Soviet Academy of Sciences, where senior physicist Igor Tamm chose his former graduate student Andrei Sakharov as a member of the team. The government put them under pressure to produce. They had until the following June to determine the feasibility of igniting heavy hydrogen to make a thermonuclear bomb.

In the ensuing months, nuclear weapons research became the "main topic" for the network Sokolov ran in America. It was useful, if not imperative, to have someone in place in Chicago with the scientific knowledge and contacts to find out how the Americans were proceeding. Mlad was the obvious candidate. But things hadn't gone at all the way Lona and Morris Cohen had envisioned when they returned to active intelligence work in mid-1947. They had been sure they could convince Mlad to forgo his progressive organizations at the University of Chicago to protect his continued clandestine activity. That hadn't happened. Then in the spring or summer of 1948, exactly the time that Moscow began focusing on the Super, they got the dismaying news from Saville Sax about Ted Hall's letter from Chicago. He had joined the American Communist Party and was departing the circle of "friends in New York."

CHAPTER 21

Rather Good Information

In the late summer of 1948, Joan and Ted Hall set out on a routine annual break back east before the fall term in Chicago. But this trip would be not at all routine, not after Soviet intelligence operatives had their say. It would utterly derail the Halls' lives of political activism. Not only would Ted Hall be drawn back into the espionage network he thought he had left for good, but according to KGB information he would bring the knowledge of two other sympathetic scientists to the cause. In the end, this surprising autumn meeting also would lead the Halls and the Cohens into a strange proximity alongside one of the legendary masters of Soviet espionage, Colonel Rudolf Abel.

By now the Halls had rooted themselves in leftist political action and they were thriving. If Joan wasn't making posters or mimeographing leaflets at the neighborhood bookstore, run by a collection of left-wing groups including the Halls' Communist Party branch, she was volunteering in the stench of Chicago's slaughterhouse district, learning about the dismal conditions in which striking workers lived as she helped their union dispense emergency aid. Collecting signatures for Progressive Party presidential candidate Henry Wallace required volunteers to haunt the often suspicious, straitlaced towns of rural Illinois to gather support from every county in the state. They both canvassed and in the end helped get Wallace onto the ballot. Joan, however, would not be able to provide the ultimate support to her candidate: She wasn't old enough to vote. Ted, who would turn twenty-three that fall, would be voting in his first presidential race.

Their political work in the American Communist Party took on greater importance to them as the other side—conservatives with a leading edge of Red-baiters—gathered steam. While people like the Halls were glad to find a candidate liberal enough to abandon mainstream two-party politics, isolationist Republicans were dismayed that the mainstream had failed to put forth a sufficiently conservative nominee. Republican candidate Thomas Dewey refused to ride the anticommunist bandwagon that many party figures were sure could cruise to victory. Dewey had argued against outlawing the Communist Party during a debate that won him the primary in moderate Oregon, but also the enmity of his party's right wing.

Even before the election the Republican right was immersed in efforts to discredit New Deal policies, hunting out communists in government and especially in institutions that helped mold public opinion. The film industry was the clearest example. The pursuit was getting more intense and was joined by conservative Democrats, who were likewise suspicious of foreign adventures and government programs that smacked of socialism or worse. Left-wingers certainly were there to be found, even communists. For years, as America struggled to kick off the Depression and then prosecute a world war alongside the Soviet ally, socialism had been a perfectly acceptable credo. But now as the domestic economy improved, and as Stalin raised fears about the aims and methods of Soviet communism through moves like the Berlin blockade, the cachet of the left was fast receding. It was not just rightist radicals who wanted to rein back communist influence as the political pendulum continued its swing back from the New Deal. More moderate citizens also were edgy, especially after events like the July 1948 indictment that accused twelve American Communist Party leaders of teaching and advocating the violent overthrow of the U.S. government. Aggressive responses to the Depression and to fascism had been one thing, but this was going too far for the American middle class.

When the Halls left Chicago for a visit to New York, they envisioned a vacation with friends and Ted's family and then their return to a vigorous autumn trying to counterbalance the growing conservative movement. They both looked forward to the presidential campaign, even though they had no hopes of success for Wallace, the onetime vice president to FDR whom Truman had dumped from his cabinet for being too pro-Soviet. The campaign was primarily a tool "to build the new party and a mass movement for the long pull," said Joan, who decades later still was astonished that some campaigners actually had believed Wallace might win the presidential election. Besides more politics, they anticipated several other agreeable changes that fall: Ted would settle into work on his doctorate in physics after passing the master's comprehensive exam earlier that year, and they would be moving into a roomier, brighter apartment. As their lease expired they had lucked into subletting a flat that a fellow communist would vacate when she moved abroad. The Halls stored their possessions with Joan's parents in Chicago before they headed to New York, planning to retrieve them and lodge themselves in the new apartment when they returned.

An early stop in New York was a visit with Saville and Susan Sax, who had left Chicago after their marriage that April. They had spent the summer with his mother, Bluma, at the family compound of rustic cottages, a simple retreat that Savy's parents had built in the Russian dacha tradition. Then they had drifted into a city apartment loaned by a family friend as they tried to figure out their future, Savy working at one or another unskilled job, Susan clerking at a bookstore in the early weeks of pregnancy.

Savy had kept up contacts with the Soviet spymasters, and now, at the end of August 1948, he had a message to deliver. The Soviets wanted Hall back. They at least wanted to talk, to present the case they apparently had been constructing since they got the first hint that Hall was distancing himself from the network, back when Lona and Morris Cohen brought the unwelcome word to Paris that he was making overtures into the world of activist politics. They wanted to reverse the decision that Ted finally had transmitted in his letter to Sax, saying Hall was making a break full and clean. Although Ted and Joan together had concluded that their out-front political work was too important to submerge under covert activities, Ted felt he at least had to pay the Soviets the courtesy of a discussion.

The evening of the meeting Savy and Ted departed under no particular cloud, and the two young women stayed behind in the Saxes' apartment on West 176th Street near the George Washington Bridge. As the hours piled up, Joan began to fidget and wonder and finally to worry. It was late, very late, when their husbands came back. Ted walked in the door, met Joan's eyes once, then silently turned and leaned his face into the wall. It was clear. He had gone back on their agreement. Initially Joan believed he still might retreat, go to the Soviets again and tell them he had changed his mind and wasn't going to rejoin their network. He didn't. The arguments plied by the Soviet agent who met Ted and Savy had been persuasive. The agent told Ted Hall that the Soviet Union was in a fight for its life in the nuclear arms race, and he was needed by the network. Despite his rebuttal that he no longer had access to secret information, the agent argued that the cause needed an ally with his background more than the American communists needed another young activist couple. One published account by a retired KGB officer said Volunteers founder Morris Cohen personally met the young scientist code-named Mlad that August and convinced him he could have a greater impact in covert work than in party politics; there are other indications that the agent who actually met Ted Hall was a Soviet.

Many years later, friends believed Hall resumed ties out of a feeling that this Soviet society he'd read about was progressing in the right direction and that concerned people had to choose sides. Sometime before the meeting Hall had seen a patriotic Soviet war film, the kind of forties movie that portrayed the heroic suffering of a people, and then pronounced that their wellspring of courage flowed from faith in communist principles. Hall would say that film made him think: "Maybe I should throw my lot in with these people."

The Halls returned to Chicago to what Joan saw as a shattered life. She felt her voice had been smothered, the equality of their marriage roles effaced by Ted's unilateral action. With Ted back in the network, they had to drop everything else. Not only did that mean leaving the Communist Party with no explanation to their friends, withdrawing from the Wallace campaign, and ending all other overt political activities, they even had to give up the cozy apartment they were supposed to move into that fall. How could they chance drawing attention by living in a flat leased to a party member? They found someone else to sublet the apartment, so at least they didn't leave their former comrade in the lurch. As for Ted and Joan, they had nowhere to turn but to her parents, ending up for several months in her old girlhood bedroom until they could find another place to live. Joan's anger and desolation at having to sacrifice her work in politics eventually smoldered into regret for the opportunities missed, but friends believe her resentment never did quite burn out.

Their lives assumed a new routine. Without politics, Joan returned to university classes. Ted plowed into his Ph.D. work. Both spent time fixing up the three-room apartment they finally found at 847 East Fifty-sixth Street, painting the kitchen yellow and caulking over the cracks in the floors to keep out the roaches. Ted Hall met only a few times for network business with Sax, who at first was a long-distance courier from New York. One visit in the dead of winter, around the Christmas holidays of 1948, came when the Halls had no nighttime heat in the flat they were trying to renovate. Sax arrived in the small hours, and there was nothing for the three of them to do but bundle up in long underwear and huddle together in bed until the heating reappeared at daylight. Such impromptu accommodations were no longer needed by the following spring, when Sax and his wife, Susan, and their newborn son, Boria, moved back to Chicago.

One sign that Hall and Sax had risen to a new level of relations with the Soviets was the espionage paraphernalia Sax carried to Chicago on that wintry trip. Savy brought tie clips that the Soviets were using as recognition signals for agents who had never seen each other. "Revolting male jewelry," someone has described it—there were golf clubs and race horses, even some tie clips with chains. That wasn't all. Wearing a fedora was requisite. Hall hated hats, not just the Army cap he had battered to no avail, but now he had to buy one. Sax needed even more outfitting. He had to purchase, at the Soviets' expense, an entire new wardrobe from suit to overcoat and hat. The ripped T-shirt he was wearing when Susan first met him at the co-op the year before was fine for a bohemian student, but not for an adult male trying to look respectable and inconspicuous.

Besides getting a dress code, Hall and Sax also were assigned cover names by which contacts would address them at face-to-face meetings. Ted became "Tom" and Savy "Sam." Soviet intelligence never shared with contacts their code names as used for internal communications, so these two young men never heard the names Mlad and Star.

All these precautions became important not only for Sax, who had been the go-between, but suddenly for Hall as well, as his renewed links with the Soviets reportedly expanded into a different realm. Although he had told the Soviet agents in New York that he could offer little help since becoming a graduate student with no nuclear clearances, the agent called Mlad did come up with something, according to KGB accounts. He brought to the network two other American scientists—a man and a woman. They were friends to whom Mlad had told the secret of his covert contacts because they, too, sympathized with the efforts to create a different kind of society in the Soviet Union. These scientists agreed to give information but feared making any clandestine contacts themselves, even with Saville Sax. A partial and admittedly altered Russian account of Mlad's work with the espionage ring says these two scientists, code-named Anta and Aden, agreed to help only if their fellow scientist promised not to reveal their names to the Soviets. At least one of them had worked at a Manhattan Project site—according to this version at the plutonium-making complex in Hanford, Washington—but precisely what the two contributed is locked in the old KGB file bearing their code names. In this one case, Mlad became a recruiter and then himself acted as courier for his friends, who have never been identified.

In his new role Hall traveled to New York at least once to meet directly with a Soviet agent from the *rezidentura,* eliminating the layer of protection Sax had provided as courier. Sometime following Sax's late-night visit that winter of 1948–49, Hall took his new hat and some information he had copied down from his scientist friends onto the New York Central's Pacemaker and headed east. Properly appareled to be inconspicuous, the inexperienced Hall arrived at the meeting site on some street corner and proceeded to surprise his contact by performing a distinctly conspicuous action. Waiting at a bus stop, Hall saw a nearby driver vainly trying to pull out of a snowbank. He watched a bit, then, having nothing better to do, Hall went over to the driver, offered his help, and managed to push a grateful New Yorker on his way. The Soviet agent surveilling the site before establishing contact watched with some small dismay. It may have been the act of a Good Samaritan, but it was not the act of a person trying to blend into the background and escape notice. Hall had to agree, sort of, that this lapse in tradecraft had been a mistake. He ended up with snow filling his shoes.

So what did Ted Hall have to offer the Soviets on those occasions when he passed something to Sax, or when he himself donned a chapeau for a meeting? Hall has never been interrogated about whether he passed information to the Soviets after World War II—because the FBI never knew of his clandestine contacts in this period. Even in conversations with close friends, Hall is not known to have acknowledged delivering any specific intelligence following his contact with Lona Cohen in Albuquerque in the summer of 1945.

Yet there is reason to suspect that in the late 1940s Hall did hand the Soviets at least one piece of secret information that made a difference in the arms race. It is now known that, during the same winter as Hall's snowy New York rendezvous, an intelligence report reached Moscow explaining an American innovation that allowed the mass production of atomic bombs. Perhaps it was only a coincidence, but the report described a secret isotope-making process then in use at Hanford, where Hall's friends Anta and Aden may have been working. The report, marked "*SOVERSHENNO SEKRETNO*" (Top Secret), was forwarded to Beria on March 1, 1949. An excerpt obtained by the authors from Russian Ministry of Atomic Energy archives shows that the report divulged an industrial process for manufacturing polonium 210, the isotope that serves as the key ingredient in the triggering mechanism of a nuclear bomb. (When put into contact with a tiny lump of beryllium inside the bomb's initiator, the polonium sprays out the burst of neutrons needed to jump-start a chain reaction in the plutonium core.)

As the report to Beria disclosed, the Americans were artificially creating polonium 210 by using a Hanford nuclear reactor to irradiate slugs of bismuth, a grayish white metal commonly used in pharmaceuticals. Once irradiated, the bismuth with its tiny added content of polonium was packed inside aluminum canisters. The casks were flown from the Hanford atomic reservation in Washington State to a new bomb-hardened underground factory in Ohio. Inside the "hot zone" of the Monsanto Chemical plant on the edge of Dayton, the polonium 210 was recovered by acid treatments inside five-foot-tall glass-lined vats. As bizarre as this process must have sounded to Beria, Americans working in the underground polonium recovery plant at the Mound Laboratory in Dayton have confirmed the accuracy of the report the Soviets received in 1949.

Up to then, Soviet geologists had found only tiny quantities of natural polonium in lead residues, not nearly enough to make weapons. Thus in designing the initiator for the first Soviet atomic bomb, Beria's physicists had reportedly been forced to substitute another naturally occurring neutron source, radium. But there was a problem: Just making one experimental A-bomb had substantially depleted the Soviet radium stockpile, and there was not enough radium-rich ore to replenish the anticipated demand for atomic, and later hydrogen, bombs. But there was no shortage of bismuth. Just four days after receiving the report on the American polonium process, Beria passed it to Igor Kurchatov and Boris Vannikov, the chief scientist and the top administrator of the Soviet atomic bomb project. By the early 1950s, the Soviets reportedly had built their own polonium recovery plant that replicated American processes used in Hanford and Dayton.

There is no evidence linking Ted Hall and his friends to any of this—either in declassified Russian archives or anywhere else. Yet what else could have been significant enough to make Hall catch the Pacemaker for that wintry encounter in New York? If they had nothing to do with it, who did? Given the timing of Hall's trip—plus the suggestion that Anta or Aden worked at Hanford—it cannot be ruled out that these three members of the Cohens' Volunteers spy ring helped the Soviet Union hold its own with America in the global arms buildup of the next four decades.

Throughout the late 1940s, getting fresh information on the U.S. atomic program remained "the main topic" of Soviet espionage networks, including the Volunteers, said Yuri Sokolov, the Russian diplomat cum spy controller in New York. "This problem of the atomic weapon is not only the problem of the initial creation, the construction of the bomb itself, but creation of the delivery, electronics, and so on. Problems of the rockets. Many problems." Sokolov recalled that sometime between 1947 and 1950, his agents retrieved information to enhance Soviet scientists' work on the hydrogen bomb, which was under way even as stepped-up development of the plutonium bomb continued to be a top priority. Whether he was referring to the 1947 data on lithium, the 1949 information on polonium, or some other as yet unknown leak, Sokolov would not clarify. He said only that some of the material came from the Cohens' sources. They supplied "not very much, but rather good information," he said. Moscow Center evaluated it "*vysoko*," he added—highly.

The Halls' closest confidants maintained he personally made only a marginal contribution, despite his proximity in Chicago to Teller and Fermi. And none of the documentation made public in Russia disputed this version. In one of his very few messages to his Soviet contacts, he gave "some little detail," from Anta and Aden, then added a philosophical note that carried the essence of his rationale behind being an informant. "The forces of peace are stronger than the forces of war," he wrote. "There will be no World War III." Hall felt willing to remain in contact, perhaps as a backup rather than as an active supplier of information, as long as he felt he somehow was advancing that cause of peace.

In the late 1940s Sokolov was meeting Lona Cohen on an average of twice a month, since she was a courier not only to the Mlad-Star team but to a few others as well. He saw Morris less often, about ten times in two years, giving instructions or getting firsthand verbal accounts of Morris's work with the sources he had cultivated back before the war. To Morris's chagrin, he was still under instruction not to expand his circle of Volunteers, a hangover of caution from the period when the Soviets constricted operations after the Canadian defection.

As the Cold War intensified in 1948, Moscow Centre began laying the groundwork for a plan to reduce the risk of exposure to its *rezidentura,* one that would rewire this network. As a Soviet diplomat, first in the consulate and then in the UN mission, Sokolov was too obvious a target for FBI surveillance. As early as November 14, 1948, the design to relieve Sokolov of at least part of his network began taking shape. That is when a Soviet spy carrying the passport of naturalized American Andrew Kayotis sailed into Quebec from Hamburg. The real Kayotis was dead, and this traveler's true name was William Fisher. He was a KGB colonel who would become most widely known under the pseudonym Rudolf Ivanovich Abel. After crossing into the United States, Abel is believed to have traveled around the country for more than six months, absorbing the sights and sounds that would give him the credibility to claim the country as his own, and quite possibly conducting espionage. He had less adapting to do than most Soviet citizens. As the son of an émigré revolutionary in Britain, Abel grew up speaking English as his native language before his family moved back to Russia when he was eighteen. In 1927 the bright young man of twenty-four, educated in art and history, but also in radio engineering, was tapped for the intelligence service. His fluency in English and knowledge of ways of the West made Abel the perfect candidate to become an illegal, living under a false identity without diplomatic status as protection from prosecution.

Abel finally checked in with Sokolov in New York in the summer of 1949, out of money and ready to start assuming control of his network. Sokolov remembered their first long talk transpired under the guise of a Sunday hike through the forested New York State park at Bear Mountain, about forty miles north of Manhattan. The infusion of cash Sokolov supplied was received as "a very good birthday present" by the older agent, who turned forty-six that July 11. Handing over money, getting Abel's report on his travels, summarizing the New York scene—all this was more comfortable for Sokolov in the camouflage of the leafy woods. By then he was getting nervous about meetings anywhere in the city. The utility of Abel's cover became apparent immediately. "I decided to check the time and wanted to ask some park officer passing," Sokolov recalled, "and he [Abel] said, 'All right, wait a minute. I'll ask him. You'd better not do it and show your accent.'"

Abel cautiously assumed command of the Volunteers network. His first face-to-face with Lona happened only after he followed her on a subway jaunt. He shadowed her before their meeting just to make sure no one else did, but at one point Lona sensed someone was at her back. Not realizing it was her new controller, the wily courier went to extra lengths to complicate her route and get rid of the suspected tail she assumed must be the FBI. It wasn't until she showed up at the designated spot, the bird house at the Bronx Zoo, that Lona discovered the man she would know as Milt had been the one following her, and her circuitous travel hadn't deceived him after all. The following week Morris Cohen showed up at the zoo. Riding to his own bird house meeting on the train, Morris sat in the back car and picked out a fellow ahead of him in a straw farmer's hat, with his jacket folded over his arm. "But he looked typically American. And something said to me, 'Very likely this is the one,'" Morris would remember. He was right. With bird song in the background, the man in the straw hat soon told him it was time to expand the network with new recruits. Morris immediately resumed efforts to recruit sources, including Spanish Civil War veterans who already had shown an ideological disposition for possible cooperation. One retired KGB officer who has read the Cohens' dossier said that in addition to Morris and Lona Cohen, the Volunteers consisted of Mlad, Star, Anta, Aden, and two other American agents who have never been identified even by code name. One of the Cohens' best sources lived in California, or so Lona was to remember in later years.

Whatever the Cohens, Hall, and the rest of the Volunteers did in 1949, the KGB rated the output of their leader, Abel, superb. The official KGB biography of Fisher/Abel said of this illegal controller and the Cohens: "They succeeded in securing the transfer to the Centre of top-secret information about work on the American atomic bomb." The only known atomic sources that any Russians have acknowledged having in America at that time were were Mlad, Anta, and Aden, though naturally there may have been others. Maintaining an appropriate attitude of intrigue, the KGB biography kept silent on the details of what Abel accomplished. But it noted that the quality of his performance is attested to by the fact that "already in August 1949 he was awarded the Order of the Red Banner for the concrete results" of his work. It may have been related not just to his work with the Cohens, but to the murky period Abel spent in America between his November 1948 arrival and his linkup the next summer with the New York network. One senior general in Russian intelligence said in 1996 that Abel's medal was awarded in connection with atomic espionage.

It is very unlikely that Abel heard about his award until months or even years later. What Abel did hear about in August 1949 was one of his first crises, a report from Morris or Lona Cohen that the young scientist Mlad again wanted out. It was a year after Ted Hall had agreed to rejoin the network, but he and Joan had never become fully reconciled to the decision and the ramifications it forced into their lives. On their annual end-of-summer visit to New York family, the Halls sent word to the *rezidentura* that Ted couldn't stick with this arrangement, and that set into motion another in the series of clandestine meetings, this time with Joan's participation.

Friends have been told that when the Halls arrived at the designated site—some New York City park where it was easy to blend in with the after-dark crowds—they found Lona and Morris Cohen had decided to double-team them. As they walked and talked, they compared experiences and views. The older couple dropped what was to the Halls the rather shocking opinion that Ted had been mistaken to tell Joan before their marriage of his involvement with the Soviets. Morris had done it differently—he had brought Lona in on his secret only after they had married. Joan was appalled that the Cohens thought such deception was a correct strategy. The Cohens' rationale apparently was that a spouse was less likely than a girlfriend to walk out in rage or to walk into the FBI with a story of spying. It was Lona who responded to Joan's misery at having to abandon political life so Ted could return to active status with the Soviets. Lona said she sympathized, for she had also had to sacrifice when she gave up union activism as shop steward for the intelligence network, for the sake of what she characterized as the route to world peace. Sometimes sacrifices were needed, said Lona, who was now thirty-six years old compared to Joan's twenty. Lona Cohen's substance and style were immediately clear to Joan, who later described her to a friend: "She felt absolutely convinced of the rightness of what she was doing. She was very militant and very disciplined. And very strong."

It wasn't a long discussion and didn't touch on political issues over which the two couples clearly would have found themselves in conflict. They did, after all, have differing views of the world and of their roles. The Cohens were Stalinists who believed in the Soviet Union as the example the world of nations must follow. The Halls had come at it differently, joining the Communist Party as a vehicle to attack the ills they saw in America. To them the party's links to the Soviet Union were an embarrassment, not an advantage. Ted always had the sense that he had volunteered his help and had given it on his own terms, choosing himself when and what to share rather than acting as an agent answerable to the demands of anyone. The Cohens had volunteered, too, but to them this had come to mean voluntarily subjecting their wills to that of the Soviets.

There was one other personal difference that at the time was scarcely apparent—a difference that may have made the Halls even less willing to continue with this dangerous liaison: Joan was four months pregnant.

Different versions suggest either that Abel showed up at this same meeting or that there was another meeting within a very few days in another New York park. "Our object was to keep him, well, with us," Morris Cohen acknowledged years afterward. The meeting was in Central Park, as he remembered in an oral history for the KGB that naturally omitted the name of the agent whose services he was so eager to retain. "He didn't want to, he and his wife, a young couple. Maybe he was twenty-six or -seven, evidently an accomplished person, a scientist, but his wife was insistent that they should not go on with this. Our people tried, but they couldn't go any further than that." According to another version, Abel was an impressive spokesman, not only because of his elegant, refined manner and beautiful command of English, but because he listened to what the Halls were saying. He disagreed that their political work was more important than Ted's remaining a covert contact; at the same time he treated the young couple's argument seriously. Abel appealed to the idealism and spirit that both Halls had shown in trying to affect American life through politics, but he tried to convince them they were on the wrong battlefield. "When you fight, you fight. And this is the real fight," Abel argued, putting politics into a global perspective. It was the geopolitical struggle of capitalism versus socialism that would determine the future, not the struggle in a Chicago stockyard. It was evident this man was an important figure and that the Soviet side was pulling out a lot of stops to keep Ted.

When they headed back to Chicago in the early fall of 1949, the Halls had not given Abel and the Cohens a final decision.

CHAPTER 22

Code Crackers

I t took six years of brilliant plodding for the American codebreakers to crack the cable that marked Ted Hall a spy.

What came to be called the Venona Project—the American military's conquest of the ciphers of America's wartime Soviet allies—originated around the time Ted Hall entered Harvard. Until then the Army codebreaking staff had been crammed into a corner of the Old Munitions Building on Washington's Constitution Avenue. There was no room to expand, and yet in June 1942 the Roosevelt administration assigned the Army's Signal Intelligence Service exclusive responsibility for breaking all foreign military and diplomatic cables. This was an outgrowth of the Army's prewar success in cracking the Japanese "purple" diplomatic codes.

Right when it needed room to grow, the Army heard about a ninety-acre secluded campus on Glebe Road just four miles west of the Pentagon. It had been the Arlington Hall Junior College for Girls, a private finishing school for 250 daughters of well-off southern and East Coast families. "They had all the social life of the time: traditional balls, active sports programs, a riding arena, equestrian events," said James Gilbert, an Army historian. Founded only in 1927, Arlington Hall Junior College never quite achieved the old-money stature of other hunt-country schools like Foxcroft. The school slid into financial trouble during the Depression. In 1942 the Army took over its rolling wooded campus and its white-columned colonial buildings for the court-imposed price of $650,000. In the same autumn that the Army Corps of Engineers was commandeering the Los Alamos Ranch School for an atomic bomb laboratory, the Army Signal Corps was converting Arlington Hall Junior College into the equally secretive Army codebreaking base. The Army's Arlington Hall Station would soon gather a brood of meteorologists, schoolteachers, missionaries, and other displaced persons to attack ciphers that many thought were insoluble. About 90 percent of the codebreakers were young women, either schoolteachers or fresh liberal arts graduates, while most of the men were newly appointed Army officers.

Early in 1943, Arlington Hall set up a "compartment" in which a few dozen analysts began picking apart coded telegrams of America's ally, the Soviet Union. It was an extremely confidential sideline to Arlington Hall's main work of breaking German and Japanese ciphers. The assistant chief of intelligence of the War Department's general staff, Army Colonel Carter Clarke, created the Russian Section after learning from a decrypted Japanese cable that Japanese codebreakers were starting to get inside Soviet coded messages. With most of European Russia under Nazi control, Clarke was fishing for some sign that Stalin might conclude a separate peace with Hitler.

Moscow's diplomatic codes used an advanced cipher system adopted by both Britain and the Soviet Union in the 1930s. Known as the one-time pad system, it produced codes that were touted as unbreakable. The drawback was that encoding a one-time pad message was slow and laborious.

To process a cable for Moscow, a Soviet code clerk in New York would begin by looking up each word in the latest edition of a Moscow Centre codebook. This was a secret dictionary in which each commonly used Russian word or syllable was assigned a four-digit code number. For example, the Russian word "everything"—*vsyo*—might have been "6729" in Moscow's codebook. To avoid ambiguities with words in foreign languages, the codebook also contained a supplementary spell table in which each Latin letter was assigned its own two-digit code group.

Here is how the phrase TO ASSURE HIM THAT EVERYTHING WAS IN ORDER might have been encoded by the New York *rezidentura*. (Soviet missions wrote their messages in Russian using Cyrillic characters; but for clarity, this hypothetical example is given in English.)

The first stage in a code clerk's labor was looking up the words in the code dictionary and writing them on a work sheet.

TO ASSURE	HIM	THAT	EVERYTHING	WAS IN ORDER
8522	7349	0763	6729	5981

Next, the clerk had to redivide the coded text into five-digit numbers. It was done by tacking the first digit of the second four-figure code onto the end of the first code group, and so on.

TO ASSURE HIM THAT EVERYTHING WAS IN ORDER
85227   34907   63672   95981

Now that the coded text had been written as fives, the clerk would apply the supposedly impregnable layer of one-time pad protection. Below each of the five-digit code groups, the clerk would write a randomly selected number. Not just any random number: a certain pre-designated five-digit number copied from a one-time pad that had been couriered to New York from Moscow Centre. A one-time pad looked like a miniature pocket notebook and consisted of dozens of pages, each bearing sixty five-digit random numbers arrayed in immutable rows and columns. Each pad was supposed to exist in only two copies—one for a Soviet diplomatic mission abroad, the other for Moscow Centre. Each number on a pad page was to be used only once, to encode a single word or letter, and then crossed off. When a sheet of numbers was used up, it was to be burned.

Now came some fancy arithmetic to lock the code inside a cipher. The Soviet clerks added the codebook numbers to the keypad numbers, using a method called non-carrying arithmetic. It meant that any number larger than nine was never carried forward.

TO ASSURE HIM THAT EVERYTHING WAS IN ORDER
85227   34907   63672   95981
67345   19650   24329   06932
————   ————   ————   ————
42562   43557   87991   91813

Even now the message wasn't ready to send. Since the Soviets sent secret cables through the ordinary circuits of RCA or other commercial telegraph companies, the numbers had to be converted into letters for simplicity in transmission. The clerks used a numeric conversion table:

0 1 2 3 4 5 6 7 8 9
O I U Z T R E W A P

Finally, the phrase "TO ASSURE HIM THAT EVERYTHING WAS IN ORDER" became "TUREU TZRRW AWPPI PIAIZ" and the message would be delivered to the RCA cable office. Once the cable was received in Moscow, a decoding clerk would laboriously strip off the disguise—first turning the letters back into numbers, then subtracting out the random numbers from Moscow's copy of the one-time pad, finally decoding the code groups into Russian text by referring to the code dictionary.

IT WAS ARLINGTON Hall's Lieutenant Richard Hallock who made the first cipher breakthrough that led to the unmasking of Ted Hall. Hallock, thirty-seven, who had been an archaeologist and scholar on the ancient Babylonian language before the war, had now been turned loose to study stacks of old Soviet coded diplomatic and trade messages. It was rather like reconstructing an alphabet from pottery shards, but the remnants Hallock was analyzing in 1943 were typewritten gibberish stretching across page after page of RCA cable blanks. At least since Pearl Harbor, American cable companies had been obliged by U.S. wartime censors to turn in duplicates of all overseas cables. U.S. counterintelligence officials had saved boxloads of messages sent not only by the Soviet Embassy in Washington but by the consulates in New York and San Francisco and by Amtorg and other Soviet trade entities dealing with the U.S. Lend-Lease Program. When Hallock started working, he had a backlog of 10,000 Soviet diplomatic and trade messages.

Hallock began by guessing the weakest link in the Soviet cipher. He deduced that the header at the top of each Soviet cable might contain repetitive patterns such as "Reference your message #." At Hallock's direction, a roomful of clerks in Arlington Hall used rudimentary IBM machines to prepare punch cards corresponding to the first five groups of numbers in each of the 10,000 Soviet messages. When Hallock had the cards sifted through a sorter in October 1943, he came upon a disastrous blunder committed by the Soviet cryptographic service. In seven cases among the 10,000 messages, the sorter detected a pattern showing that two unrelated Soviet messages seemed to be enciphered using the same cipher key. More duplicates were discovered later.

From this clue Arlington Hall came to believe that the discipline of the Soviet one-time pad system had broken down. This had evidently happened for only a few months, while Nazi tanks were encamped on Moscow's northern perimeter during that desperate Moscow winter of 1941–42. Short of machines and staff, the NKGB's cryptographic division apparently couldn't keep up with demand for the fabrication of one-time pads for Soviet missions around the world.

Under the pressure of the moment someone in the NKGB cryptographic unit had obviously cut corners. To preserve the sanctity of the one-time pad system, the Soviet clerks should have made just one original and one carbon copy of every cipher pad. Instead, they evidently began churning out random-number sheets using three sheets of carbon paper rather than one. This doubled the output of one-time pad pages without having to increase the number of machines to generate the random numbers. However, the result was that Moscow Centre distributed hundreds of duplicated random-number pads to Soviet embassies and consulates overseas. This meant that, until these defective one-time pads were used up, thousands of potentially vulnerable Soviet messages would be sent.

It was nineteen-year-old Arlington Hall research cryptanalyst Cecil Phillips who spotted a second loose thread in the Soviet code system and began unraveling it. Growing up in the Blue Ridge Mountains of North Carolina in the 1930s, Phillips had become intrigued by codes after his parents gave him a toy called the Little Orphan Annie Decoder Pin when he was about eleven. After he finished his sophomore year at the University of North Carolina, a lieutenant on a recruiting tour from Arlington Hall gave him an IQ test in June 1943. Phillips was immediately offered a job as a civilian junior codebreaker for the Army with the title of cryptographic clerk. He was just one year older than Ted Hall when he reported a few days later to Arlington Hall. After beginning in the Japanese meteorology section, Phillips was transferred in May 1944 to the Russian compartment. He was equipped with paper and pencil and set to work trying to spot patterns in columns of raw digits. After half a year of immersion, Phillips noticed an odd coincidence: At the start of some of the Soviet coded messages there would occur a number that had a relatively high proportion of 6's.

Phillips had stumbled onto a trapdoor into the cipher. He had discovered that the Soviets had begun including a non-random number "en clair" at the start of each coded intelligence message, deviating once again from the safety of their supposedly unbreakable code system due to an overload of wartime traffic. The number with too many 6's turned out to be an unciphered marker to help the recipient. It was the first number on the page of a one-time pad that had been employed to encipher the message. Using the numbers with too many 6's to sort, it was now possible to pick out pairs of Soviet messages that had been enciphered using the same one-time pad. After finding a pair of messages, Phillips and a staff of eight other cryptanalysts began back-calculating the Soviet one-time pads, one digit at a time, gradually peeling away the cipher. The task seemed like trying to push a gigantic snowball down a gentle slope, Phillips felt: The hardest part was getting it started. After the war, work accelerated when scores of new readers (the in-house slang for cipher strippers) joined the Russian Section. They were delighted to find that many of the Soviet messages used the same format to transmit lengthy order lists of Lend-Lease supplies, including part numbers and quantities. "The repetitious nature of the trade texts made it possible for the large cryptanalytic staff of fifty to seventy-five people (mostly young women) to slowly recover the code text," Phillips remembered. At this point, the brigade of women readers led by Katie McDonald and Gene Grabeel could uncover nothing more than the underlying four-digit number groups that Soviet code clerks had found in Moscow's secret code dictionaries. By the middle of 1946, they still couldn't translate those coded numbers into any intelligible language.

The next breakthrough came when some of their partially stripped messages wound up on the desk of Meredith Knox Gardner, one of Arlington Hall's premier linguists. Along with a gift for languages, Gardner brought what he described as "a sort of magpie attitude to facts, the habit of storing things away that did not seem to have any connection at all." A shy and gangling language teacher at universities in Texas and Wisconsin before the war, Gardner had been grabbed up by the Army Signal Corps shortly after Pearl Harbor. He not only was fluent in German and Spanish but had also studied Middle High German, Old High German, Lithuanian, Sanskrit, and Old Church Slavonic. Once recruited, Gardner dumbfounded his colleagues by learning Japanese in three months, and he spent the rest of the war on German and Japanese codes. Early in 1946, the thirty-four-year-old Gardner joined the Russian Section as a book-breaker, or linguist. His job was to hunt for the language meaning of code groups after the readers had stripped away the cipher. His work was called book-breaking because it meant intuitively trying to reconstruct the secret code dictionaries the Soviet clerks had used. It was like trying to create a diagramless crossword puzzle in the dark, but in 1946 and 1947 Gardner had two crucial clues from which to work. One was an outdated Amtorg codebook, probably seized in an FBI raid in the 1930s; the other was an obsolete codebook of the Soviet NKVD border police, quite possibly passed on to Arlington Hall by

British intelligence. Gardner used the old codebooks as models of how the Soviets might have structured their newer codes.

Ted Hall was the first of more than 100 wartime Soviet spies whose trails were struck by Meredith Gardner. After working for less than a year in the Russian Section, Gardner succeeded in reconstructing the code for the spell table for the Latin alphabet. On December 20, 1946, Gardner was startled to see emerging from his work sheets a list of Manhattan Project scientists—names including Hans Bethe, George Kistiakowski, Emilio Segrè. It was Hall's list of atomic physicists that he had supplied to Kurnakov during his furlough just two years earlier. This was not just the first whiff of atomic espionage, it was the first time Arlington Hall had even realized that NKGB intelligence cables were interspersed with the repetitive trade traffic that Hallock had begun studying three years before.

Over the next two years Gardner progressed from Latin letters to Russian words to phrases, but he was not able to read full messages until late 1948. By then, the Army's G-2 section had been sharing parts of the Venona breakthrough with the FBI for more than a year. In the fall of 1947 Colonel Clarke summoned S. Wesley Reynolds, the FBI's liaison agent to Army Intelligence, to the Pentagon and cautiously told him that Arlington Hall had begun to penetrate Soviet espionage traffic. The following October, Gardner began regular liaison meetings at Arlington Hall with Robert Lamphere, another FBI counterintelligence agent. Lamphere remembered receiving an odd request at one of their first meetings: Could the FBI provide the plain-text originals of documents that had been transmitted in ciphered form to the Soviet Union back in 1944? "With the lapse of four years, I didn't hold out much hope, but I told him [Gardner] I'd investigate the possibility," remembered Lamphere. "To my surprise, by return mail I received a mass of material, all in Russian except for a few translations into English. . . . This material had been photographed by New York FBI agents in the course of an investigation into Soviet operations in New York in 1944." What kind of an investigation could have given the FBI access to confidential cables of a wartime ally? No one ever told Lamphere, but long afterward he said he had come to suspect it was through a "black-bag job"—the FBI's terminology since the 1930s for a burglary sanctioned by FBI headquarters and carried out by trained FBI teams.

How much help the Army codebreakers got from Lamphere's suspected bag job remains an ardently disputed issue inside Arlington Hall's successor agency, the National Security Agency (NSA). By the 1990s,

Gardner had no recollection of receiving Lamphere's cache of plain-text messages, but Lamphere would distinctly remember giving them. If Lamphere did speed up the translations by delivering to Gardner the hidden fruits of an FBI black bag, no record of it survives in NSA files. This is a patch of uncertainty about the ancestry of the Venona decryption that would complicate any attempt by the U.S. Justice Department to establish a chain of evidence to permit the introduction of a decoded Soviet cable in any future spy trial.

Whether or not FBI black-bag-job material arrived on Gardner's desk, there is no question that Arlington Hall was desperate in the late forties to accumulate all the raw material it could. Indeed, the Army even appealed to the Commerce Department for plain-text Soviet information similar to that which Lamphere remembered giving Gardner. In the late forties or early fifties, Commerce did give Arlington Hall piles of manifests for World War II ships that had transported Soviet cargo. Wherever the plain-text Russian trade documents came from, their extraordinary length and repetitive content worked in Arlington Hall's favor. More and more often, the Arlington Hall readers found it possible to match up an uncoded shipping manifest with a Soviet coded message of the same length sent on approximately the same date. If the coded message was one that had been previously identified as using a duplicated one-time pad, the readers were now able to strip away the final layer of protection. By comparing the plain text and the enciphered version, it was possible to back-calculate the digits that the Soviets had added from their cipher pads. Once a reader had determined which random numbers had been used to encipher one of a pair of messages, it was no trouble to subtract out the same random numbers to unlock the cipher from the second coded message. Often enough, the second message was not another boring trade manifest but an NKGB intelligence cable.

Arlington Hall's labors paid off big just as news was spreading within the U.S. government that radioactive samples collected over the Pacific hinted at a Soviet atomic explosion. Early in September 1949, Gardner informed Lamphere of something he had just translated. "It became immediately obvious to me that the Russians had indeed stolen critical research from us and had undoubtedly used it to build their bomb," Lamphere remembered. "I dropped everything and began to work intensely on the deciphered message." The FBI opened an all-out investigation on September 22; the following day Truman announced the Soviet atomic explosion. The AEC almost immediately identified the

Arlington Hall decryption as a document that Klaus Fuchs had drafted while he was working for the British Supply Mission in New York in 1944. Within a few days of the Truman announcement, Lamphere informed the MI-6 liaison officer at the British Embassy that the prime suspect was Fuchs, who was now the chief scientist at Britain's top secret Harwell nuclear center.

Truman was never told about the Venona Project and wouldn't even be briefed on the Fuchs investigation for another few months. But thanks to the pervasive contacts of its Cambridge Five intelligence ring, Moscow Centre learned almost immediately that Fuchs was under suspicion. The Cambridge Five leader, Kim Philby, had just been assigned to take over as the MI-6 representative in Washington, and he learned during briefings in London that the Harwell scientist was a suspect. Philby covertly relayed the news to Moscow in late September; Fuchs probably received a tip-off from his Soviet contact in early October. On October 13, Fuchs stopped to see Harwell's security officer and said that perhaps he should resign from the lab. The only reason, Fuchs maintained, was that he might be a security risk now that his father was about to move to East Germany.

The British security services assigned the Fuchs espionage investigation to MI-5 officer William Skardon, a rumpled former Scotland Yard detective whom Lamphere likened to a "British Columbo figure." Fuchs denied everything but Skardon persisted. Skardon couldn't let on that the Soviet codes had been penetrated, but he kept dropping in at Harwell every week or ten days for further chats with Fuchs. The MI-5 man had one pressure point to tweak, and that was Fuchs's worry that his sister Kristel would be hounded by the American police. With hopes of shielding her from aggressive questioning, Fuchs confessed to Skardon on February 2, 1950.

FOR THEODORE HALL and Saville Sax, it was a stroke of wild and inexplicable luck that the FBI's investigative searchlight turned on Fuchs instead of on them. That September, Hall was still vacillating about whether to break with Soviet intelligence. Joan Hall, now five months pregnant, kept pressing Ted to throw off the clandestine layer of his life. Not realizing that Soviet intelligence viewed her husband as a primary asset, she kept arguing that she and Ted could be more effective if they resurfaced as political activists.

Hall's departure from the Volunteers occurred just about the time he was also deciding to switch out of nuclear physics, but these two life-changing decisions were apparently unconnected. Hall had already begun thinking about changing his field in the spring of 1949, while he was still in the Soviet network. That April, Hall exchanged letters with Bruno Rossi, his former Los Alamos group leader, who was now back at MIT. Rossi had mapped out a new phase of his cosmic ray studies and was looking for a postgraduate researcher to take observations from the bottom of a pit hundreds of feet in the earth. Working at MIT clearly interested Hall. "Thanks for your very encouraging letter of April 21," he wrote Rossi eight days later. "I would like to work on cosmic rays in your group." Hall explained that he was thinking about applying for an AEC fellowship that would start when he concluded his Ph.D. work at Chicago. That spring, Hall was slogging to finish his dissertation on atomic processes that occur when high-energy beams of hydrogen ions pass through four different metals, including beryllium. In his answer to Rossi, Hall went so far as to ask about how to find housing for him and Joan in Boston. But for reasons nobody can remember, the MIT prospect either wasn't pursued or never turned into a concrete offer. By the fall of 1949, Ted Hall's mind had turned to biophysics, and he had decided the best place to pursue postdoctoral research was across the University of Chicago campus.

"Nuclear physics had become pretty dull stuff to some of us young people," Ted Hall explained long afterward. "It was getting sort of boring to set up collision experiments. You know, you take a beam of particles and hit something and see what comes out. After you've done that for several years, you get a little tired of it. But biology—that was exciting new territory. It was full of really fascinating questions that were just inviting you to explore them.

"And we nuclear physicists had a very snobbish and conceited view that there was nothing there before we arrived—that the biologists were all a bunch of clucks, all they knew how to do was to classify and define things."

That decided, the vexing issue of Hall's Soviet connection persisted. The Halls were very disciplined about leaving their Fifty-sixth Street apartment whenever they had to discuss their on-again, off-again secret life. But if the FBI had installed listening devices while they were still wavering over whether to break ties, there was a chance the eavesdroppers might have caught them agonizing out loud about whether to leave the network. Truman's announcement saved Hall from that risk by stimulating him to quit espionage just in the nick of time. Not long after that day when Ted and Joan sat in their sunny kitchen and heard that the American atomic monopoly was broken, they resolved to get on with their lives. Shortly after Truman's announcement, Hall told Saville Sax to inform the Soviets that his spying days were finished.

Ted Hall's timing was a miracle from the gods of espionage. With no warning from the Soviet *rezidentura,* not even a premonition, Hall decided to end his double life just at the moment he was about to come under FBI surveillance. It was probably in the spring of 1950 that Meredith Gardner prepared the first U.S. government document that pointed toward Hall as having been a spy at Los Alamos. It was a partial translation of the NKGB cable five years earlier reporting that a nineteen-year-old physicist named "Teodor Kholl" from Harvard had given information on "Camp 2" to Sergei Kurnakov. It wasn't conclusive, but this one document naming Kholl was more damning than any single decrypted cable that Arlington Hall could ever find on Fuchs.

C H A P T E R   2 3

Espionage-R

In the spring of 1950 the Venona codebreakers dropped the Theodore Hall–Saville Sax espionage case into the lap of FBI agent Robert K. McQueen. As clever as Ted Hall was, he was now up against a formidable and righteous opponent who would love nothing more than to nail his scalp to the goalposts of Stagg Field.

Some agents hated the drudgery of spy investigations. There was no crime scene to rope off, no aggrieved witnesses, usually no paper trail to follow. There was only one guarantee: endless waiting in doorways to shadow some Soviet diplomat who was probably taking his ambassador's pants to the cleaners. But McQueen cherished the challenge of espionage. Trim, broad-faced, and about five-foot-nine, McQueen was on his way to becoming an FBI supervisor and then a judge. He would retire from the Bureau in 1969 to become a law teacher in Wisconsin, then an Illinois county prosecutor and a circuit court trial judge in Chicago's northern suburb of Waukegan, Illinois. Later he would be the chief trial judge of Illinois's nineteenth judicial circuit. Whatever else he would do, Robert McQueen would never have a job that intrigued him more than working a good espionage case.

Bob McQueen was already an espionage specialist by the time he was made the case agent running the Hall-Sax investigation. His profile had paralleled many in Hoover's FBI in the late 1940s: born in small-town America, schooled on the conservative campus of Northwest Missouri State University, accepted into the patriotic bosom of the FBI as a fingerprint clerk a month after Pearl Harbor, broadened with a B.A. in 1944 from George Washington University, hardened with a year and a half as a Navy lieutenant—junior grade. When McQueen took off his blues in the spring of 1946, the FBI assigned the twenty-six-year-old from Farragut, Iowa, to the espionage squad in the Washington Field Office.

McQueen was quickly seen as a comer. For the first two years he worked as a leg man helping the FBI case agent in charge of surveillance of the Soviet Embassy, the beaux arts mansion on Sixteenth Street, five blocks north of the White House. When he was twenty-eight, he was promoted to case agent in charge. The case had ramifications known to only a few agents: The FBI had secretly recruited as an informant someone who handled paperwork behind those gray-shuttered windows. The U.S. government had almost never developed a real human source inside the Soviet compound. Now, during the bellicose buildup to the Berlin crisis, the Soviet Embassy was Bob McQueen's territory, and J. Edgar Hoover was watching.

With his clearances for counterespionage, McQueen was introduced early to the Venona secret. Late in 1948 he was drawn into the brigade of agents shadowing Justice Department employee Judith Coplon. "This was the only instance I ever knew when the Army had broken the Russian code," McQueen remembered. Early the following year Coplon was arrested with classified documents in her purse during a New York encounter with a Soviet diplomat. The Coplon investigation ended badly for the FBI when an appeals court overturned her conviction, and for McQueen it was a path to unwanted prominence. Over the FBI's outraged objections, a federal judge allowed several dozen FBI investigative reports into evidence, including one of McQueen's intelligence memos. *The Washington Post* printed a front-page story about McQueen's report, which included his name and hinted that the FBI might have a counterspy inside the Soviet Embassy. Even without such attention, McQueen was due for a transfer as soon as he finished his night school law studies at George Washington University.

After picking up his degree, he transferred to the espionage squad in the Chicago Field Office in November 1949. The following spring, he landed in the most frustrating spy case of his life when his supervisor assigned him to investigate two new names turned up by Arlington Hall: Teodor Kholl and Savil Saks. "In our office, in Chicago, it was the biggest case we had in espionage," remembered McQueen. "It was an important case. I lived it."

The Hall-Sax investigation entered its earliest, most secretive stage while the country was in an espionage feeding frenzy. It began when Alger Hiss was convicted of perjury in late January after a jury decided the former State Department official had lied in denying that he had passed diplomatic papers to a Soviet agent in the 1930s. Hiss was only "a small part of the shocking story of communist espionage in the United States," declared the young California congressman Richard Nixon.

With spy rumors roiling the nation, news reached Hoover's headquarters on February 2 of Klaus Fuchs's confession in Britain. "All hell broke loose at Bureau headquarters," remembered Lamphere, the liaison with the Army codebreakers. Fuchs had told not only about passing atomic secrets to the Soviets but of a previously unknown American courier who picked up documents from him in New York, Boston, and New Mexico. "The information that Skardon got out of Fuchs turned what had been a quiet and careful investigation of Fuchs's connections in the United States into a raging monster of a quest," remembered Lamphere. Overnight, FBI teams mobilized across the country with orders to compile lists of possible couriers. Anyone on the FBI's security index of those with leftist connections was a potential suspect—especially those whose paths might ever have crossed Fuchs's.

The spy quest took a new and uncontrollable turn on February 9, when Wisconsin's junior senator, Joseph McCarthy, told the Wheeling Women's Republican Club in West Virginia, "While I cannot take time to name all the men in the State Department who have been named as members of the Communist Party and members of a spy ring, I have here in my hand a list of 205 that were known to the Secretary of State as being members of the Communist Party and who, nevertheless, are still working and shaping policy in the State Department." Magazines exploded with exposés including "HOW COMMUNISTS GET THAT WAY," "HOW THE RUSSIANS SPIED ON THEIR ALLIES," and even "REDS ARE AFTER YOUR CHILD." Hollywood joined the chase, churning out movies for the drive-in theaters like *The Red Menace* and *I Was a Communist for the FBI.*

Hoover responded by heating up the hunt for Fuchs's courier. Within two weeks his agents had identified 104 possible suspects and the number was multiplying. The best lead was Fuchs's statement that he had met his courier in Santa Fe in June 1945. FBI agents began collecting old registers for every hotel in New Mexico, checking the alibis of every guest. When an agent found the name of Gerson "Gus" Gusdorf on a registration card of the La Fonda Hotel in Santa Fe, teletypes flew. Lamphere knew from Army decryptions that the Soviet cables referred to Fuchs's contact as either Gus or Goose. Thinking that Gus might be the courier's real first name, Lamphere had agents scouring the Southwest for Gusdorf. After two weeks the FBI found their man. With the help of a credit bureau, agents in Albuquerque discovered that he was a seventy-year-old dairy farmer who ran a curio shop in Taos. Except for the time his farm burned down, nothing notable had happened to him in nineteen years. Gusdorf's name was scratched, but other suspects now numbered more than 500. Based mainly on the New Mexico hotel records, the list included General Leslie Groves's wartime assistant Colonel K. D. Nichols, as well as best-selling author John Gunther and historian Daniel J. Boorstin.

The Fuchs case had raged inside FBI field offices for three weeks when the oracle of Arlington Hall produced another sensation. On February 21, Lamphere opened a new investigation into the unknown subject code-named Kalibr. From what Lamphere could tell from the latest decryptions, "unsub Kalibr" had worked at Los Alamos and had a wife or sweetheart with pro-communist sentiments—a woman whose Soviet code name was Osa. One decryption showed that Osa and Kalibr had spent a week together near Los Alamos during his leave late in November 1944. Another showed that Kalibr had returned to his home in New York on another furlough in January 1945.

Pressed by Hoover, agents combed the leave records of the more than 2,600 Los Alamos soldiers and civilians. Agents from the Albuquerque FBI office found names of sixty-two people whose furloughs overlapped the known dates of Kalibr's leaves. The list did not include Ted Hall, but it did name David Greenglass, who would turn out to be the actual Kalibr. Greenglass was initially passed over by investigators in favor of two other suspects deemed more promising. One was Professor Edward Teller, who had two strikes against him: He was known to have relatives in communist Hungary, and his wartime trips away from Los Alamos coincided perfectly with those of Kalibr. The other was William Spindel, a young SED from Brooklyn College who also happened to have gone on furlough at suspicious times. Of the two, Teller was taken far more seriously, for by now he was back at Los Alamos with a go-ahead to develop the H-bomb.

Against the backdrop of the pandemonium touched off by multiple spy hunts, the FBI was plunged into yet another search. This one began in late April, probably just days after Gardner broke the cable in which the *rezidentura* told Moscow Centre about Kurnakov's initial contacts with Kholl and Saks. Of the 2,900 messages ever decoded in the forty years of the Venona Project, none contained a more explicit description of an actual NKGB recruitment. On April 21 the FBI's chief of domestic intelligence, D. M. "Mickey" Ladd, informed Hoover of the Army's decryption. Four days later Ladd followed up with a top secret report telling the director that the Chicago field office "is attempting, on a discreet basis, to locate Theodore Alvin Hall and determine his present whereabouts." The case file already carried the "Espionage-R" tag, an internal symbol that meant that FBI headquarters believed it involved spying by the Soviet Union. A nationwide investigation of Ted Hall was now inevitable. While Chicago agents planned their surveillance, the New York and Albuquerque FBI field offices were already assigned to find Saville Sax and "ascertain the identity of his mother, and particularly if she is identical with Bluma Sax." Meanwhile, the Boston office was sorting out Hall's biography from Harvard University.

Within two weeks everything in the Hall-Sax case seemed to click into place. The breakthrough was the discovery that Ted Hall had gone on leave to New York in late October 1944, exactly when the Soviet cable said Teodor Kholl had met Kurnakov. After that it took only a few days for the FBI to begin suspecting that Hall might match the profile of one of the scores of unidentified spies on Meredith Gardner's burgeoning list of code names: Mlad. One clue was that Mlad seemed tied to a friend from Harvard, just as Hall was. Almost immediately, the FBI found something even more revealing in one of Gardner's decryptions. It was a passage from the January 1945 cable informing Moscow that Mlad had just "been called up into the army" and then returned "to work in the camp [a Soviet code name for Los Alamos]." Some personnel files from the Manhattan Project were missing or destroyed, but after more than a week of searching agents did find Hall's records around May 10. They showed Hall had been drafted into the Army in late December 1944, then returned to work to Los Alamos after only a week away from the Hill. The timing of Mlad's entry into the U.S. Army matched Hall's precisely and also eliminated almost every other scientist on Oppenheimer's staff. Probably by this time, the Boston FBI office had also confirmed that Sax had returned to study at Harvard in early 1945, exactly when the decrypted cable said Star had. On May 11, the FBI counterintelligence unit informed Meredith Gardner that Mlad had been tentatively identified as Theodore Hall, and Star as Saville Sax.

In one of Hall's personnel files, the FBI came up with information dangerous to Edward Teller. It was his four-year-old letter recommending Ted for graduate work at the University of Chicago. By now the FBI knew that Teller and his wife, Mici, had been close friends of Klaus Fuchs at Los Alamos—so close that Mici Teller had driven to Mexico City with Fuchs and another couple for a post-Hiroshima vacation. Already under suspicion because his wartime travels coincided with those of Kalibr, Teller now seemed to be tied to Mlad as well. "Hall has been identified as a Soviet espionage agent while at Los Alamos," Percy Wyly, the agent in charge of the Albuquerque FBI office, wrote to Hoover on May 18. Teller's acquaintance with Hall, along with everything else in his background, made Teller "a most logical suspect" as Fuchs's courier, Wyly concluded. He stretched his string of speculation even further: "As HALL was an associate of Dr. TELLER at Los Alamos, he may have mentioned his name as a possible prospect to furnish information when he [Hall] was in New York City in October 1944."

For McQueen, the biggest question that spring was whether Hall and Sax were still spying. He had organized surveillance requiring a dozen agents for morning-to-night coverage on Hall, plus another twelve agents to cover Sax. The problem was that shadowing Ted and Joan Hall seemed all too easy. They were living like typical graduate students with an infant daughter and garden-variety radical ideas.

Within weeks after their baby was born in February, Ted and Joan ended their eighteen months of lying low and resurfaced in activist politics. Instead of rejoining the Communist Party, they signed up as members of their neighborhood branch of the Progressive Party, for which they had canvassed in 1948. If they had been looking for a disguise, this would have been a perfect choice. The Chicago FBI regarded the Progressive Party as "Communist controlled or infiltrated," but most people on campus saw the Progressives as mainstream pinkish liberals. The Progressives' youth affiliate was described by the campus newspaper *The Chicago Maroon* as "the largest and most active of the avowedly political groups" at Chicago. As the Young Progressives' campus chairman, Frank Rosen, explained their objectives, the Progressives were fighting against "discrimination" and for "full employment, housing, peace and civil liberties." The Halls were also active in the Chicago Tenants Action Council, a liberal group that had been described by one Chicago FBI informant as a "Communist front." In the upside-down world of FBI counterintelligence, the fact that the Halls had any overt left-wing political ties stymied the investigators. If McQueen had learned anything about the pattern of Soviet operatives in America, it was that real spies never joined anything.

The Sax family must have been even harder to figure out than the Halls. Savy and Sue and their year-old son, Boria, were still living near the University of Chicago, but their connections with the university had withered. Savy tried to run a small mimeographing business out of his apartment at 6516 South Minerva Avenue. In his spare time he wrote philosophical essays that nobody published. In the fall of 1949 Sax had registered as an undergraduate at Roosevelt College, a less demanding school than Chicago. He had signed up for child psychology, elementary statistics, and animal behavior, but then taken an incomplete in child psychology. In the first half of 1950 he didn't sign up for any courses; by then the Saxes were so strapped for money that Sue Sax was grading college papers and working nights as a waitress. The only thing Sax seemed to have in common with Hall is that the two were making no effort to conceal their radical politics. This became clear to McQueen as soon as he got the first results of the FBI's "mail cover" on Sax's apartment and on the nearby Black and White Mimeo Shop, a basement copying store at Fifty-sixth and Harper Streets where Sax sometimes received letters. Surveillance on Sax's incoming mail even showed that he was receiving the Sunday edition of the Communist Party's paper *The Worker*. In a decade of trailing suspected Soviet espionage agents, the FBI had devoted a lot of time to trying to distinguish which American leftists were involved in espionage. One element of the pattern never varied: Real spies didn't subscribe to *The Worker*.

On May 22, as McQueen was puzzling over the brazen activism of his suspects, the FBI located Fuchs's courier. Confronted with the map of Santa Fe that agents found in the closet of his home in Philadelphia, Harry Gold confessed: "I am the man to whom Fuchs gave the information." Nine days later Gold made a second admission, that while in Albuquerque in June 1945 he had also collected an envelope from a young soldier, "either a corporal or a non-comm," and later delivered it to his Soviet control agent. Could this soldier be the mysterious Kalibr? Could Kalibr simply be an alternate code name for Mlad or Star? To Special Agent T. Scott Miller, who was interrogating Gold, everything now made sense. Miller telephoned Washington to suggest that Hall might be the soldier whom Gold had met in Albuquerque.

Mickey Ladd immediately informed Hoover of the suspected link between Gold and Hall. Late on the morning of June 2, New York agent Robert Granville added to the suspense when he called Washington to say that a file check showed that Gold's soldier contact might be either Hall or Sax.

The next day in Holmesburg Prison on the outskirts of Philadelphia, a desperate and frightened Harry Gold viewed the photos of Ted Hall and Saville Sax. Their futures hinged on Gold's visual acuity. It didn't matter that the Albuquerque FBI had long since determined that Hall was not among the sixty-two Los Alamos employees whose furlough record matched Kalibr's; if Gold picked Hall as the "unknown soldier" he had met in Albuquerque, Hall would surely have been arrested. It would have been the right charge—espionage—but the wrong particulars. In fact, Hall and Sax were never part of the same spy ring as Fuchs. But if Gold had identified either of them, the FBI would surely have thrown the book at them—after all, the counterintelligence unit had just identified them as probable Soviet spies. The false trail to Fuchs would have seemed compelling: Imagine the excitement if Fuchs's courier Gold had pointed to Hall's picture, and then an agent had been sent to Los Alamos to check for some documentary link between Hall and Fuchs. There in the library was a mimeographed copy of the 1945 lecture notes of Peierls and Fuchs at Los Alamos University. On the title page of the report Ted Hall was listed as the note taker. All this would have led the investigators away from the actual story of Hall's espionage; yet the pressure from headquarters to close the case would have been immense. Who knows what would have happened if a facile interrogator had been armed with a Los Alamos document saying Hall and Fuchs knew each other? Would Sax have cracked under questioning, implicating Hall about their real acts of espionage?

What happened in Holmesburg Prison on June 3, 1950, is that Harry Gold told the truth: He had never seen Ted Hall or Saville Sax. Less than two weeks later, the Chicago FBI office air-mailed Hoover a report that was far from optimistic about the outlook for prosecuting McQueen's suspects. It concluded that in light of their surprisingly overt involvement in the Progressive Party and the Chicago Tenants Action Council, "it is even more imperative that corroborating evidence be obtained." As the report bearing McQueen's initials explained:

> SAX subscribes to the DuSable (Chicago) edition of *The Worker* and HALL has apparently been in contact with known Communists. His wife definitely has been in contact with known Communists. Their actions on behalf of the Progressive Party and the Chicago Tenant's Action Council have revealed a disregard for adverse publicity and there appears to be nothing of a covert nature in their current activity. In view of this information it appears likely that neither Hall nor Sax is presently engaged in surreptitious espionage work.

A few days later Hoover got news from Philadelphia that further weakened the hypothesis that Hall had been Harry Gold's soldier informant. Hoover was told that Gold had positively identified Technical Sergeant David Greenglass as the GI he met in Albuquerque. "I said 'bingo!'" said Gold later, describing how he reacted on June 15 when he was shown a snapshot of Greenglass taken in Albuquerque. That night, FBI agents in New York confronted Greenglass with Gold's identification. Greenglass broke down and confessed, saying he had passed information and accepted $500 in return. He told the agents he had been recruited by his wife, Ruth, who had in turn been drawn into espionage by his brother-in-law, Julius Rosenberg. Two days later Ruth Greenglass extended the circle of guilt by naming Julius's wife, Ethel Rosenberg, who was David's sister. Once the Rosenberg family tree was sorted out at FBI headquarters, the case was wrapped up and ready for the grand jury. On June 27, Lamphere dispatched a counterintelligence memo to Arlington Hall saying that "it is now believed that David Greenglass is identical with the individual described as KALIBR, and that Ruth Prinz Greenglass is identical with the individual known under the code name OSA."

Once Greenglass confessed that he was the Albuquerque soldier, the Hall-Sax investigation wasn't quite as riveting for Hoover's office. Hoover had the evidence he wanted to try "the crime of the century," as he hyped the case the FBI developed against Julius and Ethel Rosenberg. From Hoover's perspective, there was still only one vital loose end: an atomic scientist in a top secret job who remained an active suspect. On July 26, headquarters sent out a message to field offices saying it was "imperative" to determine if Edward Teller was a Communist Party member or sympathizer, since "subject presently asst. director for weapon development, Los Alamos." FBI offices were ordered to devote "continuous attention and all logical investigative steps," and especially to check whether he was the same Edward Teller whose name had appeared on a roster of teachers at a New York City party-affiliated workers' school in 1941. Hoover's Teller inquiry churned on for several months; then he was cleared.

WITH A HALF century of hindsight, it is clear that Agent Bob McQueen was cursed with spectacularly bad timing. He missed masterminding the biggest arrest of his life by only a matter of weeks. Not only did he open the investigation just after Hall and Sax emerged from the underground to be political activists, but there is also reason to believe that either Hall or Sax had one last espionage meeting with Lona Cohen in the early months of 1950, even as Meredith Gardner was decoding the Kholl-Saks cable. The meeting probably took place in Chicago, just about the time McQueen put them under observation.

Judging by the accounts of three KGB veterans, Colonel Rudolf Abel decided to organize one last risky encounter with either Hall or Sax because he was still determined to draw Ted back into espionage. The most persuasive of these three somewhat conflicting versions was offered by Lona Cohen. Though she was vague about the details, Lona told how she and Abel traveled to Chicago to meet the same scientist who had been her contact at Los Alamos. Their goal, she said, was to persuade him to continue to work for the Soviet Union. "He said, 'No more. I helped you during the wartime, and now it is over,'" remembered the historian of the Russian Institute of the USA and Canada to whom Lona told the story.

Morris Cohen related much the same story to another historian who worked for the Russian Foreign Intelligence Service. Morris also didn't specify when or where the meeting happened but said it was a follow up to the New York encounter known to have occurred in the summer of 1949 when he, Lona, and Abel met the "young scientist" who had been her contact at Los Alamos and tried to talk him out of withdrawing from the network. As Morris recalled in a videotaped interview, "There was one more time when we went to the home of the fellow with whom she [Lona Cohen] had met, from whom she received the materials. We did go once to his house, where he and his wife and child were living. We thought, well, we should go, perhaps we could do some good that way. That was about the last that we heard of them. It may be that Abel had something to add to this. I am not sure." His description seems to place the meeting in Chicago very close to the time McQueen started his investigation—sometime after the Halls' first child was born on February 2, 1950.

A third version of that final meeting, this one partly disguised in order to protect the KGB's sources, appeared in a recent book published in Paris by retired Colonel Vladimir Chikov. His story contains some of the same basic facts as the reminiscences of Morris and Lona Cohen—no doubt accompanied by false details added as disinformation.

According to the Chikov account, Lona Cohen held one last meeting with Mlad in the spring of 1950, shortly before she and Morris were ordered to flee from New York. Chikov's version says that Mlad arrived unexpectedly from Chicago with some "alarming information." Mlad told her that generals in the Pentagon, with the help of scientists, had marked a map of the Soviet Union with small flags designating targets for a future nuclear war. Citing what he presented as a transcript from KGB files, Chikov quoted Lona as reminiscing: "Following Abel's instructions, I informed him of the high appreciation with which Russia had received the information he had furnished. At the same time, I wanted to offer him, as a form of recompense for his services, $5,000 which I had removed from a safety deposit box. He categorically refused the money, declaring with firmness that he had not acted to get some reward, but rather to prevent a world catastrophe."

Following the appearance of Chikov's book in Paris, a longtime confidant of Hall insisted to the authors that Hall never saw Abel or the Cohens after their meeting in the New York park in the summer of 1949. However, Hall's acquaintance considered it possible that, unbeknown to Hall, Saville Sax did in fact meet with the Cohens or Abel— and did turn down a $5,000 Soviet reward.

CHAPTER 24

A Certain Animus

The link the FBI was searching for in the summer of 1950—the evidence that would tie Theodore Hall and Saville Sax to Soviet espionage—was about to disappear before Agent McQueen had any idea it had ever existed.

Even though Morris and Lona Cohen had received a cryptic order "in the third month of 1950" to lie low, to stop seeing their controller Abel, and to prepare to depart from the United States, they didn't think that in the end they would have to confront the bleak prospect of running. As Morris was trying to operate his Volunteers at some reduced level of action, the Korean War broke out on June 25 and further soured relations between the Americans and Soviets. "It came like a bombshell from the sky, what was going to face us," was how Morris Cohen described the news of hostilities in Asia. "We knew our own work would be harder and harder. Then came the information from a comrade that the best thing would be for us to leave." The spring alert had turned into a directive. The immediate concern wasn't the fighting, but the net the FBI was tightening: Klaus Fuchs, Harry Gold, and David Greenglass—one was already convicted, the second arrested, the third hauled in for questioning. Who could tell what lines would be followed, what evidence uncovered? Morris and Lona Cohen finally acquiesced that hot day at the end of June when their friend Yuri Sokolov unexpectedly showed up at their apartment with the unwelcome order to flee.

In the muddle of visiting relatives, closing bank accounts, and cashing in $1,075 worth of savings bonds, the Cohens had to help Sokolov plan their escape. On one mixed-up day they forgot at which of two sites they were supposed to appear to give him their passports, which he needed to make false travel documents. There was a main site and a fallback meeting place for the next day. Morris guessed wrong and took the passports to the secondary site, while Lona went to the main site and greeted a frustrated Sokolov empty-handed. "But it was urgent, and I said, 'All right, you have to return home and tell Morris that he or you must come to a secure place, another place, with the passports,' " Sokolov would recall. This time it worked.

It was 1 A.M. when the Soviet finally got the documents, and he was hurrying to get home. As he sped through a changing traffic light on 149th Street in the Bronx, Sokolov saw a police car loom out of nowhere, then pull him over. With the Cohens' passports sitting under his seat, he was panicked at the prospect of the kind of search traffic cops in Moscow routinely demanded. He quickly got out to divert the officer, making jokes and trying to answer the questions posed by the policeman, who saw he was a diplomat and seemed more interested in life in the Soviet Union than traffic regulations. The policeman gave him a speeding ticket, but never noticed the documents in the car. After driving a mile, Sokolov found he was so unnerved that he had to pull over till the wave of weakness passed.

That was the worst glitch. The Cohens devised a cover story that they were off to California, where Morris said he had a job with a movie company. They reportedly threw themselves a farewell party on July 5, and Cohen left a letter telling the school board he was quitting teaching because he had found "a very desirable writing job." Leaving their families was much harder. Lona's sister Ginger said they didn't even tell her they were going anywhere that last time they came to visit. "They seemed to cling. When they were leaving, they seemed to linger, linger, linger. And after that, I didn't know what happened to them. And of course I was very upset because I loved her dearly." It was hard, too, on Sonya and Harry Cohen, Morris's parents, who were now in their early sixties. One friend who had been close to Cohen since their days fighting in the Spanish Civil War said his mother "was devastated," and later appealed to Morris's friends to help her find him. "My father understood that we were leaving for good," Morris later told a Russian interviewer, to whom he described an emotional farewell.

Back then, Morris and Lona didn't know whether they ever would return to America or even precisely where they would be heading. They knew only that Moscow Centre wanted them gone, to keep themselves and others in the Volunteers out of prison. Surely Morris had never envisioned this end to a decision made in the heat of idealism fighting against fascism in Spain. But after submitting to the dictates of Moscow for more than a decade, the Cohens were in too deep to balk. One day

Yuri Sokolov felt the smooth head of a thumbtack pressed into the underside of the wooden railing at an elevated train stairwell and knew that his part of this assignment had been accomplished. "I felt it, in a certain place, [and it meant] that everything's all right for leaving. And goodbye." Lona later would talk about arriving in Mexico on July 22.

The Cohens never saw how the Korean War reverberated through American politics and society, but Ted and Joan Hall were in the middle of the protest against it. It was exactly the kind of activity that put the FBI sleuths off track.

News of the outbreak of war in Korea was the deflating end to what had been a lovely day for the Halls, a summer picnic with the baby and friends from the Progressive Party. Although the picnic was most likely surveilled by the Chicago FBI espionage squad, none of the picnickers would have been aware of that. When they got home they heard about the war, which American troops quickly entered under the protective coloration of a UN force. "We were all furious," Joan would recall, "and much of our political activity was then directed against the American so-called 'police action' in Korea."

From the FBI's viewpoint, it seemed crazy that spies would agitate openly against American military action or get into an altercation with police, as Ted did while collecting signatures to put a black trade unionist on the ballot as a congressional candidate. Savy's wife, Susan, remembered another time he and Ted ran into trouble on the Lake Michigan shorefront while circulating the Stockholm Peace Petition urging America not to use the atomic bomb again. The seemingly innocent Stockholm appeal, which was signed by millions around the world, was the invention of a Soviet-front group, and the FBI knew it. Although Susan became aware of the espionage involvement of Ted and Savy, she always thought their petition work was the spark that kindled the attention of the FBI. The truth was just the opposite. The more open Sax and Hall became in their activities in the summer of 1950, the less fodder Agent McQueen had for an espionage case. "It was never the policy of the Soviet Union to allow their undercover agents to 'blow' their cover by attracting attention to themselves by having connections with public Soviet front organizations," McQueen remembered. He was exactly right.

Another investigative lead to Hall's past in Los Alamos collapsed when David Greenglass, locked up in the Tombs in New York, said he didn't recognize the photos of Hall and Sax that FBI agents had shown him. "He said that it is possible that he may have seen some individual who resembles Hall, but if so he is unable to place this individual," said the stiff FBI account of Greenglass's questioning in September.

McQueen tracked down all the places Hall and Sax had lived, where they were schooled and worked, watched whom they met, where they went, what they read, and even to whom they wrote. The FBI put mail covers on both families and apparently tapped their phones. "We were trying to tie him [Hall] up with anybody, anything that would corroborate the information from the 'source,' " McQueen said. Investigators found nothing to alert them to the relationship with Lona and Morris Cohen, and after July 1950, it was too late. Even had they unearthed some scrap of paper with an address or record of a phone call that conceivably might have connected Sax or Hall to the Cohens, it would have led to a New York apartment on East Seventy-first Street where no one was in residence. Agents likely watched as the Halls packed up and moved out of their own Chicago apartment that fall, but they weren't fleeing the country; they were becoming part of the all-American post-war migration. As Ted began his post-doctoral studies, the Halls moved to a university-owned prefab house across the campus at 6002 South University Avenue. If the agents checked with their former landlord on Fifty-sixth Street, the worst they would have found was that the landlord was furious because the Halls had transferred their lease to some leftist friends who didn't pay the key money deposit.

The FBI watchers didn't find many leads, but may have gotten a little entertainment out of the Halls, who were hardly one-dimensional political drudges. Ted Hall's penchant for tweaking authority popped out in satirical letters like the one he wrote to the Gillette company, which had invited consumers to give their opinions of a new razor. "The day before yesterday I shaved with it. My sex life has now become unnecessary," he wrote in a mocking letter that April. "I find it ecstatic like a sexual experience. Oh how grateful I am to you." He signed it "Westling Pursby." It was not the kind of correspondence that would link the Halls to espionage. Nor did the FBI uncover anything else to make the connection.

For more than a year, McQueen kept up the search. He found that Sax "had a background," confirming that his mother had worked with Russian War Relief, and that Hall held what he termed "leftist sympathies." But McQueen still could not produce anyone with usable evidence that either had handed secrets to the Soviets. Hall worked in his own lab at the Institute of Radiobiology and Biophysics on Fifty-sixth and Ellis Streets, which was only a five-block walk from their prefab.

From what McQueen could tell he wasn't working on anything that might compromise the security of the nation. Sax was student-teaching and driving a cab. In the agent's view, Sax was "kind of a pseudo-intellectual" who didn't have access to any information, period. "We had to make a decision," McQueen said. "We decided to interview them, hoping we might possibly get a confession, and if we didn't get a confession, we might at least get some leads, something we could investigate. And if we got nothing, we hadn't really lost anything anyway in terms of making it known that they were suspects. . . . We had nothing, really, to lose."

He boned up on the backgrounds of the suspects, but McQueen also knew that tactical issues of surprise, turf, and isolation from accomplices all can be useful. In this case, he used them. "We didn't want to give them an opportunity to think it over before we began asking questions. So, in the language of the vernacular, we grabbed them off the street," McQueen said. At 2 P.M. on March 16, 1951—a typical Chicago Friday—McQueen and Special Agent J. Baird Reynolds approached Raymond Zirkle, the head of Hall's laboratory on the university campus. They got Zirkle's permission to see Hall, then "invited" him to come down to the FBI office to explain "his connection with a matter pertaining to the security of the United States." Simultaneously—at 1:58 P.M.—Saville Sax was being stopped at the southeast corner of Sixty-second and State Streets by Special Agents H. Rulon Paxman and L. Hoyt McGuire, who issued a similar invitation. FBI documents relate that both Hall and Sax "willingly" took the half-hour ride downtown to FBI headquarters in the Bankers Building on West Adams Street, each unaware the other had been hauled in for questioning.

Hall immediately tried to lessen the agents' home-court advantage. To put them on the defensive, he accused the agency of conducting fishing expeditions and trying to trick people into making damaging statements. He told McQueen he had been reading about the FBI, including a new book by Albert E. Kahn that charged that Hoover himself had helped organize illegal anti-Red raids in the 1920s. And he berated the authorities for giving his brother, Ed, and sister-in-law, Edith, what he considered an unjustified case of heartburn, after she wrote the joking wartime letter from Britain asking him to send something for Guy Fawkes Day. All this was in response to McQueen's preliminary question of whether Hall would consent to an interview. "He had a certain animus about the FBI," as McQueen put it many years later. When the agents then told Hall they wanted to discuss the crime of espionage, he agreed to answer questions. "I think he was very bright," McQueen said. "I don't think there is any question about that. Very, very bright."

Closeted in a separate interview room in the Bankers Building, Sax adopted a more relaxed strategy. Like Hall, he made no demand to see a lawyer. Instead, he quickly agreed to answer the agents' questions while issuing repeated warnings about the sorry state of his memory for dates, names, and addresses. It was part of an approach Hall and Sax had conceived long before in anticipation of such a grilling. Sax had specialized in both psychology and theater in college and so was primed to perform. In any event, it was an easy claim for Sax to make convincing, since it was largely true. He proceeded to demonstrate by misremembering not just the date of his marriage three years earlier, but the month and year. Some things about real-life details always had eluded him, although in this case Sax exaggerated his eccentricity to assure the agents he was incapable of anything so sensitive as espionage.

Having rehearsed for exactly this occasion, the two young men came up with largely congruent accounts of their friendship, activities, and assessments of each other, parts of which were fabricated. The one new bite of information they fed the FBI was a fictionalized account of Savy's trip to Albuquerque. They must have feared the FBI would be onto Sax's journey to New Mexico, so they devised a story explaining it. In fact, the FBI hadn't known, and their genuinely odd version of what happened made the G-men even more suspicious. Savy, they both said, simply decided to study anthropology at the University of New Mexico and had come to check out the prospects. The two ran into each other on the street, Hall having dropped in from Los Alamos to buy some Victrola records. Although Hall said they had been corresponding, he maintained that Sax hadn't bothered to tell him he was heading for New Mexico. What did they do at this happenstance meeting? Hall said he thought they talked about Dante's *Inferno* and the philosophy of Nietzsche. Sax's version had a more bizarre twist. He was very depressed and living in "a dream world" after flunking out of Harvard, he said, and remembered little about that period. He went to New Mexico to look around the school, and chose the place partly "because Ted Hall was the only person he could rely on to get him out of his state of depression." Sax gave no indication, however, that he tried to reach Hall in advance, and said he could not remember if he even contacted this friend he had traveled 2,000 miles to see.

Another fact on which they diverged was whether Hall had visited with Sax on his October 1944 trip to New York. The FBI questioners

obviously nipped out from time to time to compare notes on their simultaneous interrogations. At one point they came back to Hall to challenge his claim that he did not see Savy during the New York trip,
advising him that Sax had told them otherwise. Hall stuck with his story,
informing the FBI that his friend "was rather forgetful and he would
prefer to trust his own memory."

The agents made it clear by their questions that they had happened
upon some damaging information, but of course Hall and Sax didn't
know where the agents got these details or how much evidence the FBI
had. The interrogators asked about the Soviet Sergei Kurnakov, the man
to whom Hall offered his services and passed his first report on Los
Alamos. They even produced his photograph. The same for the two
men Sax had tried to contact: Earl Browder, the Communist Party
leader, and Nicola Napoli of Artkino. And what about this fellow Anatoly Yakovlev (i.e., Yatskov)? they asked. He was the Soviet vice consul
and spy handler, and Sax had met him twice.

Hall allowed that he might have read something by Kurnakov, or
"bumped into him" at a Harvard campus meeting. Other than that,
both claimed not to know, not to have seen, and never to have tried to
contact any of these people. Just the sound of those names must have
sent their heartbeats skipping, but Hall and Sax showed nothing as they
withstood the long interrogation in what Ted remembered as an over-
heated FBI office. "He [Hall] gave considerable thought to his answers,"
McQueen said in retrospect. "He was just very bright, quite calm for his
age. And being snatched on the street by two FBI agents for an interview, I thought he handled it pretty well."

In three hours of questioning, Hall admitted to nothing. He had
never had any contact with anyone either officially or unofficially connected with the Soviet government, he said, except for some letters requesting the Soviet Embassy to send literature to his scientific study
committee. He didn't think Sax would pass secret information to the
Soviets, he said, and claimed the two had never discussed committing
espionage. Sax gave the same kinds of answers. Sure he had gone "once
or twice" to the Soviet Consulate, Savy admitted, probably acknowledging the visits because he suspected he had been photographed there.
But nobody asked him about secret data, he claimed. He had just gone
to find out if his mother's relatives in Russia had survived the war.

"I believed they were guilty then, and I didn't necessarily believe
what they said, of course," McQueen remembered. In addition to what
he knew from the secret Soviet cables, McQueen found Hall's de-

meanor suspicious. "That is the curious thing, that he has never expressed resentment that he was questioned about this. An innocent man
usually says, 'Why are you asking me these questions?' There was not
any outraged denial. Just calm, matter-of-fact statements."

Suspicion wasn't enough to make a case, especially since the Venona
evidence was a precious discovery that couldn't be revealed in court.
Hall refused to let the FBI search his house, except on the condition that
agents not take or even note any left-wing literature they might find;
McQueen said no to that. Before Hall walked out of the FBI office at
5:21 P.M., he agreed to come back the following Monday. When he returned, however, he said he had discussed the matter with his wife and
with Sax and had decided, first, that he had nothing more to say, and
second, that he didn't trust the FBI anyway. In explanation, he told
McQueen he had read an appellate court opinion that accused the FBI
of purchasing perjured testimony against the leftist labor leader Harry
Bridges. "This statement was refuted by interviewing agents," read
McQueen's March 31, 1951, report to Washington. Sax had permitted a
search of his apartment, but there had been no smoking guns hidden in
a closet, nothing like the map of Santa Fe that so crumpled Harry Gold's
composure that he confessed just a year earlier. "We didn't have that
luck," said McQueen, who took part in the search. "Saville Sax admitted, of course, that he had gone down there [to Albuquerque]. And he
had just the typical left-wing periodicals, and that was it."

Hall, then twenty-five, and Sax, twenty-six, may have looked cool
to the investigators, but inside they were churning. Ted had called his
wife that afternoon to warn her he had been detained by the FBI. When
he finally returned to an anguished Joan hours later, he recounted a day
far more antagonistic than McQueen's report to Washington would
suggest. They later would tell how the agents directly accused Ted of
spying and threatened to lock him up.

The timing of the interrogation hardly could have been more in-
timidating, coming the very week of testimony in the trial of Julius and
Ethel Rosenberg in New York. They were accused of conspiracy to
commit espionage in wartime, and prosecutors had just let it be known
that they well might seek the death penalty. To make sure Sax and Hall
didn't miss the connection, the FBI interrogators showed them photos
of "the Rosenberg ring" and asked if they knew these people. Sax said
he recognized neither the names or faces, explaining that he hadn't been
reading the papers lately. Hall said he had read about the prime prosecution witness, David Greenglass, Ethel Rosenberg's brother, but in-

sisted he didn't "remember having heard of him" while they were both in the SED unit at Los Alamos. Just four days before, Greenglass had described to a jury the explosive lens mold design that he said he copied from Los Alamos and handed over to Julius Rosenberg for transmission to the Soviets. Front-page headlines exclaimed news of the "SERGEANT WHO STOLE DATA" and "TESTIMONY ON THEFT OF ATOM BOMB SECRETS." It was less than Ted Hall had given away.

The evening of Ted's FBI interrogation the Halls made a furious search through all their papers and books, through their whole small house, for any scrap that might be used to compromise them should the FBI come back with a search warrant. As friends were told the story, the Halls were especially concerned about all the Progressive Party files sitting around their house. Joan was membership chairman; she had all the names. Membership in the party was no crime, nor was possession of such a list. But they acted on an understandable worry in those times when hunting expeditions broadly targeted Americans with left-wing connections. Grand juries and congressional committees were routing supposed "pinkos" out of offices and classrooms from California to New York. That same Friday night they gathered anything at all revealing and packed it and the snow-suited baby into the old Chevy Joan's mother had donated to them. Ted was certain he saw an FBI agent standing on the corner, but no one followed them. They drove the Chevy to the home of some Progressive Party friends, where they gave a vague account of Ted's interrogation and dropped off the party records. The Halls also made a brief explanation to their stunned friends of why they again felt obligated to withdraw from politics. Then they drove through dark streets to a bridge over the Drainage Canal. They dumped the rest of their papers into the water below them.

The next day an unbidden telephone repairman, a big jovial guy dressed like a lumberjack, came to their house to repair their perfectly functioning telephone. The Halls, unaware they had been under surveillance for nearly one year, were sure he planted a listening device. Both the Halls and Saxes had no doubt after the interrogation that they were being followed, wired, and intercepted. "We were afraid our car might be bugged," Joan later recalled. "Ted would look in the mirror and make a little wig-wag with his finger to tell me we had a 'tail.'" Susan Sax, then twenty-three, believed that FBI visits got her husband fired from several jobs. "There was very obvious surveillance. They'd stand across the street staring at our doorway. It was intended to be obvious. . . . They went around kind of smearing us. Asking questions.

People I'd known in high school, even just vaguely. Old acquaintances and so forth. The main impact was economic. But also of course we were frightened. We were very young."

In late winter of 1951 the Halls and Saxes spent hours walking in the cold, lugging along their babies, because they only felt safe enough to talk out on the street. Sometimes they'd stop in a café for a coffee warm-up, but even that didn't seem private enough for their sensitive conversations. They were anxiously looking for some way to make contact again with the Cohens or with the Soviets, to let someone know they were in trouble. There was the aborted plan to cross-dress one of the men for a disguised visit to the Soviets and the unsuccessful effort to stage a meeting at the Chicago Art Institute with the Cohens, who they didn't realize had fled nine months before. The Halls and the Saxes wondered if they would have to leave America to escape jail or even execution. It was only weeks after their interrogations that Julius and Ethel Rosenberg were convicted and, on April 5, 1951, sentenced to death. "It was an awful time, really," remembered Susan Sax, thinking back on the fear and the talks about their dangerous situation, their seemingly stunted futures. "I remember thinking that I wouldn't leave the country, no matter what Savy chose to do."

No longer having to worry that Hall and Sax would find out they were being watched, FBI agents rushed to contact friends and associates to continue seeking the link that so far had eluded them. "We were certainly stymied at that point," McQueen recalled. "Unless we were able to develop information from somebody else or get additional information from the 'source,' we weren't going to get a prosecution. We didn't have enough information to get an indictment." They did keep putting out leads, working with bureau field offices in New York, Washington, D.C., Los Angeles, San Francisco, Albuquerque, and Boston.

Roy Glauber got the call at Harvard, when FBI agents came to ask about his old roommates. They posed what seemed to be strange questions about whether Glauber himself had been asked to give anybody information when he worked with Ted at Los Alamos. "I wondered during this time what in the world was going on," he said later. The FBI in Los Angeles also interviewed Sam Cohen at his Rand Corporation office about his Los Alamos buddy Hall. He recalled they expressed suspicions over Hall's involvement with "some off-center Yugoslavian communist group."

"Obviously those [interviews] weren't productive of any information that could lead to an indictment," McQueen said in 1996. "We needed a Harry Gold, a Greenglass, even a Fuchs." McQueen didn't second-guess the decision not to present the Venona evidence to a grand jury and then to a court. Street agents didn't have a full perspective on the nation's intelligence needs, he said, and he accepted the decision to keep the decryptions secret. Besides, as a former state prosecutor and later a judge, McQueen questioned whether the decryptions would have been admissible as evidence, let alone sufficient to get a conviction without eyewitnesses or a confession. Nor did he have complaints about the FBI's approach to this case, rejecting any suggestion that it got swamped in the wake of what was clearly the agency's highest-priority case and trial, the Rosenbergs. He had all the manpower and resources he needed to pursue what was Chicago's biggest espionage case of the time, he said.

Without access to the full FBI file, it is hard to assess how much effort the FBI pumped into the Hall/Sax investigation as compared, for example, to the intensive search Hoover mounted to identify Gold and then Greenglass. Gold himself was about as composed as Ted Hall during his first FBI interrogation. It wasn't until the third visit from agents—when they found the incriminating Santa Fe map in his closet—that he broke. Fuchs, too, was questioned multiple times by Skardon before he confessed. But then Gold and Fuchs cooperated, agreeing to continue talking with the FBI or MI-5. Ted Hall refused to cooperate after the first interview, so continued probing for his pressure point would have been more difficult. As for Sax, there is no indication in the released documents that the FBI ever tried to pry more information from him. One wonders how Hall might have responded if confronted with the Venona cables in 1951 instead of hearing about them only four decades later.

In late 1951, McQueen was taken off the Hall/Sax investigation and promoted to command an internal security squad. The case remained open, but in his new job he was too busy to monitor developments. "You certainly aren't going to close a case when you have information such as we had that these people had been involved in atomic espionage," McQueen said. Within months, however, Hall and Sax would become a back-burner case.

CHAPTER 25

We Have No Guns

Ted Hall led his twenty-two-year-old wife into the bathroom, the one place they could be sure there were no hidden cameras. He was carrying a clandestine writing device that the NKGB would have been proud to have invented. Press the wooden stylus against the cellophane cover—words showed up in black against a gray background. Lift the cellophane—the message disappeared forever. It was the Magic Slate that belonged to their two-year-old daughter.

"A Friend," Ted wrote in the top corner.

"From," he wrote in the middle.

"N.Y." he printed at the bottom.

Joan Hall had known something was up. Earlier that day Savy had come pounding on the door of their prefab on South University Avenue. He said Ted must come out for a walk "right now." Ted departed with hardly a word, leaving Joan to wait with their daughter. It was late in 1951 or early in 1952, the most frightening time the Halls and Saxes had ever lived through. For nearly a year since the FBI interrogation, Ted and Joan had noticed cars tailing them and the families were sure their houses were bugged. It looked as though it was only a matter of time until Ted and Savy were dragged into court like the Rosenbergs. When the U.S. Court of Appeals rejected the Rosenbergs' appeal in late February 1952, it was easy to imagine that the two ex-Harvard roommates might one day follow Julius and Ethel to the Sing Sing electric chair.

Ted was gone for two or three hours, maybe longer. When he finally returned and wrote on the Magic Slate, Joan knew better than to ask questions.

First they had to act as though nothing had happened while they packaged their two-year-old for the weather and left the house. In those days their stroller route followed the Midway, the strip of parkland between Fifty-ninth and Sixtieth Streets that led east along the campus toward Lake Michigan. It was right along the same Midway, not far from where Ted and Joan went walking, that Ted said a man from "one of the Russian organizations" had met and talked with him a few hours earlier. People very familiar with the episode said years later that the Soviet agent had been startled to hear that the FBI had interrogated Hall and Sax the previous spring. Even after grasping that everything was much riskier now, the agent affirmed that the Soviets wanted to resume contact with Hall. Ted's glum response reflected his certainty that he would soon be arrested. Hall asked him whether his whole family should be "picked up and transported lock, stock, and barrel to the Soviet Union."

Friends said that Joan was stunned by Ted's reprise of the conversation. The Halls had toyed with moving abroad, but they had never seriously considered Russia. At one point, she expressed curiosity about why no messenger had appeared at the Art Institute after they mailed that emergency postcard to Manhattan, and also wondered what ever happened to those two stalwart Soviet loyalists, the couple they had met in the park in 1949? By one account, Ted said he had been told, "They are safe and sound—and gone."

The Soviet agent was not proposing that the Halls leave America; not right away, at least. "The upshot of that meeting was that Ted and I must move to New York and resume our connection with them," Joan would explain to a friend. "Perhaps the rationale was that we might need them for protection, a quick getaway or something—or that since we were no longer doing political work, we might as well work for them." At least for the present, the plan was for Savy to remain in Chicago and pursue his latest dream of becoming a schoolteacher. In January 1952, Sax had finally received his B.A. in elementary education from Roosevelt College. Savy was now twenty-seven, and for once in his academic career, he had made the dean's list.

The Magic Slate message turned out to be Hall's passport into the most mysterious period in his decade of intermittent dealings with Soviet intelligence. This third stage would stretch from mid-1952 to the end of 1953, yet there is not a single known Russian document or published memoir hinting that it ever happened. What makes this all the more intriguing is that his third round of contacts with Soviet intelligence coincided with the last lap in the race between the United States and the Soviet Union to create a hydrogen bomb. Now that Fuchs was in a British prison, Hall was one of only three known Soviet assets in the West with enough knowledge of nuclear physics to comprehend a thermonuclear reaction. The two others were Hall's associates, Anta and Aden. Who Anta and Aden really were, and where they were working in the early 1950s, remains unknown.

Hall has insisted to close friends that he couldn't conceivably have helped the Soviet Union on thermonuclear weapons. He said he never worked on the H-bomb in his life, and that he never had any kind of clearance for classified research after he left Los Alamos in the spring of 1946. In Hall's view, he was nothing but a "sleeper" being held in reserve by the Soviets for the future. If he had occasional contacts with the Soviets in New York, it was only because they "kept stringing him along" in hopes that he might some day get a job with access to classified material. Hall gave this version with great conviction in at least two private conversations with friends in England in the mid-1990s. And there is no evidence to disprove him.

Yet if Soviet intelligence didn't see Ted Hall as a source of atomic intelligence, it is hard to see why clandestine meetings with him were worthwhile. By mid-1952, when the meetings began, Hall must have looked like a giant security risk to the Lubyanka. By then, Moscow had to assume the worst: If Hall and Sax had been interrogated by the FBI but not arrested, the chances were that the FBI had turned them into double agents. From Kim Philby the Soviets knew perfectly well that Arlington Hall had cracked the NKGB's wartime codes. That was enough for Moscow to deduce that the Americans probably viewed Hall and Sax as Soviet spies. How could the Harvard roommates have possibly avoided prosecution unless they had been turned by the FBI?

Viewed from the other side of the looking glass, some in the West have also wondered whether Ted Hall really did escape prosecution by becoming a double agent. "Based on how previous espionage cases have been handled, one possibility is that the authorities gave Hall immunity in return for information about the KGB," correspondent Michael Dobbs of *The Washington Post* wrote in 1996. After the Dobbs article, Hall was adamant that Western authorities had never suggested such a thing. His contention that he was never a double agent is consistent with the recollections of three FBI veterans involved in major espionage investigations of the 1950s. In separate interviews, all three said that as far as they knew, Hall never furnished information.

. . .

SOON AFTER THE Magic Slate episode, Ted Hall altered his career plan and moved as fast as possible to New York. It meant detouring from pure research at the peak of his most creative years.

After the 1951 FBI interrogation, Ted was still on a post-doctoral fellowship from the National Cancer Institute, doing research at the University of Chicago's Institute of Radiobiology and Biophysics. His academic supervisor, Ray Zirkle, was one of the most eminent radiation biologists in the country, a veteran of the early Oak Ridge radiation studies during the Manhattan Project. With Zirkle's help, Hall was trying to understand the "survival curve" for cells or chromosomes or even pieces of DNA when subjected to "hits" by radiation. The point was trying to pin down whether biological material has a cumulative sensitivity to radiation. Even after Zirkle learned that Hall was being questioned by the FBI, he encouraged him to stay on at Chicago and launch a career in academic biophysics. Instead, Ted found a bulletin board notice early in 1952 about an opening in New York for a research biophysicist at Memorial Sloan-Kettering. When he applied for the job, the FBI somehow found out. Agents in New York dropped in on one of Sloan-Kettering's top administrators, making it clear that the applicant was under a security investigation. Nonetheless, Hall was hired shortly before his Chicago research fellowship expired in June 1952. The following month he reported for work at the biophysics department of Sloan-Kettering at 410 East Sixty-eighth Street.

Ironically, Ted and Joan Hall were acting on a false premise when they moved to New York. They thought Ted couldn't refuse the Soviet agent's offer of an escape route because he was about to be arrested. But as it turns out, the FBI had just downgraded Hall from its list of the most urgent espionage suspects. The Halls never knew about a secret FBI memo written by William Branigan, chief of the FBI espionage section in Washington. In late January 1952, Branigan wrote a recommendation to his superior Al Belmont that Hall and Sax be "removed from the special section of the security index and placed in the regular section." The special section of the index was reserved for active spies and others suspected of being current security threats. When Branigan's call for reclassification of Hall and Sax was accepted, it was a signal within FBI headquarters that the espionage section saw little reason to continue aggressive surveillance.

Around the same time, the FBI returned to Saville Sax the materials seized from his house the previous March. One day, probably early in 1952, Sax is said to have shown Joan Hall exactly what the FBI had returned. She was reportedly horrified to find a packet of letters that Ted had sent to Savy while the Saxes were living in New York in 1948 and 1949. "I was absolutely furious at Savy, but Ted did not seem perturbed," Joan wrote to a friend years later. "Finally, he said angrily, 'Well, what do you want to do?' I grimly replied, 'We could kill him.' Ted said, 'Yes, why don't you just go ahead?' " What most upset Joan was Ted's letter asking Savy to inform "our friends" that he and Joan had decided to enroll in the American Communist Party. There on Savy's table was the letter, complete with Ted's embarrassing postscript: "Destroy this letter I guess." In retrospect, it seems the agents would never have returned potential trial evidence to Sax unless the FBI or Justice Department had concluded there was no chance of getting an indictment. But in 1952, this didn't occur to the Halls. For one thing, Ted Hall had deliberately refrained from discussing his legal status with an attorney. Just speaking with a lawyer would have been a sign of weakness, a signal to the FBI that they were hiding something—at least, that is how the Halls appraised their predicament in that less litigious decade.

Once Hall reached Sloan-Kettering, he slipped into comfortable obscurity. He was put to work studying whether there is a cause-and-effect relationship between the concentration of certain chemical elements in a cell and the onset of cancer. For the first three or four years, the work was slow going. Except for his post-doctoral paper left over from the University of Chicago, he published only two scientific articles between 1953 and 1956. One was a half-page long and the other two pages, and neither one attracted much attention. The main thing he reported was a method of generating the iodine 124 isotope by bombarding the element tellurium in a cyclotron—something that was a curiosity to nuclear physicists but had little to do with Sloan-Kettering's cancer research.

Obscurity was just what the Halls wanted in the 1950s. After the first scorchingly hot summer in their un-air-conditioned apartment at Sixty-eighth Street and Second Avenue, they moved in the fall of 1952 to a garden apartment on Main Street in Flushing, Queens. Ted commuted forty-five minutes by subway to Sloan-Kettering and Joan became an officer of their daughter's co-op nursery school. "It was a weird time," Joan Hall once wrote to a friend. "Most of the time, of course, we just got on with living—there was nothing to be gained by letting the threat gnaw our vitals and spoil our happiness. But at the back of our minds we thought of maybe leaving the United States one day."

Not long after they arrived in New York, Ted made contact with a Soviet intelligence officer who worked out of the Soviet UN mission. Joan and Ted later told friends about how tense they felt the day they approached a meeting with a Soviet near the Coney Island amusement park. As best the chronology can be pieced together, the Coney Island encounter took place in the summer of 1952. One detail that stuck in Ted's mind is that someone stole their parking place as he and Joan were about to park their Chevy near the amusement park. Joan wanted to argue with the driver, but Ted cut her off, saying it was hardly a time to be noticed. Ted's stomach had been tormenting him all day, he'd even been throwing up, but he felt the meeting had to go ahead. While Joan waited at the car, Hall found the Soviet around the corner.

That clandestine session led to another, and then another. "I seem to remember little isolated episodes where I traveled to this part of New York City or that part," Ted Hall later told a friend. He met the Soviets quite infrequently, perhaps every six months or so, as though his controllers simply wanted to see if he was safe from the FBI. Typically, their talks lasted only a few minutes, not long enough for real conversation. Hall and his main contact, "Jimmy Stevens," agreed to a mechanism for arranging impromptu meetings without using the telephone. "They had a system of writing a signal, maybe it was the number ten, on a poster in the subway," said Ted's friend. "It was in a station on the Eighth Avenue line, the third poster from the stairs or something like that." After the Coney Island meeting, there may have been no more than three or four more meetings between Hall and the Soviets over the next two years. One was in Queens just off the Van Wyck Expressway, somewhere between Jamaica and Idlewild Airport (since renamed after John F. Kennedy). Another meeting was in a black neighborhood in the Bronx. That time, there were only three white people on the street: Hall and the two Soviet agents who met him. "I don't know how they picked these crazy sites," the friend remembered Hall saying. "This one [in the Bronx] seemed absolutely mad."

Along with almost all New York City leftists, the Halls believed the defining issue of the 1950s was how to save Julius and Ethel Rosenberg. Because of Ted's clandestine connection, the Halls couldn't attend the rally in the theater district when Paul Robeson, Ruby Dee, and Rockwell Kent collected thousands of dollars for the National Committee to Secure Justice in the Rosenberg Case. Nor could they join the chartered eight-car train that ferried protesters to Ossining to a Rosenberg rally over Christmas of 1952. Ted Hall was gripped by guilt as the date of the Rosenbergs' execution neared. He and Joan debated whether he shouldn't try to do something to derail the government case. When President Eisenhower denied clemency in February 1953, the cause of Julius and Ethel began to look hopeless.

Ever more conscience-stricken, Ted Hall went against Joan's objections and made a poignant offer to his Soviet control officer: "You know, if it comes to that, perhaps I should give myself up and say, 'Don't pin it all on the Rosenbergs because I was more responsible than they were.' " Long afterward, Ted Hall said to a friend, "Yes, I meant it. I would have done it, I felt that strongly about it. But he felt it wasn't a good idea at all," he said of his Soviet contact. "And so it came to nothing."

By bizarre happenstance, the Halls were driving within a few miles of death row on June 19, 1953. "The road went right by Sing Sing prison, where the Rosenbergs were electrocuted at sunset, around 8 o'clock," Joan remembered. They were heading to a dinner party at the home of Ted's Sloan-Kettering department head. "The sun was setting as we drove past the prison, glowing huge and red on the horizon across the Hudson River," she said, "and the car radio happened to be playing the last movement of Mahler's Ninth Symphony. We drove along without speaking, stunned and desolate."

Julius was electrocuted at 8:06 P.M. and Ethel a few minutes later. The Halls drove on to their dinner party, where they had to go through an evening of small talk without letting on how devastated they felt. "We were painfully aware that there, but for some inexplicable grace, went we," Joan much later wrote to a friend. "Julius and Ethel could so easily have been Ted and Joan; Michael and Robbie [the Rosenbergs' children] could have been our little girl. And Ted would have been forced to claim innocence just as they did."

VIEWED FROM THE perspective of the Lubyanka and the Kremlin, the effort to save the Rosenbergs was a sideshow. The really important campaign of that decade was the Soviet Union's drive to overtake the United States in thermonuclear weapons. On November 1, 1952, the Americans pulled dangerously ahead when they detonated the world's first thermonuclear device, the nine-megaton "Mike" test at Eniwetok, an atoll in the Pacific. But once again, the Soviet Union caught up much faster than the CIA predicted. Avram Zavenyagin, a Soviet intelligence

Top left: Theodore Hall at age thirteen, in his bar mitzvah photo. *(courtesy Theodore Hall)* *Left:* Hall at sixteen, the whiz already a junior at Harvard. *(courtesy Theodore Hall)* *Top:* At home in Forest Hills, New York, c. 1943. From left: Ted Hall; his sister Frances Holtzberg; his father and mother, Barney and Rose Holtzberg. *(courtesy Theodore Hall)* *Bottom left:* Hall at a Chicago park in 1947 *(courtesy Theodore Hall)* *Bottom right:* Hall with his first daughter, also in Chicago, c. 1950–51, *(courtesy Theodore Hall)*

Morris Cohen (on right in family photo, c. 1930)
accepted the principles of communism held by his parents,
though his brother did not. *(Russian Foreign Intelligence Agency)*

Morris Cohen, c. 1941, was recruited as a spy for the Soviet Union
and soon convinced his wife Lona, shown in a 1943 picture,
to become a Soviet agent too. *(courtesy of the Cohen family)*

Left: NKGB officer Semyon Semyonov was the Cohen's first spy controller in New York. *(Russian Foreign Intelligence Agency)*
Middle: Soviet diplomat Stepan Apresyan, the NKGB station chief in New York. *(National Security Agency)* *Right:* Alexander Feklisov, also an NKGB undercover officer at the Soviet consulate in New York. *(Russian Foreign Intelligence Agency)*

Anatoly Yatskov (on right) was a family man but also a spy who took over part of Semyonov's network. *(courtesy of the Yatskov family)*

Top: Saville Sax, his bride Susan and their mothers on their wedding day in April 1948. *(courtesy Sarah Sax)*

Left: Ted Hall, looking the disgruntled soldier in Santa Fe, 1945. *(courtesy Theodore Hall)*

Bottom: Los Alamos Technical Building 412, an isolated cabin of the sort where Hall conducted Ra-La static experiments in 1945. *(Los Alamos National Laboratory)*

TOP SECRET

USSR

Ref. No:

Issued: 25/4/1961

Copy No: 204

DECISION TO MAINTAIN CONTACT WITH THEODORE HALL (1944)

From: NEW YORK

To: MOSCOW

No: 1585   12 Nov. 44

To VIKTOR.[i]

BEK[ii] visited Theodore HALL[TEODOR KhOLL],[iii] 19 years old, the son of a furrier. He is a graduate of HARVARD University. As a talented physicist he was taken on for government work. He was a GYMNAST[FIZKUL'TURNIK][iv] and conducted work in the Steel Founders' Union.[a] According to BEK's account HALL has an exceptionally keen mind and a broad outlook, and is politically developed. At the present time H. is in charge of a group at "CAMP-2"[v] (SANTA-FE). H. handed over to BEK a report about the CAMP and named the key personnel employed on ENORMOUS.[vi] He decided to do this on the advice of his colleague Saville SAX[SAVIL SAKS],[vii] a GYMNAST living in TYRE.[viii] SAX's mother is a FELLOWCOUNTRYMAN[ZEMLYaK][ix] and works for RUSSIAN WAR RELIEF. With the aim of hastening a meeting with a competent person, H. on the following day sent a copy of the report by S. to the PLANT[ZAVOD].[x] ALEKSEJ[xi] received S. H. had to leave for CAMP-2 in two days' time. He[b] was compelled to make a decision quickly. Jointly with MAY[MAJ],[xii] he gave BEK consent to feel out H., to assure him that everything was in order and to arrange liaison with him. H. left his photograph and came to an understanding with BEK about a place for meeting him. BEK met S. [1 group garbled] our automobile. We consider it expedient to maintain liaison with H. [1 group unidentified] through S. and not to bring in anybody else. MAY has no objection to this. We shall send the details by post.

No. 897   [Signature missing]
11th November

Top: A Ra-La bomb mockup at Los Alamos from 1947, very similar to the devices Hall and others in Rossi's group used in 1944–45. (Los Alamos National Laboratory) Bottom: U.S. Army codebreakers got their clearest lead ever to an American spy when they deciphered this November 12, 1944 Soviet cable reporting the recruitment of Hall and Sax. (National Security Agency / Central Intelligence Agency)

Top left: Army codebreakers at work in the mid-1940s, including the
legendary Meredith Gardner (second row, at left). *(National Security Agency)*
Top right: Codebreaker Cecil Phillips, c. 1946. *(National Security Agency)*

Arlington Hall, c. 1942, the former girls' school outside
of Washington, D.C., that was transformed into the headquarters for the
U.S. Army codebreakers. *(National Security Agency)*

Top left: Lavrenti Beria, who masterminded Soviet internal and external intelligence for Stalin, also was put in charge of the Soviet atom bomb development program in 1945. *(Russian Foreign Intelligence Agency) Left:* NKGB intelligence chief Vsevolod Merkulov informed Beria of the secret of implosion in February 1945. *(Russian Foreign Intelligence Agency) Above:* NKGB officer Yuri Sokolov, who masqueraded as a Soviet diplomat in New York, with his daughters on Long Island, New York, c. 1949. *(courtesy of the Sokolov family)*

The most important Soviet intelligence officer ever convicted in America, Colonel Rudolf Abel. *(courtesy UPI/Corbis-Bettmann)*

Left: Ted Hall, c. 1990, retired in Britain
and assumed he had finally outlived the
danger that his espionage would be discovered.
(courtesy Theodore Hall)

Top: Morris and Lona Cohen (c. 1970) finished their
intelligence careers in Moscow, training young Soviet
officers. *(Russian Foreign Intelligence Agency)*

Bottom: The American Fat Man bomb.
(Los Alamos National Laboratory)

official and deputy head of the atomic project, gave the Central Committee plenum a preview in July 1953: "[Our] hydrogen bomb is tens of times more powerful than an ordinary atomic bomb, and its explosion will mean the end of a second monopoly for the Americans." A month later, Zavenyagin proved his point when the Soviets exploded what *Pravda* and *Izvestia* openly called "one of the types of hydrogen bomb." Using lithium deuteride as a booster, the Soviet bomb designers had managed to achieve a yield of 400 kilotons, more than thirty times as strong as the Hiroshima bomb. The Soviets had exploded a boosted fission bomb, not a full-fledged thermonuclear weapon. Nonetheless, U.S. intelligence realized the Soviets were on the right track because traces of the thermonuclear fuel tritium were found in rain samples.

Not long afterward, Ted Hall reportedly held one of his most important meetings with Jimmy Stevens. It was the only time Ted had ever met the Soviet agent long enough for a real conversation. They discussed what both saw as the dangers of an American nuclear monopoly, with Stevens echoing fears that had troubled Ted since Los Alamos. As long as the Soviet Union was behind in the arms race, the agent said, the Americans could always issue a nuclear ultimatum. Had it not been for the Soviet bomb, the Americans might have even tried to abort the 1949 Chinese revolution, the agent told Hall; it was a "good thing that the world had made it through" this dangerously unstable period.

The meeting after the 1953 Soviet bomb test was one factor that helped Hall decide to break off contacts with the Soviets—just as he had done a few months after the first Soviet atomic bomb test in 1949. Another factor that was probably more decisive was that the threat of FBI arrest seemed to have receded. There were no more signs of surveillance squads, no more interrogations, no indications that their phones were tapped. Then, too, the Halls were thinking of making a permanent home. In the fall of 1953, Joan learned that she was again pregnant. At his next meeting with his Soviet contact, Ted broke the news that he was quitting the network—this time forever. The following year the Halls moved into a $14,000, two-bedroom house in a new development on the edge of affluent Greenwich, Connecticut.

"I just said good-bye," Ted told friends later, recounting that last meeting with the Soviet. "He said, 'All right, if that is how you feel about it. Thank you very much for all that you have done. We have no guns. We wish you the best.' "

. . .

JUST AS TED Hall was leaving the network, the FBI field office in New York was beginning to investigate a new lead that potentially could break the Volunteers ring wide open.

Three blocks from Hall's office at Sloan-Kettering, a team from the FBI anti-communist squad was going door-to-door trying to find "a very radical Communist" named Morris Cohen. The FBI had been told that Cohen was an Abraham Lincoln Brigade veteran and that he had lived until 1950 in an apartment around East Seventy-first Street and Second Avenue. An informant "of unknown reliability" had reported that Morris Cohen and his wife, Lona, "had Communist Party meetings in their home." The tipster said nothing about the Volunteers network, let alone about the Cohens' flight to Moscow. All the same, the FBI opened an investigation on October 14, 1953.

Agents found that Morris had no New York police record. But through his employment record with the New York Board of Education, they found that he had played football in the Bronx, gone to college in Mississippi, and later worked in a cafeteria. From the Veterans Administration came evidence that he had soldiered in World War II. The investigation spread to California after the FBI found a witness who remembered Morris saying he was leaving in 1950 for a job on the coast. Other agents were dispatched to rural Connecticut to check Lona's background; nobody knew where she was.

When no sign of the Cohens turned up for more than a year, the FBI ordered a mail cover on the apartment of Morris Cohen's father at 2020 Walton Avenue in the Bronx. Agents found that nobody was cashing the $15.75 disability checks that were arriving for Morris Cohen every month from the Veterans Administration. When the FBI called on Cohen's father, he insisted he didn't know where Morris and Lona had gone. Morris had always been "a fine son and a good boy," Harry Cohen lamented to one agent. After a year and a half of sporadic checking produced nothing more, the FBI lost interest. "It is felt . . . that no further investigation is warranted at this time," the special agent in charge of the New York Field Office wrote to Hoover on October 19, 1956. With that, the FBI closed its investigation into the missing "radical Communist," never guessing that he was a spy.

Three blocks from the Cohens' old apartment, Ted Hall continued his cancer research at Sloan-Kettering, feeling more secure than ever. Even though the FBI had apparently stopped scrutinizing Hall, he did everything possible to avoid attention. When he was asked to write his biography for the 1955 edition of *American Men of Science,* Ted fully described his education and his biophysics career, but omitted the wartime years he had worked for the Manhattan Project.

By then, Los Alamos was a phase of life Ted didn't feel like remembering. And he certainly didn't want to have it remembered by anybody else.

CHAPTER 26

Up to the Hilt

While the FBI was hunting from New York to California for Morris and Lona Cohen, the two were far beyond the reach of the dragnet. Their harrowing escape across ten countries ended in Moscow in November 1950. Then their Soviet sponsors sent them to Poland to be trained in the fine points of spycraft. After learning about microdots and radio transmission, the Cohens set out to travel in 1954, partly getting the feel of Europe and partly on spy business. The following year Moscow Centre sent them all the way to Hong Kong and Tokyo for reasons still unknown. By the time the New York FBI was closing the books on Morris and Lona Cohen, they were well established as illegal Soviet communications specialists in the leafy London suburb of Ruislip, under the guise of antiquarian bookseller Peter Kroger and his chatty wife, Helen.

One man in America who knew what the Cohens had been up to was Rudolf Abel. He had become their friend in the more than seven months they had worked together. Abel missed his wife and daughter back in the Soviet Union; somehow he clicked with the Cohens. They knew him as "Milt," and they socialized as well as spied. There had been the New Year's Day dinner at the Cohens' East Seventy-first Street apartment, for example, when Lona roasted a goose because it was Abel's favorite. As guest of honor, Abel carved, but somehow as he stuck in a fork the bird flew off the table, up against the newly repapered wall, and onto the floor. They ate it anyway. When the Cohens had to leave for the Soviet Union, he missed his close friends. From the Cohens' point of view, the Abel connection would turn out to be a bit too close.

Abel had continued working from his New York base after the uproar surrounding Fuchs, Gold, and the Rosenbergs quieted. Unluckily for Abel, the young ethnic Finn whom Moscow Centre sent to be his assistant in the fall of 1952 didn't like the work or the boss. After nearly five unproductive years, Abel dispatched Reino Hayhanen back to Moscow for a vacation that the deputy rightly sensed would be anything but. Hayhanen's defection midway home—at the American Embassy in Paris—led to the arrest on June 21, 1957, of Abel, the boss Hayhanen knew only as "Mark." At first the U.S. Immigration and Naturalization Service detained him in Texas as an illegal alien, but Abel later was indicted on charges of conspiracy to gather and transmit military information to the Soviet Union.

The New York trial was a sensation. Unlike earlier cases, this was a real Soviet spy sitting at the American hearth at a time when cold warriors were warning that the Soviet Union was intent on destroying America. The tall, thin man with balding head and spectacles, a.k.a. Emil Goldfus, Martin Collins, Milton, and Mark, was a colonel in the KGB. The appropriate accoutrements had been found in his room and Brooklyn Heights art studio: hollowed-out flashlight batteries for concealing information, a cipher pad for encrypting messages, a birth certificate for Martin Collins that an expert witness said was forged. One diligent trial watcher described the tenor of the publicity: "Everyone was happy those days, for it had been proven that there really were spies and subversives under every mattress. Anti-communism, vindicated, with a clean bill of health: We were not paranoid. The menace was real." Jurors had no trouble believing this worn-looking photographer and artist was a primary agent of forces trying to destroy their country. Abel was convicted, and on November 15, 1957, sentenced to thirty years in prison on conspiracy charges, although the prosecution never even alleged that he succeeded in completing any specific act of espionage.

Abel's trial stirred much of America, but it evoked little interest from two Americans who had a personal stake in his continued silence. There is reason to believe Ted and Joan Hall dimly recognized newspaper photographs of the "elegant Russian" they met in a park one night after sundown in 1949. Perhaps they read press reports that Abel wasn't talking and were confident he never would break, never would unravel the strands of his network for the FBI. For whatever reason, the Halls didn't return to their Soviet contacts for protection as they had in 1952. Once they left the network and moved to Greenwich, they felt far removed from the spectacle playing out at the Brooklyn federal court.

The Halls might have taken more interest had they known of the investigation Hoover spun off from the Abel arrest. Much of the evidence that persuaded him Abel was a leading Soviet spy was not disclosed at the time. It included a safe-deposit box with $15,000 in four bundles, to which Abel held the keys. In the dumpy Latham Hotel room on East Twenty-eighth Street where Abel was arrested, agents found a similar cache of $4,000, also wrapped in plain brown paper. But this bundle had two photographs slipped under the flap. Abel told the authorities that the man and woman pictured were a married couple he met in a New York park in 1949 and saw occasionally at museums or parks or restaurants. They talked about literature and art, he said. But the FBI couldn't help being suspicious about the strange phrases written on the backs of the photographs. "How are Joann's murders?" were the words on the woman's picture, and "Have you taken a trip to Frisco since we last saw you?" was written on the man's. Abel knew the couple only as "Shirley" and "Morris," he said. Within weeks, the FBI identified them as the missing Lona and Morris Cohen.

Interrogated days after his arrest at the INS Detention Facility in McAllen, Texas, Abel had an explanation. "Joann's murders" was a reference to his penchant for detective stories; the Frisco trip related to his having told his friends of plans to travel to San Francisco. He kept the photos simply because they were the only pictures anyone ever gave him in the United States.

The FBI quickly surmised a different explanation:

> The fact that "Mark" had 2 photographs in the $4,000 package in his hotel room would indicate a connection between these individuals and the money. It is possible this money was to be turned over to them through a cutout [a third party] and the writing on the back of each was part of a parole to be used for identification purposes. The disappearance of the Cohens . . . might indicate they became a part of "Mark's" network at that time and left New York City to take up residence in another part of the state or the country to further the business of the network.

The investigation was reopened now that the Cohens were suspected as more than simply communists. By August 15, a memorandum from Hoover told agents to handle this case as a "special" and to pursue all leads "on a five-day deadline basis." One of the main reasons for urgency was that the Cohens had disappeared almost exactly when David Greenglass was arrested, a fact that Hoover said "may indicate they may have been involved in the Rosenberg network." The FBI knew nothing of the Volunteers but had caught the scent of espionage.

Agents went back to visit many of the same friends, neighbors, and relatives they had questioned in the first phase of the Morris Cohen investigation, which had closed less than a year earlier. They also tried other avenues; one of the few relevant witnesses they unearthed was a friend who said he had met Abel at a February 1950 dinner party given by the Cohens, when they introduced him as their British friend Milton. Other than that, agents found Morris hadn't attended the funeral of either parent, nor had he ever claimed the inheritance his father, Harry, left him. David Greenglass and Harry Gold, separately shown the Cohens' pictures by agents visiting them in prison, said they had never heard of the Cohens. Investigators learned that Quartermaster Company C served Private 1st Class Morris Cohen roast turkey with giblet gravy for Christmas dinner in 1942, but found nothing to point to his current whereabouts.

Sometime after the Cohens' case was reopened in 1957, FBI agent Robert Beatson sat on a wiretap and occasionally helped track down a clue. After a year of listening, he was assigned to be lead agent on what he remembered had become "an 'old-dog case,'" namely a case in which there is very little hope of anything happening." He said he inherited the case from "a couple of real tigers" who had covered lots of ground without digging up any startling evidence. One thing they had found was the Cohens' fingerprints—his from Army records and hers from one of her war-plant jobs—and sent copies to police around the world. "There was a lot of good-natured joking going on in New York—'Boy oh boy, that's like throwing a stone at the moon.' I mean, what are the chances of anything happening from that? Slim and none," Beatson recalled thinking. There wasn't a lot left to do when Beatson got the case; this wouldn't be like the time Beatson and his partner searched Abel's hotel room and right away hit the mother lode in the wastebasket: the KGB cipher pad. Beatson was so determined not to miss anything that he recovered old ground and plowed some new—even arranging for an agent from Detroit to interview Hank Greenberg about his recollections of Morris at James Monroe High. Nothing changed the end result: Either nobody knew where the Cohens were, or nobody was talking.

. . .

OUT IN GREENWICH, the Halls were blithely unaware of the Abel-Cohens tempest. A second baby had been born just before their move from Flushing, and a third followed in 1958. The Halls had chosen Greenwich because they preferred not to live where many of their Jewish friends lived—in the upper-middle-class suburbs west of the Hudson. As Joan would explain, "We hated what we saw as the chauvinism or elitism of our Jewish friends, who kept trying to co-opt us into a set of attitudes we did not share (with overtones of Zionism). We thought we would be happier in a mainstream kind of environment." But waspy Greenwich meant culture shock for Joan, who wanted neither to play bridge nor to become a Republican. She had her babies and her home, and that was enough to keep her occupied for a while. Politically the Halls did no more than subscribe to a couple of leftist publications, *The Guardian* and *Monthly Review.*

Ted had his work at Sloan-Kettering, and occasionally there was also a bit of news from Ted's brother. Ed Hall was now a full colonel in the Air Force, designing rocket engines in California. Because Ed's work was all top secret, Ted and Joan said they didn't know much—except that the government had given him the 1955 Goddard Award, a prize for pioneers of rocketry. They said it was only after Ed retired that they learned he'd been designing the liquid-fueled Atlas and the Thor, then become program director and chief engineer of the first American solid-fueled ICBM, the Minuteman.

From their vantage point in Greenwich, Ted and Joan Hall got inklings that the wholesale assault against left-wingers was beginning to ease up, and by the summer of 1959 they even felt comfortable enough to walk into the exhibition of Soviet achievements and technology at the New York Coliseum at Columbus Circle in Manhattan. They wanted to see the face the Soviets were showing to the world after Nikita Khrushchev's denunciation of Stalin at the Twentieth Party Congress.

It turned out some things didn't change: Soviet intelligence made another pass at Ted. This Soviet was on the exhibition staff, supposedly just a young student lucky enough to be studying medical technology in New York. At least two young undercover officers of the KGB (as the NKGB was now called) and one from GRU military intelligence worked at the exhibition. Whoever the student was, he called himself Leonid Petrov and chatted up the Halls. They found him appealing, and

Ted arranged to meet again one afternoon in a park near the exhibition, hoping to learn more about the country that the Halls thought had a go at making a decent society. When Leonid Petrov showed up, he pulled out a piece of KGB signature jewelry like the tie clip Sax had brought back to Chicago in 1948. Hall was startled. By this second meeting, the Soviet obviously had been briefed by one of his bosses about the earlier contacts and wanted to know if Ted wouldn't like to come back into service. No thanks, Hall said with some vehemence, that phase of his life was done. "I have to ask you if you need any money," Petrov interjected, to which Hall said no even more vehemently. Yet Hall agreed to a third meeting, so long as Petrov agreed it would be purely social. Both Halls subsequently had dinner with Petrov, at the Russian Tea Room by one account, and the trio reportedly talked about music and the Soviet Union, about the young man's apartment in Moscow, and about a student's life in New York. The final word on espionage was Petrov's genial riposte: "Okay, we've lost you as an agent. We don't want to lose you as a friend."

IT WASN'T UNTIL early 1961 that one of the many lines the FBI had flung out for the Cohens finally got a strike. "It just made you realize the amazing power of something like fingerprints," Beatson said. Without the fingerprints circulated around the world by the FBI, the British MI-5 would never have discovered that this American pair had been masquerading for six years as Peter and Helen Kroger. According to their passports the Krogers were two New Zealanders; their Ruislip neighbors thought they were a nice Canadian couple. MI-5 had just arrested the Krogers as part of a Soviet spy ring, which had been caught sneaking submarine technology out of the Portland naval research base for delivery to Moscow.

Lona and Morris Cohen had turned out to be masters at their job. Not only had they conquered the fine points of creating microdots, making successful drops, photographing stolen documents, and operating a high-speed radio transmitter, they had also turned themselves into the apolitical, slightly eccentric Krogers, making friends and running a profitable antiquarian bookselling business.

Peter Kroger clearly didn't have a clue about the rare-book business when he opened his shop opposite St. Clement Danes Church in London. "They took him for a ride," acknowledged fellow bookseller Fred Snelling, recalling his friend's early deals with the sophisticated selling crowd. But Kroger specialized in Americana and plugged on till he learned the trade well enough to fit himself into the tight circle of English antiquarian dealers. They even invited him to play on their Bibliomites cricket team. What the other Bibliomites didn't know was that literate, hard-working Peter was mailing antique volumes hiding stolen information in microdots and disappearing ink to certain clients.

Helen Kroger was the loving wife who nipped a bit too much gin, but was exceedingly friendly and generous, especially with children in the quiet neighborhood of single-family homes thirty miles northwest of London. One neighborhood girl, Gay Search, was to describe Helen as "an exotic creature" in gray post-war Britain, a woman who not only wore trousers and could whistle like a stevedore, but offered her young friend forbidden fruits—false fingernails painted scarlet. Gay Search's mother, Ruth, chatted almost daily with Helen and sometimes talked art with the clearly more intellectual Peter Kroger. Ruth sent over baked goods—Helen was reputed to be an awful cook—and once made a black velvet hat for her close friend from Canada. One strange note was that the Krogers would "get utterly frantic" if one or the other was late coming home, Search said. Her parents attributed it to their being childless and having only each other to rely upon. "They were obviously both very frightened that one of them would be picked up," she later concluded.

When the Krogers did get picked up by MI-5 on January 7, 1961, the news jolted their friends and on a broader scale the complacent British public. "They had been such open, careless, easy, relaxed people," recalled Sheila Wheeler, the daughter of a bookseller friend. The notion that Helen manipulated elaborate communications and photographic equipment seemed ludicrous, since the neighbors used to tease her for zealously shooting snapshots that cut off heads or feet or slanted a perfectly normal horizon. "If ever you have met two people who seemed so totally transparent, to the point of naïveté, it was those two," said Wheeler. The fenced bungalow with apple trees in back could have housed anybody's neighbor—that's what shocked average Britons who read about the "spy nest" in a cozy suburb. Who else's neighbor could also be concealing a radio transmitter in a hole under the fridge?

The seemingly innocent Krogers/Cohens got caught not because they stepped outside their careful disguise but because their colleagues in crime were discovered. The initial tip-off to British intelligence was routed through the CIA, which had been receiving unsigned letters from a source called "Sniper," who was assumed to be a disgruntled official in Polish intelligence. Sniper told of a Royal Navy clerk who had supplied secrets to the Poles back in 1952, when he had been assigned to the British Embassy in Warsaw. Now, the source said, this same Englishman had returned home to Britain, was working in naval intelligence, and was reporting to the KGB. By the spring of 1960, MI-5 had identified a suspect: retired Chief Petty Officer Harry Houghton, now a clerk at the Portland Underwater Weapons Establishment, where Britain's first nuclear-powered submarine was being perfected.

After weeks of surveillance, the hard-drinking Houghton and his girlfriend, Ethel "Bunty" Gee, another civil servant working at Portland, led watchers to London, where they met the man who would turn out to be their KGB contact and the chief "illegal" in Britain. Dashing Gordon Lonsdale, whom Houghton knew as "Alec Johnson," passed a small envelope to Houghton, and in return he handed over a bag. Lonsdale, supposedly a Canadian businessman, was also put under surveillance. When Lonsdale left on a trip to the Continent, MI-5 penetrated his safe-deposit box and found a Ronson lighter with a one-time cipher pad concealed in the base, a Minox miniature camera, and enough other paraphernalia to convince them this was "a full-blown KGB operation." After that, it was simply a question of time. Authorities put a watch on Bunty Gee and became convinced she took home with her one night a drawing marked "Secret," depicting a sonar array of the atomic submarine H.M.S. *Dreadnought*. There were more London meetings with Lonsdale to observe. Then came the discovery that Lonsdale was a frequent visitor to a certain bungalow in Ruislip.

Lona and Morris Cohen, alias the Krogers, had become quite fond of Lonsdale, whom they called Ben. The relationship was not unlike their earlier friendship with Abel, except that they worked in closer contact with this thirty-seven-year-old comrade-in-espionage and ebullient ladies' man. It was Ben who helped them expand the small cellar-like space under the Ruislip kitchen, lining it with concrete and then covering the floor with new linoleum. Together they put wheels on the refrigerator so Lona could move it by herself, to get to the trapdoor and the transmitter they stashed underneath. "I had to go down, because I was thin," Lona remembered. There would be long nights in the bungalow when Lona and Ben did the tedious work of photographing documents and turning them into microdots that Morris would send out of the country hidden in a book or even under a stamp.

To be sure which house Lonsdale was visiting, MI-5 posted full-time agents across the street from 45 Cranley Drive in the home of Gay

Search's family. The agents didn't reveal that they were hunting evidence against the Krogers, saying only that a mysterious Soviet spy was believed to be visiting someone. Evidence has since suggested the authorities knew exactly where Lonsdale was going, but they needed to chronicle his visits and feared these neighbors—these friends—might be unwilling to help ensnare the Krogers. To the Search family, it quickly became apparent who was under surveillance, and Gay's mother, Ruth, had to endure a two-month charade at MI-5's behest. "I think what she was asked to do was criminal," said Gay Search, still angry more than thirty years later. Ruth still visited almost daily with Helen; then, as a proper and patriotic Britisher, Ruth Search fixed tea for the agents staring all day out the upstairs bedroom window at her friends' house. Gay Search believed the stress led to the early death of her mother, who agonized over her part in the Krogers' arrest.

On January 7, 1961, Houghton, Gee, and Lonsdale were finally arrested as the two Britons were passing documents to their Soviet contact outside the Old Vic theater. Helen and Peter Kroger were picked up the same day in their Cranley Drive home, charged with conspiring to violate the Official Secrets Act.

Shortly after, Lonsdale and Morris Cohen had a chance to talk when they were put in side-by-side cells. "He said, 'Let's pull a Milt on them,'" Morris related much later. "Milt meant M-I-L-T, Milton. He knew that our name for Abel, Rudolph Ivanovich, was Milt. Pulling a Milt meant that we would say nothing. So that we said nothing at all about any of these activities, see. Nothing at all." That is what Abel had done at his trial in America, said nothing.

In this case, though, it meant Lonsdale was going to take the blame while his friends feigned ignorance. Morris objected. "He argued, argued, argued, and finally I gave in. I said, All right, we'll do it, we'll pull a Milt," Morris recalled. Neither the Cohens nor Lonsdale testified, and in the end a jury took one hour and twenty-three minutes to convict all three.

Questions still cloak the activities of the Krogers/Cohens and Lonsdale (whose real name, according to his Soviet intelligence biography, was Konon Molody). What did the Cohens do on their travels to Japan, Hong Kong, Spain, and elsewhere? What other information did they transmit besides the Portland naval data? The 1995 KGB biographies of both Lona and Morris Cohen lauded them for providing unspecified but highly valued rocket information obtained in Great Britain. In addition, the best-selling memoir by retired British intelligence executive Peter Wright raised questions about whether Lonsdale, at least, had been warned that MI-5 was onto him. Did Lonsdale sacrifice himself and the others rather than reveal that the Soviets had a British mole—a still undiscovered source within MI-5 itself—who tipped them to the investigation? At least according to Wright, the answer was a painful yes.

Another of the mysteries that remains goes back even further, to why Rudolf Abel was carrying photographs of Lona and Morris Cohen seven years after they stopped working with him. Nearly forty years later, veterans of the old KGB, including some of Abel's colleagues, still sounded puzzled. Everyone questioned considered his possession of the pictures to be unacceptable spycraft, an indiscretion out of character for the meticulous Abel. "That's what gave us away," Lona Cohen remarked many years later with no bitterness toward her friend. "Otherwise they would never have known that there was any connection between Abel and us. Abel made the mistake. He should have gotten rid of the pictures. It's the little mistakes like that that can catch you."

At the close of their 1961 trial, Lonsdale made an unsworn statement in which he tried to take the full blame. The Krogers were unwitting accomplices, he claimed, friends who kept his cameras and valuables because he lived in an insecure hotel apartment. They had him house-sit in Ruislip while they traveled, he said, and he had secreted all this incriminating equipment in their home without their knowledge—the cipher pads, false-bottomed cigarette lighter, and fake passports.

Lonsdale's story might have caused Lord Parker, the lord chief justice at Old Bailey Central Criminal Court, to wonder about the role of Helen and Peter Kroger, had it not been for the FBI's fingerprints identifing them as the Cohens and connecting them to Abel. This background on the Cohens/Krogers convinced Lord Parker "that you both are in this up to the hilt, that you both are professional spies."

On March 22, 1961, Lord Parker sentenced Lonsdale to twenty-five years, the Krogers to twenty years each, and Houghton and Gee to fifteen years each. These were the harshest sentences ever meted out for peacetime espionage in Britain.

CHAPTER 27

Lasting Contribution

An article he published in the summer of 1961 signaled Theodore Hall's rise toward wider recognition as a scientist. At the age of thirty-five, he had finally outlived his connection with the Volunteers—or so he thought.

His piece for the journal *Science* helped him return to academia at the legendary British physics laboratory known as the "nursery of genius." There, in the same room at Cambridge University where J. J. Thomson had discovered the electron, Hall was to reach his most productive stage as a scientist and achieve world stature in his field of biological microanalysis.

"Only a few chemical elements are abundant in living materials," Hall began. In eight lucid pages, he described what had occupied his mind most of the last nine years at Sloan-Kettering. Borrowing techniques from nuclear physics to solve problems in cell biology, he had developed a technique of X-ray microanalysis to measure the concentrations of zinc or other minor components in minute biological specimens. He began working on this problem around the same time urologists at Sloan-Kettering became curious about why the concentration of zinc is typically ten times higher in a human prostate gland than in other soft tissues such as the kidney. It might be possible to control prostate cancer by injecting a zinc-binding chemical in order to manipulate the organ's zinc concentration, the urologists speculated. Hall's procedure modified an existing technique that involved training an X-ray beam on a minute specimen of tissue and analyzing the resulting fluorescent X rays. Using a set of equations he had devised, Hall was able to deduce the concentrations of chemical elements from the fluorescence spectra emitted by the specimens.

During the late fifties, some specialists learned of Hall's method from two early accounts that he published in technical books aimed at physicists. Now in his 1961 article, he explained his technique to a broader audience. To analyze delicate organic matter, he had mounted sections of quench-frozen tissue on very fine strips of nylon. "Even the widely used ¼ mil Mylar film [1/4,000 of an inch thick] would produce an intolerable background," he wrote. Instead, Hall employed home-made single-layer nylon films no more than 1/100,000 of an inch thick. To the disappointment of the Sloan-Kettering urologists, zinc did not prove to be the key to prostatic cancer. But Hall's method had successfully determined the concentrations; he had evolved a technique that would measure many of the trace elements that biologists wanted to analyze.

By the time the *Science* article appeared, Hall was looking for another position—perhaps one that would take the family overseas. Foreign travel had been impossible up to then because of their former Communist Party membership. There had been a period in the early 1950s when Congress made it illegal for Americans to leave the Western Hemisphere without a passport. The State Department followed up by denying passports to known communists and many other leftists, including the singer Paul Robeson and the philosopher Corliss Lamont. But now the Supreme Court had cleared the way for the Halls to get passports. Rockwell Kent, the artist and book illustrator who was one of the icons of the Old Left, had trailblazed the way by pressing an appeal after the State Department refused him a passport to attend a pro-Soviet peace conference in Finland. Kent had refused to say whether he had ever been a communist, arguing to the Supreme Court that the government had violated his First Amendment rights to gather peaceably with others. In 1958 the court ruled five to four that Kent and others like him had the right to travel. Afterward, the Halls sent Kent a victory bottle of champagne.

Once they were free to go abroad, the Halls became increasingly dissatisfied with their life in Greenwich. Besides disliking the suburban homogeneity, they found the politics of the 1950s uncomfortable. "Part of our motive, of course, was to get away at least partly from the threat that seemed to hang over us," Joan later wrote to a friend. "But also, we found the general atmosphere of the States oppressive, and we had no idea the civil rights movement was about to burst out." They were worried, too, that their oldest daughter would be unhappy in junior high school, especially now that her schoolmates were starting to go out on dates. In their perception, their eleven-year-old daughter was less mature physically and more of an intellectual than her classmates.

Simultaneously, Ted Hall was feeling a tug of professional curiosity that wasn't being satisfied at Sloan-Kettering. He was eager to work with an electron microprobe of the kind that metallurgists had been using to analyze extremely small samples. Biologists were beginning to use the $100,000 electron-probe instruments that had been developed for oil geology and other industrial applications, and Hall wanted an instrument with more sensitivity than the older X-ray probe at Sloan-Kettering. "I had developed a certain line of work at Sloan-Kettering and wanted to continue in that general field," Hall recalled. "Microanalysis of biological specimens is not the most glamorous or attractive field, but it is very solid and sound and I could reliably make a decent contribution."

Only a few universities in the world specialized in analytical electron microscopy. The two in America were Cornell and Stanford, and Hall considered applying to both. He also sent out feelers to an institution in Sweden. But his first choice was the Cavendish Laboratory at Cambridge University, so he wrote to one of the early prophets of electron microscopy, Dr. Vernon Ellis Cosslett, who had built the Cavendish into a world center of electron microscope research. Hall's letter led to a meeting with Cosslett during a conference of the New York Academy of Sciences. There followed an invitation for Hall to spend the 1962–63 academic year at the Cavendish—an invitation that would be extended and extended.

The Cavendish was a crucible where the past fused with the future. Fittingly, the laboratory was housed in a nineteenth-century neo-Gothic stone structure that blended into an architectural continuum with landmarks going back to the Middle Ages. The Cavendish was the department that taught Cambridge students physics, but it also had a reputation for nurturing outside researchers "with genius in their fingertips." With apparatus made of little more than string and beeswax, Cavendish researchers discovered the electron (1897), heavy hydrogen (1919), the neutron (1932), and the artificial splitting of the atom (1932). Since World War II, the laboratory had edged away from atom-smashing and toward solid-state physics and the inner structures of molecules of living organisms. It was there in 1953 that James Watson and Francis Crick built the first accurate model of a DNA molecule. The year

Theodore Hall joined the laboratory, Watson and Crick won a Nobel Prize for their "double helix" model. Through the 1950s, there was a quest to understand smaller and smaller bits of living tissue, making a biophysicist like Hall desirable. Ted and Joan and their three daughters crossed on the *Queen Mary* and arrived in Cambridge on July 17, 1962. At the Cavendish he inherited Thomson's lab space, along with a jury-rigged scanning electron probe that performed just about as well as the $100,000 American machines.

Hall's lasting contribution to science was conceived over the next five years in Cambridge. From the first day, he set out to find a way to map the concentration of chemical elements in thin or ultra-thin sections of biological specimens. Working with frozen sections of human arteries, Hall perfected an excruciatingly demanding technique for mapping concentrations of calcium, sulfur, and other elements. With an electron microscope, it was no challenge to determine the total quantity of an element. All that took was to measure the strength and wavelength of the X-ray signal kicked off by a beam of electrons that was bombarding the tissue sample. The real problem was measuring the element's concentration within a minute zone inside a cell. This required knowing the total mass of the tiny, irregularly shaped tissue samples, and that was much harder than it sounded. Hall published his solution in 1964, then revised it four years later in collaboration with his graduate student D. J. Marshall. The result came to be known by microbiologists as the Marshall-Hall Method, later simply the Hall Method. Colleagues scarcely ranked Hall's achievement with that of Watson and Crick, but they had little doubt that the Hall Method had filled a gap in the field of cell biology.

For Ted and Joan, the move to Britain was liberating in more than just professional ways. The Cuban missile crisis erupted that first autumn; by chance, their friend Ralph Miliband, the fiery Marxist lecturer at the London School of Economics, was visiting them. Miliband must have emboldened them. With nuclear war looming between the Soviet Union and America, Hall felt safe enough to take his two oldest daughters to a Cambridge peace demonstration, his first overtly political act in a decade. Joan was equally inspired by the life in Cambridge. "The atmosphere seemed so free—nobody telling you what to think, what to wear, to go to church," Joan wrote to a friend. "I was thrilled to see Africans, probably academics, walking around in gorgeous robes, tall and elegant and proud and without the rather downtrodden, defensive and suspicious look we saw in Black people in the States. We felt very anti-American. We didn't like to see signs of American presence in Cambridge. We wanted to be the only ones, I guess."

With her youngest daughter in kindergarten, Joan Hall resumed her education at Cambridge. She was on her way to a Cambridge degree in Russian and Italian, and then to a job as a lecturer in Italian at Cambridgeshire College of Arts and Technology. Officially Ted Hall was not a professor, but a "technical officer" at the Cavendish. In addition to his research, he was adviser to some graduate students getting Ph.D. degrees in physics. Meanwhile, he was openly participating in the Cambridge branch of the Pugwash anti-bomb movement.

ALL THIS TIME their freedom was in far more jeopardy than they realized. The Halls knew, of course, that Morris and Lona Cohen were serving twenty-year sentences in separate British prisons. The Halls never imagined what was about to happen: Authorities would offer Hall's former comrades-in-espionage an enticing deal in exchange for truth about the past. Morris Cohen recalled receiving the first, short-lived overture when two guards brought him to the deputy governor of Manchester Prison: "He said to me: 'There is a member of the American intelligence service who wants to see you. Do you want to see him?' Those were his exact words. Short like that. I thought a moment and said, 'No sir, I don't want.' " After that 1961 episode, the Americans gave up. On February 10, 1962, Colonel Abel walked free across the Glienicke Bridge in Berlin in exchange for U-2 pilot Francis Gary Powers.

British intelligence wasn't through with Morris and Lona Cohen, however. In 1962 or 1963, British agents told Lona that all she had to do was "cooperate" and she would get freedom, a new identity, a new home, plus a "stipend." Lona answered that she wouldn't talk without Morris. Two weeks later, the British agents arranged for them to rendezvous in prison. "Nothing doing, you have to bring Lonsdale," Morris Cohen said. So Lona was dressed in her street clothes and driven in a minibus to a negotiating meeting with Morris Cohen and Lonsdale. "They presented some kind of typewritten page with four or five conditions," Morris Cohen recounted. "They offered to send us to Christmas Island if we would talk about the Soviet services."

Nowhere on the globe would the Cohens be safer from Soviet hit men than Christmas Island, the deep-sea fishing resort atoll in the Indian Ocean 1,000 miles northwest of Australia. But Lona refused, Gordon Lonsdale refused, Morris refused—and the Halls had no idea what was happening. The British gave up on Lonsdale early in 1964, trading him to Moscow for Greville M. Wynne, a jailed British businessman who had been a courier to the most valuable Western spy in Moscow, Soviet Colonel Oleg Penkovsky.

The FBI had not forgotten about Ted Hall. Toward the middle of 1963, British authorities held up his application to renew his labor permit to work at the Cavendish. Cleveland Cram, then a CIA official handling liaison with British intelligence, heard from his counterpart in the FBI about the plan to interrogate Hall using the renewal of the labor permit as a pretext. When Hall appeared at a British office to retrieve his U.S. passport, he found himself confronting a persuasive British interrogator. "Don't worry, we are not the FBI," he remembered the officer saying. "But we know exactly who you are and what you did." The questioner knew all about Hall's supposed contacts with Kurnakov. Hall could tell the British questioner didn't believe the denials he had spun out for Agent McQueen. Yet the Briton seemed willing to forget Los Alamos if Hall would only get the whole story off his chest. The most insistent questions revolved around whether Hall was in Cambridge on an espionage mission. "What are you here for, really?" the officer asked.

With as much assurance as Hall could muster, he said he was only there to do research and rattled off the aims of his Cavendish microanalysis projects. When Hall returned to the inconspicuous little brick row house he and Joan owned at 11 Chedworth Street, he was shaken. Over the next twenty-four hours, Ted and Joan talked about it. Perhaps they should get it over with: just make some careful admission about contacts with the Soviets. Joan couldn't see any advantage in this, and after a day or two, Ted Hall decided to tell the British nothing.

The Halls waited. Finally, in the summer or fall of 1963, his labor permit came through as if nothing had ever happened. "I did not learn the result," recalled Cleveland Cram. "The FBI had jurisdiction over this matter. It was a question of American national security domestically, so it was their jurisdiction." It was the last time anyone from either Soviet or Western intelligence is known to have spoken with Theodore Hall. Yet for a long time, the Halls took care not to call attention to themselves. When Ted's Harvard class held its twenty-fifth reunion in the summer of 1969, his tongue-in-cheek note for the reunion yearbook made it sound as though his whole life had been devoid of adrenaline. "My wife and I have three children, and I am doing technical work in biology and physics in a local university," Hall wrote. "I do not believe anything is worth noting in our personal histories."

IN THAT SUMMER of 1969, the lives of their former comrades in the Volunteers, Morris and Lona Cohen, were becoming a lot more noteworthy. In their ninth year of imprisonment, help was finally on the way.

The KGB had already hinted that Peter and Helen Kroger (the Cohens) were worth a czar's ransom. The first feeler had come when Wolfgang Vogel, the East German lawyer who had orchestrated the Powers-Abel trade, flew to London in 1965 and tried to interest the British in a comparable deal for the Krogers. The British refused but the Americans were interested. As Lyndon Johnson struggled in 1967 to keep American support for the Vietnam War, American diplomat Francis Meehan transmitted to Vogel a list of eleven U.S. Navy and Air Force pilots shot down in Indochina. The Berlin-based Meehan asked if the Soviets might trade the pilots as part of another spy swap. It took Vogel a year to come back with Moscow's counteroffer. Finally, he passed the word that East Germany was willing to release two wounded pilots "currently in an East German hospital" in exchange for the Krogers. The State Department wavered, responding at first that the Krogers were "not available for exchange." When an American official tried a few months later to reopen talks, the word came back from Vogel that the offer had been withdrawn.

The next overture came in December 1967 from the exiled Kim Philby, the former British diplomat then living in Moscow. The Krogers' health was deteriorating because of "inhumanely severe" conditions, Philby told a British visitor. Philby threw out the idea that the Krogers might be exchanged for Gerald Brooke, a British lecturer imprisoned in Moscow for distributing subversive literature. "It's a pity about Brooke," said Philby. "He really was a silly fellow." When London again resisted, Moscow hinted that Brooke would be locked up for life if there was no trade.

Philby was right about one thing: The Cohens were not healthy. "From day to day I live with the fervent hope that she [Lona] won't lose her mental stability," Morris wrote after one of their prison visits. Along with depression, Lona suffered from a host of physical ailments. Her body throbbed with rheumatism or arthritis, and once she had to fight off an attack from another prisoner, suffering a broken and then permanently deformed finger. In his separate prison, Morris had chronic out-breaks of boils. "I counted 65 big ones but lost count of the little ones," he wrote a friend after one three-month bout of skin problems in 1964. Later he twice underwent surgery for Dupuytren's contracture, a rare syndrome he developed in which the tendons of his hands contracted and his fingers were drawn into loose fists. By 1969, even Morris's morale was withering in his maximum-security cell on the Isle of Wight. "I catch myself pondering what would happen to Helen or my-self if the other were to pass away while in here," he wrote to a book-seller friend. "It's a grim thought and I try not to succumb to it, but neither can I ignore it."

If the Cohens ever came close to cracking, British and American in-telligence never noticed. Instead of renewing attempts to get their con-fessions, Britain decided to take up Philby's offer of a trade, and by the fall of 1969 the deal was set. The Soviet Union would free Brooke along with two young Britons who were serving on Soviet drug charges. The Krogers/Cohens would be released to Poland, which they now claimed as their motherland.

The Cohens' departure "will be surrounded with the sort of secu-rity one would expect if the crown jewels were being flown out of Britain," a British official source told *The Times* of London in the fall of 1969. Morris and Lona boarded a British European Airlines Trident, then sipped champagne and held hands as journalists clambered around them pressing questions. When the plane landed in Warsaw, the Cohens were hustled to a Polish guest house in a waiting car. The next day they flew to Moscow, resuming their life work in the KGB.

ANOTHER FORMER VOLUNTEER, Saville Sax, was also trying to shed his past in the fall of 1969.

Throughout the sixties, Sax was terrified that the FBI was watching his house and tapping his phone in Chicago. Especially after the Cuban missile crisis, he was obsessed with nuclear war. His son Boria remem-bered when Saville Sax took the whole family in 1964 or 1965 to see the movie *My Fair Lady*, which had recently opened in the Loop. The gai-ety of Rex Harrison and Audrey Hepburn at the Michael Todd Theater couldn't cheer his father. "He remarked to the family that he wondered what would happen if an atomic bomb dropped and everyone was trapped in the theater," remembered Boria. "He said he was sure that cannibalism would break out."

Sax became so depressed that he came close to blowing his brains out. "My mother said he spent a number of months sort of confining himself to the bedroom with a revolver, threatening to shoot himself if anybody tried to call the police," Boria remembered. After a while, suicide became a weird family joke in the Sax family. "It became an ongoing theme that would come up every year or so," remembered Boria's younger sister, Sarah. "One time he told me if I wasn't home for dinner by six o'clock, he was going to fast until death," Sarah remembered. Savy's wife, Susan, believed that part of his moroseness derived from his fears of the FBI. "I think that all his life he suffered from anxiety and depression, and this certainly exacerbated his anxiety," said Susan.

Susan Sax paid a price for Savy's weirdness. She raised three children and waitressed nights to help Savy finish his education. They lived on almost no money, so rootless that once they lived in five apartments within a two-and-a-half-year stretch, all of them on Chicago's South Side on the edge of a black and Puerto Rican slum. As a part-time Checker Cab driver, Savy took eight years to earn his master's degree, but finally in 1960, at the age of thirty-six, he got an M.A. in education from the University of Chicago. After that he got a job as a psychologist at the Chicago Humane Society, a shelter that put lost dogs and cats up for adoption. Later he was hired as a school counselor and psychologist at the Pennoyer School District in Norridge, a suburb near Chicago's O'Hare Airport. Meanwhile, Susan also finished college and found work at the University of Chicago. Their modest success may well have been too much of a load for the marriage. "Well, he fell in love with one of my close friends and moved out," remembered Susan. After eighteen years of marriage, Susan and Saville Sax were separated in about 1966, later to get divorced.

In 1967, Sax got a lucky bounce. He landed a position at Southern Illinois University in Edwardsville, Illinois, just across the Mississippi from St. Louis. He was hired as program director of the New Experimental Teacher Education Program (NEXTEP), which was funded by Lyndon Johnson's Great Society to re-train teachers to be "change agents." Education Professor Merrill Harmin, the thirty-year-old visionary who ran NEXTEP, had developed what was to become a controversial theory of education called values clarification. "When I got this project under way, I started to search around for creative folks," Harmin remembered. Word of mouth led him to Saville Sax because of Sax's experimental teaching at Pennoyer. "When I interviewed him, I said, 'Wow, yeah. He's a winner,'" Harmin said.

Savy emerged as a campus counselor and guru under Harmin's patronage. His job was instructing teachers in small-group dynamics, and that meant teaching such things as "how do you listen better?" and "how do you distinguish when the task is more important than personal needs?" The underlying theory at NEXTEP was that teachers must avoid imposing values on students—even such fundamental values as fairness and compassion. Sax's specialty was mantras, and he became known for his seminars on how to dissolve inner tension. "Get in touch with your love feelings," Sax wrote in one of his meditation manuals. "Bring this love energy to any part of your body that still feels tense or hurting. Bring it as love, as warmth, as healing. Continue until you feel good in every part of yourself. Then systematically bring the energy to every portion of your body starting with the toes, the feet, the calves, the knees, the upper part of the leg, the thighs, the hips, the genital region, your abdomen, the lower chest and back. . . ."

To Harmin, there was no question Sax was extraordinary: "He was a genius, I tell you. I don't know if you've been around many geniuses, but if you get to be exceptional in one area, it twists around other areas." Harmin felt Sax had a gift for understanding other people's psychological needs. "He [Sax] was a natural just like an artist who never went to art school could be excellent. He had a knack for helping people make tough decisions between personal and social concerns." However talented he felt Sax was, Harmin didn't choose to socialize with him. "My wife thought he was weird," Harmin said. "He was clearly unusual. He often didn't wash. His house was chaotic, disorderly." Another teacher who worked under Harmin at NEXTEP remembered Sax as "a very mystical person [who] would make mystical statements." Because of Sax's unusual first name and dark complexion, the English teacher thought Sax might have come from India. To this colleague, Sax not only "looked like an Indian guru," but seemed to delight in Delphic pronouncements. "A normal person would say, 'What if we start Thursday?' He [Sax] would say, 'But are we perpetuating the continuation of reality?' "

NEXTEP died in 1972, when the Nixon administration stopped its funds. Savy Sax caught on at the university's School of Dental Medicine, teaching future dentists how to use his mantra techniques to lessen the pain of drilling. In that period Savy was also a heavy user of LSD— or so his son Boria was convinced. Whether or not Sax was actually tripping on hallucinogens, his writings were illustrated by psychedelic drawings and amounted to a mishmash of the simplistic and the visionary. "I experience myself as a warm loving person," Sax wrote. "I like to get really involved in things, and when I am, I'm quick, playful, creative, imaginative and joyful. I have very powerful love and beauty feelings. They are with me when I write, when I paint, when I walk in nature."

People at Southern Illinois came to think of Assistant Professor Sax as a storyteller, or maybe a shaman, someone who was not expected to tell the linear truth. Even when he did tell the truth, people were skeptical. So no one paid much attention when Sax began to tell an amusing story in the late seventies about the time he helped the Soviets build the atomic bomb. Saville Sax was fifty-six when he was found dead of a heart attack on September 25, 1980. At the funeral, his daughter, Sarah, was startled that so many of his friends had heard his quaint anecdotes about how Savy was once a Soviet agent. "It was no secret," Sarah Sax remembered. "I'll tell you, after he left my mother, everybody knew. They were all talking about it at his funeral. I was kind of surprised. It seemed every single person Saville knew, knew about it. He seemed to have no fear."

NEWS OF SAVY'S death did not reach Theodore Hall in England. All he knew was that his letters tapered off in the seventies and then stopped.

Hall had his own past to deal with, but that seems to have become easier as soon as he and Joan saw the footage of the Cohens flying off from Britain. In the month after the Cohens' departure, the My Lai massacre was big news in the British papers, and it elicited the first and only statement on world affairs that Hall ever published in his life. In a five-paragraph letter that appeared in *The Times,* Hall railed against the war in Vietnam with considerable eloquence. "When the manner of warfare identifies the population as a whole as the enemy, the war is not being waged with the intention of helping them," Hall wrote. "The [My Lai] massacre is significant as further powerful evidence that the war is waged by the United States Government for the domination of Vietnam." The letter caught the eye of the producer of a London TV panel show, who called and invited Hall to air his views in a round-table. Hall declined, deciding it might not be prudent to expose himself to such a wide audience. But within the confines of Cambridge, Ted felt comfortable. When some of his colleagues and students organized a one-day Free University in March 1970, Hall spoke out in public against big-money science with its conference-hopping, honorarium-collecting scientists who had joined what he called "a privileged exploiting class." He unabashedly entitled his talk "A Socialist View of Science Today."

The early seventies were years of inexorable progress in Hall's career, only to be followed by a puzzling series of setbacks. The decade started with a promising assignment when the Cambridge Department of Zoology asked the Cavendish if it could borrow Hall to work on a biological problem. Professor Torkel Weis-Fogh wanted to study how chemical elements and water pass through the wall of biological barrier membranes known as epithelia. With funding from the British government's Science Research Council, the zoology department set up the Biological Microprobe Laboratory and Hall became one of its five principal scientists. Meanwhile, Hall won another British grant to purchase one of the new EMMA-4 electron microscope microanalyzers for his own Cavendish lab. Now that he had perfected the Hall Method, research papers poured out of his lab on topics ranging from muscle regeneration to heart damage to the concentration of calcium in a squid membrane.

The first hint of trouble came in 1976 when the Cavendish decided to de-emphasize biological research. Hall could see the point. "It wasn't a physics problem anymore," he remembered. "We and other people in the field had solved everything that could be called a physics problem. Now it was up to the biologists." Hall took his EMMA-4 microanalyzer to the zoology department and became head of the Biological Microprobe Laboratory. The peak of international acclaim for the Hall Method came in 1977, when Hall's name appeared as a co-author on eleven academic papers. But trouble arose the following year when several physiologists in another Cambridge University faculty challenged the legitimacy of some results obtained by Hall's closest scientific collaborator, the Indian-born zoologist Brij L. Gupta. Gupta's research, dealing with the concentration of ions in narrow spaces between cells in a rabbit's intestine, had evoked criticism after it was reported in *Nature*. "To defend against private accusations of fraud and grossly exaggerated claims, Ted and I even published our X-ray data," Gupta remembered. But by Gupta's account, the results were such a "discomforting threat to the established dogmas" that senior physiologists in Cambridge began opposing continuation of the grant for Hall's lab.

Hall and his Biological Microprobe Laboratory were on the defensive from then on. After a series of reviews by British funding committees, the budget was ravaged and the laboratory had to close in 1984. Though Hall never quite shared his view, Gupta blamed everything on a clique of "domineering physiologists" who couldn't bear to accept the findings of a competing laboratory. "It may be that in the modern age of commercial advertising and aggressive marketing, the genuine and almost self-effacing modesty of Ted Hall, hitherto considered a virtue in science, is now punished as inadequacy," Gupta wrote. Rather abruptly, Theodore Hall took early retirement in 1984 at the age of fifty-nine.

It had been twenty years since Hall had had to answer questions about Los Alamos. All his connections to the Volunteers were finally severed, and he planned to begin his retirement tying up loose ends in his biological research. His list of professional papers would eventually reach 166, including eleven he published after retiring. He and Joan continued living in the same neighborhood in Cambridge, around the corner from the Chedworth Street row house where they had moved in 1962. As the eighties progressed, Hall occupied his mind more and more with the mysteries of quantum mechanics, the same questions about the behavior of matter on a very small scale that had fascinated him as a junior in Harvard's Class of 1944.

There were times, of course, when Ted and Joan would talk about those terrifying forties and fifties, when the network was still active. Once, the Halls even felt comfortable enough to visit Albuquerque. That was where the Electron Microscopy Society of America was holding its annual meeting with a session dedicated to Hall's life work. The conference happened to open on August 10, 1986. It was the day after the forty-first anniversary of Nagasaki—forty-one years since Theodore Hall had met Lona Cohen. During one break, nostalgia overcame caution and Ted and Joan walked around the University of New Mexico campus, looking for the spot where he had met Lona. "It was all completely different, I didn't find anything at all," Hall would somewhat plaintively tell a friend. Joan suggested a drive up the highway to see Los Alamos. Ted said no, that would be going too far.

CHAPTER 28

The Perseus Myth

Retired Colonel Vladimir Chikov of the KGB described almost poetically the silky new face the Soviet Union's spy center tried to present to the world in 1989: "When the curtain of glasnost was lifted and the fresh air began to blow, it reached these one-meter-thick walls of the building on Lubyanka." Suddenly a KGB press office materialized, and its occupants were not merely answering the odd question now and again; they were shepherding journalists through facilities that used to be resolutely off limits, badgering high-level officers to give interviews, and even helping produce an unprecedented piece of fluff called *The KGB Today,* a "documentary" film showing regular guys at their jobs defending the motherland. The KGB was determined to justify and defend itself, to revamp an image based on its years as an instrument of repression. In exposing some of its successes and focusing on its devotion to national patriotism, it also began an inexorable, inch-by-inch lifting of the curtain on the clandestine role of Ted Hall and the Volunteers.

The public relations business was certainly alien to the KGB, but the *chinovniks*, the functionaries who always have kept Russia's behemoth bureaucracies slugging along, saw that this modern path of openness was the only route to follow. Life was changing in unpredictable and, for the KGB, often unpleasant ways, making the feared agency the target of alarming criticism that would have been unthinkable just a few years earlier. It was time for a counteroffensive to divert attention from the brutish arrests and repressions of fellow countrymen that had continued well into the 1980s.

Enter Colonels Igor Prelin and Vladimir Chikov, catalysts of the counteroffensive. Both had backgrounds in journalism and in intelligence, a common combination for the KGB, although Prelin specialized in film and his comrade in the new press office was a word man. It was

Prelin who masterminded *The KGB Today* and was the on-camera tour guide, extolling the faultless pearl barley dished up by a cook at the notorious Lefortovo Prison. Recognizing that the old guard of espionage was dying off, Prelin also began videotaping the reminiscences of some of the foreign "greats" who had betrayed their governments for the sake of the Soviet Union—Britisher George Blake, for example—before their memories were lost to history. Prelin spent two days at a Service dacha taping two people about whom he knew much less, a couple who had lived in Moscow in total secrecy for two decades. The video of Morris and Lona Cohen was made in honor of the twentieth anniversary of their arrival from Britain, where they had been known by the pseudonyms Peter and Helen Kroger. Prelin liked what he saw. "I gave it to Chikov, and I said it's interesting," he remembered.

The two men decided this was the perfect story to showcase the KGB before a disenchanted Soviet audience. Here was a pair of engaging agents involved in one of the KGB's most spectacular successes: snatching the secrets of the American atomic bomb. It was a tale of love, of communist idealism, of bravery and commitment to the Soviet cause. And they were Americans, to boot. The two press aides drafted a letter to KGB director General Vladimir Kryuchkov, who had done his bit promoting the new image by answering occasional questions from Western journalists, meeting with U.S. Ambassador Jack Matlock, and talking about the wonders of Gorbachev's glasnost. "We did it just on the chance something might come of it," Chikov said in an interview. "To our great surprise, Kryuchkov signed it."

At the close of 1989 Chikov found himself planted at Yasenevo, the KGB foreign department headquarters on Moscow's southern outskirts, scribbling notes from 6,500 pages of files brought to him volume by volume. Chikov remembered the day he actually got to look through the first pages of what he called file No. 13676, the KGB's records on the Cohens/Krogers. "Of course I was excited. My hands were trembling. I thought, What if the situation changes and they deprive me of the possibility to look at this?" Glasnost, after all, was a product with an unknown shelf life. Even though Chikov had been a KGB domestic counterintelligence officer, he wasn't sufficiently trusted to sit alone and finger these jewels of the KGB foreign directorate archives. As he described the process, an unsmiling KGB minder sat across the table and eyed him, hour after hour, day after day for months. "Of course he was watching to see if I tore a page away or anything else. He was responsible for this file," Chikov explained.

The documents that were part of what the KGB called the Enormoz file were a cornucopia: biographical material on each of the Cohens going back to the Spanish Civil War, copies of the first cables confirming Morris Cohen had come back to New York and was making good on his Barcelona commitment. He had become the agent he'd promised. The most important documents Chikov copied into his thick notebook were the *spravki,* the summaries of information contained in coded cables sent between Moscow Centre and its far-flung nodes of espionage. These chronicled every contact the Cohens made. The first mosaic that appeared as he pieced together the documents was a picture of the Volunteers, dominated by Lona Cohen's Kleenex charade at the New Mexico train station in 1945. Then came the Portland spy ring and the other activities that occupied the Krogers in their high-tech bungalow outside London. From the other side, the *spravki* held Moscow Centre's instructions and evaluations of work done.

Chikov's bosses naturally were wary of how he would use this secret trove of detail. They couldn't have him exposing a foreign agent whose crimes had never been discovered. They were just as intent on hiding tracks that could reveal to other intelligence services the intricate spycraft system the Soviets had built. General Yuri Drozdov, the head of the illegals section of KGB foreign intelligence, took upon himself the task of neutralizing Chikov's notebook. He often demanded that dates and names, even code names, be changed. He simply deleted some characters. He looked at the *spravki* and compared them with Chikov's notes to be sure he had conveyed nothing about the structure of the Soviet code. As Chikov remembered, "If he noticed that I just copied it out directly, which was not allowed, he changed it. Because American codebreakers comparing American [intercepted] cables with this could break the codes. It was absolutely forbidden."

While Chikov sifted through his wealth of material and scouted for supplemental documentation, the drive to remold the KGB's image was conducted from other quarters. One of the first hints of the publicity barrage to come was dropped by General Vadim Kirpichenko, then deputy chief of the KGB's First Main Directorate—Foreign Intelligence. He helped the daily *Moskovskaya Pravda* (*Moscow Truth*) observe the seventieth anniversary of the foreign intelligence service with an interview for the December 20, 1990, paper. Kirpichenko explained several years later that the interview was part of a conscious plan. "We understood that we must make some publicity to open some pages of our history. Why? Because all the books about the Russian intelligence service were published in the West, and not one book had we prepared ourselves," he recalled. The Western portrait, which was anything but flattering, now was circulating at home. "At that time our press was strictly against all activities of the KGB and intelligence service. We were obliged to defend ourselves and to explain to our people why the intelligence service existed."

The KGB leaders were certainly capable of withstanding the verbal blows, but they suddenly faced a more pressing issue. For the first time they were in a position not so different from their American counterparts: They had to worry about justifying a budget. In the 1990 interview Kirpichenko started out by assuring readers that since the demise of Lavrenti Beria, KGB agents had stopped killing people. Then he made what appears to be the first assertion that "practically the whole time when atomic weapons were being developed in the West, detailed information was reported to the Soviet leadership and our scientists." He went on to name some retired Soviet intelligence colonels formerly stationed in America and Britain who had procured data from foreign informants. This was astonishing stuff from an agency that had denied having links to Klaus Fuchs, despite the fact that he had confessed to working for the Soviets. The same month one of the colonels, Alexander Feklisov, published the first of a two-part article in the monthly *Voyenno-Istoricheskii Zhurnal* (*Military History Journal*) detailing parts of Fuchs's cooperation with the Soviets, including Feklisov's own contacts with him while in Britain in the late forties. Perhaps the most controversial statement appeared in the *Moskovskaya Pravda* article. The paper quoted a previously secret memorandum by Igor Kurchatov, the late head of the postwar Soviet bomb program, in which he marveled that the data received from the spies were "of immense, invaluable importance for our state and our science." Until then Soviet scientists had been just as loath as the spies, though for different reasons, to confirm that the fruits of espionage had fed any atomic development in the Soviet Union.

By the following April, Chikov was ready to make his contribution. His first articles appeared in the weekly magazine *Novoye Vremya* (*New Time*). More followed. The life and times of Morris Cohen turned out to be only a fraction of Chikov's story, and only a part of that was accurately told. Beginning with the creation of the scientific-technical branch of the intelligence agency in the thirties, Chikov went on to tell how Soviet operatives sent a stream of top-secret information from the British and American bomb projects to Beria during World War II.

Beria had it vetted and turned over to Kurchatov, who then was able to shoot questions back through the spy network to get more data or clarifications from the Western scientist-informants, Chikov wrote. This was an assertion that the first Soviet bomb was created largely on the basis of the work of spies, and it quickly churned up controversy in Gorbachev's dying Soviet Union.

It was the fraction related to Cohen that grabbed a bit of attention in America. For the first time, Chikov spun out the story of a principled American scientist—code-named "Perseus"—who volunteered to give the Soviets details of the top secret work proceding in Los Alamos. He made it clear that Klaus Fuchs was not the only spy on the mesa. The American Perseus had been a comrade-in-arms of Morris Cohen during the Spanish Civil War and tracked down Cohen at Amtorg to offer his services, according to Chikov's version in three respected Soviet magazines. His account called the scientist Arthur Fielding, which he has since acknowledged was not even a real code name. To humanize the story he inserted enough background on Morris and Lona to confirm for the FBI that the couple had been engaged in espionage for more than a decade before they fled America.

Whether the FBI began a hunt for Perseus remains the agency's secret. But the news soon sent a few Western historians and journalists scurrying to archives or laboratories in efforts to pinpoint that unknown scientist. The problem was the KGB excelled at fabrication. Chikov and friends had sufficiently smudged the story with disinformation to make it impossible to identify Perseus or verify most of the other critical elements of the espionage tale. That had been precisely their intention. "The main goal was to make the story unclear, so when the intelligence of other countries began to analyze this, it would not reveal the forms and methods of the work of Soviet intelligence," Chikov later admitted in an interview. Such invention would turn out to be a typical tactic. A look at the original manuscript of Alexander Feklisov's guarded memoirs would show that he wrote it using several real code names that would disappear when the book was published. In the case of Perseus, the veiling had been a group undertaking. Early in 1991, Chikov and General Drozdov first changed various dates and cables. Then Prelin sat down with Anatoly Yatskov, Lona Cohen's former controller, to fake the story of how Perseus was recruited. The cover that Morris Cohen had signed up an old war buddy as a Soviet agent in Los Alamos was such a clever tale that for five years it diverted researchers down false trails.

As for the Cohens, they hadn't even been warned that they were about to be put on parade. After they moved to Moscow in 1969, their letters to British friends maintained the fiction that they were living in Poland. Set up in a large apartment on Patriarch's Ponds, just six blocks from the American Embassy, the Cohens were happy to have their home become a classroom for KGB recruits trying to absorb the ways of the West. The young students learned how to talk and eat and behave. Lona taught them how to swear like Americans and Morris what to read. But the Cohens' lives and contacts, even with friends, were regulated by the Centre. Semyon Semyonov, Morris's first spy boss and the couple's longtime friend, had been fired by Soviet intelligence during an upsurge of official anti-Semitism in 1953. Because he was still on tenuous terms with the KGB, he was off-limits. "They [the Cohens] were very persistent people," recalled Semyonov's widow, Glafira. "They probably told the Service that they wanted to meet us first of all. A year and a half later, they insisted." And so the two families finally did get back together, first in the Cohens' apartment and later for visits to the Semyonovs. Blake, who had been serving time with Morris Cohen until his infamous escape from Wormwood Scrubs prison, told a similar story. One day on a Moscow street the former British diplomat simply ran into Morris. They talked and agreed they must meet, but the KGB keepers refused. Only years later "the ban was lifted," Blake said, when the KGB asked him in about 1990 to make visits to the aging couple to keep them company in English. Blake would suggest that the Cohens had been so closely managed because they still were engaged in sensitive work as part of the KGB school. But it was routine for the KGB to keep control of its foreign assets who defected. The Centre never quite trusted them. They might have been turned by an enemy agency. Or they might get homesick and make overtures to their own people, promising to feed information in exchange for a trip home and amnesty.

While Chikov was crafting the story of the Cohens and the bomb, Prelin had been busy. Early in 1991 he approached British documentary producer Frances Berrigan, who had ties to the Soviet broadcasting system through her work at Siberia's Lake Baikal. First he sold her on a documentary about Kim Philby, using file footage of the agent and newer videos that Prelin's crews had taken—Philby's funeral in 1989, interviews with his widow and comrades. "We presented it as the KGB view of Philby," Berrigan said. When Prelin later brought her the idea of a story on the Cohens/Krogers, she agreed. But she demanded new videos be taken of the Krogers, turning down his dacha interviews from 1989 as too static and unprofessional.

Prelin and Chikov had not originally told the Cohens they were about to become a KGB promotional item because Soviet doctors predicted in 1989 that they wouldn't live long enough to enjoy the limelight. Yet they both rebounded from their illnesses. After the initial shock, they agreed to cooperate with the KGB publicists and Prelin was able to get the film he needed for the British documentary. Morris Cohen, who by this time was eighty-one, was confounded by this fellow Perseus he was supposed to have recruited, but the KGB keepers helped him sort out the story. The vigilant KGB refused to let Berrigan send her own crew or meet the Cohens herself, claiming they were too ill for an interview by strangers. Under the control of a Soviet film crew and questioner, the KGB allowed mostly personal queries—and none about their espionage adventures.

They did grant one request of both Berrigan and the Cohens, however, which was a visit from the couple's British friend Sheila Wheeler. She was the daughter of a bookseller whose family had assiduously attended the Krogers' trial, visited them in prison, and corresponded for years after their release.

"I felt as if I was abusing our friendship," remembered Wheeler, who had gone to Moscow at the invitation of Frances Berrigan, then was pumped full of questions the producer wanted answered. But as Wheeler brought up one seemingly sensitive subject after the next, she realized this was precisely what the Cohens wished to discuss. "It dawned on me that Helen [Lona] couldn't wait to tell me all this. In fact she jumped at the chance to justify herself, to explain her motives and everything. So she in that sense was using me as well. So we were all quite happy about it." Morris was too deaf to participate much, mostly leaving Lona to talk during Sheila's visit to the KGB hospital in Moscow where the Cohens were staying in what resembled a hotel suite. Wheeler was convinced that they had discussed these questions many times themselves, finding a justification for years spent in the service of an idealized society that had never really existed, a justification for lives that were nearing their end rather sadly, without family, without free access to books or movies or travel, and even without control over whom they could see or to whom they could speak.

Yet, Wheeler found, Lona seemed satisfied that some thread of idealism connected the multiple lives of deception that she had led:

She claimed she had always been a pacifist and that everything she did, the whole business of stealing atomic secrets and everything, was to ensure world peace. The object being that she believed if Russia had atomic weapons as well as America, that that would result in a balance of power and we would have world peace. And I said to her at one point, "Do you think your life has been a success?" And she said, "Well, we've had forty years of world peace. That's the achievement of my life." She really felt she had secured that. So yes, she did have this sense of achievement. Why she thought she had been adequately rewarded for that, I don't know, because I think their life, when they went back eventually after being released from prison, I think their life was pretty awful.

In the end Berrigan's documentary got made, melding elements of the Cohens' atomic espionage in America and the Krogers' covert communications center in Britain. The most titillating news was that an American scientist-spy, whose code name the British filmmakers translated as Percy, was still alive and at large. It was the first time a general audience in the West had heard the story, and for a while it caught the attention of British television viewers in November 1991. Little did they know that that very American scientist was living among them in Cambridge, anxiously watching to catch any hint that his secret was in danger of being exposed.

More and more of the story would burble up in an increasingly freewheeling Soviet press, leading ever closer to that exposure. What would turn out to be a critical, yet almost unnoticed, clue appeared in 1991 in an ambitious publication of the KGB itself. The *Kur'yer Sovyetskoi Razvyedki* (*Courier of Soviet Intelligence*) did a blow-out premier edition on "people and personalities" of the Service. The monthly billed itself as "the first and only reportage till now from the intelligence museum of the KGB, USSR." A feature detailing the KGB's atomic espionage feats offered three intelligence documents as proof, including the message to Beria describing how to build the bomb. This middle document of the trio bore the handwritten notation in Russian: "Sources, Mlad, Charl'z." Although Charl'z was known from Chikov's articles as the code name for Fuchs, this was the first time the code name Mlad had been made public. The document left the unmistakable impression that this Mlad was a source with extraordinary connections deep inside the Manhattan Project. The Soviets had been boasting of just such an atomic source, but had labored mightily to hide any clue to his identity.

The *Kur'yer* had made a huge gaffe. "When they realized it, it was too late," recounted Chikov. "*Kur'yer* has never come out since then. It was banned." It was a missing link of potentially great significance. If anyone had an inkling of who Mlad was, this documentation would be critical evidence of what he had done. But nobody, it seemed, could pin down the connection.

The aborted coup attempt in August 1991 led to the end of communism as state ideology, the dissolution of the Soviet Union, and the relaxation of policies limiting free speech and press. The KGB was shaken up when its chief was detained for his part in the coup plot. Soon the brawny intelligence empire would be subdivided into more controllable fiefdoms of counterintelligence, foreign intelligence, and border guards. These changes accelerated the process of opening doors on the past, though in chaotic and unpredictable ways. As seen in the case of the *Kur'yer,* sometimes the change came a bit too swiftly to be controlled.

Formerly secret archives were becoming hunting grounds for happy researchers. Parts of the Communist Party records, of Stalin's letters, of the old Comintern archives all were shedding light on Soviet machinations that had been under black-out for decades. When the Institute of the History of Natural Science and Technology decided at the beginning of 1992 to study the development of the Soviet atomic program, Yatskov responded with a personal visit and a file full of documents. Yatskov himself wrote an article for a spread in the institute's scholarly journal, *Voprosy Istorii Yestestvoznaniya i Tekhniki* (*Questions of Natural History and Technology*), outlining the role of Soviet intelligence agents. V. P. Visgin, a historian and member of the journal's editorial board, explained the accompanying documents. It was an unprecedented publication of the actual data spies had collected and delivered back to Moscow Centre and then to the scientists. The documents explained down to the millimeter how the Americans had built the atomic bomb.

Physicists from Moscow's Kurchatov Institute, who had cooperated with the historians in preparing the publication, panicked when they saw the galley proofs. They appealed to Boris Yeltsin's government to stop the material from being disseminated. From the United States, *The Bulletin of the Atomic Scientists* asked two Russians to examine the controversy later, and it published two possible reasons for the scientists' clamor. "The papers could have been useful to any aspiring nation," wrote the former head of the Soviet space program Roald Sagdeev. "Information on the first bomb might have provided valuable clues to bomb development. In fact, the older the design, the easier it would be to reproduce it somewhere in the Third World. Someone like Saddam Hussein would love to have these materials." But another view came from *Izvestia* journalist Sergei Leskov, who suggested this was part of "the struggle for a place on the Mount Olympus of history rather than a concern with nuclear nonproliferation." He thought the scientists didn't want the world to know how much information had been pilfered from the Americans. Whatever the reason, the Foreign Intelligence Service, one of the KGB successor agencies, was charged with recalling the journals that already had been printed and were being distributed to libraries and campuses around Russia. It didn't get them all.

By 1993, Prelin had aired his own television documentary on spies and the bomb in Russia, expanding on the material prepared for the British documentary. Both intelligence officers and scientists were giving interviews to everyone from Japanese television to Michael Dobbs of *The Washington Post*'s Moscow bureau. Freelance Russian researchers were making available more documentation, beyond what had appeared in the "canceled" historical journal *Voprosy*. More bits of information tumbled into the public realm.

The first publication to put together Morris and Lona Cohen, the code name Mlad, and the *Voprosy* documents was the 1994 book *Special Tasks, The Memoirs of an Unwanted Witness—A Soviet Spymaster*. It was the autobiography of the veteran secret agent Pavel Sudoplatov, who held intelligence credentials stretching back before the Spanish Civil War, written in collaboration with his son Anatoly and two probing American writers, Jerrold and Leona Schecter. Sudoplatov's chapter on atomic espionage shifted many puzzle pieces into place. However, it contained a number of small errors, as well as what most Western critics thought were some giant bloopers. Now it turns out that Sudoplatov was right that a source in Los Alamos called Mlad supplied valuable information to Lona Cohen. But Sudoplatov misidentified Mlad as Bruno Pontecorvo, who at the time was working in Canada and did not have direct access to the details of bomb design that came from Mlad. And Sudoplatov had only ambiguous documentation for his assertion that Robert Oppenheimer, Enrico Fermi, and Leo Szilard passed information to Soviet agents as well and that Oppenheimer and Fermi were jointly code-named Star. The NSA's Venona decryptions were released a year after the Sudoplatov book, and they weakened the grounds for believing that Oppenheimer, Szilard, or Fermi was a Soviet informant. When Sudoplatov republished his memoirs in Russian after the Venona release, he did not repeat the most important allegation he had made in the American edition: that he personally set up networks of illegals who convinced Oppenheimer, Fermi, and Szilard "to share atomic secrets with us." The aging Sudoplatov, who died in 1996, got much of the Enormoz story right, but he had also misremembered or confused strands of the espionage network. And there is another possibility: Even in his last years he may have adhered to the professional ethics of the intelligence trade, which forbid exposing living sources—especially to a perceptive foreign co-author like Jerrold Schecter, a former Moscow correspondent for *Time* magazine who had also worked on the staff of the U.S. National Security Council.

In any event, the Russian Foreign Intelligence Service denied Sudoplatov's claims about Oppenheimer, Fermi, and Szilard when his book first appeared. The spymasters of the 1990s probably felt secure then that the real story of Mlad and Star never would be revealed, for by 1995, almost all of the people with first-hand knowledge were dead. That included Lona Cohen, who died in Moscow of cancer in 1992 shortly after the British documentary was aired, and Morris Cohen, who followed her to Kuntsevskoye Cemetery in the summer of 1995.

The real Mlad had less and less to fear that he would be uncovered, or so it seemed in Moscow. As Morris Cohen had said in 1994 in the only newspaper interview he ever gave: "I assume even in 100 years his name won't be exposed."

CHAPTER 29

Accountings

In the spring of 1994, Theodore Hall wrote a capsule of his recent life for the fiftieth anniversary report of the Harvard Class of 1944: "I'm afflicted with Parkinson's disease and an inoperable cancer, and I recently experienced the death of a dearly loved daughter. Some of the horrors in the world scene are incomprehensible. But life still seems amazing and beautiful."

It had been a huge stretch for Ted Hall to reach the emotional resolution expressed in those last seven words. This energetic man, who walked for pleasure and played tennis for sport, suddenly found his body betraying him when kidney cancer appeared in 1989, followed by the Parkinson's. A course of immunotherapy kept him from the 1989 scanning microscopy conference in Salt Lake City, where he was honored in absentia with another special panel devoted to his life's work. By the time of that 1994 biographical blip for Harvard, Hall was rather surprised still to be alive and getting about, creaky though he was.

But disease was not the big catastrophe. The road accident that killed the Halls' second daughter, Deborah, on March 13, 1992, was the anguish of their lives. At thirty-seven, Debby Hall was a law student, a violinist with talent enough to play classical or jazz—and to play them well—and a single mother of two girls. Long a radical activist, she was biking to a law class when she was crushed by a truck in West Hampstead, just moments away from her north London home. Debby had absorbed the principles of her parents' politics and when she was just fourteen started putting them into practice with her own flair—organizing against the Vietnam War, in solidarity with the Palestinians, against the bomb and the British poll tax. For two years, she had shown up every Wednesday evening outside South Africa House on the non-stop picket protesting Nelson Mandela's imprisonment. "She made music as she did everything else—without observing the usual conventions," wrote her friend Barbara Rosenbaum. It was part of the wave of tributes not just to her tireless activism but to her compassion as well that flowed from friends and colleagues at Debby's death.

"We think about her every day. We still do," her mother said almost five years later. "It was like she brought the world to life and gave it color." The death of a child can be an event of unfathomable pain. Maybe it was harder for the Halls because finally, in that private, deep place survivors probe when they ponder their role in the irrational ending of a life, the Halls had to wonder if Debby would still be alive had they made different choices. Joan acknowledged that those painful thoughts intervened, thoughts about how life would be different if the consequences of Ted's past hadn't threatened, leading them to leave Chicago and then contributing to their decision to leave New York. What if they never had brought Debby to Cambridge? But that was a murky pit without bottom, that series of answerless questions. Their girls could have been randomly shot in Chicago or run down in New York or lost to any of the tragedies that afflict without warning or reason.

It was hard to imagine any further jolts to their placid days of books and music and gardening, friendships with neighbors and colleagues, the occasional trip to Italy. "Somehow the place suits me deeply," Ted Hall said of Cambridge. The couple had lived there more than thirty years and felt no yearning to return to America, where they now had few living roots and less familiarity. Joan sometimes missed what she called "a certain expansiveness and generosity in many Americans," but allowed that she had found similar qualities in the friends in Italy met through her work as a college teacher and translator. "Of course we don't feel totally integrated here [in England], but then we never belonged unequivocally to the main stream anywhere—Jews don't—nor were we ever part of the 'Jewish community,' " she wrote in a letter. Their politics and personalities also kept them a bit separate, she said, citing "an innate streak of nonconformity" in them both. "This is where we have our home, friends, family, professional interests; we fit in here better than we would anywhere else," she said. "We feel privileged to live in Cambridge—it's a lovely place, where difference is welcomed."

They expected no rude surprises in their retirement, but Ted and Joan Hall hadn't counted on the double whammy of the Russian KGB and American NSA. After the British documentary on Morris and Lona Cohen aired without repercussion in 1991, they figured Ted was probably safe. The scientist source the Russians called Percy or Perseus was so well disguised that even the Halls couldn't decipher who he really was from that film. Then in July 1995 the NSA released the first tranche of the Venona decryptions that had been so closely held for decades. The Cold War was over, and America's intelligence agencies were under increasing pressure to justify their operations and budgets. At the same time, a few historians and one elected leader—Senator Daniel Patrick Moynihan of New York—kept pressing the agency to give up its secrets of the past. Once the decision was made, the NSA proved just as proud to disseminate news of its intelligence coups as the KGB had been to trumpet its own successes.

Among the first decryptions released was the November 1944 cable saying Americans "Teodor Kholl" and "Savil Saks" had made overtures to Soviet intelligence. Amazingly, Hall escaped initial notice, as media attention focused on other decoded cables that verified the case against the Rosenbergs. Hall did hear something about what the NSA had distributed when he got a letter in the fall of 1995 from the scientist-author Arnold Kramish, who had been Ted's acquaintance at Los Alamos and later worked for the U.S. Atomic Energy Commission. The first nigglings of fear reached their brick row house.

Within weeks this interest materialized into visitors. Ralph Kinney Bennett, a senior staff writer for *Reader's Digest,* phoned and then showed up in Cambridge with Soviet expert and critic Herbert Romerstein, but the two didn't publish an article for a year. Then in September 1995 came our knock on Hall's door, and he got a closer look at how the evidence filtering out of the Russian archives dovetailed with the newest Venona decryptions. After two more meetings in Cambridge, Hall began giving us his side of the story in January 1996, with the stipulation that nothing could be published for at least a year. When *The Washington Post*'s Michael Dobbs appeared on their doorstep a month later, the Halls knew they finally were in for a shot of publicity. They didn't know if the inevitable news story would trail a stream of tabloid and television journalists in its wake or perhaps carry an even more menacing aftermath of renewed investigation. Though aware that the potential for prosecution had been raised again after forty-five years, the Halls could see nothing to do about it. They did little to protect themselves; they did not even have their telephone number unlisted. Their one concession to reality was to hire Benedict Birnberg, a London lawyer of the political left.

The media frenzy they found to be mercifully brief, if largely unpleasant—a few more uninvited visitors, a spate of phone calls, a single ambush by a British photojournalist lying in wait on their street. The two-page spread by Dobbs, including photos of everyone from Josef Stalin to Robert Oppenheimer, was written as the posing of a mystery rather than a call to indict. It included history on the American bomb project and Soviet spy operations, as well as what could be gleaned about Hall himself from interviews and the smattering of available records. Combining earlier reporting in Moscow with new spadework and the NSA revelations, Dobbs hypothesized that Hall, mentioned in a single cable, was actually the agent Mlad who had been cited in half a dozen Venona decryptions. The NSA confirmed within weeks that it had indeed identified Mlad as Theodore Alvin Hall, and Star as Saville Savoy Sax. But neither Dobbs nor any other journalist discovered what Hall and Sax really had done or found the reasons behind their decision to pass America's most important military secret of the twentieth century to the Soviet Union.

People magazine published one of the most unsympathetic followup articles, headlined "A SHY SCIENTIST IS EXPOSED AS A TRAITOR," but it contained nothing more about what Hall had actually done. In Britain the early publicity was soft. *The Guardian* ran a non-judgmental piece after Hall gave a short interview to British correspondent Jonathan Steele, who not only described the Venona evidence, but quoted the scientist's leftist viewpoints and said colleagues in Cambridge referred to him as "the great historical figure of biological microanalysis." The local *Cambridge Evening News* said Hall's fellow scientists at the university found it all rather unbelievable, and its headline labeled him a "GREAT GUY ABSOLUTELY DEVOTED TO HIS SCIENCE."

But some did call for an accounting. In America, historians John Haynes and Harvey Klehr, conservative chroniclers of the American Communist Party, said the Venona documents confirmed that Soviet-inspired communism had been a true threat in the United States, not just the product of right-wing hysteria. The new NSA documents revealed that Hall was among scores of Americans who broke the law and got off scot-free, they wrote in a scornful article in the neoconservative *The Weekly Standard*. "These men betrayed the United States and the rest of the Free World. They abetted a totalitarian and expansionist state ruled by Josef Stalin," they wrote. Rather than demand prosecution of Americans such as Hall so many years later, which Haynes and Klehr acknowledged might not be possible, they said simply that the passage of time "should not relieve them of the responsibility to account for their acts." They admonished journalists and historians not to "ignore the dishonorable and villainous conduct of the spies still among us." *The Daily Telegraph* in London went a step further, suggesting in October 1996 that Hall deserved the same fate as the Rosenbergs. "He assisted one of the two great enemies of civilisation [Stalin], and did so by deceiving colleagues and country," said the *Telegraph* editorial. "If he merits mercy, it is only because he is now ill, not because his crime is somehow diminished by time."

These were hard indictments to read, but their effect was fleeting. The Halls had surrounded themselves with family and friends whose outlook made them at least forgiving of what Ted Hall had done, if not thoroughly supportive, so he confronted no angry harsh accusers face-to-face. And it increasingly appeared that nobody with the power to demand an accounting in a court of law was going to press for one. With the deaths of Sax, Yatskov, Kurnakov, and the Cohens, there were no living eyewitnesses who could directly tie Hall to espionage.

OF COURSE THERE was a personal accounting for Hall to render, the internal debate pitting the slippery adversaries of right versus wrong. In one ruminant moment, Ted Hall was thinking out loud with a friend about what he had done and the reasons. The aim, as he had said many times, was breaking the monopoly of nuclear weapons. In retrospect, the issue was more complicated than building two piles of bombs in two different backyards to assure that none would be hurled from either. One salient factor was the nature of the country receiving the bomb data, a Soviet Union run by a dictator who ordered mass killings of his own people and the subjugation of others. "In 1944 I did not realize the nature and scale of the atrocities perpetrated in the Soviet Union during and after the 1930s," Hall said. "Many reports about these things had been proved false, and they seemed incompatible with the obvious dedication of the Soviet Army and people during the war. If I had seen the whole picture in focus, I feel quite convinced that I would have acted differently."

But then he puzzled over whether that was a logical approach, on grounds that the need for a global balance of power was unrelated to the nature of the regime in charge of whatever country was acting as the balance. In the end he concluded that he wouldn't have been able to ignore the human aspect. "On reflection," he said, "I think my emotional revulsion against Stalin's terror would have stopped me in my tracks. Simple as that."

Tied up in this intellectual package was Ted Hall's acknowledgment: not that his action was wrong, but that it had been based on faulty information. He may have been not entirely comfortable with his decisions, but late in life he still believed that what he did, considering the circumstances of the times as he knew them, was right. And he still felt some pride at having summoned the daring to take what he saw as a necessary step. The only regret he has expressed is that his choices caused hard times for his wife, Joan. Hall's code of ethics was painted from a very personal palette, his own shapes from his own colors, independent of society's legal definitions of right and wrong. He came to his position from the conviction that the laws in the 1920s and 1930s and beyond hadn't worked. He saw a dysfunctional democracy and nonfunctional economy and didn't trust either. So he did what he did.

Ted Hall was not the first or last to break a law he thought was wrong. But the impact on a society is both explosive and unpredictable when people choose not to accept the rule of law. Such rejection can leave a nation balancing on the tip of chaos, like post-Soviet Russia in the absence of a legal system its people respect; it can result in anything from ripples of crime to a cleansing tide of revolution. Civil disobedience has been a tool of dissent from Ghandi's India to Martin Luther King's American South, a tool of people who have no choice but to break laws that crush their lives. But civil disobedience is a public protest by people whose commitment is defined by their willingness to go to prison. Anti-nuclear activist Rotblat, who himself has put in the public domain much information that governments would rather keep hidden, said he could understand the goal of eliminating a nuclear monopoly fifty years ago. But he faulted the means used by Los Alamos spies, saying a scientist should be bound by the scientific tradition of openness. "If you feel something is wrong . . . come out in the open and say this is what you are doing and do not do it by clandestine means, regardless of the consequences," said Rotblat. "Take the punishment."

No formal judgment is likely to close the case of Theodore Hall. Even on the scales of history, it is hard to weigh the consequences of putting American atomic research in the hands of the Soviet Union in the mid-1940s. There is no question that an arms race quickly followed, but so did a balance of power. Brush fires and regional wars flared, but no third world war. Anxiety seeped down to the level of second graders flattened against school walls in air-raid drills, but in the end the real air raid never happened. Nuclear weapons were kept sheathed after the first deadly blasts because both sides had them. In all likelihood, the Soviets would have developed their bomb anyway, though probably not until the mid-1950s at the earliest. Without details from a second source like Hall, the suspicious Beria would have had information only from one scientist named Fuchs, who had the drawback of being German. The material from Greenglass was too naïve and garbled to substitute for Ted Hall's scientific formulations. With the Cold War declared over, archives are cracking open everywhere and may lead astute researchers to some clarifications. What no one will ever know is if the bomb would have demolished other cities and peoples, had America managed to monopolize it for a decade longer.

The mix of morality and politics that makes up Ted Hall's story is complicated and colored in a spectrum of varying shades, depending on the eyes of the viewer. We have laid out the facts as we found them for the court of historical hindsight, not tried to judge them.

THE EMOTIONAL RESPONSE to espionage, the passing of clandestine information about one country to another, ebbs and rises with the intensity of one's loyalty to nation.

Theodore Hall wouldn't call himself "patriotic" in any conventional sense, though he maintained he never lost his affection for America. Both he and Joan held American passports, but they were citizens in name only. They were passionately loyal to broader principles of political life—justice and equality, for example—that they believed weren't being observed in their native country. Ted Hall always believed the breaking of the atomic monopoly was in the best interests of Americans, even if it meant breaking American law. "If you care very much for the well-being of the people of your country and you take a step with the intention of keeping them from a horrible catastrophe, that is not disloyalty," Hall said in early 1997. "The experiences of Auschwitz and the Gulag and Vietnam remind us that blind obedience to authority is not always a good kind of loyalty."

The ideals and worries that made the Halls leftists pushed the Cohens into becoming ideologues who considered themselves lifetime revolutionaries. The Cohens never apologized for spying against America or Britain, and in the 1980s took citizenship in the Soviet Union. A few years before his death, Morris fondly quoted a film in which a young intellectual was telling Robespierre he could not quit the French revolution: " 'If you are a revolutionary you don't stop here. You go to the very end.' That's all." And so the Cohens did. They accepted the existence of past mistakes and even horrors that were being uncovered in their adopted country in their last years of life, welcomed the regime's loosening grip, and professed satisfaction as the new Russia turned toward social democracy. Russia was the only revolution they had known, and they stayed with the program to the end. For their loyalty they did receive some thanks. President Boris Yeltsin posthumously designated Morris and then Lona Heroes of Russia, the only Americans ever known to have been awarded the Soviet or the Russian hero's medal.

To the Halls in their later years, no attractive government loomed on the horizon. "We can't fill the role of political exiles longing for home," Joan wrote one time. They had considered Sweden as a potentially congenial place to live, but never moved there. Joan was among the disillusioned radicals still quietly wondering, without much hope, if there ever would materialize a political movement in which she could feel at home. Ted expressed a strong belief that "human beings are naturally intelligent, compassionate, and competent creatures, that they will find ways out of the present mess and into a decent future—although I am worried about the mass dementia systematically induced by the mass media." The Halls weren't looking for a country to love, just some peace of mind.

To the keenest of American patriots like Haynes and Klehr, that was the last thing Ted Hall deserved. They wrote that "peace should not come easily to Hall and others like him, who have been exposed at last by the American government's release of the 'Venona files.' " Haynes and Klehr were absolutely right that the Venona decryptions identified a web of Soviet espionage in America that had entangled scores of American citizens. But they overstated the case when they went on to write about those who denied their espionage: "They contributed to the miseducation of millions by helping to perpetuate the illusion that it was hysteria, not real evidence of treachery, that prompted the hunt for spies in the early years of the 'twilight struggle.' " Considering the slash-and-burn approach of McCarthyism, the suggestion that hysteria and political opportunism were not integral to the purges of the fifties is impossible to swallow.

The NSA's point in releasing its decryptions was not to justify McCarthyism. Nor was it simply to identify Americans whose acts had never been disclosed, or to paint black marks over the lives of those who had been merely under a shadow. It was to let Americans draw lessons about a troubling chapter of their national experience. William P. Crowell, deputy director of the NSA, warned that it will take time for historians and the public to "sort out the full meaning of Venona." Crowell noted with some wonderment that more than 100 people were shown to have served as Soviet spies in one short period from 1944 to 1945. "I think it is very important to the United States that we have an accurate understanding of that espionage and the reasons for it," he said, "so we know how to protect American democracy."

The country must know what happened, to figure out why it happened and to keep it from happening again. This period of widespread espionage was not born of the lust for money; the big-price-tag spies like Ames came later and were fewer. Nor were the Soviets so clever that they found a cache of weak people in the 1940s and twisted them to perform acts violating their consciences. They linked up with volunteers such as Theodore Hall, Saville Sax, and Morris and Lona Cohen, people who were smart and bold and convinced that American democracy wasn't functioning for the good of the people. As Crowell said, one must search for the reasons that people end up adversaries of the nation—whether propelled by disaffection with what is, or by attraction to a system that looks better—if one hopes to advance American democracy.

CHAPTER 30

Aftershock

Early in 1997, as we were finishing the manuscript for this book, Theodore Hall finally gave us the statement we had been urging him to compose since our first discussion with him at the tearoom of the Cambridge railroad station in the fall of 1995.

During fifteen full days of interviews over the intervening eighteen months, Ted and Joan Hall had churned up memories and emotions that in many cases had lain dormant for decades; they were sometimes puzzling, occasionally painful, and often humorous. But never once in that time did Ted Hall allow himself to utter a direct on-the-record acknowledgment that he had been involved with Soviet espionage agents. He needed more time to think about it, he would often tell us. More time to fill in the blanks in his memory: to consider what had been done so long ago by a nineteen-year-old Harvard physicist whom he had a hard time remembering.

On the sixteenth day of interviews, Hall handed us the two-page statement that he and his wife had composed on their home computer. He had obviously chosen his words with the care of a diamond-sorter. While he left no doubt that he was proud of what he had done, his objective was to acknowledge and justify it without actually confessing to specific acts of espionage. But taken together, his words constituted a historic assumption of responsibility. To our knowledge, it is the first time an American scientist even came close to acknowledging that he helped another nation build the atomic bomb.

Frugal as always, the Halls had printed out the document on the backs of two spoiled pages of a philosophical essay that one of their friends had given them. He handed us his statement on February 22, but a few days later he told us he wanted some time to reflect on his wording, and on March 24 he gave us a slight revision. This is what Theodore Alvin Hall finally wrote:

> I am grateful to the authors and publishers of this book for giving me the opportunity to express my present views.
>
> During 1944 I was worried about the dangers of an American monopoly of atomic weapons if there should be a postwar depression. To help prevent that monopoly I contemplated a brief encounter with a Soviet agent, just to inform them of the existence of the A-bomb project. I anticipated a very limited contact. With any luck it might easily have turned out that way, but it was not to be. Now I am castigated in some quarters as a traitor, although the Soviet Union at the time was not the enemy but the <u>ally</u> of the United States; the Soviet people fought the Nazis heroically, at tremendous human cost, and this may well have saved the Western Allies from defeat.
>
> It has even been alleged that I "changed the course of history." Maybe the "course of history," if unchanged, would have led to atomic war in the past fifty years—for example the bomb might have been dropped on China in 1949 or the early fifties. Well, if I helped to prevent that, I accept the charge. But such talk is purely hypothetical. Looking at the real world we see that it passed through a very perilous period of imbalance, to reach the existing slightly less perilous phase of "MAD" (mutually assured destruction).
>
> My fears of a severe postwar economic depression were not justified at the time. I might have realised that at the end of World War II, pent-up demand would keep the factories humming for several years at least. But the dangers have not really abated: automation and economic globalization are generating an intractable world-wide crisis of unemployment, and this has led to an unholy alliance between the weapons industry and the military, some of whom have been quite prepared to blow up the world in their Messianic zeal (General Thomas Power, former head of the U.S. Strategic Air Command, has been quoted as saying that he would regard it as victory if two Americans and one Russian survived World War III).
>
> There is now persuasive evidence that until 1956, and during the Cuban missile crisis of 1962, military flights over the Soviet Union were ordered without the knowledge of the President or

any civilian agency of the nation's elected government, and against their stated policies. The Strategic Air Command circulated a "Joint Strategic Capabilities Plan" for all-out nuclear war, with explicit instructions to conceal the very existence of this plan from all civilian authorities. All this was not merely an illegal usurpation of power, it was horrifically dangerous—the overflights were a provocation which put the fate of the world potentially in the hands of any Rambo on either side of the Cold War. Presumably through some quirk in the application of the rule of law, the perpetrators of this program were not punished but were awarded medals and retired with honor. I refrain from spelling out comparisons and conclusions which are all too obvious.

In 1944 I was nineteen years old—immature, inexperienced and far too sure of myself. I recognize that I could easily have been wrong in my judgement of what was necessary, and that I was indeed mistaken about some things, in particular my view of the nature of the Soviet state. The world has moved on a lot since then, and certainly so have I. But in essence, from the perspective of my 71 years, I still think that brash youth had the right end of the stick. I am no longer that person; but I am by no means ashamed of him.

I would like to add one strongly felt point about the fallout from the Venona documents. Those who have used revelations of espionage to support their view that McCarthy was right are a real threat to American democracy. In McCarthy's time the damning label of "Red" was applied not only to Communists but to all progressives and their organizations—to all political activity in support of trade unions, minority rights, academic freedom, secure medical care and in fact the whole apparatus of the Welfare State. All this was condemned as part of a sinister plot inspired by foreign devils—exactly the kind of claim that dictators use to suppress dissent. The truth is that while spies no doubt existed, they were never an integral part of American progressive movements. It would be terrible if that cycle of repression happened all over again.*

Theodore Hall
24/03/97

---

*See Hall's sourcing in Notes, p. 366.

Sources and Methods

This book could not have been written without the understanding and tolerance of our editors at the Cox chain of newspapers, for whom we worked as Moscow correspondents all the time this book was being researched and written. We are particularly indebted to Arnold Rosenfeld, Andrew Glass, Andrew Alexander, and Matt Vita for assigning us to Moscow under an arrangement that allowed us to devote part of our time to historical research.

Nor would this book have happened without the persistence of six talented researchers whom we recruited to gather documentary sources (and in some cases to conduct interviews) in the United States while we were working in Russia. They are: Andrei Cherny, for Harvard University background; Julie Gamill Gibson, for scientific background and for Lona Cohen's stay in Arden, Delaware; Dusty Horwitt, for FBI records and Saville Sax's life in Illinois; Helen McMaster, for background on espionage; Judy Jacobsen, for Morris Cohen's years at Mississippi A & M; and Mark Kennedy Windover, for genealogical records and Lona Petka's background in Massachusetts. For help in Moscow with technical translations, we often relied on Pavel Kustov.

This book began in the fall of 1994, when we happened to read an interview in *Komsomol'skaya Pravda* with an eighty-four-year-old American spy living in Moscow, Morris Cohen. We had never heard of Morris Cohen; his veiled story about Los Alamos espionage sounded intriguing. By then we were beginning our second year as Moscow correspondents, and we thought that an interview with Morris Cohen would make a good Sunday feature. We soon made the first of three trips to Los Alamos and began researching the Manhattan Project scientists' movement to oppose the use of the bomb.

Try as we might, we never quite could set up that elusive interview with Cohen, though we came close. After months of negotiations, the press bureau of the Russian Foreign Intelligence Service finally gave us permission to meet Cohen sometime around his eighty-fifth birthday, which was coming up on July 2, 1995. Twelve days before his birthday, Cohen went into a coma and died. We wrote his obituary and packed away our notes. But then the story took another turn. Just a few weeks later, the U.S. National Security Agency began releasing the fifty-year-old Venona Documents, and for the first time there was proof from Western archives that Cohen's claims of a major undetected spy at Los Alamos were not a KGB invention.

It took several months for a full set of those first Venona papers to reach us in Moscow; we happened to read the Teodor Kholl/Savil Saks cable late one evening in September 1995. Given all the time we had invested in researching the Morris Cohen story, we decided we couldn't let this clue pass. On September 19, 1995, one of us flew to England and knocked on Theodore A. Hall's door in Cambridge. After awkward introductions and a brief, inconclusive conversation, we left behind copies of the relevant Venona cables and the Russians' Mlad/Charl'z document, as well as samples of our previous writing. Several more meetings in Cambridge ensued, and we signed an agreement with Joan and Ted Hall providing for a series of embargoed interviews. To demonstrate their abhorrence of "checkbook journalism," the Halls insisted on the addition of a clause stating that no money had been, or would be, exchanged in connection with the interviews.

Ted and Joan Hall opened up only partway during a series of interviews held in Cambridge from November 1995 to March 1997. Even in those areas of their lives they agreed to discuss freely, their memories had sometimes faded or played tricks during half a century in which they had rarely discussed this story with any outsider.

To fill in the rest of the story, we have relied heavily on Russian intelligence and Ministry of Atomic Energy documents that briefly became available to researchers in Moscow during the post-perestroika period of 1991–1993, but that have since been reclassified and locked away by Russian authorities. We have also found confirmation and elaboration of the story of the Volunteers' spy ring through interviews with more than seventy-five other people who participated in or came to know bits of what happened. A dozen of these were professional Soviet intelligence officers, well versed in creating cover stories to protect secret sources. We have accepted their information gratefully, but with an extra dash of skepticism as we undertook to double-check the facts. As the Notes indicate, many of the passages describing acts of espionage are based on sources whom we have agreed to describe only as "confidential sources." In some cases, this confidential information came "on a background basis" from persons on the following list of interviewees; in other cases it is from people who have asked that their names not be mentioned at all. In addition, we have honored the requests of those who did not want their place of residence identified. Interviewees included:

D. W. Aiken, Starkville, Mississippi; Steven Anders, Fort Lee, Virginia; Harold Argo, Los Alamos; Colonel Vladimir Barkovsky, Moscow; Robert J. Beatson, Maryland; Valentin Belakogne, Moscow; Robert Louis Benson, Fort Meade, Maryland; Frances Berrigan, London; David Bibb, Las Vegas, New Mexico; Morris Brier, New York; Jack Bjoze, New York; George Blake, Moscow; Robert Bleiberg, New York; Jean Brachman, Arden, Delaware; Peter Carroll, San Francisco; Svetlana Chervonnaya, Moscow; Colonel Vladimir Chikov, Moscow; Claire Cohen, U.S.A.; Sam Cohen, Los Angeles; Cleveland Cram, Washington, D.C.; William Crowell, Fort Meade, Maryland; Martin Deutsch, Cambridge, Massachusetts; Nikolai Dolgopolov, Moscow; Alexander Feklisov, Moscow; Meredith Gardner, Washington, D.C.; Roy Glauber, Cambridge, Massachusetts; Edith Hall, U.S.A.; Edward Hall, U.S.A.; Joan Hall, Cambridge, England; Theodore A. Hall, Cambridge, England; Merrill Harmin, Illinois; Terry Hawkins, Los Alamos; Don Holcomb, Arden, Delaware; David Kahn, New York; General Oleg Kalugin, Washington, D.C.; Vladimir N. Karpov, Moscow; Gary Kern, California; General Vadim Kirpichenko, Moscow; Arnold Kramish, Virginia; Boris Labusov, Moscow; Robert Lamphere, Arizona; Edward Lending, Florida; Robert McQueen, Illinois; John A. Miskel, California; Donald Moore, Virginia; Sophie "Ginger" Petka Olson, U.S.A.; Jacques Penn, New York; Stanislav Pestov, Moscow; Cecil Phillips, Fort Meade, Maryland; Colonel Igor Prelin, Moscow; Thomas Reed, California; W. L. "Buddy" Richmond, Starkville, Mississippi; Joseph Rotblat, London; Arkady Rylov, Moscow; Boria Sax, U.S.A.; Sarah Sax, U.S.A.; Susan Sax, U.S.A.; Walter Schneir, Pleasantville, New York; Gay Search, London; Ilya Semyonov, Moscow; Glafira Semyonova, Moscow; John H. Simpson, Chicago; Yuri Smirnov, Moscow; Sam Smith, Edwardsville, Illinois; O. F. Snelling, London; Morton Sobell, San Francisco; Leya Sokhina, Dubna, Russia; Colonel Yuri Sokolov, Moscow;

Gilbert Steiner, Washington, D.C.; Yelena Stuken, Moscow; Anatoly Sudoplatov, Moscow; Edward Teller, Stanford, California; Sheila Wheeler, London; Clyde Wiegand, Oakland, California.

In addition to thanking those interviewed, we must express gratitude to people who took time to advise us, or guide us, or correct us, or share copies of documents with us, or point us to others who knew what happened. Foremost among them were two people: Roger Meade, the archivist of Los Alamos National Laboratory, and General Yuri Kobaladze, chief of public affairs of the Russian Foreign Intelligence Service. Others who have our thanks include: Vladimir Antonov, Moscow; Robert Conquest, Stanford, California; Robert T. Crowley, Washington, D.C.; Michael Dobbs, Washington, D.C.; Judi Emmell, U.S. National Security Agency press office, Fort Meade, Maryland; Peggy Engel, Maryland; FBI press office; Elliott Friedman, Chicago; Harvey Klehr, Atlanta, Georgia; Nerses Krikorian, Los Alamos; Jack Platt, Virginia; Ronald Radosh, Maryland; Retired FBI Officers Association, Quantico, Virginia; Herbert Romerstein, Washington, D.C.; Jerrold and Leona Schecter, Washington, D.C.; Jeffrey M. Smith, U.S. Department of Energy, Washington, D.C.; Carl Stern, director of public relations, U.S. Department of Justice; Oleg Tsarev, Moscow; Veterans of the Abraham Lincoln Brigade, New York; David Washburn, New York; Alvin Weinberg, Oak Ridge, Tennessee.

Blessed are the collectors. Institutions where we or our researchers assembled written materials included: Adams Historical Society, Adams, Massachusetts; Akron Public Library; Boston Public Library; *The Bulletin of the Atomic Scientists* library, Chicago; Central Polytechnical Library, Moscow; FBI Freedom of Information reading room, Washington, D.C.; Foreign Literature Library, Moscow; George Washington University Library; Harvard University archives; Henry George School archives, Philadelphia; Kuntsevskoye Cemetery register, Moscow; Kurchatov Institute archives, Moscow; Kvasnikov family archive, Moscow; Library of Congress; Los Alamos archives; Los Alamos library; Ministry of Atomic Energy archives, Moscow; Mississippi State University archives, Starkville, Mississippi; National Archives branches in Washington, D.C., San Pedro, California, and Chicago; New York Public Library; Nexis; Roosevelt University Alumni Office archives, Chicago; Russian Center for the Preservation and Study of Documents of Recent History, Moscow; Russian Foreign Intelligence Service archives, Moscow; Tarashcha municipal archives, Tarashcha, Ukraine; University of

California (Berkeley) Library; University of Chicago library; Wilmington Free Library, Wilmington, Delaware.

Finally, for turning a book idea into a book deadline, we thank our agent, Esther Newberg of International Creative Management. For refining our ideas and whittling our words, we are indebted to the creativity of people at Times Books/Random House, including our editor, Geoff Shandler; our copy editors, Sarah Polen and Nancy Inglis; and our publisher, initially Peter Osnos and then Peter Bernstein.

For those with suggestions on further lines of inquiry, our e-mail addresses are: joea@coxnews.com and marciak@coxnews.com.

Notes

PROLOGUE

XI   Background on Truman announcement: Rhodes (1995), pp. 371ff;
     McCullough (1992), pp. 747ff.

XII University of Chicago campus and Stagg field in 1949: *The Chicago Ma-
     roon,* various issues, September–October 1949; photographs from Univer-
     sity of Chicago archives; confidential sources.

XIII That was a traumatic . . . "those Asiatics": McCullough (1992), pp. 747ff;
     Rhodes (1995), pp. 368–379.

XIII Edward Creutz, Arthur Snell, and Otto Hahn quotations: *Chicago Daily
     Tribune,* Sept. 24, 1949.

XIV "viper in our bosom": West (1964), p. 365. West's phrase was "this viper
     in their bosoms," and she used it to characterize the Soviet spy Kim
     Philby as well as his former employers in British intelligence who had
     permitted him to continue unofficial ties with British security agencies
     long after he had come under official suspicion.

XIV Legal justifications for illegal acts: One of the clippings Mlad kept in his
     files was a front-page newspaper story in *The Guardian* (London and Man-
     chester), July 31, 1996. It told of one of the few instances when a Western
     law court upheld the defense that it is legally permissible to commit a
     crime in order to prevent a greater one. As *The Guardian* reported, a jury
     in Liverpool, England, cleared four women peace campaigners of crimi-
     nal charges after they acknowledged having plotted and caused $2.5 mil-
     lion in damage to a British Hawk fighter that they attacked with
     hammers. The jury verdict, which did not constitute a binding precedent
     for other cases, accepted the women's argument that they "had lawful ex-
     cuse to disarm Hawk ZH955 because they were using reasonable force to
     prevent a crime." The Hawk was one of twenty-four British fighters
     being prepared in a Liverpool factory for export to Indonesia, and pro-

testers contended that Indonesia would use the planes in acts of genocide in the Indonesian-occupied former Portuguese colony of East Timor.

xiv–xv Terry Hawkins quotations: Terry Hawkins interview, April 3, 1996; eighty-odd million killed: Hawkins's estimate of war fatalities in 1900–1945 is probably not much of an exaggeration. According to Gilbert, *The First World War* (New York: Holt, 1994), p. xv, approximately fourteen million soldiers and civilians were killed in World War I, while in World War II, Weinberg (1994), p. 894, says military and civilian deaths "probably reached sixty million."

xv   "A whole bunch . . . lot of significance": confidential source.

CHAPTER I. BABES IN THE WOODS

3   It was a steamy . . . : Unless otherwise noted, descriptions of events in this chapter are from retired KGB Col. Yuri Sokolov (interviewed Feb. 7, 1995, and April 26, 1996) and from confidential sources further discussed in Sources and Methods.

3   Scores of agents: Williams (1987), p. 167, citing headlines in the *New York World Telegram and Sun* and the *New York Mirror,* May 29, 1950.

4   Morris Cohen . . . Rudolf Abel: Morris Cohen interview, *Komsomol'skaya Pravda,* Oct. 4, 1994.

4   Young woman he had never met: FBI Gold file 100-81002 p. 2. The FBI said Gold told them the woman lived "in upper Manhattan, in the neighborhood of Lexington Avenue, near 62d, 72d, 58th, or 68th Street, and she may have been Russian-born or of Russian descent, although he never met her."

4   Percy Pyne mansion: The New York landmark at 680 Park Avenue was built in 1911 for Wall Street banker Percy Rivington Pyne by the architectural firm of McKim, Mead & White (*The New York Times,* Dec. 12, 1982). Percy Pyne has been described in *Sports Illustrated* as "an enormously rich playboy" who went to St. Paul's and Princeton, where he was a close friend before World War I of the Princeton football and hockey star Hobey Baker (*Sports Illustrated,* March 18, 1991). The Soviets bought the Pyne mansion for "close to a half a million dollars" in about 1947 (*The New York Times,* Aug. 20, 1948, p. 8) and occupied it until 1965.

4   Cohens' Seventy-first Street address in 1950: FBI Cohens file 100-406659-53, p. 6. The building has since been torn down and replaced by an apartment building.

5   Knew too much . . . Los Alamos: Morris Cohen interview, *Komsomol'skaya Pravda,* Oct. 4, 1994. Cohen said: "We understood that if we did not leave, we would risk to fall under suspicion. And it would lead them to Los Alamos."

6   FBI showing up: FBI Hall file 65-59122-241.

6   Hall was Mlad: Venona Documents, New York–Moscow No. 1699, Dec. 2, 1944.

7   A way to get back in touch: This account and subsequent information on how the Hall and Sax families responded to the FBI interrogation is from confidential sources.

7   Sax's relationship with Hall: Theodore and Joan Hall interviews, including Jan. 12–13, 1996, and July 30–31, 1996; Susan Sax interview, July 23, 1996; confidential sources.

8   There was talk . . . execution: Radosh (1983), p. 173, noted that after the emotional opening statement by U.S. Attorney Irving Saypol at the Rosenbergs' trial in early March 1951, "it is hardly surprising that editorial writers and newspaper columnists all over the country seemed confused about the actual charges against the Rosenbergs or that so many of them took the occasion to urge the death penalty for treason."

CHAPTER 2. ROOTS OF REBELLION

10   Three-story house: Edward Hall interview, July 23, 1996.

10   Always remembered the shock: Theodore Hall interview, Jan. 12, 1996.

10   On timing of Holtzberg family's move to Manhattan: *Trow's General Directory of Boroughs of New York, Manhattan and Bronx, 1933–34,* reported that the Holtzberg family was living in apartment 38 at 725 West 172d Street. Theodore Hall said (interview Dec. 7, 1996) he is sure his family was living in Washington Heights by the time the nearby George Washington Bridge opened to traffic in October 1931. By one Holtzberg family legend mentioned in a July 30, 1996, letter from Joan Hall to the authors, Governor Franklin D. Roosevelt kissed the six-year-old Theodore Hall during the ceremony for the opening of the George Washington Bridge.

10   Holtzbergs on Grand Street: U.S. Census, 1900, New York/Manhattan, Enumeration Dist. 273, sheet 33B, 34A. Jacob Holtzberg's occupation was listed as "furrier."

10-11   Lower East Side conditions: Howe (1989), p. 69ff.

11   Situation of Russian Jews in 1880s and 1890s: Lincoln (1981), pp. 592–593.

11   Population in Pale of Settlement: Howe (1989), p. 5.

11   Immigration and Holtzberg family background details: U.S. Census 1900, New York/Manhattan, Enumeration Dist. 273, sheet 33B, 34A; U.S. Census 1920, New York/Queens, Enumeration Dist. 279, sheet 8B. Full name of Barnett Holtzberg's mother, Terza Kutner, is taken from his March 31, 1908, license for his marriage to Rose Moskowitz: Municipal Archives, New York City.

11-12   Jacob Holtzberg's fur business: *New York City Directory, 1900–01;* Edward Hall interview, July 23, 1996. According to the 1900–1901 edition of the *New York City Directory,* the firm's address was 173 Mercer Street.

12   He was remembered . . . whimsical humor: Edward Hall interview, July 23, 1996; Joan Hall letter to the authors, July 30, 1996.

12   Rose Moskowitz background: According to her son, Rose Moskowitz was born in the United States and her parents ran a Hungarian restaurant in Manhattan (Theodore Hall interview, Jan. 12, 1996). This description is consistent with her listing in a 1925 New York State census (N.Y. 1925 Census, Queens County, Far Rockaway, ED73, AD5, Ward 5).

12   1926 strike: Howe (1989), p. 339.

12   But their success . . . 20 percent: McElvaine (1984), pp. 23, 39.

12   J. Holtzberg & Sons did go under: Edward Hall interview July 23, 1996.

12   Same neighborhood where . . . lived: *New York City Directory, 1910–1911,* showed them living at 508 W. 180th Street after their marriage.

12-13 Americans everywhere . . . 24.9 percent: McElvaine (1984), p. 75.

13   New fur partnership: Edward Hall interview, July 23, 1996. The new company came into existence no later than 1933, according to *Trow's General Directory of Boroughs of New York, Manhattan and Bronx, 1933–34.*

13   Mother was secretary: Theodore Hall interview, Jan. 12, 1996.

13   He was a latecomer . . . already forty-four: Hall's birth certificate (under the name Theodore A. Holtzberg) is listed in "Index of Births in Queens County, 1925," Certificate No. 10043, at the New York Public Library.

13   Rose adored . . . Theodore happened: interviews with Theodore and Joan Hall, Jan. 12, 1996.

13   Butcher stories: Theodore Hall interview, May 5, 1996.

14   "I simply had . . . the boy": Edward Hall interview, July 23, 1996.

14   "I worshiped . . . all that stuff": Theodore Hall interview, Jan. 12, 1996.

14   Playing curb ball: Joan Hall letter to the authors, July 30, 1996.

14   Macy's rebellion: Theodore Hall interview, Jan. 13, 1996; Joan Hall letter to authors, July 30, 1996.

14   "Just do it . . . defeated her": Theodore Hall interview, Jan. 12, 1996.

14   Punched his father: Theodore Hall interview, Oct. 5, 1996.

15   Philosophical argument of falling tree: Theodore Hall interview, Jan. 12, 1996; Edward Hall interview, July 23, 1996.

15   His older brother . . . "and end-all": Theodore Hall interview, Jan. 12, 1996.

15   Bodily ejected: Edward Hall interview, July 23, 1996.

15-16 From the Comintern . . . utterly sensible: Klehr and Haynes (1995), pp. 8–9.

16   "Our country . . . ideas of communism": Edward Hall interview, July 23, 1996.

16   Ed brought home: Edward Hall interview, July 23, 1996.

16   The writings of muckraking ". . . in rule": Theodore Hall interview, May 5, 1996.

16   By the time he was twelve . . . "discussing them": Theodore Hall interview, May 5, 1996.

16   Holtzbergs not Orthodox . . . feared by many: Theodore Hall interview, May 5, 1996.

16   Religious practices of Jewish immigrants: Howe (1989), p. 61.

17   "I went . . . I begin": Edward Hall interview, July 23, 1996.
      Change from Holtzenbecker to Holtzberg on Ellis Island: Edward Hall interview, July 23, 1996.

17   In the fall of 1936 . . . "inestimable benefit": application of Edward N. Holtzberg to change his name to Edward N. Hall, Supreme Court of Queens County, petition granted by Judge Burt Jay Humphrey on Sept. 15, 1936. Theodore Hall's name change was granted around the same time by another court, presumably one that handled cases involving minors.

CHAPTER 3. A REVOLUTIONARY YOUNG GIRL

18   Though she was . . . convert to socialism: Morris and Lona Cohen interview, KGB oral history (1989), tape 3, p. 26.

18   "We lived in the . . . opportunities there": Sophie "Ginger" Olson interview, July 14, 1995. She also said the Petkas had ten children.

18   Lona Petka leaving home at twelve or thirteen: N.Y. City Voting Register from 33rd election district of 9th assembly dist., 1949, in which Mrs. Lona Petka Cohen stated she had lived in New York City twenty-three years.

18   Lona Cohen wearing high heels to look older: KGB historian Gen. Vadim Kirpichenko interview, Feb. 28, 1996.

18   "She was only twelve . . . clothing factory": Morris Cohen interview with Spanish Civil War historian Peter Carroll, May 27, 1993.

18   Both her parents . . . weavers: Their occupations are listed as weavers in the marriage license of Feb. 6, 1901, found in records office at Adams, MA. Her father was listed as an employee of Berkshire Cotton in the 1901–02, 1910–11, and 1918–19 editions of *Adams Town Directory*. Her father was listed in both 1910 and 1920 U.S. Census records as a weaver in a cotton mill; the 1910 and 1920 Census records state that her mother had no paid employment. Petka 1910 Census record: Sup. Dist. 119, ED 19, Sheet 16A. Petka 1920 Census record: 1st Sup. Dist., 7th Enum. Dist.

18   Lona Petka birth date: FBI Cohens file 100-406659-5.

19   "Mfrs . . . goods and lawns": *Adams Town Directory, 1901–02*.

19   McKinley . . . stayed with Plunkett: letter to authors from local historian and genealogist Mark Kennedy Windover, Dec. 1, 1995.

19   Background on Ladislaus "Walter" Petka and Mary Czupryna: As with many immigrants, their names appear with different spellings on various documents. These spellings are taken from the first FBI background investigation of Lona Cohen in December 1954: FBI Cohens file 100-

406659-5. Dates of her parents' immigration to the United States from the 1910 U.S. Census for Adams Town, MA, Sup. Dist. 119, ED 19, Sheet 16A.

19   Sister paid passage: Sophie "Ginger" Petka Olson interview, July 14, 1995.

19   Came from . . . Belarus: Boris Labusov interviews, July 12, 1995, and March 7, 1997. Labusov, an official of the Russian Foreign Intelligence Service and longtime friend of the Cohens, said he had found that Lona Cohen's family and his came from the same area—the region of Brest, which is now the main Belarussian city bordering on Poland.

19   Marriage of Lona's parents: marriage certificate of Feb. 6, 1901, Adams Town records office.

19-20   Petka real estate transactions: from North Berkshire Registry of Deeds. 1915 purchase of Albert Street property, deed book 286, p. 530, and deed book 323, p. 214; 1916 transfer to Walter Petka and subsequent joint re-mortgage, deed book 329, p. 671, and deed book 315, p. 360; 1923 sale of property: deed book 349, p. 62, and deed book 367, p. 362.

19   Practice of houses being purchased in name of head of household: local historian Mark Kennedy Windover, Dec. 1, 1995, letter to authors.

20   Mary's pregnancy and birth of sixth child, Dellia: U.S. 1920 Census for Adams Township, MA, 1st Sup. Dist., 7th Enum. Dist.

20   "I was only . . . the war": videotape of Lona and Morris Cohen at Soviet state hospital in Moscow, July 1991. Collection of Sheila Wheeler. Lona Cohen also told a Russian historian in 1992 that her father took her to a parade of disabled war veterans in 1918, and this contributed to her pacifism. Svetlana Chervonnaya interview, March 6, 1997.

20   "Because she questioned God": Morris Cohen interview with historian Peter Carroll, May 27, 1993.

20   Petka family in Taftsville, CT: the *Adams Town Directory* of 1925–26, published in 1925, listed the Petkas as having already left Adams for Taftsville. Also, Sophie "Ginger" Petka Olson, Lona Cohen's sister, described in an interview on July 11, 1995, growing up on the Petka farm in Taftsville.

20   "Wasn't particularly happy": George Blake interview, July 12, 1995.

21   "cruelly" treated: Glafira Semyonova interview, July 18, 1995.

21   Her father drank a lot: George Blake interview, July 12, 1995.

21   Drunk driving arrest: Berkshire County (MA) Superior Court Case No. 1802, Book 12, p. 85. Petka was convicted and fined $100, but appealed the sentence. A jury ruled in his favor, but the court records are unclear whether jurors overturned the guilty verdict or the sentence.

21   Could not afford a car: Sophie "Ginger" Petka Olson interview, July 11, 1995.

21   "She was always . . . change the world": Sophie "Ginger" Petka Olson interview, July 11, 1995.

21   "had a hell of a good time": FBI Cohens file 100-406659-29.

21   "I was a revolutionary . . . are they?' ": Morris and Lona Cohen interview, KGB oral history (1989), tape 3, p. 26.

21   Lona in single-tax commune: She spoke about it with her friend George Blake, the British defector, in Moscow in the late 1980s or early 1990s. Interview with George Blake, July 12, 1995.

21-22   Henry George movement in Arden: *The Delmarva Star* (Wilmington, DE), June 21, 1925; *The Sunday Star,* Wilmington, DE, Sept. 6, 1931; *The Philadelphia Inquirer Magazine,* May 31, 1970; Henry Wiencek, *Smithsonian,* Vol. 23, No. 2, p. 124, May 1992.

22   Lona working at Mary Bruce Inn: Sophie "Ginger" Petka Olson interview, May 8, 1996. Mrs. Olson remembered that she was about eighteen when she visited Arden, which would place her visit in about 1937.

22   Mary Bruce Inn as a former brothel: interviews with longtime Arden residents Jean Brachman and Don Holcomb, July 29 and 30, 1996.

22   Upton Sinclair's involvement with the house: *Journal Every Evening* (Wilmington, DE), April 5, 1941.

23   Eating weeds, breadline chaos, River Rouge conflict: McElvaine (1984), pp. 80, 92–93.

23   Tugwell convinced, intellectuals endorsed: McElvaine (1984), pp. 126, 204.

23   Lona Petka . . . Communist Party: The 1935 date was given by Morris Cohen in KGB oral history (1989), tape 1, p. 14. Lona Cohen, who was present during that interview, did not dispute his statement. This date conflicts with data reported earlier by British journalist Arthur Tietjen, who wrote in 1961 that the earliest trace the FBI could find of Lona Cohen's American Communist Party membership was an application to join the party she allegedly signed in 1940—five years after Morris Cohen said she became a member. See Tietjen (1961), p. 62.

23   Lona Petka as a good cadre: Morris and Lona Cohen interview, KGB oral history (1989), tape 3, p. 26.

24   Rally with 20,000 people: *The New York Times,* July 20, 1937; *The Daily Worker,* July 20, 1937. Morris Cohen described the meeting, without a specific date, in Morris and Lona Cohen interview, KGB oral history (1989), tape 1, p. 30.

24   Lona had wanted to go . . . only for men: Col. Yuri Sokolov interview, Feb. 7, 1995.

24   "That was the first time . . . like a little bit . . .": Morris and Lona Cohen interview, KGB oral history (1989), tape 1, p. 30.

24   "Her only disadvantage . . . by all means": Morris Cohen, quoted in *Novoye Vremya,* No. 16, April 1991.

24   "Until that time . . . very, very kind": Lona Cohen, quoted in *Novoye Vremya,* No. 16, April 1991.

CHAPTER 4. ILLEGALS

25   "It was principally . . . in Spain": MacKenzie-Papineau Battalion questionnaire for new recruits filled out in August 1937 in Spain by "ISRAEL Pickett ALTMAN (name in the U.S. Morris Cohen)," deposited in Russian Center for the Preservation and Study of Documents of Recent History (RTsKhIDNI), fond 545, opis 3, delo 509.

25   Harry Cohen arrested with leaflets: Central State Historical Archive of Ukraine, fond 274, opis 1, delo 1275, p. 19. The arrest record named one of the defendants as "G. Kogan." G. Kogan was a contemporary Russification of "H. Cohen." The G. Kogan named in the czarist police document not only was from the same small Ukrainian town of Tarashcha but also was the same age as Morris Cohen's father, Harry Cohen. In addition to the 1905 document from Ukraine, a Cohen family member in the United States said in 1995 that according to family lore Harry Cohen was involved in revolutionary activities in Russia around the time of the 1905 revolution. The family member declined to be named for publication.

26   Fifty-seven anti-Jewish pogroms: Ascher (1988), pp. 130–131.

26   Immigration details and address of Harry and Sonya Cohen: U.S. 1920 Census for New York, Borough of Manhattan, Enumeration District 1107, sheet 17.

26   A fiery communist: 1995 interview with a Cohen family member who declined to be identified.

26   "Moishe got . . . did not": 1995 interview with Cohen family member who declined to be identified.

26   Morris Cohen at John Reed speech: Morris Cohen interview with historian Peter Carroll, May 27, 1993, and Morris Cohen interview, *Komsomol'skaya Pravda,* Oct. 4, 1994.

26   Seventy years later: George Blake interview, July 12, 1995.

26   Talmudic school: George Blake interview, July 12, 1995.

26   Moved away: Claire Cohen interview, July 11, 1995.

26   "the sun . . . and set with him": Claire Cohen interview, July 11, 1995.

26   Bronx championship: *The New York Times,* Oct. 30, 1927, p. 6.

26   Rubbed shoulders: Robert J. Beatson, former FBI special agent, confirmed in an interview (April 12, 1996) that Morris Cohen knew Hank Greenberg in high school. Beatson said the FBI questioned Greenberg about his acquaintanceship with Cohen in the late 1950s or early 1960s, and Greenberg said he had not kept in touch with Morris Cohen after James Monroe.

27   Couldn't pay all the bills: Claire Cohen interview, July 11, 1995.

27   Renamed: Bettersworth (1953), p. 305. Mississippi A & M was renamed Mississippi State College in 1932 and later renamed Mississippi State University.

27   Morris Cohen football career in Mississippi: Morris Cohen interview with historian Peter Carroll, May 27, 1993; *The Reflector* (Mississippi A & M student newspaper), Oct. 14, 1931.

27   "He got good . . . team": D. W. Aiken (former assistant freshman coach) interview, June 30, 1995.

27   On the cusp of bankruptcy: Bettersworth (1953), pp. 292–300.

27   "He was very evasive . . . liberal, you know. . . .": W. L. "Buddy" Richmond interview, July 14, 1995.

28   Spoke openly about the merits: FBI Cohens file 100-406659-1076, quoting sources whose names have been deleted.

28   Secret societies critiqued: *The Reflector,* May 16, 1934, p. 4.

28   "that there are members . . . a chance": *The Reflector* (Mississippi A & M student newspaper), May 18, 1932, p. 7.

28   Situation of blacks: Wier (1977), pp. 30–34.

28   Cohen and *Memphis Press-Scimitar:* Morris Cohen's employment records in the late 1940s with the N.Y. City Board of Education stated that he worked for the *Press-Scimitar* from 1933 to 1936 and also for an unspecified period for *The Jackson Daily News* in Jackson, MS. Cohen's board of education records are summarized in FBI Cohens file 100-406659-2, p. 3.

28   Organized waiters' strikes: Morris Cohen Spanish Civil War questionnaire, RTsKhIDNI, fond 545, opis 3, delo 509.

28   "At that time . . . into the river": Morris and Lona Cohen interview, KGB oral history (1989), tape 1, pp. 11–12.

28   Cohen at University of Illinois: FBI Cohens file 100-406659-542, pp. 1–5.

28   Football trainer at Illinois: Morris Cohen interview with historian Peter Carroll, May 27, 1993.

28   "Building a cooperative . . . students": Morris Cohen Spanish Civil War questionnaire, RTsKhIDNI, fond 545, opis 3, delo 509; Morris and Lona Cohen interview, KGB oral history (1989), tape 1, p. 13.

28   "Russia in fact . . . new just society": Morris Cohen political autobiography, quoted in *Novoye Vremya,* No. 16, April 1991.

29   "We were considered" . . . kicked out: Morris and Lona Cohen interview, KGB oral history (1989), tape 1, p. 14.

29   Kicked out of Illinois University: FBI Cohens file 100-406659-1081.

29   Morris's pseudonym Bruce Pickett and becoming branch organizer: RTsKhIDNI, fond 545, opis 3, delo 509. Also, Edward Lending, "Morris Picket . . . Né Morris Cohen" (1992). (The authors used the spelling "Pickett" since this was how Morris Cohen spelled his pseudonym on his August 1937 Spanish Civil War questionnaire.)

29   Spanish Civil War background and chronology: Thomas (1986), p. 595ff.

29   Israel Altman as head of group of seventeen volunteers that departed July 25, 1937: RTsKhIDNI, fond 545, opis 6, delo 856, p. 78.

30   "Finally we . . . "Internationale": Morris and Lona Cohen interview, KGB oral history (1989), tape 1, p. 31.

30   Many years later . . . the loyalists: George Blake interview, July 12, 1996.

30   "When the war . . . would go there": RTsKhIDNI, fond 545, opis 3, delo 509.

30   Cohen wounded: RTsKhIDNI, fond 545, opis 3, delo 509.

30-31   Cohen in hospital, elected agitprop leader: evaluation of Oscar Hunter, hospital political commissar, RTsKhIDNI, fond 545, opis 6, delo 856, p. 79.

31   "Boy Scout" faction: Lending (1992) and authors' 1995 interviews with Edward Lending.

31   "special school": *Novoye Vremya,* No. 16, April 1991, and *Komsomol'skaya Pravda,* Oct. 10, 1994; interviews with fellow "special school" student Jack Bjoze, April 7 and July 10, 1995.

31   General Alexander Orlov . . . "school is illegal": Costello and Tsarev (1993), pp. 275–277.

31   One war account . . . "its release": Carroll (1994), p. 197.

32   Morris Cohen on joining the special school: Morris and Lona Cohen interview, KGB oral history (1989), tape 1, pp. 31–34; *Novoye Vremya,* No. 16, April 1991; *Komsomol'skaya Pravda,* Oct. 4, 1994.

32   General Orlov's NKVD file credited . . . : Costello and Tsarev (1993), p. 276.

32   Jack Bjoze on Morris Cohen: Jack Bjoze interviews, April 7 and July 10, 1995.

32   Cohen bumped into Hemingway: Cohen Prison Letters, April 4, 1972, to Nora and Sheila Doel. Cohen wrote the Doels about a time when he was teaching English after he had been released from a British prison in 1969: "Suddenly I recalled that once upon a time, I had been close enough to Hemingway to be able to say something about the man as well as the author." Cohen's letter offered no explanation of his encounter with Hemingway.

32   Cohen assigned to Albacete: notation on letterhead of "Base de las Brigadas Internacionales Albacete," April 3, 1938, RTsKhIDNI, fond 545, opis 6, delo 856, p. 77.

32   Judging from the reminiscences: interviews with Jack Bjoze, April 7 and July 10, 1995, as well as other unidentified veterans interviewed by historian Peter Carroll, as reported in Carroll (1994), p. 197. Also, author Herbert Romerstein, a former U.S. House Un-American Activities Committee investigator, searched Russian archives on the Spanish Civil War and wrote a chapter entitled "Spain and the NKVD" in his book, *Heroic Victims,* that described Morris Cohen's recruitment as a Soviet spy. Romerstein's inquiry did not turn up a link between Cohen's unit in Spain and the executions of suspected Trotskyists, which Romerstein de-

scribed in detail in a separate chapter entitled "Persecution of Dissidents." See Romerstein (1994), pp. 53–62 and 68–74.

32 Sailing on *Ansonia:* FBI Cohens file 100-406659-1075.

33 One day at lunch . . . said much later: Morris Cohen interview, *Komsomol'skaya Pravda,* Oct. 4, 1994.

33 Dates of Semyonov's studies at MIT: MIT registrar's office.

33 Cohen work at Amtorg in the late thirties: FBI Cohens file 100-406659-559, pp. 3–4.

34 A document in . . . "prewar years": quoted in Semyonov official biography in Samolis (1995), p. 136.

34 "Lona and Morris . . . everything there": Glafira Semyonova interview, July 18, 1995.

CHAPTER 5. QUIRKY TALENT

35 In that summer . . . physicist: Theodore Hall remembered (interview, Nov. 16, 1995), "There were times when I wondered what I would like to be when I grew up. There were three things. One of them was a comedian, one was a journalist, and one was a physicist."

35 Theodore Hall at Townsend Harris: Townsend Harris yearbook of June 1940; Theodore Hall interview, Jan. 12, 1996.

35 James Jeans book: Theodore Hall interview, Feb. 17, 1996; inscription from copy of the James Jeans book in Hall's library in England.

35 "fired my imagination . . . bottom of it": Theodore Hall interview, Jan. 12, 1996.

35 Matrix multiplication: Motz and Weaver (1993), pp. 151, 152.

36 Ed Hall's background: Edward and Edith Hall interview, July 23, 1996.

36 "I had the feeling . . . theoretical physicist": Theodore Hall interview, Jan. 12, 1996.

36 Background and composition of Townsend Harris: *Newsday,* April 14, 1995; Gilbert Steiner interview, May 7, 1996.

36 "You could always . . . short pants": Gilbert Steiner interview, May 7, 1996.

36 Ted joined . . . Newton and Einstein: Townsend Harris yearbook of June 1940; Theodore Hall interview, Jan. 12, 1996.

36 Hall's baseball favorites: he recalled (interview, Jan. 28, 1997) that one was Henry Manush, who hit .378 for the Detroit Tigers in 1926.

36 Hall doubts about religion and his bar mitzvah: Theodore Hall interview, Jan. 12, 1996; Joan Hall letter to authors, July 30, 1996.

37 Theodore Hall's parody and bar mitzvah: Theodore Hall interview, Jan. 12, 1996; Edward Hall interview, July 23, 1996; Joan Hall letter to authors, July 30, 1996.

37 Sixth Avenue El controversy: *The New York Times,* June 11, 1995, section 13, p. 2. The article quotes *722 Miles,* a subway history by Clifton Hood,

as saying it was a persistent but unfounded "myth" that the steel from the 1939 demolition of the Sixth Avenue El was later used by the Japanese military in World War II.

37-38   Hall's involvement in anti-Miermann protest: Theodore Hall interview, Jan. 12, 1996.

38   "I am not sure . . . virtually nonexistent": Gilbert Steiner interview, May 7, 1996.

38   Bob Bleiberg . . . recalled: Robert Bleiberg interview, June 11, 1996.

38   Spanish Civil War as a formative event: Theodore Hall interview, May 4, 1996; Joan Hall letter to authors, July 30, 1996.

38   Hall joining, later drifting away from American Student Union: Theodore Hall interview, Jan. 12, 1996; Joan Hall letter to authors, July 30, 1996.

38   ASU chapter was founded by Julius Rosenberg: Radosh and Milton (1983), p. 3.

39   Ted Hall encounter with Columbia admissions officer: Theodore Hall interview, Jan. 12, 1996; Joan Hall letter to authors, July 30, 1996.

39   Even if they . . . would be fewer: Theodore Hall interview, Jan. 12, 1996; Joan Hall letter to the authors, July 30, 1996.

39   "Calculus was a delightful . . . no apparent use": Theodore Hall interview, Jan. 12, 1996.

40   Frisch-Meitner experiments and discovery of fission: Rhodes (1986), pp. 250–260; Libby (1979), pp. 54–55.

40   Enrico Fermi . . . Uhlenbeck: Kevles (1971), p. 324.

40-41   William Laurence article: *The New York Times,* May 5, 1940.

41   Coming atomic Garden of Eden . . . : Dr. R. M. Langer, *Collier's,* Vol. 106, No. 1 (July 6, 1940), p. 18.

41   "I read that . . . nuclear chain reaction": Theodore Hall interview, Jan. 12, 1996.

42   Unofficial Soviet theme song: *People's Songbook* (New York: Boni and Gaer, 1948), p. 48.

42-43   Hall following dispatches from Eastern Front, and his outrage at Truman remark: Theodore Hall interviews, Jan. 12, 1996, and May 4–5, 1996.

43   "If we see that Germany . . . as many as possible": *The New York Times,* June 24, 1941, cited in McCullough (1992), p. 262.

43   "For all military . . . is done with": Bullock (1992), p. 734.

43   "If they want a war . . . shall have one" and Otto Dietrich quotation: Bullock (1992), p. 735.

43   Moscow saved by Soviet counterattack: Weinberg (1994), p. 292.

CHAPTER 6. COMRADES

44   Lona's work with the Winstons: interview (April 12, 1996) with retired FBI agent Robert Beatson, who agreed to discuss his investigation of

Lona Cohen's work, but would not talk about the Winstons by name. However, the Winstons were named in an earlier account by author Sanche de Gramont, in which Alan Winston was listed as a source. See de Gramont (1962), p. 322, which says the Winston family lived at 1035 Park Avenue. When contacted by the authors June 24, 1996, Alan Winston confirmed Agent Beatson's description of Lona Cohen as a "tomboy" but said he would prefer not to discuss his recollections of his former governess on the grounds that his memory of her had dimmed over half a century.

44   Winstons involved in bedsheet-manufacturing business: Morris Cohen interview with historian Peter Carroll, May 27, 1993.

44-45 "She was kind of flighty" . . . scarcely "pretty": Jack Bjoze interview, April 7, 1995.

45   Morris's parents liked . . . "Polish shiksa": 1995 interview with a Morris Cohen relative who declined to be identified.

45   "Once I told him . . . attract attention": Lona Cohen interview in *Novoye Vremya,* No. 16, April 1991.

45   His second job was substitute teaching . . . "footballs and bats": Weidman, quoted in de Gramont (1962), p. 321.

45   Cohen was Semyonov's main . . . at Amtorg: interview with Glafira Semyonova (Semyonov's widow), July 18, 1996. Morris Cohen also said Semyon Semyonov served as his controller in New York: Cohen interview in *Komsomol'skaya Pravda,* Oct. 4, 1994. According to U.S. government records, Semyonov was in the United States in 1938–1940 and again from March 20, 1941, through Sept. 29, 1944. Source: U.S. government's footnote [v] to Venona Documents, New York–Moscow No. 1054, July 5, 1945.

45   Morris's initial assignment . . . German Nazi supporters: Lona and Morris Cohen interview, KGB oral history (1989), tape I, p. 35.

46   One of Semyonov's agents . . . Eastman Kodak: Alfred Dean Slack's confession to FBI, June 27, 1950, FBI Gold file 65-57449-666.

46   Operating manual for making nylon: Harry Gold statement, cited in FBI Gold file 65-57449-666.

46   Semyonov also . . . penicillin: Semyonov official biography in Samolis (1995), p. 135.

46   "I couldn't make . . . I thought about it": Lona and Morris Cohen interview, KGB oral history (1989), tape 1, pp. 2–3.

46   On July 3 . . . retreat if necessary: Bullock (1991), p. 730.

46   Petka-Cohen marriage license: Connecticut State Department of Health, Bureau of Vital Statistics, Town of Norwich.

47   "It wasn't really" . . . was there: Sophie "Ginger" Petka Olson interview, July 11, 1995.

47   The wife of . . . "for it": Claire Cohen interview, July 11, 1995.

47   To one of the men . . . "dick": 1995 interview with a member of Morris Cohen's family who declined to be identified.

47   "It was really . . . the Soviet Union": Morris and Lona Cohen interview, KGB oral history (1989), tape 1, p. 35.

47   Gottesman opposition to racketeer takeover: *The New York Times,* Oct. 22, 1937.

47   Benny Gottesman–Morris Cohen interchange: de Gramont (1962), p. 321.

47–48   "One day he came . . . made up my credo": quoted in *Novoye Vremya,* No. 16, April 1991.

48   Helen as Lona Cohen's cover name: She used this cover name in dealings with clandestine contacts at least from the late 1940s to the 1990s. According to a recently declassified CIA memo dated Feb. 6, 1948, a "Soviet agent of importance" with the cover name Helen was operating in the United States as early as 1937 (Benson and Warner [1996], p. 109). Yet according to this memo, American intelligence had established that this Helen was actually one of the cover names of Elizaveta Yulyevna Zubilina (whose actual family name was Zarubina), a captain in the Soviet NKVD stationed in Washington in the early 1940s. It remains a mystery whether American intelligence erroneously concluded that Zubilina/Zarubina's cover name was Helen. It is conceivable that Helen was Lona Cohen's cover name from the late thirties, or conversely that Helen was used in the late 1930s and early forties by Zubilina/Zarubina, then reassigned to Lona Cohen following Zubilina's August 1944 departure from the United States. Or it is possible that for a time, both women used the cover name Helen.

48   Lesli as Lona Cohen's internal Soviet code name: U.S. codebreakers found only one reference to Lesli in Soviet cable traffic: Venona Documents, New York–Moscow No. 50, Jan. 11, 1945. A U.S. government footnote to this cable identified Lesli as Lona Cohen. Lesli was still Lona Cohen's internal code name between 1947 and 1950, according to KGB Col. Yuri Sokolov, who was her controller in New York during that period (Sokolov interview, Feb. 7, 1995). Helen remained her cover name throughout the 1960s and on into the 1990s.

48–49   Machine-gun incident: described by KGB Col. Vladimir Chikov in *Novoye Vremya,* No. 16, April 1991, after Chikov was given access to a file on the Cohens known as KGB File 13676. In an interview in Moscow in May 1995, after he had retired from the KGB, Chikov explained that while the machine-gun incident occurred essentially as he described it, he deliberately falsified some details to protect the identity of KGB sources. Another retired KGB officer, who declined to be identified, confirmed that classified KGB files do contain references to Lona's machine-gun episode.

49   One KGB veteran . . . before the war: 1996 interview with retired KGB officer who declined to be identified. The story that Morris Cohen and Julius Rosenberg occasionally worked in tandem before the war is plausible, but not supported by documentary evidence.

49   Billions of dollars under Lend-Lease: According to *The New York Times,* Feb. 1, 1946 (pp. 2 and 22), a report sent to Congress by President Harry Truman in late January 1946 showed that the Soviet Union had received approximately $11 billion worth of American Lend-Lease aid from March 1941 through 1945. Deliveries to the Soviet Union included 14,795 planes, 7,056 tanks, 131,653 submachine guns, 1,951 locomotives, 2.8 tons of steel, and 15,417,000 pairs of combat boots. The report showed that the Soviet Union was the second largest recipient of U.S. Lend-Lease aid, behind Great Britain, which received about $32 billion of the total of $46 billion in Lend-Lease war aid.

49   Radar terminology: The term radar, officially adopted by the U.S. Navy in November 1940, was an acronym for Radio Detection and Ranging (Guerlac [1987], pp. 1–12).

49   Morris Cohen as recruiter of "radar source": Feklisov (1994), p. 76.; Col. Alexander Feklisov interview, July 27, 1995. A second source, Col. Vladimir Chikov of the KGB's public relations staff, described Cohen as the recruiter of an American "radar-sonar source" in an article in *Novoye Vremya,* No. 16, April 1991. Feklisov said he learned of Cohen's role when he was Soviet intelligence's controller of the radar source in 1944–45; Chikov said he learned of it in 1989 or 1990 by reading KGB archives on Morris Cohen.

50   Morris Cohen's U.S. Army service: FBI Cohens file 100-406650-1066. Whereabouts of 241st Q.M. Service Battalion in World War II: U.S. Army Quartermaster Corps historian Dr. Steven Anders, Fort Lee, VA, interview, April 19, 1995.

50   "I went in the Army . . . this work": Lona and Morris Cohen interview, KGB oral history (1989), tape 1, p. 37.

CHAPTER 7. HARVARD EGG ROAST

51   It was Ted's older brother . . . return mail: interviews with Theodore Hall, Jan. 12, 1996, and May 4, 1996, and interview with Edward Hall, July 23, 1996.

51   Conant and Harvard in 1942: Album of 1945, p. 16; "frame their college career": Album of 1946, p. 75, both from Harvard University archives.

51–52   "A flag pole rose . . . own daily ceremony": Album of 1946, p. 76.

52   "Have you seen . . . stand politically, etc.?": Theodore Hall to Edward Hall, Sept. 6, 1942, Hall Letters. His question referred to Sir Stafford Cripps, the British ambassador to Moscow in the early 1940s whose pro-Soviet views eroded while in the Soviet Union; to Prime Minister Win-

ston Churchill; and to Ernest Bevin, a trade union leader and figure in the Labour Party.

52–53   "Moscow-on-the-Charles" and Granville Hicks appointment: Album of 1943–44, p. 76.

53   "My roommates . . . quite brilliant": Theodore Hall to Edward Hall, Oct. 5, 1942, Hall Letters.

53   "are tops—absolutely exceptional": Theodore Hall to Edward Hall, April 4, 1943, Hall Letters.

53   Barney Emmart and Jake Bean: description of their interests from interviews with Theodore Hall (Jan. 12, 1996) and Roy Glauber (May 9, 1996). Barney Dunan Emmart died in Salem, MA, July 20, 1989, according to the Harvard Class of 1945's anniversary report published in 1990. William Jacob Bean died on Sept. 8, 1992, according to an obituary in *The New York Times* (Sept. 9, 1992).

53   Bean's invitation to the Paul Sachs course: Bean obituary in *The Independent* (London), Oct. 15, 1992.

54   "They regarded . . . passionate devotion": Theodore Hall interview, Jan. 12, 1996.

54   He was on duty: Theodore Hall interview, May 4, 1996.

54–55   Cocoanut Grove fire: *The Patriot Ledger,* Quincy, MA, Feb. 15, 1996.

55   Fourteen affiliated with Harvard: Album of 1945, p. 14.

55   "I was used . . . different standard": Theodore Hall interview, Jan. 12, 1996.

55   "Personally I have been . . . continue that way": Theodore Hall to Edward Hall, Feb. 3, 1943, Hall Letters.

55   Hall in Furry's statistical mechanics course: Theodore Hall to Edward Hall, Feb. 3 and April 4, 1943, Hall Letters; Theodore Hall interview, Jan. 12, 1996. Interestingly, Professor Furry was to acknowledge to Harvard officials in 1953 that he had been a member of a small unit of the Communist Party at Harvard from 1938 until at least 1946, when he began to become disillusioned with the party. However, Hall said (interviews, Jan. 12, 1996, Jan. 25, 1997) that he had no idea about Furry's leftist political leanings. For Furry background, see "Summary of Wendell H. Furry's Political Troubles," unpublished chronology by his wife, Susan Furry, May 1989, Harvard University archives.

55–56   "The special is . . . hardly dazzling": Theodore Hall to Edward Hall, April 4, 1943, Hall Letters. For a concise background on quantum mechanics, special and general theories of relativity, see Motz and Weaver (1993), pp. 273–284.

56   Trying to . . . to recall: Theodore Hall interview, Jan. 12, 1996.

56   "I remember . . . anti-communist": Theodore Hall interview, Jan. 12, 1996.

56   "As to other . . . active politically": Theodore Hall to Edward Hall, April 4, 1943, Hall Letters.

56   "Our youth is spent . . . off to war": quoted in Album of 1945.

56–57   On Theodore Hall teaching physics at Harvard: Mrs. Martin Landesberg (Theodore Hall's late sister) to Edith Hall, Sept. 15, 1943: "Ted has been teaching at Harvard. . . . Imagine a seventeen year old lecturing in physics. It's all Ed's fault."

57   On death of Theodore Hall's mother: Theodore Hall interview, Jan. 12, 1996; Theodore Hall cablegram to Lt. Edward Hall, July 2, 1943, Hall Letters.

57   Hall's term paper on relativity and atomic physics: Theodore Hall to Edward Hall, Oct. 24, 1943, Hall Letters.

57   "He was burning" . . . in the living room: Roy Glauber interview, May 9, 1996.

58   Sax arrived in September 1942: Album of 1946, p. 202.

58   Dark, wiry, and bohemian: interview with Sax's son Boria, May 7, 1996. According to Boria Sax, when Saville Sax was in his late teens or early twenties, he occasionally visited bars in Harlem with Baldwin and was accepted as black.

58   Saville Sax family background, upbringing: interviews with Boria Sax (son of Saville Sax), May 7, 1996; Susan Sax (ex-wife of Saville Sax), July 23, 1996; Sarah Sax (daughter of Saville Sax), Oct. 16, 1996; *The Washington Post,* Dec. 25, 1996.

58   "He had wild and . . . find his way": Joan Hall interview, May 4, 1996.

58   Sax's involvement in John Reed Society: confidential source. In addition, his son Boria Sax said in an interview (May 9, 1996) that Saville Sax was almost certainly a communist by the time he arrived at Harvard.

59   Van Vleck and quantum mechanics: "But only a few matched John Van Vleck in attempts to resolve theoretically the problems of atomic theory." Kevles (1971), p. 168.

59   Hall and Van Vleck's course: Theodore Hall interview, Jan. 12, 1996; Roy J. Glauber interview, May 9, 1996.

59   Van Vleck and Berkeley conference: Rhodes (1986), p. 416.

59   Van Vleck as 1943 Los Alamos consultant: Hewlett and Anderson (1990), p. 236.

59   Van Vleck and Kemble selected: FBI Hall file 65-59122-76, FBI Fuchs file 65-58805-1318.

60   Trytten background: Trytten obituary in *The Washington Post,* Sept. 17, 1978.

60   Poison gas . . . priority projects: Kevles (1971), p. 320.

60   Select group of rarities: J. Hammon McMillen of Kansas State College, quoted in Kevles (1971), p. 320.

60   Three secret crash projects: Kevles (1971), pp. 307–308.

60   "That room had . . . he'd ever lived": Roy Glauber interview, May 9, 1996.

60   Timing of Trytten visit: Roy Glauber estimated (interview, May 9, 1996) that it was about one month after his own eighteenth birthday, which was Sept. 1, 1943.

60–61   Ted Hall's recruitment by Trytten: Theodore Hall interviews, Jan. 13 and July 30, 1996; Theodore Hall March 1951 interview with FBI, Hall FBI file 65-59122-241.

61   Hall's "light-hearted" conversation in Lowell House: confidential source.

CHAPTER 8. AWFUL MAGIC

62   Date of Hall's arrival: Theodore Hall 3″ × 5″ index card, Dorothy McKibben personnel files, Los Alamos archives.

62   "this somewhat . . . project": Hoddeson et al. (1993), p. 131.

62–63   Description of 109 Palace Avenue: Bernice Brode, in Badash (1980), p. 134.

63   Glauber, Hall, von Neumann arrival: Roy Glauber interview, April 8, 1996.

63   Ranch School: Truslow (1991), p. 3.

63   To the Army . . . the Hill: Truslow (1991), p. 3.

63   "When we were . . . next door to U-235": Theodore Hall interview, Jan. 13, 1996.

64   Los Alamos Primer: LA 1 (April 1943), full text published in Serber (1992), pp. 3ff. Manhattan Project scientists devised an internal code for referring to fissionable isotopes. The code for an isotope consisted of a numerical shorthand in which the first digit was an abbreviation for an isotope's atomic number within the periodic table. The second digit was an abbreviation for its atomic weight. Thus plutonium—element 94 in the periodic table, with an atomic weight of 239—was code-named "49." U-235—element 92, with an atomic weight of 235—was called "25."

65   Average age: Hawkins (1983), p. 483, stated that as of May 1945, the most likely age for a member of the scientific staff was twenty-seven and the "average age" was 29.4. Bernice Brodie, who lived in Los Alamos from 1943 to 1945 as a scientist's wife and part-time computing machine operator, wrote that the "average age at Los Alamos was twenty-five" (Brode in Badash et al. [1980], p. 150).

65–66   "None of us . . . salaries!": Laura Fermi, quoted in Badash et al. (1980), p. 93.

66   Testing paraphernalia: Hoddeson et al. (1993), pp. 62–65.

66   On February 4 . . . Project sites: Hewlett and Anderson (1990), p. 243.

66   Painting thermostat box: LAMS 93 (April 15, 1944), p. 22.

66–67   Case and Glauber assignments: Hoddeson et al. (1993), p. 181.

67   "That was all right . . . Rossi's lab": Theodore Hall interview, Jan. 12, 1996.

67   Rossi assignment from Oppenheimer: Rossi (1990), p. 76.

67   "double ionization chamber": Rossi (1990), p. 77; LAMS 54 (Feb. 15, 1944), pp. 7, 17.

67   First few grams: "It is planned to measure the 25 spectrum using 2 g of enriched material," LAMS 50 (Jan. 15, 1944), p. 6. "25" was the Manhattan Project code name for uranium 235.

67   Soundproof metallic shield: LAMS 50 (Jan. 15, 1944), p. 6.

67–68   "The results . . . encouraging": LAMS 93 (April 15, 1944), pp. 7, 21.

68   "It wasn't . . . other way": Theodore Hall interview, Jan. 12, 1996.

68   Progress report of April 15, 1944: LAMS 93.

68   Rossi's May 15 report: LAMS 96 (May 15, 1944), p. 20.

68–69   It was a relief . . . reduced: Hewlett and Anderson (1990), p. 243.

69   Within the confines . . . writers: LA 128 (Aug. 26, 1944), p. 1.

69   "as a standard . . . laboratory": LA 150 (Oct. 5, 1944), p. 2.

69   Fifty years . . . neutrons: Hoddeson et al. (1993), p. 191.

69   Rossi's July 1 . . . "experiment": LAMS 117 (July 1, 1944), p. 15.

70   1,600,000 spontaneous fissions: LAMS 131 (Sept. 8, 1944), p. 4.

70   Oppenheimer considered resigning: Rhodes (1986), p. 549.

70   July 4, 1944, colloquium: Hoddeson et al. (1993), p. 240.

70   "It was decided . . . at it": quoted in Rhodes (1986), p. 549.

CHAPTER 9. CLUES TO ENORMOZ

71   Semyonov recalled to Moscow: he departed from the United States September 29, 1944, according to U.S. government records cited in footnote to Venona Documents, New York–Moscow No. 1054, July 5, 1945.

71   Lona Cohen heard nothing: Venona Documents, New York–Moscow No. 50, Jan. 11, 1945, said the last Soviet contact with Lesli had been a meeting with Tven (i.e., Semyonov) about six months earlier.

71   Two rosters: Venona Documents, New York–Moscow No. 1251, Sept. 2, 1944, and New York–Moscow No. 1404, Oct. 5, 1944.

72   For more than . . . Grand Concourse: Claire Cohen interview, July 11, 1995.

72   Lona's first war-plant job: This was the job listed on her November 1942 voter registration form with the New York City Board of Elections, according to FBI Cohens file 100-406659-33.

72   By November 1943: Lona Cohen listed this job on a November 1943 voter registration form with the New York City Board of Elections. FBI Cohens file 100-406659-33.

72   Move to 178 East Seventy-first Street: FBI Cohens file 100-406659-53.

72   "My in-laws . . . around with men": Claire Cohen interview, July 11, 1995. She was relating the story as it was told in Morris Cohen's family in the early 1950s, shortly after she married into the Cohen family.

72   Lona Cohen injury: FBI Cohens files 100-406659-34 and 100-406659-551.

72 "Lona Cohen definitely . . . loose morals": FBI Cohens file 100-406659-29. Although the identity of the interviewee was deleted, the retired FBI agent who conducted the interview, Robert Beatson, has told the authors (interview, April 12, 1996) that it was with a wartime neighbor of Lona Cohen's.

72 "mannish attire . . . year round": FBI Cohens file 100-406659-29.

72 "dozens" of moles: Semyonov official biography in Samolis (1995), p. 136. The Russian word *desyatki,* translated here as "dozens," can also be translated as "tens."

72–73 "I was in touch . . . our comrades": Lona and Morris Cohen interview, KGB oral history (1989), tape 1, p. 40.

73 "There was a seaman . . . That's wonderful": Lona and Morris Cohen interview, KGB oral history (1989), tape 1, pp. 41–42.

73 Lona made courier to OSS official: Lona and Morris Cohen interview, KGB oral history (1989), tape 1, p. 43.

73 Lona Cohen and "Zveno": Venona Documents, New York–Moscow No. 1239, Aug. 30, 1944. The cable fragment said: "Through Volunteer's wife we learned from [NSA translator's note: word indistinct, probably the word "Link" in English, or in Russian "Zveno"] brother at Link." This was one of only three references to "Zveno" in the Venona Documents. If Lona Cohen was really a go-between to Zveno, she was involved with one of the most intriguing of the scores of unidentified Soviet agents whose code names turned up in wartime cable traffic. A historical publication of the NSA and CIA (Benson and Warner [1996], p. xxviii) speculated that Zveno was William Weisband, a U.S. Army signals intelligence specialist who served in signals intelligence posts in North Africa and Italy during the war and later returned to the Army codebreaking staff in Virginia after the war. In 1950, Weisband was identified by an FBI informant as a Soviet mole, suspended from codebreaking duties and sentenced to a year in prison on contempt of court charges. Weisband was suspected, but never charged, of a more serious offense: disclosing to the Soviet Union in the late 1940s that the Americans had broken the Soviet wartime codes.

74 Lona Cohen as "Volunteer's wife": The Aug. 30 cable (Venona Documents, New York–Moscow No. 1239, Aug. 30, 1944) was the last trace of Lona Cohen in Soviet cable traffic before Semyonov left for Moscow and Lona Cohen was consigned by the *rezidentura* to "cold storage." By then Lona's code name Lesli may have been retired, for she was referred to in the August 30, 1944, cable as "Volunteer's wife." (Volunteer was the code name that had been assigned to Morris Cohen after the Spanish Civil War, according to Yuri Sokolov, a retired Soviet intelligence officer interviewed by the authors on Feb. 7, 1995.)

74 "evidence . . . atomic weapons": Kvasnikov official biography in Samolis (1995), p. 50.

74   M.A.U.D. report: A declassified copy was later reproduced as Appendix 2 of Gowring (1964), the authorized history of Britain's wartime atomic research. *Voprosy* (1992), documents 1 and 2, were copies of two October 1941 Soviet intelligence cables reporting the NKVD's clandestine receipt of the M.A.U.D. report.

74   Most likely leaker: This was also the judgment expressed in the two most current and important books on Soviet atomic history, Holloway (1994), p. 82, and Rhodes (1995), p. 52. On the other hand, Russian intelligence veterans have given credit instead to another member of the Cambridge Five, the late Donald Maclean.

74–75   "In a number . . . critical mass: *Voprosy* (1992), document No. 3, p. 109.

75   Molotov-Pervukhin meeting: *Khimiya i zhizn'* No. 5 (1985), "The First Years of the Nuclear Project," based on a 1978 interview with Mikhail G. Pervukhin.

75   Kvasnikov, the Moscow Centre . . . the New York *rezidentura:* Kvasnikov 1993 taped interview with his granddaughter, Yelena Stuken, Kvasnikov family archive, Moscow.

75   Because of . . . Japan: Kvasnikov 1993 taped interview with Yelena Stuken, Kvasnikov family archive, Moscow.

75   "One evening . . . acquaintances": Gold's Sept. 24, 1965, memorandum to scholar Augustus S. Ballard, quoted in Rhodes (1995), p. 91.

75–76   "a full report . . . end of January 1943": Sudoplatov (1994), p. 182. The memoirs of the eighty-seven-year-old former secret police general were greeted with much skepticism in 1994 because they included his allegation (p. 3) that unknown Soviet agents "convinced Robert Oppenheimer, Enrico Fermi, Leo Szilard, . . . and other scientists in America to share atomic secrets with us." Sudoplatov died late in 1996 without having substantiated his charges. Nevertheless, fresh documentary evidence from Russian archives does vindicate Sudoplatov on his other assertion that Soviet intelligence found out about Fermi's secret Chicago chain-reaction experiment early in 1943. See Ovakamian document, quoted below in this chapter.

76   Molotov turned . . . Kurchatov: At first, Kurchatov told Molotov he couldn't see how to overcome the difficulties of separating uranium. "I then decided to provide him with our intelligence data," Molotov recounted. "Our intelligence agents had done very important work. Kurchatov spent several days in my Kremlin office looking through this data. . . . He said, 'the materials are magnificent. They add exactly what we have been missing.' " Molotov, quoted in Rhodes (1995), p. 71.

76   Three weeks later . . . March 7, 1943: *Voprosy* (1992), document No. 4, p. 111.

76   Soviet Consulate: The balconied town house at 7 East Sixty-first Street was leased by the Soviet Union from Mrs. M. Hartley Dodge, a member

of the family that had founded the Dodge Brothers motorcar company. In 1948, Mrs. Dodge declined to renew the lease on the consulate, and all Soviet diplomats in New York consolidated their operations for the next several years in the Soviet mission to the United Nations, which was in the Percy Pyne mansion (*The New York Times,* August 20, 1948). The old consulate has since been torn down. Col. Alexander Felklisov (interview, March 7, 1997) said the intelligence *rezidentura* was in a metal-shuttered fourth-floor room.

76 "At first he" . . . Feklisov: Yelena Stuken interview, May 28, 1996.

76 NKVD and NKGB: The first is the Russian acronym for People's Committee for Internal Affairs, the second for People's Committee for State Security.

77 At the beginning . . . will begin: "About Works on a New Source of Energy—Uranium," classified top secret, July 29, 1943, signed Colonel of State Security Gaik Ovakamian, chief of the third department, first directorate, NKGB USSR (Russian Ministry of Atomic Energy archives).

77 One Soviet intelligence cable . . . put it: Venona Documents, New York–Moscow No. 961, 21 June 1943.

77 The next day . . . "vaporization": Venona Documents, New York–Moscow Nos. 972, 979, 980, June 22–23, 1944.

77 The seven-month gap . . . in 1945: The timing of atomic intelligence was traced by the authors through two sources—decrypted Soviet intelligence cables known as the Venona Documents, and top secret commentaries on atomic intelligence written in Moscow in 1943–1945 by the Soviet physicists Igor Kurchatov and Isaak Kikoin, some of which appeared in *Voprosy* (1992) and others that are on file in the archives of the Russian Ministry of Atomic Energy.

77–78 Near the end . . . Gold remembered: Rhodes (1995), p. 93; Williams (1987), p. 197.

78 Late in January . . . in England: Williams (1987), pp. 20ff.

78 Hitler's invasion . . . Manhattan Project: Williams (1987), pp. 46–63; Moss (1987), pp. 52–53.

78 First evidence of Fuchs contact with Soviets: Venona Documents, London–Moscow No. 2227, Aug. 10, 1941.

78 The material . . . diffusion membranes: The most complete account of the timing and content of material Fuchs passed to his Soviet contacts was in Fuchs's confession to FBI Agents Hugh H. Clegg and Robert J. Lamphere on May 19, 1950, at a prison in England following Fuchs's conviction for violation of the Official Secrets Act. See FBI Fuchs file 65-58805-1412, especially pp. 30–34.

78 $500 bonus: Venona Documents, New York–Moscow No. 1049, July 25, 1944.

78-79 Soviet agent Fogel: The identity of this unidentified Soviet atomic agent, whose code name was changed to "Pers" in September 1944, is one of the important remaining questions about World War II espionage. The first known reference to Fogel/Pers in Soviet cable traffic was a partly de-crypted report from Fogel on Enormoz about a chemical process involv-ing "neutralization" of a certain "weak" substance (Venona Documents, New York–Moscow No. 212, Feb. 11, 1944). His report may well have dealt with the layout of a heavy water plant then under discussion at Oak Ridge, for two weeks later in Moscow, Kurchatov wrote an evaluation for Soviet intelligence on new "materials" he had reviewed describing a heavy water plant that made use of "electrolysis and reaction columns" (Igor Kurchatov memorandum, Feb. 22, 1944, Russian Ministry of Atomic Energy archives). Four months later, a Soviet cable (Venona Doc-uments, New York–Moscow No. 834, June 16, 1944) reported the dis-patch to Moscow of "two secret plans of the layout of the ENORMOZ plant from FOGEL." Shortly thereafter, Kikoin wrote a commentary in Moscow describing recently received plans of an Enormoz factory as "ex-tremely important" (undated memo, second half of 1944, from I. K. Kikoin to M. G. Pervukhin, people's commissar of the chemical industry, Russian Ministry of Atomic Energy archives). Agent Fogel was men-tioned in two Soviet intelligence cables later in 1944, once when the agent's code name was changed to Pers (Venona Documents, No. 1251, Sept. 2, 1944) and once when the New York *rezidentura* was considering which courier should have contacts with Fogel/Pers (Venona Documents, Nos. 1749 and 1750, Dec. 13, 1944). As of this December 1944 cable, Fogel/Pers was evidently at "Camp 1," which has been identified in a So-viet document as the code name for Oak Ridge (V. Merkulov to L. P. Beria, Feb. 28, 1945, reproduced as *Voprosy* [1992], Document 7). After December 1944, Fogel/Pers never turned up again in decrypted Soviet cable traffic.

79 "somewhere in Mexico": Harry Gold confession to FBI, May 22, 1950, in Williams (1987), p. 198.

79 Fuchs and Gold agreed . . . he had disappeared: Venona Documents, New York–Moscow No. 1223, Aug. 29, 1944; Gold confession in Williams (1987), p. 198; Rhodes (1995), p. 113.

79 "A Review on the Uranium Problem": Kurchatov, memorandum of Dec. 24, 1944, on NKGB letter No. 1/3/16015.

79 Mechanism for clandestine contacts: Venona Documents, New York–Moscow No. 915, June 28, 1944.

79 Maclean's Washington assignment: Rhodes (1995), 129.

79 "the extremely curious remark on page 9": Kurchatov, memorandum of Dec. 24, 1944, on NKGB letter No. 1/3/16015. In fact, there was

no "Laboratory V" in the Manhattan Project, but either Kurchatov or some unknown NKGB translator may have misread the actual American code name for Los Alamos—"Laboratory Y"—and translated it as "Laboratory V."

CHAPTER 10. IMPACT OF THE GADGET

81   On Sundays . . . too late?: Theodore Hall interview, Jan. 13, 1996.

81   As he lay on his bed . . . to humanity: Theodore Hall interview, July 13, 1996.

82   Hall interest in Richard Strauss: Theodore Hall interviews, July 31, 1996; Jan. 26, 1997.

82   A month before . . . Oppenheimer: Rhodes (1986), p. 569.

82   "sniveling winds and pompous tubas": description from a review by Valerie Scher, *The San Diego Union,* Nov. 14, 1994, p. E-6.

82   There were times . . . he was duping them: Theodore Hall interview, July 31, 1996.

82   "People had . . . work that off ": Roy Glauber interview, May 9, 1996.

82   "Luis Alvarez . . . billiards table": Theodore Hall interview, Jan. 12, 1996.

83   "Hans Staub . . . 'world out?' ": Bernice Brode, quoted in Badash (1980), p. 141.

83   One of Hall's . . . restart it: Theodore Hall interview, May 4, 1996; Sam Cohen interview, Sept. 30, 1996.

83   To Cohen . . . Hall's attention: Sam Cohen interview, Sept. 30, 1996. See also Sam Cohen's recollection, quoted in "Secrets of Venona," by Ralph Kinney Bennett and Herbert Romerstein, *Reader's Digest* (September 1996).

83   Best contemporary snapshot: Theodore Hall to Edith Hall, May 20, 1944, Hall Letters.

84   "his prima donnas be happy": John H. Manley, in Badash (1980), p. 26.

85   In 1946 . . . about them: Badash (1980), p. 99.

85   Ted Hall was aware: Theodore Hall interview, July 31, 1996.

85   Would not be remembered . . . those talks: Martin Deutsch interview, May 9, 1996; Joseph Rotblat interview, July 30, 1996.

85   "There was considerable . . . than afterward": FBI Fuchs file 65-58805, Boston FBI report BS 65-3319 of Feb. 15, 1950.

86   A number of scientists . . . "Washington authorities": FBI Fuchs file 65-58805, Boston FBI report BS 65-3319 of Feb. 15, 1950. The FBI agents had come to question Deutsch because Klaus Fuchs had told agents after his spying conviction that Deutsch had been among his close friends at Los Alamos. During the 1950 FBI questioning, Deutsch refused to name any scientists who allegedly shared Fuchs's inclination to give nuclear secrets to the Soviets, and his description was packed away for four decades in FBI archives.

86   Alliance in disarray: Johnson (1983), p. 433; Weinberg (1994), p. 676.

86   "I know . . . the Russians": Joseph Rotblat interview, July 30, 1996.

86   Later that year . . . atomic research: Joseph Rotblat interview, July 30, 1996.

86–87   "I always thought . . . problems": Joseph Rotblat interview, July 30, 1996.

87   But another . . . "the gadget": Smith (1965), p. 61.

87   "The word came back . . . at all": Roy Glauber interview, May 9, 1996.

87   In his Delphic . . . control over it: Smith (1965), pp. 5–9.

87   "It was there . . . was made": Joseph Rotblat interview, July 30, 1996.

87   "I cannot see . . . present bombs": quoted in Rhodes (1986), p. 530.

87–88   "scolded us . . . Soviet Union": Rhodes (1986), p. 537.

88   "The President and I . . . mortal crimes": Rhodes (1986), p. 537.

88   "George Kistiakowsky . . . surrounded": quoted in Rhodes (1986), p. 574.

88–89   Ra-La experiment: Hoddeson et al. (1993), p. 269; Rossi (1990), pp. 86–87.

89   On October 15 . . . annual leave: The dates of Hall's leave were given in a June 1950 FBI document cited in FBI Hall file 65-59122-107.

89   However, by the time . . . bomb project: confidential source.

89–90   I have . . . quite differently: Theodore Hall statement, released to the authors Feb. 22, 1997.

CHAPTER 11. ADVENT OF MLAD AND STAR

91   Hall en route to tell Soviets: confidential source.

91   "The U.S. Congress . . . couldn't vote": Theodore Hall interview, Jan. 13, 1996.

92   Sax and Hall met: In FBI Hall file 65-59122-241, Sax acknowledged to the FBI that he met with Hall several times during a vacation from Los Alamos.

92   Sax's apartment description: Susan Sax interview, July 23, 1996.

92   Bluma Sax's character and activities in Russian War Relief: Susan Sax interview, July 23, 1996.

92   Sax and Hall plotting touchy logistics: confidential source.

92   Bluma Sax beliefs and fears: Susan Sax interview, July 23, 1996.

93–94   Sax's efforts to make Soviet contact: Venona Documents, New York–Moscow No. 1699, Dec. 2, 1944. A partial decryption by American codebreakers described efforts of an unnamed person to meet with Napoli and with "Helmsman" (Earl Browder's code name). According to the decryption, Napoli sent the unnamed person to talk to Bek (Kurnakov). Sometime before 1961, the American cryptanalysts concluded on the basis of what they termed "collateral" information (probably meaning material supplied to them by FBI counterintelligence officers) that the unnamed person who visited Helmsman was "Star" (Saville Sax's code name). Sax himself later told his wife he believed he had been photographed during at least one visit to some Soviet-related office in search of a Soviet intelligence contact (Susan Sax interview, July 23, 1996).

93   Background on Sergei Kurnakov: Venona Documents, New York–Moscow Nos. 929, 930, June 17, 1943.

94   Browder's situation in late 1944: Romerstein and Levchenko (1989), p. 235. Browder had been leader of the Communist Party USA, until it was temporarily dissolved at a convention in May 1944. It reappeared as the Communist Political Organization, which is what Browder headed in October 1944.

94   Browder's imprisonment: Klehr, Haynes, and Firsov (1995), p. 11.

94     $1.5 billion in import/export: Junius B. Wood, *Nation's Business Magazine,* March 1945, p. 46. This was a cumulative figure as of the end of 1941 and did not include the additional $11 billion in American Lend-Lease aid during the war.

94   Provocateurs at Amtorg: *American Mercury,* January 1940, p. 81.

94   Hall's encounter at Amtorg: confidential source.

94   "politically developed": Venona Documents, New York–Moscow No. 1585, Nov. 12, 1944.

94-95 Hall's "recruitment" meeting with Kurnakov: confidential source; *Komsomol'skaya Pravda,* Oct. 4, 1994; *Novoye Vremya,* No. 16, April 1991; Vladimir Barkovsky interview, Feb. 2, 1995. However, Hall, in a 1951 interview with the FBI (FBI Hall file 65-59122-241), denied he ever met Kurnakov.

95   Pressed vodka on him: confidential source.

95   Hall handed over a report to Kurnakov: Venona Documents, New York–Moscow No. 1585, Nov. 12, 1944; confidential source.

95   Policy dictated: Venona cables are filled with requests for permission to take day-to-day actions—recruit Americans, make contacts, use photo equipment, bring other Soviets into the network. Major decisions had to be cleared in Moscow. Examples are found in New York–Moscow No. 1657, Nov. 27, 1944; Nos. 1749 and 1750, Dec. 13, 1944; and No. 1773, Dec. 16, 1944.

95   Snapped a photograph: confidential source.

95   Hall and Sax went rowing: In FBI Hall file 65-59122-241, Hall told the FBI about boating with Sax in Central Park, p. 6; Sax also talked about it, p. 19.

96   Inquire about the fate: Sax statement in FBI Hall file 65-59122-241.

96   No one survived: Susan Sax interview, July 23, 1996; authors' interviews in Vinnitsa, Ukraine; reported in *The Atlanta Constitution,* March 21, 1994.

96   Sax got file to Soviets: Venona Documents, New York–Moscow No. 1585, Nov. 12, 1944.

96   Background on Yatskov: In America he used the fake surname Yakovlev, and that is what he is called in FBI files and in transcription of the Venona messages.

97   "To feel out . . . with him": Venona Documents, New York–Moscow No. 1585, Nov. 12, 1944.

97   Luncheon at Bonat's, Penn Station episode: confidential source. Bonat's Café is no longer in business, but the Summer–Fall 1944 edition of the New York telephone book listed the restaurant at 330 West Thirty-first Street.

97-98   Cable on Hall's meeting with Bek (Kurnakov): Venona Documents, New York–Moscow No. 1585, Nov. 12, 1944.

98   "simply wrong": Theodore Hall interview, Feb. 22, 1997.

CHAPTER 12. MOLE HUNT

100-101   CIC investigation of Rotblat: FBI Fuchs file 65-58805-616, March 7, 1950, summary; Joseph Rotblat interview, July 30, 1996; "Joseph Rotblat—The Road Less Traveled. Founder of the Pugwash Conferences on Science and World Affairs," *Science,* Vol. 52, No. 1, p. 46.

101   "Of course . . . question mark on me": Joseph Rotblat interview, July 30, 1996.

101   Allied intelligence report: Powers (1993), p. 364, notes that the Joint Anglo-American Intelligence Committee distributed a 5,000-word report on November 28, 1944, summing up what it had gleaned about German nuclear developments. It concluded no large-scale Nazi atomic bomb program was under way.

101   Rotblat confronted with dossier: quotes and description of episode from Joseph Rotblat interview, July 30, 1996.

101-2   Elsbeth Grant role: FBI Fuchs file 65-58805-1118; 65-58805-616, March 7, 1950, report; Joseph Rotblat interview, July 30, 1996.

102   O'Bryan told CIC: FBI Fuchs file 65-58805-1118.

102   "Although most . . . bureaucracy": Joseph Rotblat interview, July 30, 1996.

102   Rotblat departure: Joseph Rotblat interview, July 30, 1996; FBI Fuchs file 65-58805-616, March 7, 1950, memorandum.

102-3   "That they didn't . . . to watch me": Joseph Rotblat interview, July 30, 1996.

103   Minimized the significance: FBI Fuchs file 65-58805-1522.

103   Site easily guarded: Groves (1962), pp. 64–67.

103   Pseudonyms and bodyguards: Fermi (1954), pp. 202, 212; Smith and Weiner (1980), p. 268.

103   Ban on British lifted: Hewlett and Anderson (1990), pp. 272–280.

103-4   "to keep . . . and processes": Groves (1962), p. 141.

104   At the end of January . . . for uranium metal: Holloway (1994), p. 101.

104   Weinberg-Nelson episode: According to a February 6, 1948, CIA memo declassified late in 1996 (see Benson and Warner [1996], p. 105), the U.S. government was obtaining verbatim transcripts of conversations inside

Steve Nelson's house in Berkeley through what the CIA memo referred to as "technical coverage of his residence." For details on Weinberg case, see Stern (1969), pp. 57, 60; *Report on Atomic Espionage,* Committee on Un-American Activities, U.S. House of Representatives, Sept. 29, 1949, pp. 4–5; Romerstein and Levchenko (1989), p. 214.

104   "the object . . . installations engaged": Brown and MacDonald (1981), p. 621.

104   Grosse letter: Aristid V. Grosse, Rubber Director's Office, War Production Board, to Conant, April 15, 1943, microfilm roll 7, James B. Conant papers, National Archives.

104   Grosse mentioned: *The New York Times,* May 5, 1940.

105   Los Alamos radio intercept system: Badash et al. (1980), p. 11.

105   Undercover agents: Manhattan District History, Intelligence & Security (1945), pp. 2.4ff.

105   Twice-daily bus: Badash et al. (1980), p. 133.

105   Feynman stunts: Feynman (1985), pp. 97–99, 101.

105   Bet he could sneak a scientist: Joseph Rotblat interview, July 30, 1996.

105   Biggest fault: Col. Vladimir Barkovsky interviews, Feb. 5, 1996, and April 5, 1997.

106   Hiskey-Adams episode: HUAC (1949), 14.

106   During the war . . . sabotage: Manhattan District History, Intelligence & Security (1945) p. 2.10.

107   Gold finding Kristel Heineman: Venona Documents, New York–Moscow No. 1606, Nov. 16, 1944; Williams (1987), pp. 206–209.

107   Fuchs call from Chicago: Venona Documents, New York–Moscow No. 1606, Nov. 16, 1944.

107   David Greenglass role: Venona Documents, New York–Moscow No. 1600, Nov. 14, 1944, and New York–Moscow No. 1773, Dec. 16, 1944. Also, interview with Retired KGB Col. Alexander Feklisov, March 7, 1997, in which he acknowledged that Julius Rosenberg helped him recruit Greenglass as a spy.

108   "A report . . . on ENORMOZ": Venona Documents, New York–Moscow No. 1585, Nov. 12, 1944.

108   Black diplomatic suitcases: Rhodes (1995), pp. 96–101.

108   Scientists working on the bomb: Venona Documents, New York–Moscow No. 1699, Dec. 2, 1944. When the U.S. National Security agency distributed a decrypted version of the cable within the British and American intelligence agencies on May 21, 1952, it appended a footnote saying the message "probably contains material derived from MLAD (Theodore Alvin Hall)."

108   On December 25 . . . Kurchatov wrote: Kurchatov's memo entitled "Conclusions on materials accompanying document No. 1/3/22500

dated December 25, 1944," written April 11, 1945, Russian Ministry of Atomic Energy archives.

109   Electron multiplier at Los Alamos: LAMS 4, July 15, 1943.

109   "On the basis . . . the bomb": Kurchatov's memo entitled "Conclusions on materials accompanying document No. 1/3/22500 dated December 25, 1944," written April 11, 1945, Russian Ministry of Atomic Energy archives.

CHAPTER 13. SAVY'S RENDEZVOUS

110   Walt Whitman code: confidential source.

110   Not many weeks after Ted's furlough: confidential source.

110   Previous use of book codes: David Kahn, author of *The Codebreakers* and historian at the National Security Agency in the mid-1990s, has noted that the ancient Greek military expert Aeneas the Tactician "suggested pricking holes in a book or other document above or below the letters of a secret message. German spies used this very system in World War I, and used it with a slight modification in World War II—dotting the letters of newspapers with invisible ink" (Kahn [1967], p. 83). Kahn also described (p. 177) how the British spy Benedict Arnold employed a book code based on using certain pages and lines from Volume I of the fifth Oxford Edition of Blackstone's *Commentaries* to transmit secret information on West Point to the British in the 1770s. Kahn said (interview, Oct. 3, 1996) that one of the few known uses of book codes in the twentieth century was by anti-British independence activists in India. After consulting with another NSA historian, Kahn told the authors he knew of no instance when Soviet intelligence agents had ever communicated using a book code such as the Hall-Sax system based on *Leaves of Grass.*

111   "state of depression": Saville Sax statement to FBI, March 16, 1951, in FBI Hall file 65-59122-241; Susan Sax interview, July 30, 1996; Boria Sax interview, May 9, 1996.

111   List of Saville Sax jobs: FBI Hall file 65-59122-241.

111   "that Ted had . . . acted as a courier": Susan Sax interview, July 30, 1996.

111   "I believe he . . . on the same side": Boria Sax interview, May 9, 1996.

111-12 "extensive discussions . . . than for states": Theodore Hall interview, Jan. 27, 1997.

112   Michael Sidorovich: Venona Documents, New York–Moscow No. 1536, Oct. 28, 1944, indicate that Sidorovich had agreed to move from New York, apparently to Cleveland, where he would be the backup agent for an important Soviet spy in a military plant. He was identified by the U.S. government in the Venona Documents as William Perl, code-named Yakov.

112   "Savy was a . . . much so": Susan Sax interview, July 30, 1996.

112   Sax perfecting a cover story: Sax later told this story to the FBI in 1951, as evident in FBI Hall file 65-59122-241.

112   "a few months": confidential source.

112   Spurt of cables: Venona Documents, New York–Moscow No. 1699, Dec. 2, 1944; New York–Moscow Nos. 1749 and 1750, Dec. 13, 1944; and New York–Moscow No. 1774, Dec. 16, 1944. These cables referred to two Moscow–New York cables evidently on related subjects—Nos. 5740 and 5797—that were not deciphered.

112-13   "We consider . . . on ENORMOUS": Venona Documents, New York–Moscow Nos. 1749 and 1750, Dec. 13, 1944. There was a compelling operational reason why Harry Gold could not take on a lengthy trip to New Mexico: Fuchs had just sent word that he would visit his sister's house in Cambridge over Christmas 1944 (Venona Documents, New York–Moscow No. 1606, Nov. 16, 1944).

113   Little Boy and Fat Man: Hoddeson et al. (1993), p. 2. As this Los Alamos technical history makes clear, there were originally plans for a third design, Thin Man. It was envisioned as a gun-type bomb made of plutonium but the design was discarded and Thin Man was never produced because of Emilio Segrè's discovery about plutonium's high rate of spontaneous fission.

113   Working in the Ra-La . . . Fat Man: Los Alamos archivist Roger Meade said of Hall's job in the Ra-La group: "G-Division did about everything associated with Fat Man. Just because they were doing completely different work doesn't mean they were physically isolated. He would have known generally what was going on. He would have had access to sizes and shapes, which were the critical components." Meade interview, Jan. 8, 1996.

113   On November 28 . . . chemical compounds: Hoddeson et al. (1993), pp. 270–271, 338.

113-14   The uranium hydride idea . . . unworkable: Hawkins et al. (1983), p. 118, said the hydride gun-type bomb was abandoned in February 1944. Hoddeson et al. (1993) said interest in the hydride gun "had disappeared" by August 1944. However, until a real bomb was tested, no design ideas were completely written off.

114   Account of Hall-Sax meeting in Albuquerque: confidential sources.

114   One of the chemicals . . . of uranium: Hoddeson et al. (1993), p. 199.

115   On December 28 . . . active service: Theodore Hall letter to authors, Sept. 2, 1996. Also, Hall's military discharge records, shown by Hall to the authors on January 27, 1997, indicated that the date of Hall's induction and the start of his active service was December 28, 1944.

115   "Wait a minute . . . you'll find out": Theodore Hall interview, Jan. 12, 1996.

115   Under pressure to fill . . . at work at Los Alamos: Manhattan District History, Personnel (1947), pp. 6.7–6.19.

115   Five hundred SEDs in December 1944: Hawkins et al. (1983), p. 484.

115   When the recruiting . . . U.S. Army private: Theodore Hall interview, Jan. 12, 1996.

115-16   Only 19 of the 2,600: Hawkins et al. (1983), p. 484.

116   "I don't know . . . sidewalks appeared": Theodore Hall interview, Jan. 12, 1996.

116   Sax family stories about Saville Sax leaving documents at consulate: Boria Sax interview, May 9, 1996; Sarah Sax interview, Oct. 10, 1996.

116-17   Cable activity: Another hint that Sax probably returned to New York near the end of 1944 is a discontinuity in the numbering of the two deciphered Moscow cables to which the New York *rezidentura* responded on January 23, 1945. The first of the two Moscow-to-New York cables was numbered 316, the second 121. It is evident from other deciphered cables that a new series of Moscow cables began in early January 1945 and had progressed to No. 121 by mid-January. No. 316 was evidently from an earlier series of Moscow cables, perhaps one that began in 1944 and ended at year's end. Venona Documents, New York–Moscow No. 94, Jan. 23, 1996.

117-18   Cable of Jan. 23, 1945: Venona Documents, New York–Moscow No. 94, Jan. 23, 1945.

118   Spelled out their conclusions: There are other reasons for identifying Mlad as Theodore Hall, as *The Washington Post*'s Michael Dobbs was the first to report in a February 25, 1996, article. Among the points of similarity between Mlad and Hall: the November 12, 1944, Soviet cable stated that Theodore Hall had met with a Soviet official code-named Bek within the few days before Hall had to return to "Camp 2" near Santa Fe. The decrypted Soviet cables contained no indications that Hall ever met anyone from the Soviet consulate but Bek. Then, a month later, the code name Mlad began appearing in Soviet cable traffic, and one of the first cables specified that Mlad had met only one Soviet representative—the same Bek. (According to a footnote to Venona Documents, New York–Moscow No. 1585, Nov. 12, 1944, Bek was the code name of Sergei Kurnakov. This identification grew out of a FBI counterintelligence inquiry in the fifties and sixties aimed at identifying code names listed in the Venona Documents.)

CHAPTER 14. PASSING THE IMPLOSION PRINCIPLE

119   "great interest": Venona Documents, Moscow–New York No. 298, March 31, 1945.

119   Hall mentioned to Oppenheimer: S. K. Allison to J. R. Oppenheimer, Feb. 20, 1945, document A-84-019-32-18, Los Alamos archives.

119-20 Background on Ra-La shots: Alvarez (1987), pp. 136–137; Rossi (1990), p. 87–88; Hoddeson et al. (1993), pp. 148–154, 268–271; LA 13044-H, appendix A; "Memorandum on Conference of 15 April 1944 Subject: Discussion of the Ra-Ba-La Experiments," document A-84-019-32-18, Los Alamos archives.

120 Hall's role in Ra-La experiments: Theodore Hall interviews, Jan. 12 and Oct. 5, 1996.

120 Use of hemispheres in early Ra-La static experiments: fax from Los Alamos archivist Roger Meade, March 8, 1997; Theodore Hall interview, March 24, 1997.

120 Between 200 and 750 pounds: LA 13044-H (1996), appendix A.

120 240 curies of Ra-La: LA 13044-H (1996), appendix A.

120 Nowhere in the world . . . "like a fishing pole": Hoddeson et al. (1993), pp. 150, 153. This Los Alamos technical history quotes Los Alamos chemist Rod Spence as saying: "No one ever worked with radiation levels like these before, ever, anywhere in the world. Even radium people normally deal with fractions of grams, fractions of a curie." The technical history added: "By today's standards, the exposures they [Ra-La experimenters] received would be judged unacceptable."

120 "We were turning out . . . build some more": Theodore Hall interview, Oct. 5, 1996.

120-21 A set . . . simultaneously: Hoddeson et al. (1993), pp. 148–154, 268–271; Rossi (1990), pp. 87–88.

121 On February 20 . . . Ted Hall: S. K. Allison to J. R. Oppenheimer, Feb. 20, 1945, document A-84-019-32-18, Los Alamos archives.

121 February 28 meeting: Hoddeson et al. (1993), p. 312.

121 At another . . . "have our bomb": Hoddeson et al. (1993), p. 271.

121 Report No. 1103/M: *Voprosy* (1992), document 8, p. 122. A team of Russian scholars, working with the aid of historians of the Russian intelligence agencies, wrote in 1992: "In this document they mention for the first time the implosion method" (*Voprosy* [1992], p. 133).

123 "Advise forthwith . . . from Charl'z": Venona Documents, Moscow–New York No. 183, Feb. 27, 1945.

123 Meaning of code name Zapovednik: According to a footnote appended in 1973 to Venona Documents, New York–Moscow No. 799, May 26, 1945, by an unidentified U.S. counterintelligence analyst, "The RESERVATION [ZAPOVEDNIK]" was "possibly" a code name for Los Alamos, and its director, "VEKSEL," was "possibly" J. Robert Oppenheimer.

123 As Fuchs would later confess . . . fission in plutonium: FBI Fuchs file 65-58805-1412.

123 How long it took to exchange messages and draft intelligence reports: For example, a June 13, 1945, cable from New York predicting the U.S. atomic test took nearly a month of deciphering, cross-checking, and typ-

ing before the intelligence reached Beria, as detailed in Chapter 16. For details on Soviet wartime encoding procedures, see Chapter 22.

124   Insisted that they never knew each other: Greenglass told the FBI Sept. 26, 1950 (FBI Greenglass file 65-59028-332), that he wasn't acquainted with Hall. Hall told the FBI on March 16, 1951 (FBI Hall file 65-59122-241), that he recognized Greenglass's photo from newspaper articles on the Rosenberg case, but he did not "know him at Los Alamos, nor did he remember having heard of him while there."

124   Both Greenglass and Hall contributed: One detail that Greenglass probably contributed was Anchor Ranch. This was where Greenglass worked as a machinist in the explosives division. Anchor Ranch was a remote, well-protected site about three miles from the main Los Alamos technical area where Ted Hall worked. As far as is known, Ted Hall never visited Anchor Ranch. Greenglass probably also contributed other descriptive information on the Los Alamos site and security, but the report included nothing about the technical work in Greenglass's explosives shop at Anchor Ranch.

124   Several dozen: Holloway (1994), p. 99, reported that twenty-five Soviet scientists were working at Laboratory 2 as of April 25, 1944.

124   On March 5 Kurchatov: Kurchatov memo to NKGB, March 16, 1945, *Voprosy* (1992), document 9.

124   Three earlier secret commentaries: Kurchatov to NKGB, March 7, 1943; March 22, 1943; July 4, 1943 (*Voprosy* [1992], documents 5, 6, 7).

124   "They are . . . the bomb": *Voprosy* (1992), document 8, p. 122.

125   "Mlad's report about work . . . great interest": Venona Documents, Moscow–New York No. 298, March 31, 1945. The U.S. codebreakers were never able to decode the five code groups between "work" and "great," so it is impossible to know precisely what "work" the cable was referring to. In the NSA parlance, each missing code group could have been a word, an individual letter, a number, or a punctuation mark.

125   The wording of another report card: Venona Documents, Moscow–New York No. 298, March 31, 1945, not only contained an appraisal of Mlad's work, it also contained Moscow's report card of materials on gaseous diffusion received from Klaus Fuchs in the spring and summer of 1944. Interestingly, the cable's evaluation of Fuchs's materials closely paralleled a February 28, 1945, memo for the NKGB from Isaak K. Kikoin, who was Kurchatov's chief expert on uranium separation. The Kikoin memo confirms that the NKGB officer who drafted the March 31, 1945, cable closely followed Kikoin's earlier written judgment. The February 28 Kikoin memo had spoken of "testing of membrane" and "the location of some buildings." The March 31 NKGB cable referred to "tests of the membrane" and "the layout of the plant" (Isaak K. Kikoin, "Review of materials received December 25, 1944," Feb. 28, 1945, Russian Ministry of Atomic Energy archives.)

125   Relative velocity: The estimate of 10,000 meters per second, which Kurchatov received four months before the first American atomic test at Alamogordo, was a highly accurate projection of how fast the critical mass could be assembled inside an implosion bomb. Two months after Alamogordo, Fuchs gave the same estimate in a document he passed to Gold in their September 1945 meeting in Santa Fe, NM. Fuchs's September mention of 10,000 meters per second is documented in "Obzor po voprosu ob atomnoi bombe" (Review on the question of the atomic bomb), Document 462, Russian Ministry of Atomic Energy archives.

125   Twice in those two months: November 28 and December 11, 1944. Hoddeson et al. (1993), p. 338.

126   The uranium hydride gun bomb: Hoddeson et al. (1993), pp. 181, 338.

126   "The materials are of great value": *Voprosy* (1992), document 10, p. 123.

126   On April 10 . . . "great value": Venona Documents, Moscow–New York No. 349, April 10, 1945.

127   What Hall gave to Sax in Albuquerque: confidential source.

127   "What we did . . . means obvious": Edward Teller interview, April 4, 1996.

127   "negligible or less": Richard Feynman, quoted in Hoddeson et al. (1993), p. 181.

128   "Here was a guy . . . a rebel": Arnold Kramish interview, May 14, 1996.

128   "He was the most . . . annoyed by the Army": Kenneth Case interview, as reported by Michael Dobbs, *The Washington Post,* Feb. 25, 1996.

128   Hall's run-ins with the military: Theodore Hall interview, May 4, 1996; Sam Cohen interview, Sept. 30, 1996.

128–29   "It was a strange . . . I was doing anyhow": Theodore Hall interview, May 4, 1996.

129   Ra-La test shots in April–June 1945: LA 13044H, p. A.1.1.

129   "You take a sphere . . . around backwards: Theodore Hall interview, Dec. 7, 1996. Hall said (interview, March 24, 1997) that his role in the Bayo Canyon during the actual test shots was assembling the radiation counters that measured signals from the explosions.

129   Tampers used in Ra-La dummy bombs: Los Alamos archivist Roger Meade wrote to the authors (e-mail, March 7, 1997): "Both cadmium and uranium were used as tamper material. I could not find any information about how many shots used tampers, but my guess is most, since this was critical in simulating implosion."

CHAPTER 15. AN INKLING ABOUT ALAMOGORDO

130   "Very gloomy . . . maybe Seventy-ninth Street": Col. Alexander Feklisov interview, July 27, 1995. During 1944–1945 Feklisov was accredited as a Soviet diplomat under the false name Alexander Fomin and had the Soviet cable code name Kalistrat. For one of several mentions of Fek-

lisov/Fomin in Venona Documents, see New York–Moscow No. 586, April 26, 1944.

130   Feklisov-Scali episode: *The New York Times,* Nov. 14, 1985; Oct. 11, 1995. According to Anatoly Dobrynin, the Soviet ambassador to Washington during the Cuban missile crisis, Col. Feklisov contacted Scali "because he regarded him, rightly or wrongly, as an important CIA agent." Dobrynin said he was briefed about Feklisov's KGB channel to the Kennedy administration, but considered it "relatively insignificant" in view of his own ongoing contacts with Attorney General Robert Kennedy. See Dobrynin (1995), pp. 94–95.

130   Messmates in intelligence school: Feklisov (1994), p. 58.

131   Kvasnikov as Julius Rosenberg's controller: Col. Alexander Feklisov interview, May 7, 1997.

131   "Yatskov had . . . being followed": Col. Alexander Feklisov interview, July 27, 1995.

131   There were only . . . hard as possible: Lamphere and Shachtman (1986), p. 20.

131   Once, Feklisov remembered . . . "very carefully": Col. Alexander Feklisov interview, July 27, 1995.

132   "Serb has . . . courier . . .": Venona Documents, New York–Moscow No. 50, Jan. 11, 1945.

132   70,000 casualties: Weinberg (1994), p. 78.

132   Morris Cohen's assignment in the Army: He served through the war as part of the 3233rd Quartermaster Service Company, which was part of the 241st Quartermaster Service Battalion: FBI Cohens file 100-406659-1084.

132   History of 241st Quartermaster Service Battalion in World War II: interview with Steven Anders, historian of the U.S. Quartermaster Corps, April 19, 1995.

133   Her fellow workers . . . "their interests": Morris Cohen said in 1993 that Lona Cohen was shop chairman in "an airplane factory" the final months of the war. He did not name the company, but FBI investigators have determined from company personnel records that from 1943 to 1945 she worked at Aircraft Screw Products. Morris Cohen videotaped interview with Russian Foreign Intelligence Service historian, July 15, 1993; FBI Cohens file 100-406659-33.

133   "He stated . . . a Communist": FBI Cohens file 100-406659-51.

133   Coming home . . . " 'Good for you' ": Lona Cohen interview, KGB oral history (1989), tape 1, p. 39.

133   After the war . . . accepted: confidential source.

133   "Part of the materials . . . such a way": Kvasnikov reminiscence (ca. 1993), Kvasnikov family archive, Moscow.

133-34 "My babushka . . . the information": Yelena Stuken interview, May 28, 1996.

134 "Remember the . . . we are connected": Lona Cohen in an aside to Morris Cohen, during their interview with a KGB historian (KGB oral history [1989], tape 1, p. 4).

134 "By orders . . . Canada": Samolis (1995), p. 71.

134 Uranium arrived . . . in late 1944 or 1945: Vladimir N. Karpov interview, Aug. 2, 1996.

134 "I was interested . . . our scientists": Kvasnikov reminiscence (ca. 1993), Kvasnikov family archive, Moscow.

134 Yatskov considered making Lona Cohen Gold's backup: FBI Yakovlev file 100-346193-63. (Anatoly Yakovlev was the pseudonym on Anatoly Yatskov's diplomatic passport.)

134 "His mother . . . they succeeded": Susan Sax interview, July 23, 1996.

134-35 Sax had flunked out . . . become a physicist: A list of Sax's Harvard courses, including Physics 111 (Mechanical Heat and Wave Motion) and Math 211 (Engineering Mechanics), is on file at the Roosevelt University alumni office in Chicago. Sax submitted his Harvard transcript to Roosevelt College (now University) when he was applying there for admission in the late forties.

135 Timing of Lona Cohen's first trip to New Mexico: It must have been sometime after January 11, 1945, for it was after that date when she was recalled from cold storage and assigned Anatoly Yatskov as controller. Col. Alexander Feklisov recalled (interview, July 27, 1995) that the coffee shop meeting took place on a cool and nasty day not long before the end of World War II—sometime before Hiroshima. A check of 1945 Manhattan weather reports in *The New York Times* finds that there were cloudy, "nasty" days of the kind Feklisov remembered on April 7, April 16, April 23, and May 3. Based simply on his recollection of the weather, Feklisov speculated that the meeting could have taken place in the fall instead of the spring. However, a check of weather reports in *The New York Times* found no "nasty" day of the sort Feklisov remembered in either August or September 1945. By October 1945, the NKGB had been forced virtually to shut down espionage activities in North America because of the defection of Soviet GRU code clerk Igor Gouzenko on September 5, 1945, in Ottawa.

135 "We looked . . . meet Lona": Col. Alexander Feklisov interview, July 27, 1995.

135 She was blond . . . "you know": Col. Alexander Feklisov interview, July 27, 1995. Feklisov didn't meet Lona again until Anatoly Yatskov's funeral in Moscow in 1992, when they took time to exchange recollections about Lona's meeting with Yatskov in the coffee shop. Their encounter at

Yatskov's funeral rules out the possibility that Feklisov had watched Yatskov meet some other courier.

135   "possibly a minute or so": Harry Gold confession, quoted in Williams (1987), p. 206.

135   "as brief a period as was necessary": Harry Gold confession, in Williams (1987), p. 197.

135   First he needed . . . each other: Yelena Stuken interview, May 28, 1996.

135   The main addition . . . atomic bomb: FBI Fuchs file 65-58805-1397. Fuchs made a detailed confession in June 1950 after his conviction, spelling out what he had given Harry Gold and when. In this confession, Fuchs said it was only in June 1945 that he informed Gold of the approximate site and date of the upcoming atomic test.

136   Kvasnikov's May 26 cable: Venona Documents, New York–Moscow No. 799, May 26, 1945. "49" was the Manhattan Project's code name for plutonium, "25" was its code name for uranium 235.

137   What isn't speculation . . . Kvasnikov insisted: Kvasnikov reminiscence, (ca. 1993), Kvasnikov family archive, Moscow.

137   Lona Cohen's two New Mexico trips: In the fall of 1992, a few months before her death, Lona Cohen told her Russian friend Svetlana Chervonnaya (a historian at the Russian Institute of the USA and Canada) that it was her "feeling" that she had made two trips to New Mexico in pursuit of atomic information—once in August 1945 and once at some unspecified earlier time. Lona Cohen told Chervonnaya that her mind was hazy on the details because she was ill. Lona Cohen's recollection was related to the authors by Chervonnaya in an interview, March 6, 1997. Morris Cohen also recalled two Lona Cohen trips in his interview with *Komsomol'skaya Pravda* (Oct. 4, 1994), but he gave details of only one of the two trips. Yatskov's version of Lona Cohen's travels was related to the authors by Col. Alexander Feklisov (interview, July 27, 1995). According to Feklisov, Yatskov told him shortly before he died that Lona Cohen made two trips to New Mexico. Feklisov said: "One trip was successful, the other wasn't successful. She hadn't contacted the person. Yatskov told me" (Feklisov interview, July 27, 1995).

137   He also . . . "from Julius": Rhodes (1995), pp. 165–166.

137   "I have been guiding . . . Albuquerque is": Yatskov, quoted in Rhodes (1995), p. 165.

138   "Already in May . . . plutonium bomb": Col. Anatoly Yatskov, 1992 interview with Japanese TV, videocassette of unedited interview, Russian Foreign Intelligence Service archives.

138   "His task included . . . of such importance": Yelena Stuken interview, May 28, 1996.

138   "on Alameda Street . . . to the street": FBI Fuchs file 65-58805-1397.

138   "considerable packet of information": Williams (1987), p. 214.

138-39   Fuchs recalled that . . . soon be tested: FBI Fuchs file 65-58805-1412, p. 32.

139   By now Greenglass had . . . mass of uranium: Greenglass, July 17, 1950, confession in FBI Rosenberg file 65-58236-150, p. 12.

139   After seeing Greenglass . . . in New Mexico: Rhodes (1995), p. 173.

139   Cable number 18956/568: The number appears on the photocopy of a memo from V. N. Merkulov to L. Beria, dated July 10, 1945, reproduced in *Kur'yer Sovyetskoi Razvyedki* (1991), p. 11.

CHAPTER 16. THE GRAUBER INCIDENT

140   "a compromise of Mlad" and "completely unsatisfactory work": Venona Documents, Moscow–New York No. 709, July 5, 1945.

140   TOP SECRET . . . this year: *Voprosy* (1992), p. 127.

141   Gold-Yatskov late June meeting: Rhodes (1995), p. 173.

141-42   Merkulov letter to Beria (the Mlad/Charl'z document): *Kur'yer Sovyetskoi Razvyedki* (1991), p. 11.

142   Every reason to believe . . . Hall: Only once between early 1943 and July 1945 is the Soviet NKGB known to have adopted new code names for its agents in America. That was in September and early October 1944, which was a time of a major personnel changeover in the New York *rezidentura*. In that instance, deciphered cables showed that all the old code names were retired simultaneously and a complete set of new ones was substituted. The *rezidentura* used the code name Mlad in a cable on May 26, 1945 (Venona Documents, New York–Moscow No. 799), and Moscow used the code name Mlad in a cable on July 5, 1945 (Venona Documents, Moscow–New York No. 709). There is no reason to doubt that these cables referred to the same Soviet source Mlad who was mentioned in the Mlad/Charl'z document of July 10, 1945. The American NSA decoded at least 126 Soviet cables sent between the United States and Moscow during the period January 1–July 31, 1945. None of these showed any indication of a new set of agents' code names.

142   Fuchs and "Composition B": Williams (1987), p. 191. Composition B was the explosive actually used in the Trinity test bomb. Composition C was an alternate explosive used in some tests after Oppenheimer froze the design of the Trinity bomb using Composition B. According to Rhodes (1986), p. 577, Composition B was a "slurry of wax, molten TNT and a non-melting chrystalline powder, RDX." Composition B was 40 percent more powerful than TNT, according to Rhodes.

142   "has not been fully worked over": Venona Documents, New York–Moscow No. 799, May 26, 1945.

143   Grauber incident: Venona Documents, Moscow–New York No. 709, July 5, 1945.

143   "It is very" . . . in the mid-1960s: Roy Glauber interview, May 9, 1996.

144   Pervukhin letter to Politburo and Stalin: Holloway (1994), p. 115.

144   Interim Committee discussions: Rhodes (1986), pp. 647–648.

144   Byrnes protested: Rhodes (1986), p. 646.

145   "The guys . . . stars": Theodore and Joan Hall letter to the authors, May 1996.

145   Hall's recollection of Trinity: Theodore Hall interviews, Jan. 12, 1996, and Feb. 17, 1996.

145–46 "who spoke . . . thought, 'Ugh' ": Theodore Hall interviews, Jan. 12, 1996, and Feb. 17, 1996. Los Alamos travel records show that Compton, who was stationed in Chicago as head of the Metallurgical Laboratory, visited Los Alamos to witness the Trinity explosion on July 16, 1945 (Hawkins et al., p. 241), and that he later returned a few days after the Hiroshima explosion for a meeting of an advisory panel on August 11–13, 1945 (document A-84-019/9-5, Los Alamos archives). Oppenheimer spoke at a number of convocations of Los Alamos scientists in that period; if Compton also spoke, his remarks were not recorded. However, at least one other scientist has memories similar to Hall's. Ted Hall's friend Sam Cohen wrote in his memoirs about a colloquium the day of the Hiroshima blast when Oppenheimer spoke to an audience of cheering scientists. "He was proud, and he showed it, of what we had accomplished. . . . And his only regret was that we hadn't developed the bomb in time to have used it against the Germans. This practically raised the roof." Quoted from Cohen (1983), pp. 22–23.

146   "Things happen . . . nuclear weapons": Theodore Hall interview, Feb. 17, 1996.

146   Truman-Stalin exchange: Holloway (1994), pp. 116–117.

146   "It was the beginning . . . 'didn't understand' ": Maj. Gen. Vadim Kirpichenko interview, Feb. 28, 1996.

146   "We shall . . . up our work": Edmonds (1986), p. 69. In his memoirs former Soviet Ambassador Anatoly Dobrynin related a story that Andrei Gromyko, then Soviet ambassador to America, told him about Stalin's reaction at Potsdam. Gromyko told him that after the meeting, Stalin called Kurchatov and ordered him to speed up work. Kurchatov reportedly complained that he didn't have enough electrical power, and not enough tractors to clear forested sites for nuclear plants. Stalin supposedly cut the power to major populated areas, except for factories, and diverted it to the atomic project, and also gave Kurchatov two tank divisions to clear the trees (Dobrynin [1995], p. 23). However, his account seems to be a compression of conversations and events that took place over the subsequent several months, since in July 1945 the atomic bomb was still a laboratory project, and no atomic-related industrial facilities got under way until the Special Committee on the Atomic Bomb was named on August 20, 1945 (Holloway [1994], pp. 134–137).

CHAPTER 17. BOMB IN A KLEENEX BOX

148   Lona Cohen's Los Alamos trip: seven accounts by KGB veterans describe her trip, but none stated the name of her American contact: Lona Cohen official biography in Samolis (1995), p. 71; Col. Anatoly Yatskov, quoted in *Kur'yer Sovyetskoi Razvyedki* (1991), p. 14; Morris Cohen interview with Russian Foreign Intelligence Service (SVR) historian, July 15, 1993; Col. Vladimir Chikov in Chikov (1996), p. 152; Col. Vladimir Barkovsky, interviews with the authors, Feb. 9, 1995, and April 5, 1997; Col. Dmitri Tarasov, interview with *Komsomol'skaya Pravda*, July 10, 1993; and Gen. Pavel Sudoplatov in Sudoplatov (1994), p. 190. Of these, three (Samolis, Yatskov, and Sudoplatov) specified that Lona Cohen's trip occurred in August 1945, and one (Barkovsky) said the trip was "after Hiroshima." Another (Cohen) said it was "about the time the Americans dropped the bomb on Hiroshima and Nagasaki." Chikov (1996) stated (p. 159) that Lona's trip occurred in late July 1943, but Chikov's co-author, Gary Kern, has told the authors (interview, Oct. 2, 1996) that he believes the 1943 date in the book is incorrect. Kern said he has reason to believe that Russian intelligence officials would not allow Chikov to publish the correct date.

148   Snag a scientist: Brode in Badash (1980), p. 158.

148   Friendlier treatment: Feld (1979), p. 302; Williams (1987), pp. 215–216.

149   Train trip, boarding house: Morris Cohen, interview with SVR historian, July 15, 1993.

149   Lona Cohen's sojourn in Las Vegas, NM: Morris Cohen, interview in *Komsomol'skaya Pravda*, Oct. 4, 1994.

149   Make a pass: Morris Cohen, interview with SVR historian, July 15, 1993.

149   Five minutes: Col. Vladimir Barkovsky interview, Feb. 2, 1995.

150   "However . . . gave her the material": Morris Cohen, interview with SVR historian, July 15, 1993.

150   Hall's description of Albuquerque meeting with Lona Cohen: confidential source.

150   Lona Cohen had seen Hall's photograph: Morris Cohen, interview in *Komsomol'skaya Pravda*, Oct. 4, 1994. Morris Cohen said she had seen a picture of the "young scientist" she was supposed to meet.

151   Front-page report on Los Alamos: *The Santa Fe New Mexican*, Aug. 6, 1945.

152   Judge for yourself . . . about this box: Col. Anatoly Yatskov in *Kur'yer Sovyetskoi Razvyedki* (1991), p. 14.

152   "had been . . . of the police:" Col. Anatoly Yatskov Yatskov in *Kur'yer Sovyetskoi Razvyedki* (1991), p. 14.

152   Five or six sheets, rough sketch, "redundant": confidential source.

153   "a thick pile . . . writing": Col. Anatoly Yatskov interview, *Kur'yer Sovyetskoi Razvyedki* (1991), p. 14.

153   What Sax told Hall: confidential source.

153   Five other veterans, official history: See first note in Chapter 17.

153   Beria appointed as early as August 7: Rhodes (1995), p. 178. However, according to Holloway (1994), pp. 116–123, Beria was not chosen until mid-August.

153–54   Beria became chairman . . . "been destroyed": quoted in Holloway (1994), p. 132.

153   Harriman-Stalin conversation: Holloway (1994), p. 128.

154   "Persons disclosing . . . Espionage Act": Groves, reprinted in Smyth (1989), p. xiii.

154   "It was far . . . been set up": Smyth (1989), p. 307. Citing "reasons of security," the unreleased forty-page draft (declassified only in 1979) still described just one method of assembling a critical mass, the gun method, and said nothing of the implosion method.

154   Provided a ceiling: Smyth (1989), p. 305.

155   "Of course . . . incredibly quickly": Arkady Rylov interview, April 22, 1995. He also provided the description of how Department S worked.

155   "The intelligence service. . . . Who knows": Arkady Rylov interview, April 22, 1995.

155   Hall had come to believe: confidential source.

155   "I never had . . . the bomb": Theodore Hall interview, Feb. 22, 1997.

155–56   Lona described one informant: Svetlana Chervonnaya interview, March 6, 1997. Col. Vladimir Barkovsky, a senior consultant working at the Russian Foreign Intelligence Service, went even further, declaring (interview, April 6, 1997) that Lona Cohen obtained all her information in New Mexico from only one source—Mlad.

156   Greenglass bomb description: FBI Rosenberg file, 65-58236-150; Rhodes (1995), pp. 193–195.

156   Also in September . . . Alamogordo: FBI Fuchs file, 65-58805-1397.

156   Expressed uneasiness: Williams (1987), p. 215.

156   This was a rare . . . same foreign government: A 1946 inventory of the "intake" of wartime Soviet intelligence, found in a Moscow archive, reveals that in the weeks after Hiroshima, the NKGB received three separate reports on the atomic bomb. The 1946 inventory is listed in Russian Ministry of Atomic Energy archives as "Col. L. Vasilevsky to Lt. Gen. P. Ya. Meshik, Ministry of State Security Document 22/c/345, Dec. 18, 1946." The first of the three reports, "About the Atomic Bomb," was thirty-six pages long and recorded on the inventory as Document No. 458. Only a brief thirteen-line excerpt has been declassified in Russia; since it mentioned the Trinity test, Hiroshima, and Nagasaki, the document could not have been prepared before Lona Cohen's August trip to Albuquerque. The authors also found a considerably longer declassified exerpt of a document entered on the inventory as No. 462, entitled

"Obzor po voprosy ob atomnoi bombe" (Review on the question of the atomic bomb). No. 462 contains information that closely corresponds to the details that Klaus Fuchs confessed he gave to Harry Gold in September 1945 (see Fuchs's confession in FBI Fuchs file 65-58805-1412). The 1946 inventory also listed a third document, No. 464. This one corresponds to what Greenglass confessed he handed to Julius Rosenberg in September 1945. See below in Chapter 18, discussion of the erroneous thirty-six-lens design described in No. 464.

157   "For example . . . of course": Kvasnikov personal memoir (1993), p. 16, Kvasnikov family archive, Moscow.

157   Information "was so detailed . . . experimental production": Yatskov 1992 interview on Russian television, quoted by the Associated Press, May 12, 1992.

157   "priceless . . . needed in Moscow": Yatskov in *Kur'yer Sovyetskoi Razvyedki* (1991), p. 14.

157   "matched page to page": Col. Vladimir Barkovsky interview, Feb. 2, 1995.

157   "When you have two . . . are reliable": Col. Vladimir Barkovsky interview, Feb. 2, 1995.

157   Sudoplatov on Lona Cohen, Pontecorvo: Sudoplatov (1994), p. 201.

158   "This document . . . four years": Sudoplatov (1994), p. 201.

158   That bedrock . . . "NKGB USSR": *Voprosy* (1992), Document 13. Authorities in Los Alamos have declined to comment on the accuracy of the bomb description in Document 13.

158   "There's the . . . by now": Theodore Hall interview, Dec. 7, 1996.

CHAPTER 18. SEEDS OF THE SUPER

159-60   Stunned by . . . disappeared quickly: Szasz (1984), p. 160.

160   Kenneth Bainbridge–Paul Aebersold radiation study: LA 359, Sept. 19, 1945. One of the ten participants is listed as "T/5 E. Hall." Evidently Aebersold, who wrote the report with the British physicist P. B. Moon, referred to Ted Hall as "E. Hall" out of a mistaken belief that his nickname Ted was for Edward, rather than Theodore.

160   "I got volunteered . . . wasn't much": Theodore Hall interview, Feb. 17, 1996.

160   Post-Trinity radiation studies, September 9 press visit: Szasz (1984), p. 117; LA 359, Sept. 19, 1945; Hoddeson et al. (1993), pp. 375ff; *Life,* Sept. 24, 1945, pp. 27ff.

161   "There was an interim . . . tolerant": Theodore Hall interview, Jan. 12, 1996.

161   "The war is over . . . hydrogen bomb": "The History of the American Hydrogen Bomb," by Edward Teller, unpublished paper sent by Teller to a conference on the history of the Soviet Atomic Project in Dubna, Russia, May 14–18, 1996.

161-62   Fermi secret lectures: Nine pages of notes prepared by Fermi in 1945 have recently surfaced in Russian Ministry of Atomic Energy archives, containing information on the hydrogen bomb that remains classified in the United States. A Russian physicist with access to the Russian archives has stated (Goncharov, translation in *Physics Today,* November 1996, p. 50) that Soviet intelligence "obtained concrete information that embodied elements of the 'classical Super' theory in September 1945." From the context of Goncharov's statement, it is clear Goncharov was describing the Fermi lecture notes although Goncharov did not mention Fermi by name. Retired KGB Col. Vladimir Barkovsky has confirmed (interview, April 5, 1997) that Soviet intelligence did obtain the Fermi lecture notes in September 1945. Barkovsky said he'd recently conferred with Goncharov about the *Physics Today* article, and therefore he was certain the document on the "classical Super" to which Goncharov referred was the Fermi lecture notes. The authors have examined both Russian and English versions of the 1945 Fermi lecture notes now in Russian files (Ministry of Atomic Energy archives, document No. 462). The Russian translation of the Fermi lecture notes was signed by "Terletsky" (probably NKGB Col. Yakov Terletsky of Gen. Sudoplatov's Department S) and dated January 28, 1946. Two veteran officials at Los Alamos, asked separately by the authors to review the Russian archives' English version of the Fermi notes, have each said they appear to give an authentic picture of American knowledge about thermonuclear research as of 1945 or 1946. It appears most likely that the Fermi notes were passed to the Soviets by Klaus Fuchs in his meeting with Harry Gold in Albuquerque in September 1945. In Fuchs's confession to the FBI in June 1950 (FBI Fuchs file 65-58805-1412), Fuchs acknowledged that he passed a copy of Fermi's Super lecture to the Soviets. However, Fuchs remembered having turned it over sometime after he returned to Britain in June 1946, which was at least nine months after it actually reached Moscow. According to Los Alamos records, the only time Fermi is known to have delivered secret lectures on the Super is at Los Alamos in the summer of 1946. Fermi's 1945 notes may have been in preparation for an earlier series of lectures he never delivered.

162   Teller was certain . . . "Germany had been": Rhodes (1995), pp. 206–207.

162   Hall's assignment to work with Teller: the F-Division progress report of October 1, 1945, showed that Hall and de Hoffmann were working in Teller's Super group, which was then part of Enrico Fermi's F-Division. A month later, Progress Report 13 of the Gadget Physics Division (LAMS 304), November 1, 1945, p. 3, said: "Hall and de Hoffmann have carried out calculations in connection with the planned experiment of neutron scattering in para-hydrogen and para-deuterium." According to Los

Alamos archivist Roger Meade, another progress report in late 1945 showed that Hall had been attached to a group in the Theoretical Division that performed mathematical calculations for various sectors of the laboratory. Results of the Hall–de Hoffmann work for Teller were issued in classified form within the laboratory as LAMS 345, "Spin-Dependent Part of the Neutron-Deuterium Cross Section," by T. Hall and F. de Hoffmann, Feb. 6, 1946, and LAMS 346, "Neutron Spectrum from a Cold Parahydrogen Radiator," Feb. 11, 1946.

162–63   "According to your Group Leader. . . . in scientific research": J. Robert Oppenheimer to T/5 Theodore A. Hall, Oct. 1, 1945, Hall's personal files.

163   "You know . . . record collection": Theodore Hall interview, May 5, 1996.

163   At the time . . . Nagasaki: Hawkins et al. (1983), p. 304.

163   Los Alamos University: Documents found in Los Alamos archives, file A-85-003, included September 17, 1945, memo "To All Technical Personnel, Subject: Catalog of Courses"; undated "Catalog Los Alamos University"; "Statistics and Comments on Academic Courses Given at Los Alamos 1945–1948."

164   Hall as Klaus Fuchs's note taker: "Hydrodynamics Lecture Notes: Peierls," Theodore Hall, editor, ca. 1946, Los Alamos library.

164   "From the very . . . had no future": *Voprosy* (1992), p. 105.

164   That October . . . too good to be true: *Voprosy* (1992), p. 105.

165   "If this is" . . . rewarded or punished: *Voprosy* (1992), p. 105.

165   Stalin-Kurchatov January 25, 1946, meeting: Kurchatov handwritten notes from Stalin meeting, document N185/18.02.60, Kurchatov Institute archives.

165   Teller's Steinway: Blumberg and Panos (1990), p. 92.

165   Teller was on . . . in physics: For Teller's list of his early collaborators on the superbomb, see Teller (1987), p. 72. For Teller recommendation of Hall: FBI Greenglass file 65-59028-38. SAC Albuquerque to Director, May 18, 1950. In an interview with the authors April 4, 1996, Teller said he had no recollection of Ted Hall; if he wrote a letter of recommendation for Hall to the University of Chicago, he said, it must have been because de Hoffmann had asked him to do so.

165   The cover sheet said: . . . "F. de Hoffmann": "Neutron Spectrum from a Cold Parahydrogen Radiator," LAMS 346, Feb. 11, 1946. After looking over the para-hydrogen paper on which he was listed as the co-author with Hall and de Hoffmann, Teller insisted that their joint work had no relation to the hydrogen bomb. "To my knowledge, the practical application of this is practically nil," Teller said of LAMS 346 (interview with the authors, April 4, 1996).

165–66 Two Hall-Koontz reports: LA 541, "Counter for Use in Scattering and Disintegration Experiments," March 20, 1946, and LA 542, "Scattering by Helium of Neutrons from 0.6 to 1.6 MeV," March 20, 1946.

166 Louis Slotin in Spanish Civil War: Leona Marshall Libby, who knew Slotin at the University of Chicago in the early forties, wrote of Slotin in her autobiography (Libby [1979], p. 204): "He had spent several years in Spain as a member of the Abraham Lincoln Brigade. It had been for him a marvelous adventure as well as a crusade. He and I were laboratory assistants in a second-year physics course. . . . Louis told wonderful tales of how, in Spain, he had mainly been keeping a mountain funicular repaired and running to supply mountain troops, in spite of attacks and sabotage."

166 Slotin had told Ted about it: Theodore Hall interview, Dec. 7, 1996.

166 "There was a sort . . . group with Slotin": Theodore Hall interview, Dec. 7, 1996.

166 Hall losing atomic clearance: Theodore Hall interviews, Jan. 12, 1996, and May 4, 1996; FBI Hall file 65-59122-241.

166 Ted had . . . considerable stretch: Arnold Kramish interview, May 19, 1996. Kramish said he heard some years later from de Silva that Ted initially refused to sign for his Army checks, but that de Silva finally managed to persuade him to sign for them. Hall told the authors in 1996 that he did not recall refusing to accept his pay.

166–67 "I hear you're . . . Manhattan Project": Edith and Edward Hall interview, July 23, 1996; FBI Hall file 65-59122-241.

167 Hall's stay in Oak Ridge: Hall told the FBI in 1951 (FBI Hall file 65-58805-241) that he "remained about two months" at Oak Ridge and finally obtained a discharge to return to college. However, Hall's clear recollection of being at Los Alamos when Louis Slotin died suggests he cannot have reached Oak Ridge until early June 1946. His discharge papers show he was discharged from the Army on June 24, 1946.

167 "You had your . . . went back: Theodore Hall interviews, Jan. 12, 1996, and Jan. 27, 1997.

167 Hall's discharge: Hall's June 24, 1946, military discharge papers, Hall's personal files in England.

167 Presidential unit citation: Harvard College Class of 1944, Triennial Report, Cambridge 1947.

CHAPTER 19. DESTROY THIS LETTER

169 Ten physics books: Theodore Hall and Joan Hall interview, Feb. 17, 1996.

169 Co-author of four of the 124 titles: *The Bulletin of the Atomic Scientists,* Dec. 1, 1946, pp. 14–16. The Nobel physics laureates listed among the authors: Enrico Fermi (1938), Emilio Segrè and Owen Chamberlain (1959), Eugene P. Wigner (1963), Hans Bethe (1967), and Luis W. Alvarez (1968).

169   Three of his . . . degree: Hall, T.A., Koontz, P.G. (Aug. 1, 1947), "Scattering of Fast Neutrons By Helium," *Physical Review*, Vol. 72, No. 3, pp. 196–202; Sutton, R.B., Hall, T.A., Anderson, E.E., Bridge, H.S., DeWire, J.W., Lavatelli, L.S., Long, E.A., Snyder, T., Williams, R.W. (Dec. 15, 1947), "Scattering of Slow Neutrons by Ortho- and Para-Hydrogen," *Physical Review*, Vol. 72, No. 12, pp. 1147–1156; Koontz, P.G., Hall, T.A. (September 1947), "Counter for Use in Scattering and Disintegration Experiments," *Review of Scientific Instruments*, Vol. 18, No. 9, pp. 643–645.

169   Metropolis wartime work with Teller: Hoddeson et al. (1993), pp. 157–161, 204, 416.

169   "This was a big . . . to predict": Theodore Hall interview, May 4, 1996. Teller's office used by Hall: Theodore Hall interview, March 24, 1997. Hall said he shared Teller's office for a brief period, probably at the end of 1946.

170   "We just didn't share . . . 'Shostakovich, oihh!' ": Theodore Hall interview, Jan. 12, 1996.

170   Switched . . . to Allison: Theodore Hall interview, Jan. 12, 1996.

170   He remembered nothing: Edward Teller interview, April 4, 1995.

170   It's true that . . . for the cause: Smith (1965), p. 291.

170   "inevitable . . . or force": Smith (1965), p. 505.

170   "expressed extreme . . . imperialistic tendencies": Blumberg and Panos (1990), quoting Marvin Goldberger, p. 93.

170   But until . . . Teller wrote: Smith (1965), p. 504.

170   Hall's connection wasn't broken: confidential source.

170-71   Hall visit to family and Sax in New York: FBI Hall file 65-59122-241.

171   Savy transfer to Chicago; dependent on Ted: Joan Hall interview, May 4, 1996; Susan Sax interview, July 23, 1996.

171   For as David . . . "atom bomb project": FBI Rosenberg file 65-58236-150, p. 7.

171   Cooperative housing project: Joan Hall personal memoir (1995).

171   Joan Krakover background: Joan Hall personal memoir (1995); Joan Hall interview, Jan. 12, 1996.

171   Hung out with him: Joan Hall personal memoir (1995).

172   Shot with water pistol: Joan Hall interview, Jan. 12, 1996.

172   "That was the damned . . . as you could": Theodore Hall interview, May 5, 1996.

172   Joan Hall political development: Joan Hall personal memoir (1995).

173   "It has been pointed . . . the other way": Theodore Hall interview, July 30, 1996.

173   "I was madly . . . clear definitions": Joan Hall personal memoir (1995).

173   They quickly . . . right away: Joan Hall personal memoir (1995).

173   One hurdle that remained: A description of this episode came from a confidential source.

173 "naïvely convinced . . . fabrication": Joan Hall interview, May 5, 1996.

173 Discovered . . . heroic dimension: confidential source.

174 Hall-Krakover marriage: marriage license 1976581, Cook County Clerk's Office.

174 "rich friends in New York": confidential source.

174 Soviet payments: According to Greenglass's confession (FBI Rosenberg file 65-58236-150), Greenglass received $500 from Harry Gold in Albuquerque; Greenglass also told of borrowing a total of about $1,000 from Julius Rosenberg later and of receiving $5,000 from Rosenberg to flee the country in 1950 after Gold's arrest. According to Fuchs's confession (FBI Fuchs file 65-58805-1397), he received £100 in 1947 or 1948.

174 Never would accept repayment: confidential source. In a related recollection, Saville Sax's ex-wife, Susan Sax, told the authors that while they were married Saville brought home an unexpected $500, probably in 1949, which he told her had come from the Soviet spy contacts, and about which she felt very uncomfortable. Susan Sax interview, July 23, 1996.

174 Hall learning about "Helen" in New Mexico: confidential source.

175 "The Cold War . . . and menacing": Joan Hall personal memoir (1995).

175 Chicago scientists' movement: Smith (1965), pp. 116ff.

175 *The Bulletin of the Atomic Scientists:* The original title was *The Bulletin of the Atomic Scientists of Chicago.*

175 Hutchins's article: *The Bulletin of the Atomic Scientists of Chicago,* March 1, 1946, p. 1.

176 Hall found himself . . . "a shock, naturally": Theodore Hall interview, Jan. 13, 1996.

176 Hall handed over letters: FBI Hall file 65-59122-241. In his 1951 interview with the FBI, Hall said he was "a member of a committee within the Committee of Atomic Scientists [*sic*], which subcommittee was set up to study the Soviet Union."

176 "We found . . . in jargon": Joan Hall personal memoir (1995).

177 "The connection . . . possibility for judging": Theodore and Joan Hall interview, May 5, 1996.

177 Halls and Wallace campaign: Joan Hall personal memoir (1995).

178 HUAC hunt: Fariello (1995), p. 255.

178 "Freddie was . . . subscribe again": Theodore Hall interview, May 4, 1996.

178 Saville Sax marriage, Susan Healy background: Susan Sax interview, July 23, 1996; Boria Sax interview, May 9, 1996.

178 "tell our friends . . . I guess": confidential source.

CHAPTER 20. PARIS AND BACK

179 "walking . . . of knife": Col. Vladimir Chikov interview, June 1, 1995.

179 Shut down for more than a year: Col. Vladimir Barkovsky interview, Feb. 2, 1995, and Col. Yuri Sokolov interview, Feb. 7, 1995.

179   Get passports: FBI Cohens file 100-406659-5 indicates Morris Cohen applied for a new passport in May 1947; 100-406659-53 says Lona Cohen got a new passport in 1947.

179   Going to Paris: Morris and Lona Cohen interview, KGB oral history (1989), tape 2, p. 3; Col. Yuri Sokolov interview, April 26, 1996.

179   "a routine visit": Moorehead (1963), p. 35.

180   Fuchs in address book: Williams (1987), p. 90. Williams noted (pp. 143–145) that Fuchs's name was one of five on a list from Halperin's notebook sent to MI-5 in 1946, and that the FBI subsequently opened a file on Kristel Heineman.

180   Bentley gave 107-page statement: Radosh and Milton (1983), pp. 229, 527.

180   "After the Canadian . . . about one year": Col. Yuri Sokolov interview, Feb. 7, 1995.

180   Honorably discharged: FBI Cohens file 100-406659-2, pp. 1–2.

180   "Although the Hitlerist . . . Soviet intelligence": Samolis (1995), p. 69.

180   "spymania": Samolis (1995), p. 69.

180   Frostbite or snow blindness: FBI Cohens file 100-406659-29, p. 3.

180   Eligible for 10 percent disability: FBI Cohens file 100-406659-8.

180   Underground leaders and Soviet soldiers: Morris Cohen interview, KGB oral history (1989), tape 1, pp. 52–53.

180-81   Morris Cohen recollections of Buchenwald: Morris Cohen interview, KGB oral history (1989), tape 1, pp. 51–52. According to U.S. Army Quartermaster Corps historian Dr. Steven Anders, Morris Cohen's 241st Quartermaster Service Battalion was stationed at Weimar, five miles from Buchenwald, April 24–26, 1945. Buchenwald was liberated by American troops two weeks earlier, on April 11. Anders interview, April 19, 1995.

181   Cohen enrolled in Teachers College: FBI Cohens file 100-406659-2.

181   Cohens fond of children: Gay Search interview, June 9, 1995; Sheila Wheeler interview, June 6, 1995.

181   "They wanted . . . discuss it": Col. Yuri Sokolov interview, Feb. 7, 1995. Former KGB Col. Vladimir Chikov, in an interview June 1, 1995, said Morris Cohen's injuries during the Spanish Civil War prevented them from conceiving children, but this has not been confirmed by other sources.

181-82   Lona is said to have complained bitterly: Chikov (1995), p. 196. He said Lona had received documents from her OSS source that were so good she took the step of calling Yatskov at the consulate from a pay phone on the street. He gave her a place to meet him, but never showed up, according to Col. Chikov's version, because he was being followed. Col. Yuri Sokolov also said (interview, April 26, 1996) that Lona Cohen was very anxious to get back to work.

182   "institute . . . Yakovlev [Yatskov]": FBI Yakovlev file 100-346193-134.

182   Gold-Yatskov December 26, 1946, meeting: FBI Yakovlev file 100-346193-64.

182   "In those years . . . tougher than before": Morris Cohen interview, KGB oral history (1989), tape 1, pp. 44–46.

182   Despite the dearth . . . with the Soviets: Chikov (1996), pp. 200, 203.

183   "I must say . . . close relations"; Bastille Day description: Morris and Lona Cohen interview, KGB oral history (1989), tape 2, pp. 8–10.

183   "rented a house . . . as tourists": FBI Cohens file 100-406659-551, p. 4.

183   "We didn't want . . . 'any strength' ": Morris and Lona Cohen interview, KGB oral history (1989), tape 2, p. 4.

183   "a movement for peace" . . . accomplish anything: Chikov (1996), pp. 198–202. While Col. Chikov has acknowledged embellishing much of his book on the Cohens, his account of the Cohens' Paris trip is substantiated by other sources. An FBI inquiry in the 1950s learned of the Cohens' trip to Paris from U.S. passport records and from interviewing the Cohens' New York acquaintances. The Cohens spoke of the Paris trip during their 1989 KGB oral history project interview, as did Col. Yuri Sokolov in an April 26, 1996, interview with the authors.

183   Political union: Susan Sax interview, July 23, 1996; Ted and Joan Hall interview, Jan. 27, 1997.

184   Cohens' new control agent: Col. Yuri Sokolov interview, April 26, 1996; Chikov (1996), p. 201.

184   Possible November 1947 meeting and postcard signal: Chikov (1996), p. 202.

184   "Anatoly . . . friendly talk": Col. Yuri Sokolov interview, April 26, 1996.

184-85 First meeting between Sokolov and Lona Cohen: Col. Yuri Sokolov interview, Feb. 7, 1995.

185   Benjamin Franklin High School: Cohen's New York Public Schools employment records showed that on May 27, 1947, Cohen registered for a course at Columbia University as a student teacher, with field work at Benjamin Franklin High School. He entered Columbia University to receive his teacher's license on February 2, 1948, and was licensed as an elementary school teacher in June 1949, a high school social studies teacher in June 1950, and a junior high school social studies teacher in July 1950. FBI Cohens file 100-406649-2.

185   Group code-named the Volunteers: the first published reference to the Volunteers appeared in an article by KGB Col. Vladimir Chikov in an official Soviet armed forces publication (*Armiya*, No. 20 [1991], p. 73).

185   Fuchs on Teller's and Fermi's work in Chicago on the Super: Goncharov (1996), pp. 14–15. (Also, English translation in *Physics Today*, November 1996, p. 51.)

186   Hall was repelled: confidential source.

186   Remarkable intelligence . . . Fuchs was not the source: Goncharov (1996),
        pp. 14–15. (Also, *Physics Today,* November 1991, in English translation, p.
        51.) In March 1997, Goncharov was pressed for clarification when he ap-
        peared at a historical conference at the Lawrence Livermore Laboratory in
        Livermore, CA, to present an updated version of his *Physics Today* article.
        According to several American participants in this closed conference,
        Goncharov stated that the information on lithium did not come from
        Fuchs. "He [Goncharov] did not dispute our claim that [Soviet] insight
        into American interest in lithium came from another, yet unnamed
        source." (E-mail to the authors, March 18, 1997, from a confidential
        source attending the Livermore conference.) Also, the authors have ex-
        amined a detailed written description of the American Super project re-
        ceived by Moscow from Fuchs in April 1948. The Fuchs document made
        no mention of using lithium as a nuclear bomb fuel. Fuchs is known to
        have visited the United States for a declassification conference and had
        dinner with Teller in late November 1949. But that was at least a month
        after the October intelligence report on lithium reached Moscow. Re-
        tired KGB Col. Alexander Feklisov, who was Fuchs's controller in Lon-
        don in the late 1940s, said (interview, March 7, 1997) that he is certain that
        Fuchs was not the source of Moscow's October 1947 information on
        lithium.

186   Edward Teller . . . at Los Alamos: Rhodes (1995), p. 306.

186–87 Hall's work with lithium: T. A. Hall and P. G. Koontz, "Scattering of Fast
        Neutrons by Helium," *Physical Review,* Vol. 72, No. 3, Aug. 1, 1947; T. A.
        Hall, "A Note on the Li $7(p,n)$ Be 7 Reaction and an Excited State of Be
        7," *Physical Review,* Vol. 77, No. 3, Feb. 1, 1950.

187   Ginsburg proposed in December 1948: Goncharov (1996), p. 20, gave De-
        cember 2, 1948, as the date of Ginsburg's proposal.

187   Sakharov on "Second Idea": Sakharov (1990), p. 182.

187   March 13, 1948, Fuchs meeting: Goncharov (1996), p. 16.

187   It would be months: Rhodes (1995), pp. 329–330.

187   Blast . . . 100,000 square miles: Soviet intelligence Document 713-a, Rus-
        sian translation dated June 10, 1948, "Konstruktsiya DTB" (Construction
        of DTB [deuterium bomb]), and Document 713-b, undated original
        seven-page document in English, entitled "Construction," Russian Min-
        istry of Atomic Energy archives.

187   A weapon of . . . Moscow: According to city maps, wartime Moscow
        covered a roughly circular area with a radius of seven miles or less. Ac-
        cording to 1977 estimates by the U.S. Defense and Energy Departments,
        a ten-megaton bomb exploded at the optimal height would cause "se-
        vere" damage to wood-frame buildings twelve miles from the point of
        detonation; to reinforced concrete apartment buildings six miles from the

point of detonation; to railroad bridges seven miles from the point of detonation. Glasstone and Dolan (1977), pp. 212–219.

187   Fuchs's material as catalyst: Andrei Sakharov conjectured in his memoirs (Sakharov, 1990, p. 94) that the work he was asked to do by Tamm involved checking information "acquired by espionage." However, not until a May 1996 historical conference in Dubna, Russia, was Sakharov's suspicion publicly confirmed. In a paper written for the symposium, veteran Russian weapons designer German A. Goncharov provided a detailed chronology (Goncharov, 1996, pp. 17–18, or *Physics Today*, November 1996, pp. 52–53, for English translation) of how the Fuchs material and the earlier 1947 intelligence report on lithium had stimulated development of the Soviet hydrogen bomb.

188   "main topic": Col. Yuri Sokolov interview, April 26, 1996.

CHAPTER 21. RATHER GOOD INFORMATION

190   Dewey against outlawing: Halberstam (1993), p. 7.

190   Indictment of twelve leaders: Fariello (1995), p. 55.

190   "to build . . . long pull": Joan Hall interview, Jan. 13, 1996.

191   Their marriage that April: The Saxes were married at Chicago City Hall by Carl H. Smith, judge of the marriage court, on April 8, 1948, according to their marriage license on file with the Cook County Clerk's Office.

191   Visit by Halls and moves of Saxes: Susan Sax interview, July 23, 1996.

192   Mlad rejoined network; Morris Cohen met Mlad: confidential sources; Chikov (1996), p. 205.

192   Account of why Hall resumed ties: confidential source.

193   Sax's Soviet-financed wardrobe: Susan Sax interview, July 23, 1996.

193-94 Account of Mlad recruiting Anta and Aden and his subsequent reporting of their information to the Soviets: Chikov (1996), pp. 200 and 205. In addition, Col. Chikov's American co-author, Gary Kern, wrote in an epilogue (p. 360) that, based on his sources, (1) Anta and Aden had worked at Hanford, (2) had been recruited to help the Soviets by Mlad, and (3) maintained contact with the Soviets through Star. Chikov later told the authors substantially this same version (interview, Oct. 31, 1996), adding that Anta and Aden passed sufficient information for the KGB to maintain a separate file on them that he had seen. Somewhat similar accounts have come from several confidential sources, including a second ex-KGB officer. The ex-KGB source confirmed that Soviet intelligence did obtain important atomic information from a still unidentified American married couple, both of whom were scientists.

194-95 March 1, 1949, report to Beria: Document No. 822-B, "Zavod po proizvodstvu poloniya v g. Daytone" (Factory for the production of polonium in Dayton), Ministry of Atomic Energy archives.

195   Report was accurate: Gus Essig, a retired physicist who worked in the Dayton laboratory, was asked in April 1997 whether the polonium reclamation process described in the Soviet intelligence document was accurate. Essig replied, "Yes, roughly." Essig recalled an atmosphere of extreme secrecy, saying "I never said anything about what I was working on to my wife." According to Essig, the underground polonium extraction plant at Dayton's Mound Laboratory was built in 1948 with seventeen-foot-thick concrete walls and was designed to withstand all but a direct nuclear hit. *Dayton Daily News,* May 4, 1997.

195   Four days later: L. Beria to M. G. Pervukhin and A. P. Zavenyagin, March 4, 1949, transmitting instructions for Kurchatov and Vannikov, Ministry of Atomic Energy archives.

196   "This problem . . . Many problems": Col. Yuri Sokolov interview, Feb. 7, 1995.

196   "not very much . . . *vysoko*": Col. Yuri Sokolov interview, April 26, 1996.

196   Halls' closest confidants: confidential sources.

196   Not to expand his circle: Morris Cohen, interview with Russian Foreign Intelligence Service (SVR) historian, July 15, 1993.

197   Fisher/Abel arrival in Quebec and Abel background: Bernikow (1970), pp. 15ff; Van Der Rhoer (1983), pp. 91–94.

197   Abel finally . . . " 'show your accent' ": Col. Yuri Sokolov interview, April 26, 1996.

197-98 Abel initial meetings with Cohens: Morris and Lona Cohen interview, KGB oral history (1989), tape 3, pp. 11–12.

198   One retired KGB officer who has read: Col. Vladimir Chikov interview, Oct. 31, 1996.

198   One of the Cohens' best sources: Morris and Lona Cohen interview, KGB oral history (1989), tape 1, p. 9. Lona Cohen said: "The last time we saw Abel, we gave him the addresses of our two contacts in California. . . . The main one was the one, I think, in California."

198   "They succeeded . . . atomic bomb": Samolis (1995), p. 158.

198   "already in August . . . concrete results": Samolis (1995), p. 158.

198   Abel's medal was for atomic espionage: Gen. Vadim Kirpichenko interview, Feb. 28, 1996.

199-200 Halls' meeting in the park with Cohens, later meeting with Abel: Morris Cohen interview, videotaped by SVR, July 15, 1993; confidential source.

200   "He didn't want . . . than that": Morris Cohen interview with SVR historian, July 15, 1993.

200   "When you fight . . . fight": confidential source.

CHAPTER 22. CODE CRACKERS

201   Early history of the Venona Project: Benson and Warner (1996), pp. vii–xvii; Lamphere and Shachtman (1986), pp. 78–98; Wright (1987), pp. 227–239.

201   Background on Arlington Hall Junior College; Gilbert quotation: United Press International dispatch, Sept. 29, 1989.

201   Early history of Arlington Hall: retired NSA official Cecil J. Phillips, e-mail to the authors, Jan. 8 and 11, 1997; "Arlington Hall: Home to the 'Puzzle Palace,' " United Press International dispatch, Sept. 29, 1989; *The Washington Post,* April 26, 1986, and Oct. 11, 1993.

202   Early in 1943 . . . with Hitler: Benson (July 1995), p. 1; Benson and Warner (1996), p. xiii; Cecil J. Phillips, e-mail to the authors, Jan. 8, 1997.

202   Workings of one-time pad system: Benson and Warner (1996), p. xv; Cecil J. Phillips, e-mail to the authors, Jan. 8 and 11 and Feb. 21, 1997; Meredith Gardner interview, Oct. 5, 1995; Kahn (1967), pp. 662–665; Lamphere and Shachtman (1986), pp. 78–82; Wright (1987), pp. 227–228.

202-3   Hypothetical example: There are several published versions by retired Western intelligence officials, including Lamphere (1986), pp. 79ff, and Wright (1987), pp. 227–239. The authors relied on their accounts, as well as corrections and clarifications from several retired NSA officials, including Cecil Phillips (Phillips, e-mail to the authors, Jan. 8, Jan. 11, and Feb. 21, 1997).

204   Hallock's role: interview with Cecil Phillips, Oct. 3, 1996; Benson and Warner (1996), p. xv. Hallock's treatise on Assyrian and Babylonian languages, "The Chicago Syllabary and the Louvre Syllabary," was published in 1940 by the University of Chicago Press.

205   Breakdown of Soviet system of preparing one-time pads: talks by Meredith Gardner, Cecil Phillips, Robert Louis Benson, and others at a Washington seminar sponsored by CIA and NSA, Oct. 3–4, 1996, devoted to the history of the Venona Project. Also, e-mail from Cecil Phillips, Jan. 8 and 11, 1997; Benson and Warner (1996), p. xv.

205   Phillips's background and role: remarks by David Kahn, Cecil Phillips, and Robert Louis Benson, Venona historical conference, Washington, DC, Oct. 3–4, 1996; interviews with Cecil Phillips and Robert Louis Benson, Oct. 3, 1996, and Jan. 6, 1997; e-mail from Benson, Jan. 8 and 11 and Feb. 20, 1997.

205   Number with too many 6's: One of the most puzzling aspects of the Venona breakthrough is why the Soviets occasionally deviated from using completely random numbers in preparing onetime pads. Whether it was due to human or mechanical failure, they sometimes did deviate. Phillips gave this explanation of how he exploited this phenomenon: "The deviation from random was not present on all [onetime pad] pages but quite variable. . . . What I observed was that if you looked at the first five-digit group of about 100 to 200 consecutive New York-to-Moscow messages . . . there were about twice as many 6's as expected. . . . In retrospect, clearly what I had found was a favorable cluster of a couple hundred [onetime pad] pages in which the same strong non-random characteristics

either persisted throughout or which were especially strong in enough pages to produce the effect. I did not have an explanation for what I had observed, but I showed it to Mrs. Feinstein (our chief cryptanalyst), who observed, 'That looked like it could be clear key!' She suggested that a couple of the clerks check these first groups against a bank of hypothetical additives which we had been producing by forcing 'opening' code groups into trade messages. The checking produced 'hits' between the KGB first groups (with all the 6's), which showed that there were duplicated [onetime pad] pages between trade and KGB messages. This confirmed that my observations were significant (i.e., that the first [five-digit] group of all messages was some form of indicator, not just the groups with lots of 6's.)" (Cecil Phillips, e-mail to the authors, June 7, 1997)

206 Role of McDonald and Grabeel: Cecil Phillips, e-mail to authors, Feb. 21, 1997.

206 Gardner's role: Meredith Gardner interview, Sept. 5, 1995; Gardner speech at Venona conference, Washington, DC, Oct. 3, 1996; Michael Dobbs, "The Man Who Picked the Lock," *The Washington Post,* Oct. 19, 1996; e-mail from Cecil Phillips, Jan. 11, 1997.

207 On December 20 . . . Segrè: Benson and Warner (1996), pp. xxi, xl. The first intelligence cable partly broken by Gardner was New York–Moscow No. 1669, Dec. 2, 1944, according to Benson and Warner (1996), p. xxi.

207 Reynolds's role: Robert Louis Benson, e-mail to authors, Feb. 20, 1997.

207 Lamphere's role: Lamphere and Shachtman (1986), pp. 83–95; Robert Lamphere interview, Dec. 10, 1996; Benson and Warner (1996), pp. xxiii–xxiv.

207 "With the lapse . . . in 1944": Lamphere and Shachtman (1986), p. 85.

207 No one ever . . . "black-bag job": Robert Lamphere interview, Dec. 10, 1996. Indeed, there is recent circumstantial evidence to support Lamphere's suspicion. Soviet cable traffic shows that Soviet security officials investigated traces of a covert entry in a Soviet Purchasing Commission office in Washington over the weekend of Dec. 19, 1942. A cable (Venona Documents, Washington–Moscow 8167 and 8168, Dec. 29, 1942) said someone had tampered with a safe in the office of Comrade Minakov, chief of the commission's Department of Marine Orders, and documents "could have been photographed." It said Minakov was reprimanded by Investigator Logachev for keeping "a big black folder" in the safe that "may compromise not only yourself and the Secret and Cipher Division [of the purchasing commission] but also the Soviet Union."

207-8 How much help . . . NSA files: e-mail to the authors from Cecil Phillips and Robert Louis Benson, Jan. 11, 1997.

208-9 Decoding of Fuchs message and reaction in Washington and London: Lamphere and Shachtman (1986), pp. 133–136; Borovik and Knightley (1994), pp. 265–268; Williams (1987), pp. 119–125; Brown (1994), p. 389.

209 Fuchs investigation, Philby's role, Fuchs confession: Benson and Warner (1996), p. xxvii; Lamphere and Shachtman (1986), pp. 132–159; Williams (1987), pp. 119–125. On Philby, see also Benson (July 1995), which states, "Kim Philby, while assigned to Washington, D.C., 1948–1951, occasionally visited Arlington Hall for discussions about Venona; furthermore, he regularly received copies of summaries of Venona translations as part of his official duties."

210 Hall-Rossi 1949 correspondence: Theodore Hall to Bruno Rossi, April 30, 1949, carbon copy in Theodore Hall files; Theodore Hall interviews, Jan. 12, 1996, and Jan. 29, 1997.

210 Hall's doctoral dissertation: Theodore Hall, "Ratio of Cross Sections for Electron Capture and Electron Loss for Proton Beams in Metals," *Physical Review,* Vol. 19, No. 3, Aug. 1, 1950 (received for publication March 2, 1950).

210 "Nuclear physics . . . define things": Theodore Hall interview, July 31, 1996.

211 Hall notified Sax he was leaving network: confidential sources.

It was probably . . . at Los Alamos: interview with NSA historian Robert Louis Benson, Jan. 6, 1997, and e-mail from Benson, April 4, 1997. Benson said this first Arlington Hall translation of the Teodor Kholl cable bears no date, but is identifiable as having been prepared in 1949 or early 1950 because it carries the American security classification stamp "COPSE" (an internal Arlington Hall code word that Benson said was used only to denote documents decrypted in the year 1949 or in the early months of 1950). Benson said the latest known decryption bearing a "COPSE" stamp was from April 1950—suggesting that the Kholl document may have been translated as late as seven months after the start of the Klaus Fuchs inquiry. Benson said the first translation of the Kholl document was unsigned, but can be identified from its content as having been prepared by Gardner. In an interview October 3, 1996, Gardner said he didn't specifically recall the document that first identified Theodore Hall.

CHAPTER 23. ESPIONAGE-R

212-13 McQueen background: Robert McQueen interviews, Oct. 15, 1996, and Jan. 3, 1997; McQueen biography in *Martindell-Hubbell Law Directory.*

213 The case had . . . windows: Lamphere and Shachtman (1986), pp. 115, 117.

213 McQueen role in Coplon case: Robert McQueen interview, Oct. 15, 1996; McQueen letter to the authors, Jan. 8, 1997.

213 Over the FBI's . . . Soviet Embassy: Lamphere and Shachtman (1986), p. 118.

213 McQueen's role revealed: *The Washington Post,* June 10, 1949.

213 "In our office . . . lived it": Robert McQueen interview, Oct. 15, 1996.

214   "a small part . . . United States": Miller and Nowak (1977), p. 27.

214   "All hell broke . . . monster of a quest": Lamphere and Shachtman (1986), p. 137.

214   Overnight . . . crossed Fuchs's: FBI Fuchs file 65-58805-642, New York report, May 9, 1950.

214   "While I cannot . . . the State Department": quoted in Halberstam (1993), p. 50.

214   Magazines exploded: Miller and Nowak (1977), p. 28.

214   Identified 104 suspects: FBI Fuchs file 65-58805-642.

214-15   Gusdorf investigation: FBI Fuchs file 65-58805-915.

215   Nichols, Gunther: FBI Fuchs file 65-58805-642. Boorstin: FBI Fuchs file 65-58805-1146.

215   "unsub Kalibr" investigation: Benson and Warner (1996), p. xxvi; Lamphere (1986), p. 175.

215   Finding sixty-two possible suspects: FBI Greenglass file 65-59028-30.

216   Start of Hall-Sax investigation: FBI Hall file 65-59122-15; Ladd to Hoover, April 25, 1950; Robert McQueen interview, Oct. 15, 1995.

216   "ascertain the identity" . . . Harvard University: FBI Hall file 65-59122-15; Ladd to Hoover, April 25, 1950.

216   Finding records on Hall's leave: the FBI has not declassified documents telling where and when Hall's leave records were obtained. SAC Albuquerque to FBI director, May 18, 1950, FBI Greenglass File 65-59028-38, includes a parenthetical remark showing that by May 18, the Albuquerque office was aware that Hall "was in New York City in October, 1944." The document contains a hint that this information may have been conveyed to Albuquerque in a May 10 letter from FBI headquarters, which was then overseeing a search of some Manhattan Project files stored in Washington. However, a later document, Chicago Field Office to FBI director, June 13, 1950, FBI Hall file 65-59122-107, said: "Information furnished by the Albuquerque Office reflects HALL was on leave from October 15, 1944, to October 29, 1944."

216   January 1945 cable: Venona Documents, New York–Moscow No. 94, Jan. 23, 1945.

216   On May 11: NSA historian Robert Louis Benson said (interview, Jan. 6, 1997) that a May 11, 1950, memo reporting on the tentative identification of Mlad as Theodore Hall has been found in NSA archives. Benson said the memo is unsigned but the format is clearly recognizable as an FBI counterintelligence memo similar to other unsigned memos known to have been furnished by Lamphere to Gardner in 1950. Benson declined to release the May 11 memo, saying its exact text is classified.

216   Post-Hiroshima vacation: FBI Fuchs file 65-58805-915, reporting Mrs. Teller's statement to the FBI. The other couple was British scientist Rudolph Peierls and his Russian-born wife, Genia.

217 Wyly memo to Hoover: FBI Greenglass file 65-59028-38, SAC Albuquerque to Hoover, May 18, 1950.

217 First weeks of McQueen's investigation: FBI Hall file 65-59122-76, report by Robert K. McQueen, June 1, 1950; McQueen interview, Oct. 15, 1996; Joan and Theodore Hall interview, May 4, 1996.

217 "discrimination" . . . "civil liberties": *The Chicago Maroon,* Sept. 20, 1949, p. 7.

217 Halls' political activities: FBI Hall file 65-59122-76, report by Robert K. McQueen, June 1, 1950; McQueen interview, Oct. 15, 1996; Joan and Theodore Hall interviews, May 4, 1996, and March 24, 1997.

217 Mimeographing business: FBI Hall file 65-59122-76.

218 Saville Sax courses at Roosevelt College: Roosevelt University alumni office archives.

218 Saxes strapped for money: Susan Sax interview, July 23, 1996.

218 FBI "mail cover" on Sax: FBI Hall file 65-59122-138, report by Robert K. McQueen, Aug. 25, 1950.

218 "I am the man . . . the information": quoted in Lamphere and Shachtman (1986), p. 151.

218 "either a corporal or a non-comm": FBI Gold file 65-40327-1B, handwritten notes of Agent T. Scott Miller in Vol. 16.

218 To Special Agent . . . in Albuquerque: FBI Greenglass file 65-59028-97.

218 Mickey Ladd . . . Gold and Hall: Ladd to Hoover, June 2, 1950, cited by Lamphere and Shachtman (1986), footnote to p. 175.

218 Late on the morning . . . Hall or Sax: FBI Rosenberg file 65-58336-4, Granville memo to files, June 2, 1950.

219 Hall as Klaus Fuchs's note taker: "Hydrodynamics Lecture Notes: Peierls," Theodore Hall, editor, ca. 1946, Los Alamos library.

219 What happened . . . Saville Sax: FBI Gold file 65-57449-332, Philadelphia FBI teletype, June 3, 1950.

219 "It is even . . . espionage work": FBI Hall file 65-59122-107, Chicago Field Office to FBI director, June 13, 1950.

220 "I said 'bingo!' ": Rhodes (1995), p. 432, quoting Harry Gold 1965 interview with Augustus Ballard.

220 Arrest of Greenglass: FBI Greenglass file 65-59028-179.

220 June 27 Lamphere memo: reproduced in Benson and Warner (1996), p. 153.

220 "imperative": quoted in two FBI follow-up teletypes, Washington Field Office cable, Aug. 14, 1950, FBI Fuchs file 116-2713-48, and Newark Field Office cable, Aug. 3, 1950, FBI Fuchs file 116-2713-50.

221 "He said . . . now it is over' ": authors' interview with Svetlana Chervonnaya, March 6, 1997, relating her conversations with Lona Cohen in the KGB hospital in Moscow, September–December 1992.

221 Morris Cohen account of final meeting: Cohen interview with Russian Foreign Intelligence Service historian, July 15, 1993.

221–22 Chikov account of final meeting: Chikov (1996), p. 220.

222 A longtime confidant: confidential source.

CHAPTER 24. A CERTAIN ANIMUS

223 Cohens told to lie low "in the third month": Morris Cohen interview, *Komsomol'skaya Pravda,* Oct. 4, 1994.

223 "It came . . . to leave": Morris and Lona Cohen interview, KGB oral history (1989), tape 1, p. 4.

223 Closing bank accounts and cashing bonds: *The Times* (London), March 23, 1961.

223 Cohens' mixed-up day: Col. Yuri Sokolov interview, Feb. 7, 1995.

224 Movie company job: FBI Cohens file 100-406659-559.

224 Threw a party: FBI Cohens file 100-406659-559.

224 "a very desirable writing job": FBI Cohens file 100-406659-2.

224 "They seemed . . . her dearly": Sophie "Ginger" Petka Olson interview, July 14, 1995.

224 Cohen's mother "was devastated": Jack Bjoze interview, April 7, 1995.

224 "My father . . . for good": Morris Cohen interview, *Komsomol'skaya Pravda,* Oct. 4, 1994.

225 Felt the . . . "And good-bye": Yuri Sokolov interview, Feb. 7, 1995.

225 Arrived July 22 in Mexico: Svetlana Chervonnaya interview, March 6, 1997.

225 "We were all . . . in Korea": Joan Hall, personal memoir, February 1996.

225 Hall's altercation with police: Joan Hall personal memoir, February 1996.

225 Hall-Sax Stockholm peace petition work: Susan Sax interview, July 23, 1996.

225 "It was never . . . organizations": Robert McQueen letter to authors, Dec. 5, 1996.

225 "He said . . . this individual": FBI Greenglass file 65-59028-332.

226 Mail covers and phone taps: FBI Hall file 65-59122-138. This August 25, 1950, report by McQueen specifies that mail covers on the work and home addresses of both Hall and Sax were renewed on July 28, 1950, for a thirty-day period. Another section of the report told of ten pieces of information on Hall and Sax that the FBI had received from "Confidential Informant T-63, of known reliability." Judging from the FBI's terminology in reports on other national security cases, it seems highly likely that Informant T-63 was either a telephone wiretap or an electronic bug. Before the Hall document was declassified in 1990, the FBI deleted all information it had received forty years earlier from Informant T-63, leaving only a set of stamp-pad markings indicating the information was top se-

cret. This was consistent with the FBI's handling of documents in other cases involving wiretapping.

226 "We were . . . the 'source' ": Robert McQueen interview, Oct. 15, 1996.

226 Halls' move to prefab, key money deposit: Joan Hall, personal memoir, February 1996; FBI Hall file 65-59122-241.

226 "The day before . . . to you": April 19, 1950, carbon copy of "Westling Pursby" letter in Theodore Hall personal files in Cambridge, England.

226-27 Sax "had a background . . . to lose": Robert McQueen interview, Oct. 15, 1996.

227 Student teaching: Sax transcript, Roosevelt University alumni office archives.

227 "We didn't . . . off the street": Robert McQueen interview, Oct. 15, 1996.

227 Hall and Sax invitations to FBI headquarters: This and subsequent details of the Hall and Sax March 13, 1951, interrogation come from McQueen's FBI report of March 31, 1951, unless otherwise noted (FBI Hall file 65-59122-241).

227 Interview was in Bankers Building: Robert McQueen, letter to authors, Oct. 29, 1996.

227-28 "He had . . . very bright": Robert McQueen interview, Oct. 15, 1996.

228 It was part . . . such a grilling: confidential sources.

228 Specialized in both psychology and theater: Roosevelt University alumni office archives show that by March 1951 Sax had taken at least two psychology courses at Harvard, then another three courses in sociology and psychology and two in theater at the University of Chicago and at Roosevelt.

228 FBI hadn't known: Robert McQueen interview, Oct. 15, 1996.

229 "He [Hall] gave . . . pretty well": Robert McQueen interview, Oct. 15, 1996.

229 Sax suspected he was photographed: Susan Sax interview, July 23, 1996.

229-30 "I believed they were guilty . . . statements": Robert McQueen interview, Oct. 15, 1996.

230 "We didn't have that luck . . . that was it": Robert McQueen interview, Oct. 15, 1996.

230 Agents accused Ted: Theodore and Joan Hall interview, Jan. 13, 1996.

231 Headlines on Rosenbergs: *The New York Times,* March 13 and March 15, 1951.

231 Account of Halls' finding and dumping of papers into canal: confidential source.

231 "We were . . . had a 'tail' ": Joan Hall interview, Jan. 13, 1996.

231-32 "There was . . . very young": Susan Sax interview, July 23, 1996.

232   "It was . . . chose to do": Susan Sax interview, July 23, 1996.

232   Rushed to contact friends: Robert McQueen interview, Oct. 15, 1996. Also, a McQueen memorandum to Washington, dated March 13, 1951, noted Hall and Sax were about to be interrogated and urged that agents in other offices be alerted to prepare to interview associates of the two "in an attempt to obtain corroborating information regarding the Bureau source allegation." It emphasized that agents should refrain from making any contact until after Hall and Sax had been questioned. (The file number on authors' copy of this report is incomplete, reading "65-59122-39." It should have an additional digit, which was cut off in the copying process.)

232   "We were certainly stymied . . . get an indictment": Robert McQueen interview, Oct. 15, 1996.

232   Glauber got the call: Roy Glauber interview, May 9, 1996.

232   "some off-center . . . group": Sam Cohen interview, Sept. 30, 1996.

232–33   "Obviously those . . . a Fuchs": Robert McQueen interview, Oct. 15, 1996.

233   McQueen didn't second-guess: Robert McQueen interview, Oct. 15, 1996.

233   "You certainly . . . atomic espionage": Robert McQueen interview, Oct. 15, 1996.

CHAPTER 25. WE HAVE NO GUNS

234–35   Magic Slate incident, the Hall-Sax meeting with a Soviet visitor on the Midway, subsequent discussions between Joan and Theodore Hall along the Midway, the Halls' decision to move to New York: confidential sources.

235   At least for the present . . . dean's list: Roosevelt University alumni office archives.

236   Account of Hall's denial of H-bomb espionage: confidential sources.

236   "Based on how . . . about the KGB": Michael Dobbs, *The Washington Post,* Feb. 25, 1996.

236   After the Dobbs . . . such a thing: Theodore Hall interview, May 4, 1996.

236   Recollections of three FBI veterans: Donald Moore interviews, April 10 and May 8, 1996; Robert Lamphere interviews, May 8 and Dec. 10, 1996; Robert McQueen interview, Oct. 15, 1996. "I think what probably happened is that the guy [Hall] just decided we had nothing on him," said Moore, the chief of Hoover's Soviet counterintelligence division from 1956 to 1973. "And we didn't—nothing that we could use. We couldn't touch anything out of Venona."

237   Hall's research under Zirkle: T. A. Hall, "Interpretation of Exponential Dose Curves," *Bulletin of Mathematical Biophysics* (1953), Vol. 15, pp. 43–47; Theodore Hall interview, Jan. 29, 1997.

237   Zirkle's career: Seaborg (1994), p. 639.

237   Zirkle encouraging Hall to stay in Chicago: Theodore Hall interview, Oct. 5, 1996.

237   "removed from the . . . regular section": FBI Hall file 65-59122-39? (authors' photocopy lacks final digit in file number and a page number). The memo dated Jan. 18, 1952, from W. A. Branigan to A. H. Belmont recommends removing Hall from the Special Section, and a hand-written notation so orders.

237   The special section . . . security threats: Robert McQueen interview, Oct. 15, 1996; Donald Moore interview, April 10, 1996.

238   Episode after Saville Sax was given back packet of letters: confidential source.

238   Only two articles between 1953 and 1956: T. A. Hall, "Chemical Analysis of Radioactive Mixtures in Biological Materials," *Nucleonics* (1954), Vol. 12, No. 3, p. 34; T. Hall, M. Siegel, L. M. Sharpe, D. Pressman, "Production of I-124 by the Deuteron Bombardment of Tellurium," *Physical Review* (1954), Vol. 95, p. 1208.

238-39   "It was a weird . . . one day": confidential source.

239   Hall's 1952–53 meetings in New York with Soviet intelligence officers: confidential sources.

239   Campaign to save the Rosenbergs: Radosh and Milton (1983), p. 329.

240   Hall's offer to turn himself in: confidential sources.

240   "The road went . . . just as they did": confidential source.

241   "[Our] hydrogen bomb . . . for the Americans": quoted in Holloway (1994), p. 308, citing a 1953 Soviet Communist Party Central Committee transcript published in 1991.

241   1953 Soviet atomic test: Cochran et al. (1989), p. 349; Rhodes (1995), pp. 524–525; Holloway (1994), pp. 306–307; Goncharov (1996) (*Physics Today* translation), p. 57.

241   "I just said . . . 'the best' ": confidential sources.

242   Morris Cohen 1953–56 investigation: FBI Cohens file 100-406659, especially folios 1, 2, 3, 4, 5, and 28.

242   Cohen's uncashed disability checks: FBI Cohens file 46659-8.

242   "a fine son and a good boy": FBI Cohens file 100-4060659-11.

242   1956 closing of Cohen investigation: FBI Cohens file 100-406658-28.

CHAPTER 26. UP TO THE HILT

244   Cohens trained in the Soviet Union and Poland: Svetlana Chervonnaya told the authors (interview, March 6, 1997) that she heard a detailed story from Lona Cohen in the fall of 1992 about the Cohens' circuitous travels through Central and South America, Africa, and Europe before they got to Moscow. Morris and Lona Cohen interview, KGB oral history (1989), tape 3, pp. 6, 11–14, describes their harrowing first weeks in the

Soviet Union. Judging from the interview, the Cohens may have been in some danger from Stalin's security forces during their initial stay in Moscow in November 1950, possibly because they were Americans or possibly because this was a period of heightened anti-Semitic activity in Moscow and Morris Cohen was Jewish. The Cohens told their interviewer of an episode when someone came banging on the door of their downtown apartment in the middle of the night. They chose to remain silent inside, not answering the door, and within days their comrades whisked them away to Poland.

244   Trip to Hong Kong and Tokyo: Morris Cohen interview with Russian Foreign Intelligence Service (SVR) historian, July 15, 1993. Judging from the interview, the trip occurred in 1955. Also, see Tietjen (1961), p. 69. A veteran CIA officer, Cleveland Cram, told the authors (interview, Sept. 1, 1995) that he had not heard of a Soviet intelligence operation in Japan in the mid-1950s that would have merited or required a visit by the Cohens. It seems quite possible the Cohens were used as couriers for a Soviet ring in the Far East of which the CIA wasn't aware.

244   Abel lonely, clicked with Cohens: Yuri Sokolov interview, April 26, 1996.

244   New Year's goose: Morris and Lona Cohen interview, KGB oral history (1989), tape 3, pp. 1–2. The Cohens did not specify when this occurred, but judging from Abel's known activities in the United States and from Yuri Sokolov's recollections (interview, April 26, 1996), the incident probably happened on New Year's Day, 1950.

245   The appropriate accoutrements: Bernikow (1970), pp. 230–231.

245   "Everyone was . . . menace was real": Bernikow (1970), p. 146.

246   FBI found $4,000 and the Cohens' photos: FBI Cohens file 100-406659-35.

246   "Shirley" and "Morris" identified as Cohens: FBI Cohens file 100-406659, message to Washington from the New York FBI office dated July 22, 1957.

246   Abel's explanation of Cohens' photos: FBI Cohens file 100-406659-53.

246   The fact that "Mark" . . . network: FBI Cohens file 100-406659-35.

246–47   "special . . . Rosenberg network": FBI Cohens file 100-406659-29.

247   Dinner party with "Milton": Lamphere and Schachtman (1986), p. 277.

247   Deaths of Harry and Sonya Cohen: FBI Cohens file 100-406659-44.

247   Greenglass and Gold shown Cohens' photos: FBI Cohens file 100-406659-41.

247   1942 Cohen Christmas dinner: FBI Cohens file 100-406659-1066.

247   Beatson tracking Cohens: Robert J. Beatson interview, April 12, 1996.

248   "We hated what . . . of environment": This and other details of the Halls' life in Greenwich are taken from Joan Hall's 1995 description written for a friend, provided to the authors by a confidential source, or from material from other confidential sources.

248 Edward Hall background in mid-1950s: Edward Hall (ca. 1995), pp. 54–84. Col. Hall's career in rocketry is further described in Neal (1962), pp. 49–70ff.

248 KGB and GRU on exhibition staff: retired KGB Gen. Oleg Kalugin interview, Jan. 7, 1997. Kalugin said that although he was one of the two KGB officers working on the staff of the Soviets' 1959 New York exhibition, he did not meet Theodore Hall and had no knowledge of a meeting involving Hall during the exhibition.

249 The Soviet exhibition: Kalugin (1994), p. 2. When the exhibition opened on June 29, 1959, *The New York Times* reported on page 1 (*The New York Times,* June 30, 1959) that First Deputy Premier Frol R. Kozlov had opened "a brilliant Soviet exhibition at the New York Coliseum," and that both President Eisenhower and Vice President Nixon had represented the United States at the opening. It said Nixon noted a "disappointing lack of progress" between American and Soviet diplomats that resulted from "basic conflicts of interest and deeply clashing ideologies."

249 Halls' meetings with Leonid Petrov: confidential source.

249 "It just . . . like fingerprints": Robert J. Beatson interview, April 12, 1996.

249-50 "They took . . . cricket team: O. F. Snelling interview, May 27, 1995.

250 "They had been . . . those two": Sheila Wheeler interview, June 8, 1995.

250-51 Sniper warns of British spy: Wright (1987), pp. 161–162.

251 Houghton passes envelope to Lonsdale: *The New York Times,* March 19, 1961.

251 "a full-blown KGB operation": Wright (1987), p. 165.

251 Put a watch on Bunty Gee: *Strange Neighbors,* a documentary film from Walberry Production aired on British Channel 4, November 1991.

251 Cohens and Lonsdale working together: Morris and Lona Cohen interview, KGB oral history (1989), tape 2, pp. 25–26.

252 "I think" . . . Krogers' arrest: Gay Search interview, June 9, 1995. Playwright Hugh Whitemore portrayed the Krogers' story and the moral dilemma of the Search family in a successful play, *Pack of Lies,* produced in London in 1983.

252 "He said . . . we'll pull a Milt": Morris Cohen interview with SVR historian, July 15, 1993.

252 Lonsdale/Molody biography: Samolis (1995), p. 103.

252 Cohens provided rocket information: Samolis (1995), pp. 69, 72.

253 Nearly forty years later . . . sounded puzzled: Col. Yuri Sokolov interview, Feb. 2, 1995; Gen. Vadim Kirpichenko interview, Feb. 28, 1996. Kirpichenko, head of the historical project of the Russian Foreign Intelligence Service, said in the interview that whatever Abel's reason for saving the photographs, "it is certainly his fault—he was obliged to destroy these photos."

253   "That's what gave . . . catch you": Morris and Lona Cohen interview, KGB oral history (1989), tape 3, p. 2.

253   Lonsdale tried to take blame: "Official Secrets Trial: Statement from Dock by Lonsdale," *The Times* (London), March 22, 1961.

253   "that you both . . . professional spies": "Official Secrets Trial: Lonsdale, 'Master Mind' Gets 25 Years," *The Times* (London), March 23, 1961.

253   Lonsdale-Kroger sentences: *The Times* (London), March 23, 1961.

CHAPTER 27. LASTING CONTRIBUTION

254   Hall's 1961 article: "X-ray Fluorescence in Biology," *Science,* Vol. 134 (Aug. 18, 1961), pp. 449–455.

255   Hall's two earlier accounts: Theodore A. Hall, "X-ray Spectroscopy," in H. Yoe and H. Koch, eds., *Trace Analysis* (New York: John Wiley and Sons, 1957), pp. 485–492; Theodore A. Hall, "A Non-Dispersive X-ray Fluorescence Unit for the Analysis of Biological Tissue Sections," *Advanced X-Ray Analysis,* Vol. I, pp. 297–305.

255   Rockwell Kent court case (*Rockwell v. Dulles*): *The New York Times,* March 17, April 27, June 17, and June 25, 1958.

255-56 Reasons for Halls' readiness to leave United States: Theodore and Joan Hall interviews, Jan. 12 and Oct. 5, 1996, Jan. 28, 1997; fax from Theodore and Joan Hall to the authors, Feb. 24, 1997; confidential sources.

256   "I had developed . . . decent contribution": Theodore Hall interview, Oct. 5, 1996.

256   Cavendish Laboratory background: Mason (1994), pp. 160–177, 193–204.

257   Hall at Cavendish: Gupta (1991), p. 360.

257   Thin or ultrathin sections: In electron microanalysis, "thin" means roughly one micrometer, whereas "ultrathin" means roughly one tenth of a micrometer. (A micrometer, also known as a micron, is a millionth of a meter.) Theodore Hall interview, Jan. 29, 1997.

257   Hall Method: Gupta (1991), pp. 369–370; Theodore Hall letters to authors, March 17 and April 12, 1996; Hall interview, Jan. 29, 1997. 1964 version of Hall Method: T. A. Hall, A. J. Hale, and V. R. Switsur, "Some Applications of Microprobe Analysis in Biology and Medicine," symposium sponsored by Electrothermics and Metallurgy Division, the Electrochemical Society, Washington, DC, October 1964 (New York: John A. Wiley and Sons, 1966), pp. 805–833. 1968 version of Hall Method: D. J. Marshall and T. A. Hall, "Electron-probe X-ray Microanalysis of Thin Films," *British Journal of Applied Physics* (1968), Series 2, Vol. 1, p. 1651.

257-58 Halls' life in Cambridge. Joan Hall's 1995 description to a friend, from confidential source; Joan and Theodore Hall interview, Jan. 28–29, 1997.

258   Morris Cohen recalled . . . "I don't want": Morris Cohen interview, KGB oral history project (1989), tape 2, pp. 1–2.

258-59   Cohens, Lonsdale rejecting Christmas Island deal: Morris Cohen interview, KGB oral history project (1989), tape 2, pp. 1–2; Morris Cohen interview with Peter Carroll, May 27, 1993.

259   Lonsdale-Wynne trade: Andrew and Gordievsky (1990), p. 47.

259   The labor permit as a pretext: Cleveland Cram interview, Dec. 10, 1996.

259   Hall anguish after 1963 session with British interrogator: confidential
sources.

259   "I did not learn . . . their jurisdiction": Cleveland Cram interview, Dec.
10, 1996.

260   "My wife and I . . . our personal histories": Harvard 25th Anniversary
Report (Spring 1969).

260   Soviet offer to trade two wounded pilots for Cohens: *The New York Times,*
June 27, 1993; Whitney (1994), p. 438. According to Whitney, the eleven
pilots on the list given to Vogel were all held by the North Vietnamese
until the United States pulled out of the Vietnam War in 1973.

260   Philby overture to trade Cohens for Brooke: *The Sunday Times* (London),
Dec. 17, 1967.

260   "From day to day . . . mental stability": Peter Kroger (Morris Cohen) letter from Parkhurst Prison to Sheila Doel Wheeler, Aug. 1, 1968, Cohen
Prison Letters.

260-61   Her body throbbed . . . deformed finger: Snelling (1982), p. 239.

261   "I counted 65" . . . in 1964: Peter Kroger (Morris Cohen) letter from
Wormwood Scrubs Prison to Sheila Doel Wheeler, April 30, 1964,
Cohen Prison Letters.

261   Cohen and Dupuytren's contracture: Snelling (1982), p. 223.

261   "I catch myself . . . ignore it": Peter Kroger (Morris Cohen) letter to
Nora Doel, Jan. 22, 1969, Cohen Prison Letters.

261   "will be surrounded . . . out of Britain": *The Times* (London), Oct. 24,
1969.

261   Cohens' arrival in Warsaw, next-day transfer to Moscow: Morris Cohen interview with Russian Foreign Intelligence Service historian, July 15, 1993.

261   His son Boria remembered . . . "would break out": Boria Sax interview,
May 9, 1996. Boria Sax said he did not know the date of the incident but
recalled that it happened at the Michael Todd Theater. Newspaper
archives show that *My Fair Lady* opened at the Michael Todd Theater in
1964.

262   "My mother said . . . the police": Boria Sax interview, May 7, 1996. Sax's
then-wife, Susan Sax, confirmed in an interview (July 23, 1996) that a
near-suicide episode occurred but declined to discuss it.

262   "It became an . . . until death": Sarah Sax interview, Oct. 15, 1996.

262   "I think . . . his anxiety": Susan Sax interview, July 23, 1996.

262   Five addresses in two and a half years: According to Sax's Roosevelt College files, between the fall of 1949 and spring of 1952, the Saxes lived at:

5520 South Kenwood Avenue; 1370 East Sixty-first Street; 5633 South Maryland Avenue; 6516 South Minerva Avenue; and 5306 South Ellis Avenue.

262 Divorce of Susan and Saville Sax: Susan Sax interview, July 23, 1996; Boria Sax interview, May 9, 1996; Saville Sax biographical note in Sax and Hollander (1975), p. 7.

262 Dates of Sax's work at Southern Illinois: interview with Sam Smith, Southern Illinois University news service, Jan. 14, 1997; Southern Illinois University Press release, Sept. 29, 1980, announcing Sax's death.

262 Sax work with NEXTEP project: Sax biographical note in Sax and Hollander (1975), p. 7.

262 Harmin's recollections of Sax and NEXTEP: Merrill Harmin interview, Jan. 16, 1997.

263 Sax as campus guru: Boria Sax interview, May 9, 1996.

263 Merrill Harmin and "values clarification": *The New York Times,* April 30, 1975; *Policy Review,* October 1986.

263 Sax and mantras: Boria Sax interview, May 9, 1996.

263 "Get in touch . . . chest and back . . .": Sax and Hollander (1975), p. 25.

263 "He was a genius . . . disorderly": Merrill Harmin interview, Jan. 16, 1997.

263 Another teacher . . . " 'continuation of reality?' ": Jan. 26, 1996, interview with a colleague of Saville Sax at Southern Illinois University in the late sixties who declined to be identified.

263 NEXTEP funds stopped: Sax and Hollander (1975), pp. 7, 47; Merrill Harmin interview, Jan. 16, 1997.

263 Saville Sax and LSD: Boria Sax interview, May 9, 1996. However, Boria's sister, Sarah Sax, said (Oct. 15, 1996, interview) that to her knowledge, her father was never a drug user.

264 "It was no secret . . . to have no fear": Sarah Sax interview, Oct. 15, 1996.

264 News of . . . then stopped: Theodore Hall interviews, Jan. 12 and May 4, 1996, Jan. 26, 1997.

264 Hall's letter on Vietnam: *The Times* (London), Nov. 27, 1969, letters column.

264-65 Hall's 1970 talk at Free University: Hall's handwritten lecture notes for "A Socialist View of Science Today," dated March 15, 1970, Theodore Hall private files.

265 The early seventies were . . . a squid membrane: Gupta (1991), pp. 370–372.

265 "It wasn't a . . . to the biologists": Theodore Hall interview, Oct. 5, 1996.

265 But trouble arose . . . Hall's lab: Gupta (1991), p. 372.

265-66 After a series . . . "as inadequacy": Gupta (1991), p. 377.

266 Account of Halls at 1986 microscopy conference in Albuquerque: confidential sources.

CHAPTER 28. THE PERSEUS MYTH

267 "When the curtain . . . Lubyanka": Col. Vladimir Chikov interview, June 1, 1995.

267-68 Prelin as tour guide: Gwertzman and Kaufman (1991), p. 152.

268 "I gave . . . interesting": Col. Igor Prelin interview, May 25, 1995.

268 Kryuchkov's role: His glasnost had its limits. He was among the coup plotters who had Gorbachev detained on his Crimea vacation in August 1991, then imposed emergency rule in an effort to block the ratification of the new union treaty that would have diluted centralized power.

268 "We did it . . . signed it": Col. Vladimir Chikov interview, June 1, 1995.

268 "Of course . . . at this?" and other details on the file: Col. Vladimir Chikov interview, June 1, 1995.

269 "If he noticed . . . forbidden": Col. Vladimir Chikov interview, June 1, 1995.

269-70 "We understood . . . service existed": Gen. Vadim Kirpichenko interview, Feb. 28, 1996.

270 "practically . . . our scientists": Gen. Vadim Kirpichenko interview in *Moskovskaya Pravda,* Dec. 20, 1990.

270 "of immense . . . our science": a short excerpt from the Kurchatov document was quoted in *Moskovskaya Pravda,* Dec. 20, 1990. Later, it turned out that this was an accurate citation from the first sentence of Kurchatov's March 7, 1943, memo to M. G. Pervukhin (*Voprosy* [1992], document 4).

271 Disappearing code names in Feklisov's manuscript: The most interesting deletion was that of a Soviet atomic agent whom Col. Feklisov originally referred to as "Pers." His Russian manuscript, partly typed and partly handwritten, was provided to the authors by a confidential source. It contained a list of four agents including one he repeatedly called Pers (for example, Feklisov manuscript, pp. 134, 135). A photocopy of his manuscript shows that someone drew lines through "Pers" and substituted the code name "Monty" for Pers. When the book appeared (Feklisov [1994], p. 84), his list of agents had been reduced to three and Pers had been omitted. Also omitted was his two-page section that had described the atomic espionage activities of Pers. In fact, Pers was the actual NKGB code name of a still unidentified Soviet agent at "Camp 1," the Soviet designation for Oak Ridge. (See Chapter 9 for the 1944 role of Soviet agent Pers.) One possibility that can be inferred from the edited Feklisov manuscript is that Chikov, Prelin, and Drozdov invented agent Perseus by combining the exploits of no fewer than three real Soviet atomic sources: Pers, Mlad, and Star. Chikov contributed to that theory in an interview October 31, 1996, when he said the KGB had combined Mlad and Pers into Perseus. However, he would not clarify whether only the name Pers had been appropriated for part of the cover, or whether the actual actions of the agents

Mlad and Pers had been collapsed into his tale of Perseus. Chikov also said he had been directed to remove most references to Star.

271   Faked the cover: Col. Igor Prelin interview, June 25, 1995.

272   "They [the Cohens] . . . they insisted": Glafira Semyonova interview, July 18, 1995.

272   "the ban was lifted": George Blake interview, July 12, 1995.

272-73   "We presented" . . . and unprofessional: Frances Berrigan interview, June 9, 1995.

273   They wouldn't live long: Col. Igor Prelin interview, June 18, 1995.

273   Refused to let Berrigan send crew: Frances Berrigan interview, June 9, 1995.

273   "I felt . . . happy about it": Sheila Wheeler interview, June 8, 1995.

274   She claimed . . . pretty awful: Sheila Wheeler interview, June 8, 1995.

274   Documentary got made: *Strange Neighbors,* a Walberry Production, aired in November 1991.

274   "people and . . . the KGB, USSR": *Kur'yer Sovyetskoi Razvyedki,* 1991, p. 3. Gen. Vadim Kirpichenko, retired first deputy chief of the KGB, who was compiling the official eight-volume history of Russian intelligence, confirmed (interview with the authors, Feb. 28, 1996) that *Kur'yer Sovyetskoi Razvyedki* had been put out by "our officers."

275   "When they realized . . . was banned": Col. Vladimir Chikov interview, June 1, 1995.

275-76   "The papers . . . these materials": Roald Sagdeev in *The Bulletin of the Atomic Scientists,* May 1993, p. 32.

276   "the struggle . . . nonproliferation": Sergei Leskov in *The Bulletin of the Atomic Scientists,* May 1993, p. 37.

276   Small errors: Arkady Rylov, one of two physicists working with Sudoplatov in Department S, said (interview, April 22, 1995) that the department started in September 1945, not in February 1944 as stated in Sudoplatov (1994), p. 184. According to Rylov's recollection and documents in the Russian Ministry of Atomic Energy Archives, Department S lasted until mid- or late 1946.

276-77   Sudoplatov's charge against Oppenheimer, Fermi, and Szilard: In the prologue to his original edition in English (Sudoplatov [1994], p. 3) Gen. Sudoplatov wrote that Soviet agents "convinced Robert Oppenheimer, Enrico Fermi, Leo Szilard . . . and other scientists in America to share atomic secrets with us." Sudoplatov's Russian-language edition, published in 1996, omitted this prologue. His Russian-language version did repeat his intriguing, but not incriminating, statement that wartime Soviet intelligence officials used internal code names to refer to certain major American nuclear scientists, including Oppenheimer and Fermi. For the Sudoplatov version in Russian, see Pavel Sudoplatov (1996).

277   "I assume . . . exposed": Morris Cohen interview, *Komsomol'skaya Pravda,*
         Oct. 4, 1994.

CHAPTER 29. ACCOUNTINGS

278   "I'm afflicted . . . and beautiful": Harvard Class of 1944 Fiftieth Anniver-
         sary Report (1994), p. 228.

278–79   "She made . . . conventions": Barbara Rosenbaum article, clipping in
         Halls' personal files from *Workers' Press* (London), April 4, 1992.

279   "We think . . . gave it color": Joan Hall interview, Jan. 28, 1997.

279   Painful thoughts: Joan Hall interview, Dec. 7, 1996; Theodore and Joan
         Hall interviews, Jan. 12 and 13, 1996.

279   "Somehow the place suits me deeply": Theodore Hall letter to authors,
         Jan. 1, 1997.

279   "a certain expansiveness . . . anywhere else": Joan Hall letter to authors,
         Dec. 21, 1996.

279   "We feel . . . welcomed": Joan Hall interview, Feb. 22, 1997.

280   Didn't recognize Perseus: Theodore and Joan Hall interview, Jan. 13,
         1996.

280   Halls heard from Kramish: Theodore and Joan Hall interview, Sept. 19,
         1995; Arnold Kramish interview, May 14, 1996.

280   Bennett and Romerstein: *Reader's Digest,* September 1996, p. 140.

281   Dobbs's two-page spread: *The Washington Post,* Feb. 25, 1996, pp. A1,
         A20–A21.

281   "A SHY SCIENTIST . . . TRAITOR": The quoted phrase was the second deck
         of the headline over a Hall profile in *People,* March 18, 1996, p. 99.

281   "the great . . . microanalysis": *The Guardian,* Feb. 27, 1996, p. 3.

281   "GREAT GUY . . . HIS SCIENCE": *Cambridge Evening News,* Feb. 27, 1996.

281–82   "These men betrayed . . . still among us": *The Weekly Standard,* April 15,
         1996, p. 17.

282   "He assisted . . . diminished by time": *Daily Telegraph* (London), Oct. 4,
         1996, p. 25.

282   Hall's thoughts: confidential source.

283   "In 1944 I . . . acted differently": Theodore Hall interview, Feb. 22, 1997.

283   "On reflection . . . Simple as that": Theodore Hall interview, Feb. 22,
         1997.

283   "If you feel . . . the punishment": Joseph Rotblat interview, July 30, 1996.

284   Theodore Hall wouldn't call . . . "kind of loyalty": Theodore and Joan
         Hall interview, Feb. 22, 1997.

285   " 'If you are' . . . That's all": Morris Cohen interview, KGB oral history
         (1989), tape 1, p. 47.

285   Cohens accepted mistakes and social democracy: Morris and Lona Cohen
         interview, KGB oral history (1989), tape 3, pp. 27–29.

285   Heroes of Russia: Itar-Tass news bulletin, June 24, 1996.

285   "peace should not . . . the 'twilight struggle' ": Haynes and Klehr, *The Weekly Standard,* April 15, 1996, pp. 15–17.

286   "sort out . . . American democracy": William Crowell interview, Dec. 28, 1995.

CHAPTER 30. AFTERSHOCK

288-89   [This note was written by Theodore Hall.] Information about unauthorized spy overflights is taken from a BBC documentary in the *Timewatch* series (a Brook Associates Production for BBC/A&E Network co-production) broadcast in Great Britain on Oct. 8, 1996. The specific points cited were mentioned by Robert Bowie (State Dept. 1953–7), Daniel Ellsberg (Pentagon analyst 1959–71), Gen. Andrew Goodpaster (White House Defense Liaison Officer 1954–60), and Prof. William Kaufmann (Rand Corp. 1954–70). Unauthorized flights during the Cuban missile crisis (in this case not spies but bombers armed with nuclear weapons) are described in Raymond L. Garthoff, *Reflections on the Cuban Missile Crisis,* Washington, D.C., The Brookings Institution, 1989, p. 62.

Bibliography

Alvarez, Luis W., *Adventures of a Physicist* (New York: Bantam, 1987).

Andrew, Christopher, and Oleg Gordievsky, *KGB: The Inside Story of its Foreign Operations from Lenin to Gorbachev* (New York: HarperCollins, 1990).

Ascher, Abraham, *The Revolution of 1905: Russia in Disarray* (Stanford, CA: Stanford University Press, 1994).

Badash, Lawrence, Joseph O. Hirschfelder, and Herbert P. Broida, *Reminiscences of Los Alamos: 1943–1945* (London, Boston, and Dordrecht, Holland: D. Reidel Publishing, 1980).

Barkovsky, Vladimir, unpublished notes for lecture given to American scientists on the role of the Soviet technical and scientific intelligence branch in the history of the Soviet atomic bomb project (Los Alamos, NM, November 1994).

Benson, Robert Louis, *Introductory History of VENONA and Guide to the Translations,* Venona Historical Monograph 1 (Fort George G. Meade, MD: National Security Agency, July 1995).

Benson, Robert Louis, *The 1942–43 New York–Moscow KGB Messages,* Venona Historical Monograph 2 (Fort George G. Meade, MD: National Security Agency, October 1995).

Benson, Robert Louis, and Michael Warner, eds., *Venona: Soviet Espionage and the American Response, 1939–1957* (Washington, DC: National Security Agency and Central Intelligence Agency, 1996).

Bernikow, Louise, *Abel* (New York: Trident, 1970).

Bettersworth, John K., *People's College: A History of Mississippi State* (University of Alabama Press, 1953).

Blumberg, Stanley A., and Gwinn Owens, *Energy & Conflict: The Life and Times of Edward Teller* (New York: Putnam, 1976).

Blumberg, Stanley A., and Louis G. Panos, *Edward Teller: Giant of the Golden Age of Physics* (New York: Scribner's, 1990).

Borovik, Genrikh, and Phillip Knightly, *The Philby Files: The Secret Life of Master Spy Kim Philby* (Boston: Little, Brown, 1994).

Brown, Anthony Cave, *Treason in the Blood: H. St. John Philby, Kim Philby and the Spy Case of the Century* (Boston, New York: Houghton Mifflin, 1994).

Brown, Anthony Cave, and Charles B. MacDonald, *On a Field of Red: The Communist International and the Coming of World War II* (New York: Putnam, 1981).

Bulloch, Alan, *Hitler and Stalin: Parallel Lives* (New York: Knopf, 1992).

California Legislature, *Sixth Report of the Senate Fact-Finding Committee on Un-American Activities,* 1951.

Carroll, Peter, *Odyssey of the Abraham Lincoln Brigade: Americans in the Spanish Civil War* (Stanford, CA: Stanford University Press, 1994).

Chikov, Vladimir, "Kak raskryvali 'atomniye sekrety,' " [How They Discovered the Atomic Secrets], *Armiya,* Nos. 18, 19, 20 (Moscow, 1991).

Chikov, Vladimir, "Kak sovyetskaya razvyedka 'rashchepila' americanskii atom," [How Soviet Intelligence 'Split' the American Atom], *Novoye Vremya,* Nos. 16 and 17 (Moscow, April 1991).

Chikov, Vladimir, "Ot Los-Alamosa do Moskvy" [From Los Alamos to Moscow], *Soyuz,* Nos. 21, 22, 23 (May 1991).

Cochran, Thomas B., William M. Arkin, Robert S. Norris, and Jeffrey I. Sands, *Nuclear Weapons Databook,* Volume IV, *Soviet Nuclear Weapons* (New York: Harper & Row, 1989).

Cohen, Morris, interview with Nikolai Dolgopolov, in *Komsomol'skaya Pravda,* Oct. 4, 1994.

Cohen, Morris, interview on videotape with Russian Foreign Intelligence Service (SVR) historian (Moscow, July 15, 1993).

Cohen, Morris, unpublished interview with Peter Carroll, American author and historian of the northern California branch of the Veterans of the Abraham Lincoln Brigade (Moscow, May 27, 1993).

Cohen, Morris and Lona, seventy-six letters from Wormwood Scrubs and other British prisons, under the pseudonyms Helen and Peter Kroger, 1961–1969, private collection.

Cohen, Morris and Lona, interview for KGB oral history project (Moscow, 1989).

Cohen, Morris and Lona, interview from the documentary *Strange Neighbors* (London: Walberry Productions, November 1991).

Cohen, Sam, *The Truth About the Neutron Bomb: The Inventor of the Bomb Speaks Out* (New York: William Morrow, 1983).

Conant, James B., papers 1943–45, microfilm (Washington, DC: National Archives).

Corson, William R., and Robert T. Crowley, *The New KGB: Engine of Soviet Power* (New York: William Morrow, 1985).

Costello, John, and Oleg Tsarev, *Deadly Illusions: The KGB Orlov Dossier Reveals Stalin's Master Spy* (New York: Crown, 1993).

de Gramont, Sanche, *The Secret War: The Story of International Espionage Since World War II* (New York: Putnam, 1962).

Dobbs, Michael, "Code Name 'Mlad,' Atomic Bomb Spy," *The Washington Post,* Feb. 25, 1996.

Dobbs, Michael, "The Man Who Picked the Lock," *The Washington Post,* Oct. 19, 1996.

Dobrynin, Anatoly, *In Confidence: Moscow's Ambassador to America's Six Cold War Presidents* (New York: Times Books, 1995).

Dziak, John J., *Chekisty: A History of the KGB* (Lexington, MA: Lexington Books, 1988).

Edmonds, Robin, *Setting the Mould: The United States and Britain: 1945–1950* (Oxford, England: Clarendon Press, 1986).

Fariello, Griffin, *The Red Scare: Memories of the American Inquisition: An Oral History* (New York: Norton, 1995).

Feld, Bernard T., *A Voice Crying in the Wilderness: Essays on the Problems of Science and World Affairs* (Oxford, England: Pergamon Press, 1972).

Feklisov, Alexander, *Za okeanom i na ostrove: Zapiski radvyedchika* [Beyond the Ocean and on the Island: Notes of an Intelligence Officer] (Moscow: DEM, 1994).

Feoktistov, L. P., "Vodorodnaya bomba: Kto zhe vydal yeyo sekret?" [The Hydrogen Bomb: Who Really Gave Up Its Secret?], unpublished paper presented at historical conference in Dubna, Russia, May 14–18, 1996.

Fermi, Laura, *Atoms in the Family: My Life with Enrico Fermi* (Chicago: University of Chicago Press, 1954; reprint, Albuquerque, NM: University of New Mexico Press, 1982).

Fermi, Rachel, and Esther Samra, *Picturing the Bomb: Photographs from the Secret World of the Manhattan Project* (New York: Harry N. Abrams, 1995).

Feynman, Richard P., *"Surely You're Joking, Mr. Feynman!" Adventures of a Curious Character* (New York: Norton, 1985; reprint, New York: Bantam, 1986).

Frisch, Otto R., *What Little I Remember* (Cambridge, England: Cambridge University Press, 1979).

Glasstone, Samuel, and Philip J. Dolan, *The Effects of Nuclear Weapons* (Washington, DC: U.S. Department of Defense and Department of Energy, 1977).

Goncharov, German A., "Osnovye sobytiya istorii sozdaniya vodorodnoi bomby v SSSR i SShA" [The Basic Events of the History of the Creation of the Hydrogen Bomb in the USSR and the USA], paper presented at a historical conference in Dubna, Russia, May 14–18, 1996. The text was published in Russian in *Uspekhi Fizicheskikh Nauk* (Moscow: Russian Academy of Sciences, No. 166, October 1996); an English translation appeared in *Physics Today* (November 1996).

Gowring, Margaret, *Britain and Atomic Energy: 1939–1945* (London: Macmillan, 1964).

Groves, Leslie R., *Now It Can Be Told: The Story of the Manhattan Project* (New York: Harper & Brothers, 1962).

Guerlac, Henry E., *Radar in World War II* (Washington, DC: Tomash Publishers, 1987).

Gupta, Brij L., "Theodore Alvin Hall: A Biographical Sketch and Personal Appreciation," *Scanning Microscopy,* Vol. 5, No. 2 (1991). Includes full citations of 166 scientific publications authored or co-authored by Theodore Hall, 1947–1991.

Gwertzman, Bernard, and Michael T. Kaufman, *The Collapse of Communism—By the Correspondents of* The New York Times (New York: Times Books, 1991).

Halberstam, David, *The Fifties* (New York: Ballantine Books, 1993).

Hall, Edward N., "USAF Engineer in Wonderland: Including the Missile Down the Rabbit Hole and How to Maintain Military Effectiveness at a Profit to the Nation," unpublished manuscript, ca. 1995, on deposit at Air Force Historical Research Agency, Maxwell Air Force Base, AL.

Hall, Theodore, nine letters from Theodore Hall to Edward Hall and Edith Hall, September 1942–May 1944, private collection.

Hall, Theodore, ed., "Hydrodynamics Lecture Notes: Peierls," ca. 1946, mimeographed manuscript in Los Alamos Laboratory Library (including Hall's notes on four lectures on hydrodynamics by Klaus Fuchs).

Hall, Theodore, "Ratio of Cross Sections for Electron Capture and Electron Loss for Proton Beams in Metals" (Hall's 1950 University of Chicago doctoral dissertation), *Physical Review,* Vol. 19, No. 3 (Aug. 1, 1950).

Hall, Theodore, "X-Ray Fluorescence in Biology," *Science,* Vol. 134 (Aug. 18, 1961).

Hall, T. A., P. G. Koontz, and B. Rossi, "Absolute Values of the Fission Cross Sections of 25 and 28 from 0.28 to 2.50 MeV," LA Report 128 (Los Alamos, NM: Aug. 23, 1944). The Los Alamos code name for U-235 was "25" and for U-238, "28."

Harmin, Merrill, and Saville Sax, *A Peaceable Classroom: Activities to Calm and Free Student Energies* (Minneapolis: Winston Press, 1977).

Hawkins, David, Edith C. Truslow, and Ralph Carlisle Smith, *Project Y: The Los Alamos Story* (edited version of LAMS 2532, an official history written in 1946 and 1947) (Los Angeles: Tomash Publishers, 1983).

Herkin, Gregg, *The Winning Weapon: The Atomic Bomb in the Cold War: 1945–1950* (New York: Knopf, 1980).

Hewlett, Richard G., and Oscar E. Anderson Jr., *The New World: A History of the United States Atomic Energy Commission,* Vol. 1, *1939–1946* (Berkeley, CA: University of California Press, 1990).

Hoddeson, Lillian, Paul W. Hendrikson, Roger A. Meade, and Catherine Westfall, *Critical Assembly: A Technical History of Los Alamos During the Oppenheimer Years, 1943–1945* (Cambridge, England: Cambridge University Press, 1993).

Holloway, David, *Stalin and the Bomb: The Soviet Union and Atomic Energy 1939–1956* (New Haven: Yale University Press, 1994).

Houghton, Harry, *Operation Portland: The Autobiography of a Spy* (London: Rupert Hart-Davis, 1972).

Howe, Irving, *World of Our Fathers: The Journeys of the East European Jews to America and the Life They Found and Made* (New York: Simon & Schuster, 1983).

Jeans, James, *The Mysterious Universe* (New York: Macmillan, 1930).

Johnson, Paul, *Modern Times: A History of the World from the 1920s to the 1990s* (London: George Weidenfeld & Nicolson Ltd., 1983; reprint, Phoenix/Orion Books, 1996).

Kahn, David, *The Codebreakers: The Story of Secret Writing* (New York: Macmillan, 1967).

Kalugin, Oleg, with Fen Montaigne, *The First Directorate: My 32 Years in Intelligence and Espionage Against the West* (New York: St. Martin's, 1994).

Kevles, Daniel J., *The Physicists: The History of a Scientific Community in Modern America* (Cambridge, MA: Harvard University Press, 1971, 1995).

KGB Museum of Intelligence, "Sovyetskaya razvyedka v litsakh i lichnostyakh" [Soviet Intelligence in People and Personalities], *Kur'yer Sovyetskoi Razvyedki*, No. 1 (1991).

Klehr, Harvey, John Haynes, and Fridrikh Igorevich Firsov, *The Secret World of American Communism* (New Haven and London: Yale University Press, 1995).

Knight, Amy, *Beria: Stalin's First Lieutenant* (Princeton, NJ: Princeton University Press, 1994).

Knight, Amy, *The KGB: Police and Politics in the Soviet Union* (Boston: Unwin Hyman Ltd., 1988).

Krivitsky, W. G., *In Stalin's Secret Service: An Exposé of Russia's Secret Policies by the Former Chief of the Soviet Intelligence in Western Europe* (New York: Harper & Brothers, 1939).

Kurchatov, Igor, memorandum of Dec. 24, 1944, "Zaklyucheniye po 'obzornoi rabote po probleme urana' k pismu N. 1/3/16015 iz 16.09.44" [Conclusions On 'A Review of the Uranium Problem' in Reference to Letter 1/3/16015 Dated Sept. 16, 1944] (Russian Ministry of Atomic Energy archives; partial text also translated into English in Sudoplatov [1994], appendix 3, p. 468).

Kurchatov, Igor, memorandum of April 11, 1945, "Zaklyucheniye po materiali k preprovoditelnoi N. 1/3/22500 iz 25.12.44" [Conclusions On Materials Accompanying Document No. 1/3/22500 Dated Dec. 25, 1944] (Russian Ministry of Atomic Energy archives; partial text also translated into English in Sudoplatov [1994], appendix 3, p. 470).

Kurchatov Institute, *Istoriya atomnogo proyekta* [History of the Atomic Project] (Moscow: Kurchatov Institute, 1994, 1995).

Lamont, Lansing, *Day of Trinity* (New York: Atheneum, 1965).

Lamphere, Robert J., and Tom Shachtman, *The FBI-KGB War, A Special Agent's Story* (New York: Random House, 1986).

Lawren, William, *The General and the Bomb: A Biography of General Leslie R. Groves, Director of the Manhattan Project* (New York: Dodd, Mead, 1988).

Lending, Edward, "Morris Picket . . . Né Morris Cohen," unpublished manuscript (Florida, 1992).

Libby, Leona Marshall, *The Uranium People* (New York: Crane Russak, 1979).

Lilienthal, David E., *The Journals of David E. Lilienthal: The Atomic Energy Years 1945–1950,* Vol. II (New York: Harper & Row, 1964).

Lincoln, W. Bruce, *The Conquest of a Continent: Siberia and the Russians* (New York: Random House, 1994).

Lincoln, W. Bruce, *The Romanovs: Autocrats of All the Russias* (New York: Anchor Books, 1981).

Lonsdale, Gordon, *Spy: Twenty Years in Soviet Secret Service: The Memoirs of Gordon Lonsdale* (New York: Hawthorn Books, 1965).

Los Alamos Historical Society, *Behind Tall Fences: Stories and Experiences About Los Alamos at Its Beginning* (Los Alamos, NM: Los Alamos Historical Society, 1996).

Los Alamos National Laboratory, "The Bayo Canyon/Radioactive Lanthanum (Ra-La) Program," report LA 13044-H (Los Alamos, NM: 1996).

Los Alamos National Laboratory, *Los Alamos 1943–1945: The Beginning of an Era,* (Los Alamos, NM: Los Alamos National Laboratory, LASL 78-78 Reprint, 1995).

Manhattan District History, Book I—General; Volume 8—Personnel, Dec. 19, 1947, Record Group 374, A1218 roll 3, National Archives, Washington, DC.

Manhattan District History, Book I—General; Volume 14—Intelligence & Security, Dec. 31, 1945, Record Group 374, A1218 roll 5, National Archives, Washington, DC.

Mason, Richard, *Cambridge Minds* (Cambridge, England: Cambridge University Press, 1994).

McCullough, David, *Truman* (New York: Simon & Schuster, 1992).

McElvaine, Robert S., *The Great Depression: America, 1929–1941* (New York: Times Books, 1984).

Miller, Douglas T., and Marion Nowak, *The Fifties: The Way We Really Were* (Garden City, NY: Doubleday, 1977).

Ministry of Atomic Energy, "Obzor po voprosu ob atomnoi bombe" [Review on the Question of the Atomic Bomb], a summary, believed to be based on a September 1945 espionage report from Klaus Fuchs to Harry Gold, prepared in Moscow in 1945 or 1946 describing how to build the American atomic bomb, as well as providing classified lecture notes prepared by Enrico Fermi describing wartime research at Los Alamos on a thermonuclear bomb (Document 462, Ministry of Atomic Energy archives, Moscow).

Ministry of Atomic Energy, *Sozdaniye pervoi sovyetskoi yadernoi bomby* [Creation of the First Soviet Nuclear Bomb] (Moscow: Moskva Energoatomizdat, 1995).

Ministry of Atomic Energy, "Zavod po proizvodstvu poloniya v g. Daytone" [Factory for the production of polonium in Dayton], a Soviet intelligence report to L. P. Beria, March 1, 1949, Document No. 822B (Ministry of Atomic Energy archives, Moscow).

Moorehead, Alan, *The Traitors* (New York, Evanston, and London: Harper & Row, 1963).

Moss, Norman, *Klaus Fuchs: The Man Who Stole the Atom Bomb* (London: Grafton Books, 1987).

Motz, Lloyd, and Jefferson Hane Weaver, *The Story of Mathematics* (New York: Avon, 1993).

Neal, Roy, *Ace in the Hole: The Story of the Minuteman Missile* (Garden City, NY: Doubleday, 1962).

Nichols, K. D., *The Road to Trinity* (New York: William Morrow, 1987).

Peierls, Rudolf, *Bird of Passage: Recollections of a Physicist* (Princeton, NJ: Princeton University Press, 1985).

Pervukhin, Mikhail G., "The First Years of the Nuclear Project," interview in *Khimiya i Zhizn* [Chemistry and life], No. 5 (1985).

Pestov, Stanislav, *Bomba: Tainy i strasti atomnoi preispodnei* [The Bomb: Secrets and Horrors of the Atomic Netherworld] (Moscow: Shans Publishers, 1995).

Physics Today, "Special Issue: New Light on Early Soviet Bomb Secrets," Vol. 49, No. 11 (November 1996).

Powers, Thomas, *Heisenberg's War: The Secret History of the German Bomb* (Boston: Little, Brown, 1993).

Radosh, Ronald, and Joyce Milton, *The Rosenberg File: A Search for Truth* (New York: Holt, Rinehart and Winston, 1983).

Rhodes, Richard, *Dark Sun: The Making of the Hydrogen Bomb* (New York: Simon & Schuster, 1995).

Rhodes, Richard, *The Making of the Atomic Bomb* (New York: Simon & Schuster, 1986).

Romerstein, Herbert, *Heroic Victims: Stalin's Foreign Legion in the Spanish Civil War* (Washington, DC: Council for the Defense of Freedom, 1994).

Romerstein, Herbert, and Stanislav Levchenko, *The KGB Against the Main Enemy: How the Soviet Intelligence Service Operates Against the United States* (Lexington, MA: Lexington Books, 1989).

Rossi, Bruno, *Moments in the Life of a Scientist* (Cambridge, England: Cambridge University Press, 1990).

Russ, Harlow W., *Project Alberta: The Preparation of Atomic Bombs for Use in World War II* (Los Alamos, NM: Exceptional Books, 1984, 1990).

Sakharov, Andrei, *Memoirs* (New York: Knopf, 1990).

Samolis, T. M., ed., *Veterany vneshnei razvyedki Rossii: Kratkiye biograficheskiye spravochniki* [Veterans of Russian Foreign Intelligence: Short Biographical Summaries] (Moscow: Russian Foreign Intelligence Service, 1995).

Satchler, *Introduction to Nuclear Reactions* (New York: Oxford University Press, 1990).

Sax, Boria, "Searching for America," unpublished manuscript about his family background (1994).

Sax, Saville, and Sandra Hollander, *Wake the Dragon: A Book on Awareness Medita-tion Centering Self-Shaping* (Evansville, IL: Reality Games Institute, 1975).

Seaborg, Glenn T., *The Plutonium Story: The Journals of Professor Glenn T. Seaborg 1939–1946* (Columbus, OH: Battelle Press, 1994).

Serber, Robert, *The Los Alamos Primer: The First Lectures on How to Build an Atomic Bomb* (Berkeley, Los Angeles, and Oxford: University of California Press, 1992).

Smith, Alice Kimball, *A Peril and a Hope: The Scientists' Movement in America, 1945–47* (Chicago: University of Chicago Press, 1965).

Smith, Alice Kimball, and Charles Weiner, eds., *Robert Oppenheimer, Letters and Recollections* (Stanford, CA: Stanford University Press, 1980).

Smyth, Henry DeWolf, *Atomic Energy for Military Purposes: The Official Report on the Development of the Atomic Bomb Under the Auspices of the United States Govern-ment, 1940–1945, with a New Foreword by Philip Morrison and an Essay by Henry DeWolf Smyth* (Stanford, CA: Stanford University Press, 1987).

Snelling, O. F., *Rare Books and Rarer People* (London: Werner Shaw, 1982).

Stern, Philip M., *The Oppenheimer Case: Security on Trial* (New York: Harper & Row, 1969).

Sudoplatov, Pavel, *Razvyedka i Kreml': Zapiski nezhelatel'nogo svidetel'ya* (Intelli-gence and the Kremlin: The Notes of an Unwanted Witness) (Moscow: TOO "Geya," 1996).

Sudoplatov, Pavel, and Anatoly Sudoplatov, with Jerrold L. and Leona P. Schecter, *Special Tasks: The Memoirs of an Unwanted Witness: A Soviet Spymaster* (Boston: Little, Brown, 1994).

Szasz, Ferenc Morton, *The Day the Sun Rose Twice: The Story of the Trinity Site Nu-clear Explosion, July 16, 1945* (Albuquerque, NM: University of New Mexico Press, 1984).

★Tchikov, Vladimir, and Gary Kern, *Comment Staline a volé la bombe atomique aux Américains—Dossier KGB No. 13676* [How Stalin Stole the Bomb from the Americans—KGB Dossier 13676] (Paris: Robert Laffont, 1996).

Teller, Edward, *Better a Shield than a Sword: Perspectives on Defense and Technology* (New York: Free Press, 1987).

Teller, Edward, "The History of the American Hydrogen Bomb," unpublished paper presented at historical conference at Dubna, Russia, May 14–18, 1996.

Thomas, Hugh, *The Spanish Civil War* (New York: Touchstone, 1986).

Tietjen, Arthur, *Soviet Spy Ring* (New York: Coward-McCann, 1961).

Truslow, Edith C., *Manhattan District History: Nonscientific Aspects of Los Alamos Proj-ect Y: 1942 Through 1946* (Los Alamos: Los Alamos Historical Society, 1991; orig-inally issued in March 1973 by Los Alamos National Laboratory as LA-5200).

U.S. House of Representatives Committee on Un-American Activities (HUAC), *Report on Atomic Espionage* (Nelson-Weinberg and Hiskey-Adams Cases) (Washington, DC: Sept. 29, 1949).

★The French transliteration of Chikov.

Van Der Rhoer, Edward, *The Shadow Network: Espionage as an Instrument of Soviet Policy* (London: Robert Hale Ltd., 1983).

Vasilevsky, L., inventory of espionage materials received and translated by the NKVD's Department S that relate to construction of the atomic bomb, Vasilevsky memorandum to Lt. Gen. P. Ya. Meshik, Ministry of State Security Document 22/c/345 of Dec. 18, 1946 (Ministry of Atomic Energy archives, Moscow).

Venona Documents (Fort George G. Meade, MD: U.S. National Security Agency, Releases 1–5, 1995–1996).

Voprosy Istorii Yestestvoznaniya i Tekhniki [Questions of the History of Natural Science and Technology], No. 3, 1992.

Weinstein, Gerhard L., *A World at Arms: A Global History of World War II* (Cambridge, England: Cambridge University Press, 1994).

West, Rebecca, *The New Meaning of Treason* (New York: Viking, 1964).

Whitney, Craig, *Spy Trader* (New York: Times Books, 1994).

Wier, Sadye H., with John F. Marszalek, *A Black Businessman in White Mississippi, 1886–1974* (Oxford, MS: University Press of Mississipi, 1977).

Williams, Robert Chadwell, *Klaus Fuchs: Atom Spy* (Cambridge, MA: Harvard University Press, 1987).

Wise, David, *Nightmover: How Aldrich Ames Sold the CIA to the KGB for $4.6 Million* (New York: HarperCollins, 1995).

Woodrow Wilson International Center for Scholars, *Soviet Nuclear History* (Washington, DC: Cold War International History Project Bulletin, Fall 1994).

Wright, Peter, *Spy Catcher* (New York: Dell, 1987).

Zaloga, Steven J., *Target America: The Soviet Union and the Strategic Arms Race, 1945–1964* (Novato, CA: Presidio, 1993).

Index

About the Authors

JOSEPH ALBRIGHT and MARCIA KUNSTEL are a husband-and-wife team who combine working as journalists and historians. Since becoming foreign correspondents in 1983, they have covered wars and upheavals in Afghanistan, Lebanon, South Africa, the Philippines, Iraq, and Chechnya. From 1993 to 1997, while researching and writing this book, they were the Moscow correspondents for the Cox Newspapers group, for whom Albright has worked since 1976 and Kunstel since 1987. Their first book as co-authors was *Their Promised Land,* a history of the Israeli-Palestinian conflict in microcosm that was published in 1991.

Albright and Kunstel won the 1988 Overseas Press Club Award for their newspaper series on worldwide child labor and the 1991 Headliner Award for their coverage of the Gulf War buildup. Albright also wrote *What Makes Spiro Run,* a 1972 biography of Vice President Spiro Agnew.